Defending Biodiversity

Imagine that you are an environmentalist who passionately believes that it is wrong to drill for oil in the Arctic National Wildlife Refuge. How do you convince someone that a decision to drill is wrong?

Debates about the environment and how humans ought to treat it have gone on for decades, yet arguments in favor of preserving biodiversity often lack empirical substance or are philosophically naïve, making them far less effective than they could be. This book critically examines arguments that are commonly offered in support of biodiversity conservation. The authors adopt a skeptical viewpoint to thoroughly test the strength of each argument and, by demonstrating how scientific evidence can be integrated with philosophical reasoning, they help environmentalists to better engage with public debate and judiciously inform public policy. This interdisciplinary and accessible book is essential reading for anyone who engages in discussions about the value of biodiversity conservation.

JONATHAN A. NEWMAN is Professor of Ecology, and Dean of the College of Biological Science at the University of Guelph, Canada.

GARY VARNER is Professor and former Head of Philosophy at Texas A&M University, USA.

STEFAN LINQUIST is Associate Professor in the Department of Philosophy and Adjunct Professor in the Department of Integrative Biology, both at the University of Guelph, Canada.

Defending Biodiversity
Environmental Science and Ethics

JONATHAN A. NEWMAN
University of Guelph

GARY VARNER
Texas A&M University

STEFAN LINQUIST
University of Guelph

CAMBRIDGE
UNIVERSITY PRESS

CAMBRIDGE
UNIVERSITY PRESS

University Printing House, Cambridge CB2 8BS, United Kingdom

One Liberty Plaza, 20th Floor, New York, NY 10006, USA

477 Williamstown Road, Port Melbourne, VIC 3207, Australia

4843/24, 2nd Floor, Ansari Road, Daryaganj, Delhi – 110002, India

79 Anson Road, #06–04/06, Singapore 079906

Cambridge University Press is part of the University of Cambridge.

It furthers the University's mission by disseminating knowledge in the pursuit of education, learning, and research at the highest international levels of excellence.

www.cambridge.org
Information on this title: www.cambridge.org/9780521768863
DOI: 10.1017/9781139024105

First published 2017

Printed in the United States of America by Sheridan Books, Inc.

A catalogue record for this publication is available from the British Library.

Library of Congress Cataloging-in-Publication Data
Names: Newman, Jonathan A., author. | Varner, Gary E. (Gary Edward), author. | Linquist, Stefan Paul, author.
Title: Defending biodiversity : environmental science and ethics / Jonathan A. Newman, University of Guelph, Gary Varner, Texas A & M University, Stefan Linquist, University of Guelph.
Description: Cambridge, United Kingdom : New York, NY : Cambridge University Press, 2017. | Includes bibliographical references and index.
Identifiers: LCCN 2017023820 | ISBN 9780521768863 (hardback)
Subjects: LCSH: Biodiversity – Moral and ethical aspects.
Classification: LCC QH541.15.B56 N49 2017 | DDC 333.95–dc23
LC record available at https://lccn.loc.gov/2017023820

ISBN 978-0-521-76886-3 Hardback
ISBN 978-0-521-14620-3 Paperback

Contents

Preface

This book has three coauthors. Jonathan Newman is an ecologist, former Director of the School of Environmental Sciences, current Dean of the College of Biological Science, and adjunct professor in the Department of Philosophy at the University of Guelph. Gary Varner is an environmental philosopher and animal ethicist, and former head of the Department of Philosophy at Texas A&M University. And Stefan Linquist is a philosopher of biology at the University of Guelph.

We want to begin by saying very clearly that:

All three of us consider ourselves to be environmentalists, and we all think that biodiversity ought to be conserved.

We emphasize this up-front, because some may view this book as an attack on environmentalists and on the view that biodiversity ought to be conserved. It is not. Throughout this book we critically analyze various popular arguments commonly offered in support of biodiversity conservation. We adopt a critical or 'skeptical' stance toward these arguments not because it is our aim to defeat them, but rather because we hope to test their strength. As the reader will soon discover, some arguments fare better than others, and none of them offer full-blown support for the extensive conservation programs that some environmentalists endorse. As we shall explore, some arguments for biodiversity conservation lack adequate empirical support in ways that challenge conventional assumptions, and sometimes they commit one to positions that have unpalatable consequences.

Nevertheless, we did not write this book to dismiss environmentalists' concern for biodiversity. Rather, our hope is that reading this book will help environmentalists *improve* the arguments they make for conserving biodiversity. This is important because promoting conservation often involves convincing others that biodiversity should be protected at the expense of some human activity such as development, and it almost always involves arguments with people who do not immediately share our views. If environmentalists are to be persuasive, then we will have to bring good arguments to these debates. And, as any seasoned debater will know, it's always important to know the limitations and weaknesses of one's arguments. Appreciating the limitations of our current arguments can help us engage more effectively in such discussions in the future. The questions we raise about various arguments have no easy answers, and, indeed, it is this fact that makes the study of them, *by environmentalists*, all the more important.

All three of us, in our teaching, in discussions with friends, family, and colleagues, and in our research, engage repeatedly in arguments about the environment and about how humans ought to treat it. These experiences motivated us to write this book. Arguments about the environment and about how humans ought to behave toward the environment have been ongoing in the academic discipline of environmental ethics for decades. All of the opening gambits in these arguments are well-known, and have equally well-known responses. In our experience, many environmentalists seem unaware of these 'moves and counter moves.' As a result, we waste a lot of time and energy exploring old ground, to the detriment of advancing the quality of our discussions. We hope that by exploring these opening moves and countermoves, the reader will be better able to see where the most fertile ground is located, and how they can best engage with the subject matter.

In writing this book, we struggled with finding the right voice for our presentation. There are places in the text where we are writing about arguments that others have advanced, some of which we agree with and others of which we do not. Indeed, we do not always agree among ourselves on every position, and we explore some of our differences in the final chapter. Nevertheless, there are (many) conclusions on which we all agree, and in those cases we will make statements along the lines of "We think that . . ."

This approach proved particularly tricky when we had to present positions that we think many environmentalists hold, even though the three of us do not necessarily hold those positions. As we said, we consider ourselves to be environmentalists, even though we don't all subscribe to each and every position that characterizes what we call 'the environmentalist agenda.' Environmentalism comprises a very broad set of personal and political positions, and it is common to find disagreement even among environmental groups in their positions on individual issues. We thought that by limiting our discussion to the conservation of biodiversity, we might perhaps narrow the agenda enough that we could find sufficient common ground on which to start our exploration of these ideas. Hence, there are many places in the book where we refer to 'environmentalists' or 'the environmentalist agenda.' These terms are not meant to be pejorative in any way; indeed, at various places in the book we will use language such as "we environmentalists" to indicate that we do not consider ourselves to be above or in any way outside the group we are labeling 'environmentalists.'

The book follows a fairly simple structure that aims to mirror conversations (arguments) about biodiversity conservation. We start out, in Chapter 1, by defining our terms (e.g. 'biodiversity,' 'intrinsic value,' etc.) and laying out something that we think approximates the environmentalist agenda. With the stage set in Chapter 1, we are ready to engage with the common arguments for why we should conserve biodiversity. We divide these arguments into two kinds, which we label:

1. **Instrumental value defenses**: That we ought to conserve biodiversity because it is valuable to humans. In economics this value is called 'instrumental value,' and we will refer to these defenses collectively as 'instrumental value defenses.' Philosophically, this type of argument is a commitment to an anthropocentric ethical position. What matters morally are human beings and their interests. Everything else, including biodiversity, has instrumental value. It is a means to an end, and that end is human welfare.

2. **Intrinsic value defenses**: That we ought to conserve biodiversity for non-instrumental value reasons. Philosophically, this type of argument involves a commitment to one of several non-anthropocentric ethical positions. Things additional to (or perhaps other than) human beings and their interests matter morally, and biodiversity is one of these things. Regardless of how useful biodiversity is (or is not) to humans, we ought to conserve it because it is the morally correct thing to do. This tactic amounts to a claim that biodiversity has what philosophers refer to as 'intrinsic value,' and we will refer to these arguments collectively as 'intrinsic value defenses.'

Part I of the book comprises five chapters and considers the instrumental value arguments. Chapter 2 is a fairly lengthy chapter (because the topic is rich and complex) that examines the argument that we should conserve biodiversity because of the ecosystem services that we derive from it. Chapter 3 is similarly lengthy, and explores 'precautionary defenses.' These defenses take the form of defending conservation over development for reasons of biodiversity's uncertain usefulness in an uncertain future. Chapter 4 explores the arguments that we ought to conserve biodiversity because it is the source of our food, fuel, fiber, and medicine. Chapter 5 looks at arguments based on the value of nature-based tourism and the power of biodiversity to transform how we value nature in general, and biodiversity in particular. We round up Part I with a brief consideration of how far the instrumental value arguments get environmentalists in their defense of biodiversity conservation. In Part I the strength of the arguments rests primarily on the empirical evidence – what the data indicate – although problems with the precautionary defenses are also philosophical in nature. We think that readers may conclude from Part I that instrumental value defenses cover a lot of biodiversity conservation but they don't cover all of it, and that these defenses also imply some fairly unpalatable, but logically additional commitments. Faced with the perhaps unsatisfying conclusion that there are parts of biodiversity that are not useful to us, or perhaps not *more useful* to us than are the alternatives, environmentalists like to claim that biodiversity doesn't have to be useful because it has 'intrinsic value,' or that people have some moral/ethical responsibility to conserve it anyway. Some environmentalists will go straight to this point without ever entertaining instrumental value arguments. For these environmentalists, the conservation of biodiversity has *nothing to do* with whether or not it is useful. These environmentalists feel that estimating the economic value of biodiversity is not only wrong, it is wrong-headed! This will be evident to some as we consider the 'implied commitments' that accompany each of the instrumental defenses.

In Part II of the book, we consider in detail the claims of environmentalists for the non-anthropocentric value of biodiversity. In Chapter 7 we provide a brief introduction to the methods that philosophers use to defend moral theories, principles, rules, and moral judgments in general. This chapter will be important as we come to grips with how to assess a claim that biodiversity has intrinsic value. In Chapter 8 we will examine arguments based on claims that (1) sentient non-human animals are worthy of our moral concern, and (2) that all living organisms have intrinsic value and are therefore worthy of our moral concern, independently of their instrumental value to humans. In Chapters 9 and 10, we tackle the broader claims that ecological wholes, such as species and ecosystems, might have intrinsic value. And finally, in Chapter 11, we consider the claim that the aesthetic nature of biodiversity has intrinsic value. We complete Part II with a summary (Chapter 12), in which we reflect on the strengths and weaknesses of the environmentalist's claim that biodiversity has intrinsic value.

We end the book (Chapter 13) with some personal and biographical reflections on our individual value commitments, why we think that humans ought to conserve biodiversity, and the implications of those views for how we live our lives.

Acknowledgments

J.A.N.: I thank Gary Comstock for setting me on this road, Tim Mawson for his help in keeping me on this road, and all of my current and former students and colleagues with whom I have discussed these ideas and issues over the years. I would also like to thank the Canadian Natural Science and Engineering Research Council for their continuing support for my research.

G.E.V.: I'm grateful to Jonathan Newman for conceiving of this project, bringing me on board, and then wisely adding his colleague Stefan to the team. Thanks also to my parents, for supporting my chosen career path, despite the mystification it caused in them. And I thank my colleague, Clare Palmer, for commenting on some parts of the manuscript for which I wrote the first drafts.

S.P.L.: I am grateful to Jonathan and Gary for involving me in this project. Thanks to Madeleine McGreer for helping me understand certain mathematical models in environmental economics, and to Nola Semczyszyn for lending her expertise in aesthetics. I appreciate the many insights from students and community members who participated in the Philosophy Field Course, which met at the University of Guelph and in Tofino, British Columbia. Finally, special thanks to Lucy, Marita, and Katarina for their inspiration and encouragement.

I Biodiversity and the Environmentalist Agenda

I.I INTRODUCTION

Edward (E.O.) Wilson, Harvard Emeritus Professor of Entomology and great popularizer of the term 'biodiversity,' eloquently said (2006, p. 91):

> The human hammer having fallen, the sixth mass extinction has begun. This spasm of permanent loss is expected, if it is not abated, to reach the end-of-Mesozoic level by the end of the century. We will then enter what poets and scientists alike may choose to call the Eremozoic Era – The Age of Loneliness.

Supposing that Wilson is correct, why should we care? In this book we will examine a number of commonly given reasons for why biodiversity ought to be conserved. These reasons can be divided into two types: instrumental and intrinsic value reasons. Before we can begin our examination, we need to do a bit of 'housekeeping.' In Section 1.2 we will take on the important, but difficult, task of discussing what biodiversity might be, and how we plan to treat the term in this book. It may come as a surprise to many, but biodiversity is not one thing, and it certainly is not well defined. In Section 1.3, we will set the scene by considering why some people think we are running out of biodiversity. Are we, as Wilson suggests, in the midst of the 6th mass extinction? What sorts of evidence is presented in support of this claim? Our next task, in Section 1.4, will be to attempt to define, for lack of a better term, 'the environmentalist agenda.' Environmentalism comprises a large and varied set of personal and collective values and policies, about which there may be much disagreement. We lay out what we think many environmentalists want when it comes to conserving biodiversity. The agenda will be important as we will assess the implications of the

1

reasons given for conserving biodiversity against the agenda itself, to see how far any particular defense gets the environmentalist in achieving her goals. Finally, in the latter half of this chapter (Sections 1.5–1.6), we introduce the notion of 'intrinsic value' and we provide a taxonomy of positions in environmental ethics.

1.2   WHAT DO WE MEAN BY 'BIODIVERSITY'?

'Biodiversity' is one of those words that have taken on meaning beyond that envisaged by the people who originally coined the term. 'Ecology' and 'ecosystem' are two other notable examples. The common perception is that the term 'biodiversity' owes its origin to E.O. Wilson (1988), although the progenitor 'biological diversity' had been around for some years before the contraction. At the time, 'biodiversity' referred vaguely, and simply, to *the diversity of life*, whatever that means. Within professional ecological and conservation biology circles, 'biodiversity' often refers to total diversity at three levels of ecological organization: genes, species, and ecosystems. Indeed, this is the definition adopted by the United Nation's Convention on Biological Diversity (CBD), signed as part of the Rio Summit in 1992:

> "Biological diversity" means the variability among living organisms from all sources including, inter alia, terrestrial, marine and other aquatic ecosystems and the ecological complexes of which they are part; this includes diversity within species, between species and of ecosystems.

This definition has the advantage of being inclusive of all manner of life forms, regardless of the level or scale at which they might be identified. Future scientific developments might one day identify new forms of biodiversity – for example, at micro-organismal or intra-genomic scales. The CBD definition provides a sufficiently broad umbrella to capture such new forms of biodiversity, in addition to the more familiar ones. However, such generality comes at the price of conceptual precision. Arguably, an adequate definition of biodiversity ought to facilitate the comparison and ranking of regions. Indeed, policy makers and conservation managers often face difficult decisions about how to strategically invest limited conservation resources. The CBD definition, for all its flexibility, offers little guidance on this front. The problem becomes acute when diversity at one level or scale trades off against diversity at some other level. It is easy to imagine cases where an investment that maximizes within-species genetic diversity, say, requires sacrifices in the number of species or distinct habitats that are simultaneously conserved. For any environmental organization whose mandate is simply to maximize biodiversity, the CBD definition potentially generates conflicting courses of action.

A related concern arises even when the focus is restricted to a specific level of the biological hierarchy. For example, conservation biologists often focus on *species richness* as a useful measure of biodiversity (i.e. the number of distinct species in a given region). But difficult trade-offs can arise even here. Consider two habitats that are equal in species richness. Perhaps one is a marine habitat containing 20 species of pacific rockfish (*Sebastes*). The other is also a marine habitat with only 5 rockfish species, but 5 species of sculpin and 10 species of invertebrates. Does one region contain more biodiversity? Intuitively, the answer seems obvious. The second habitat, containing both invertebrate and vertebrate species, is the more diverse region. The implication of this argument is that species richness alone cannot serve as a definition of biodiversity – even though it is often used as a convenient proxy for measuring it. Notice that this same thought experiment can be run with any number of different properties besides phylogenetic distance:[1] morphological diversity, diversity in ecological roles, diversity of ecosystem functions, metabolic diversity, or diversity in developmental mechanisms, to name but a few. One can imagine holding all other factors constant while varying just one of these properties and the result will be a corresponding change in the amount of biodiversity that one intuitively identifies among two otherwise identical regions. We recognize that, in practice, two regions are unlikely to vary along just

---

[1] See e.g. Vellend et al. (2011): 194–207.

one of these dimensions. However, the point of the thought experiment is to show that any number of biologically salient properties might be taken to contribute to differences in total biodiversity among regions. The CBD definition offers no instruction whatsoever on how to rank the importance of these potentially contributing factors.

Such concerns have motivated various attempts to sharpen the definition of biodiversity. One general strategy for redefining biodiversity is the reductionist approach. Reductionists propose to define biodiversity in terms of one core property or a limited set of properties whose relationships are clearly defined. For example, philosophers James Maclaurin and Kim Sterelny (2008) review a wide range of scientific contexts in which biodiversity plays some important role. These include a number of different projects in evolutionary biology, ecology, and conservation biology. Maclaurin and Sterelny argue that, in most of these cases, species richness is an adequate definition of biodiversity. Occasionally, this definition needs to be qualified by some secondary factor, such as the phylogenetic distance among species or the diversity of ecological roles that they occupy. But, generally speaking, species richness is the core property that most scientists are tracking when they investigate the biological significance of biodiversity, or so it is argued.

A second general strategy for defining biodiversity is the pluralist approach. According to this view, no core property or limited set of properties is picked out by the various uses of this term. Instead, there are many distinct properties or property clusters being identified on different occasions. A reasonable objective for pluralism is to disambiguate 'biodiversity' into several sub-concepts. For example, one sense of biodiversity might apply to comparisons of aquatic systems. A different biodiversity concept might apply to micro-organisms, and so on. Part of the challenge for pluralism, however, lies in selecting the appropriate goals for this categorization schema. For example, the philosopher and conservation biologist Sahotra Sarkar, and conservation biologist Chris Margules, maintain that the biodiversity concept is inherently bound up with the practices of conservation biologists. According to Sarkar and Margules (2002), the precise goals of conservation biology tend to vary from one conservation project to the next: one day it might be preventing the intrusion of an invasive species, the next day the goal might be preventing the extinction of a precious subspecies, and on yet another occasion the goal might be to conserve a diversity of habitats. This openness of conservation objectives makes it impossible, Sarkar and Margules argue, to identify a limited set of biodiversity definitions that are suitable to all conservation aims. This predicament leads Sarkar and Margules to conclude that 'biodiversity' should be defined operationally as whatever property a given group of conservationists happen to be interested in maximizing on a given occasion.

Taking a step back from these debates, we suspect that many lay persons and non-experts would find it surprising that there is no scientifically agreed upon definition of biodiversity. In public debates about conservation, environmentalists often appeal to the notion of biodiversity as a way of lending scientific credibility to their agenda. Regions are characterized as a conservation priority simply because they contain 'high levels of biodiversity.' Such uses of the term give the impression that one is talking about a scientifically established property whose definition and quantification is beyond reproach. In fact, this is far from true. To be clear, in saying that biodiversity admits of no clear scientific definition we are not suggesting that environmentalists' arguments are therefore lacking in substance. On any given occasion it is usually possible to identify which properties of a biological system are threatened by a particular course of action. Perhaps the important lesson is that we environmentalists need to be as clear as possible in our use of this term. Otherwise, we risk committing the 'fallacy of equivocation.'[2] For example, suppose that it has been demonstrated that one form of biodiversity (e.g. within-species genetic diversity) is valuable because it buffers against extinction. It would be mistaken to infer that other forms of

---

[2] This logical fallacy occurs when one employs a word that has two or more meanings, but glosses over the distinction in order confuse the listener as to the true meaning. For example: "Doctors know a lot about medicine. We are doctors. Therefore we know a lot about medicine." This looks like a logical inference, but 'doctor' might mean a medical doctor, or a PhD (doctor of philosophy). The first sentence uses the former meaning, whereas, in our case, the second sentence means the latter.

biodiversity (e.g. species richness or habitat heterogeneity) are likewise valuable for the same reason. The same fact might not apply to other forms of biodiversity. Species richness does not buffer against extinction in any obvious way. Nor does habitat heterogeneity have this effect, generally speaking. This is one of the problems that can arise when subtly distinct concepts are associated with the same term: one can easily slide from saying something true to something false, often without notice.

What, then, do we authors mean by 'biodiversity'? The problem with providing a clear definition that we can stick to throughout this book is that we are unlikely to find one that enjoys universal approval. An alternative approach would be to look at what legislation and actual conservation projects seek as goals, and to use those to derive a de facto definition. However, this sort of investigation would take us beyond the scope of our current discussion, the aim of which is to assess the various reasons for valuing biodiversity, however it might be defined. We have thus made an effort to be clear about how we are using this term in the chapters that follow, highlighting occasions when alternate definitions of biodiversity might make a difference to its valuation.

I.3   WHY THINK THE EARTH IS RUNNING OUT OF BIODIVERSITY?

In the 3.5 billion years since life evolved on this planet, biologists estimate that approximately 4 billion species have evolved, and about 3.96 billion have gone extinct. This amounts to approximately 99% of all species that have ever existed (Barnosky et al., 2011). This means that, to a first approximation, about one species has gone extinct every year. As long as that extinction rate is balanced by a similar speciation rate, the number of species currently extant on the planet remains constant. Of course, neither extinction rates nor speciation rates have been constant over time. There have been exactly five periods in the past where extinction rates were much higher than the 'background' rate of extinction. These higher extinction rates were sustained long enough to result in so-called mass extinctions. Such mass extinction events occurred a long time ago (see Table 1.1), the last one approximately 65 million years ago.

Table 1.1 *Past mass extinction events*

The **Ordovician Event** ended ~443 Myr ago; within 3.3 to 1.9 Myr 57% of genera were lost, an estimated 86% of species.
The **Devonian Event** ended ~359 Myr ago; within 29 to 2 Myr 35% of genera were lost, an estimated 75% of species.
The **Permian Event** ended ~251 Myr ago; within 2.8 Myr to 160 Kyr 56% of genera were lost, an estimated 96% of species.
The **Triassic Event** ended ~200 Myr ago; within 8.3 Myr to 600 Kyr 47% of genera were lost, an estimated 80% of species.
The **Cretaceous Event** ended ~65 Myr ago; within 2.5 Myr to less than a year 40% of genera were lost, an estimated 76% of species.

Redrawn from Barnosky et al. (2011).
Myr = million years, Kyr = thousand years.

Not only were these events a long time ago, but they happened over long periods of time (with the possible exception of the Cretaceous Event). For example, the Triassic Event occurred over a period from 600,000 years to 8,300,000 years. To put that in perspective, the entire history of our species (*Homo sapiens*) is around 300,000 years. Mass extinction events are variously defined, but, roughly speaking, they are times when the Earth loses >75% of its species in a 'geologically short period of time.'

Current extinction rates are said to be 1,000 to 10,000 times higher than the background rate of extinction, leading some to declare that we are in the midst of a 'sixth mass extinction event' (e.g. Barnosky et al., 2011). This suggestion has inspired grave concern among many environmentalists. Such numbers are indeed alarming, but it is important to understand how they are derived.

1.3.1   How Do Scientists Estimate the Background Rates of Extinction?

This is an important question because the lower the estimate of this rate, the worse current extinction rates look. First, the background rates are estimated from the fossil record. This already makes such an estimate problematic since not all species fossilize. Second, the notion of a 'species' used in the fossil record is different than that commonly used in contemporary taxonomy. The fossil record uses the notion of a 'morphospecies'; if two fossils look similar, then they are described as being the same species. In modern taxonomy we have many examples of two (or more!) species looking similar but actually being classified as different. These are sometimes called 'cryptic species.' And third, the fossil record can usually only be resolved to the level of genus or sometimes family, rather than to species. To get a number of species, scientists take estimates of the number of species per genus (or family) from well-resolved groups, such as mammals and birds, and apply them to other groups, such as marine invertebrates. Finally, extinction rates estimated from the fossil record are often estimated over very different time scales (millions of years) than are contemporary extinction rates (tens to hundreds of years).

Using these admittedly somewhat problematic methods, common estimates range from 0.1 to 1 extinction per 10,000 species per 100 years. Ten thousand species times 100 years gives something called a 'million species-years.' Historically, estimates of the background rate of extinction have ranged from 0.1 E/MSY (extinctions per million species-years) to 1 E/MSY. Past estimates of background extinction rates were usually based on marine invertebrate species (Raup, 1991), which may persist longer than terrestrial species (Ceballos et al., 2015). Anthony Barnosky and colleagues (2011) used a more complete mammalian fossil record to estimate the background rate of extinction at approximately 1.8 E/MSY. Note that this estimate is between 1.8 and 18 times higher than that previously used.

1.3.2 How Do Scientists Estimate Contemporary Extinction Rates?

The International Union for Conservation of Nature (IUCN) is the definitive source of information for contemporary extinctions and extinction threats. According to the current database (see Table 1.2) approximately 20% of the species that have been evaluated are either extinct, extinct in the wild, critically endangered, or endangered (according to the IUCN definitions of these terms). Assuming that all of the endangered or worse-off species will go extinct in the near future, and assuming that this relative extinction rate carries on unabated for a few thousand years, then Barnosky et al. (2011) estimate that the global extinction rate will approximately equal the 75% definition used for a mass extinction event[3].

More recently, Gerardo Ceballos and colleagues (2015) looked at just the vertebrates. They estimated that extinction rates varied from 8 to 100 times higher than a very conservative background rate of extinction of 2 E/MSY (rounded up from Barnosky et al., 2011). An estimate of 100 E/MSY, coupled with the very important assumption that speciation rates change very little (certainly a contested assumption), gives a 1% decline every 100 years. If unchanged for about 14,000 years, we would achieve the 75% species loss required for the 6th Mass Extinction event (McGill et al., 2015).

There are obviously lots of data problems and assumptions necessary to arrive at this conclusion, for estimating even contemporary extinction rates is difficult. One reason even our contemporary extinction rate estimates are crude is that we don't actually know how many species there are currently extant on the Earth. There are currently about 1.5 million species identified, and we are advancing that number by about 20,000 species a year (Costello et al., 2013). The total number of non-microbial species has been estimated to be somewhere between 2 and 100 million. More recently Mark Costello and colleagues (2013) estimate that the number of non-microbial species is between 2 and 8 million, and assess that larger previous estimates "now seem highly unlikely." One of Costello's coauthors, Robert May, has remarked on many occasions that we know more about the number of stars in the universe than we know about the number of species on the Earth. That

---

[3] Note that there is a lot more to Barnosky et al.'s calculation than presented here, but that is roughly one way that they arrive at this conclusion.

Table 1.2 *Threats to biodiversity*

	Extinct	Extinct in the Wild	Critically Endangered	Endangered	Vulnerable	Near Threatened	Least Concern	Wikipedia
Animalia	**731**	**32**	**2524**	**3740**	**5613**	**3547**	**29752**	**>18,000**
Annelida (segmented worms)	1		1	2	1	2		
Arthropoda (insects, arachnids, myriapods, and crustaceans)	81	2	370	550	1,024	345	3,817	>6,000,000
Chordata (mammals, fish, amphibians, reptiles and birds; salps and sea squirts; and lancelets)	337	16	1,566	2,649	3,498	2,494	23,094	>63,000
Cnidaria (sea anemones, corals, jellyfish)				28	204	176	301	>6,100

Echinodermata (starfish, sea urchins, sand dollars, sea cucumbers, sea lilies)	310	14		7	9	1	111	950
Mollusca (snails, slugs)			576	501	872	528	2428	>69,000
Nemertina (ribbon worms)	1		1	1	1		1	650
Onychophora (velvet worms)	1		1	2	4	1		180
Platyhelminthes (flatworms)	1							4,500
Plantae	99		2,205	3,352	5,310	1,583	5,762	
Anthoceratophyta (hornworts)				2				100
Bryophyta (mosses)	2		12	13	10	1	3	14,502
Charophyta (green algae)							8	
Marchantiophyta (liverworts)	1		11	14	14		4	9,000

Table 1.2 (cont.)

	Extinct	Extinct in the Wild	Critically Endangered	Endangered	Vulnerable	Near Threatened	Least Concern	Wikipedia
Rhodophyta (red algae)	1		6		3		4	5,500
Tracheophyta (clubmosses, horsetails, ferns, gymnosperms (including conifers) and angiosperms (flowering plants))	95	37	2,176	3,352	5,283	1,581	5,736	259,656

Data from International Union for Conservation of Nature (IUCN) on threats to biodiversity. IUCN 2016. The IUCN Red List of Threatened Species. Version 2016–1. www.iucnredlist.org. Definitions for the individual categories can be found here: www.iucnredlist.org/technical-documents/categories-and-criteria. The column labeled 'Wikipedia' denotes the number of known species in that plant or animal group.

may be an exaggeration, but one certainly can appreciate the spirit of May's sentiment.

Another way to look at this is that regardless of the number of species on Earth, if the extinction rate were, say, 5% per decade, then in 150 years we would have lost 54% of the species. However, if the rate were more like 0.5% per decade, then in 150 years we would have only lost about 8% of our species. Current extinction estimates are closer to the latter than the former figure (May et al., 1995).

1.3.3 Biodiversity Trends on Different Scales

Biodiversity can be discussed on different spatial and temporal scales. Brain McGill and colleagues (2015) recently reviewed '15 forms of biodiversity trend in the Anthropocene.'[4] Their conclusions are summarized in Table 1.3.

McGill et al.'s assessment of the evidence shows that besides the number of species on Earth, patterns of biodiversity are sometimes declining, but sometimes increasing, and often are not known with much certainty. Indeed, McGill et al. conclude:

> Probably the most striking fact from an examination of [Table 1.3] and the corresponding literature is how little we know. Even patterns that seem well established, like the global decline in biodiversity [α diversity], have never been directly measured and rely on models to estimate the changes. Many trends are almost completely unstudied, including temporal and spatial ß diversity and changes in net abundance at the community level. Additionally, for the credibility of future generations of biodiversity scientists, we also believe it is important to communicate the currently very large error bars in estimates of biodiversity trends. A second striking fact that emerges is that, even faced with dramatic environmental change, species richness [α diversity] can remain, on

---

[4] The proposed name of a new geological epoch to denote the influence of humans.

Table 1.3 *Assessment of fifteen trends in contemporary biodiversity*

Scale	Temporal ß diversity: change in community composition through time	α diversity: the number of species present	Spatial ß diversity: change in community composition across space	Number or biomass
Global: the entire planet	Probably increasing	Declining		Unknown
Biogeographic: a scale within which speciation and global extinction are dominant processes	Unknown	Increasing	Probably declining	Unknown
Meta-community: a scale that includes spatial heterogeneity and within which dispersal is the dominant process	Unknown	Probably increasing	Probably declining	Probably declining
Local: a scale dominated by species interactions and environmental constraints	Probably increasing	On average unchanged	Probably declining	Probably increasing

Adapted from McGill et al. (2015). The table shows the authors' assessment of 15 trends in contemporary biodiversity. Trends assessed as 'probably' indicate that they are commonly hypothesized based on anthropogenic influences, but not often measured empirically. There are only three trends for the spatial ß diversity because this measure is a comparison from one spatial scale to the next. Trends assessed as 'unknown' indicate that there is little empirical evidence or speculation about the trend. Only the trends shaded gray are based on substantial empirical evidence.

average, constant. However, this apparent constancy hides
enormous turnover in the identities of the species present.

(McGill et al. 2015, 110–111)

1.4   THE ENVIRONMENTALIST AGENDA

Throughout this book we will be referring to 'environmentalists' and
the sorts of outcomes that they advocate as matters of public policy, as
matters of law, and as desired states of the world. It was far from clear
to us, when starting this book, whether 'environmentalists' could be
clearly defined. Environmentalism embraces many disparate groups
who are motivated by a variety of environmental problems, and who
hope to achieve their possibly conflicting goals through a number of
different means. We thought that, perhaps, by focusing on the issue of
biodiversity it might be possible to throw a sufficiently large net over
these many different flavors of environmentalism. But even this very
general goal might fall short of capturing a shared ambition among all
of the very different individuals and organizations who self-identify as
'environmentalists.' Instead, in what follows we offer a list of outcomes that environmentalists tend to support. These should not be
regarded as a checklist of requirements for environmentalism, but
rather as a somewhat tentative description of the goals that (we
authors think) most environmentalists are striving to realize.

We should also say that we presume that you (the reader) would
probably consider yourself to be an environmentalist. We (the authors)
consider ourselves to be environmentalists as well. We don't subscribe
to all of the positions listed below, and we wouldn't be surprised to
find that you don't either. In fact, the three of us don't all agree on
what we should conserve and why, and we will explore these differences briefly in the final chapter. All this is by way of saying that it is
not our intention to set up a 'straw man' in our characterizations of
what we think environmentalists want. We think that most people
who think of themselves as being environmentally minded will find

some points of connection with at least some of these positions, and that is all that will be necessary to follow on with the rest of the book.

1.4.1   Preference for Preventing Extinction

> In democratic societies people may think that their government is bound by an ecological version of the Hippocratic oath, to take no action that knowingly endangers biodiversity. But that is not enough. The commitment must be much deeper – to let no species knowingly die, to take all reasonable action to protect every species and race in perpetuity.

> E.O. Wilson (1999, p. 326)

As we saw in Section 1.2, conserving biodiversity might mean many different things, but there is a great deal of agreement that foremost among them is preserving individual species. Conserving species is an explicit goal of many of the major conservation organizations: for example,[5] the World Wildlife Fund, the California Native Plant Society, and Nature Canada, just to name a few. Often these organizations focus on reducing the rate of species extinction as a means of preserving biodiversity. Preventing extinction is Target 12 of the Aichi Biodiversity Targets. These targets are contained in the United Nations' Convention on Biological Diversity's Strategic Plan for Biodiversity 2011–2020.[6]

1.4.2   Preference for 'Natural' over Modified Habitats

> Something will have gone out of us as a people if we ever let the remaining wilderness be destroyed; ... if we drive the few remaining members of the wild species into zoos or to extinction.

> Wallace Stegner [1909–1993] (Wilderness Letter,[7] 1960)

Our sense is that environmentalists favor natural over human-modified habitats, even if those human-made habitats are analogs or reconstructions of some natural habitat. Grazed meadows, constructed wetlands,

---

[5] www.worldwildlife.org/species/index.html   [6] See www.cbd.int/sp/targets/default.shtml
[7] http://stanford.io/2bsoqPF

old fields,[8] these are not appropriate habitats for conservation concern for many environmentalists. That's not to say that we can't find people, or even whole organizations, dedicated to the conservation of, for example, hedgerows in England[9] or pastoral countryside in Europe. While such habitats are certainly preferable to shopping malls and car parks, they generally do not excite the majority of environmentalists. Nor do such people think that precious conservation funds should be diverted away from natural habitats to protect those that have been significantly modified by humans.[10] Preserving natural habitat is Target 5 of the Aichi Biodiversity Targets.

1.4.3 A Preference for Preservation over Conservation

> By an environmental ethic I mean a preservationist ethic, not merely a conservationist one. The goal of environmentalism is to leave much of nature in its original state or to restore it to that state.
>
> J. Robert Loftis (2003, p. 42)

Contemporary use of the word 'conservation,' at least biological conservation, probably encompasses both the concept of conservation and the concept of preservation, but this has not always been so. Indeed, some might disagree that it is currently so. The distinction may trace its origin to philosopher John Passmore's [1914–2004] book *Man's Responsibility for Nature*. In that book, Passmore (1974) makes the distinction that conservation is about the wise use of renewable resources so that they will continue to be available for generations to come, and preservation is about leaving nature alone, unspoiled by human activity. Passmore

---

[8] A type of habitat formed when agricultural fields are abandoned and allowed to 'return to nature,' so to speak. These ecosystems are often characterized by a high proportion of non-native species, but are otherwise functionally similar to native grasslands.

[9] See e.g. http://tinyurl.com/79kgmfn

[10] Of course, there is an obvious criticism to the suggestion that unmodified habitats are a worthy conservation goal. In North and South America, humans have been impacting their environment for several thousand years. In Australasia, the duration of human impact extends back to perhaps 45,000 years before present. Our impact on habitats in Africa, Europe, and Asia go back even further. Technically speaking, outside of a few lakes in Antarctica and perhaps some regions on the bottom of the ocean, there are no habitats on this planet that have avoided human modification. Does this mean that environmentalists are chasing an illusion? This issue will resurface at various points throughout this book.

explicitly linked these two views to particular ethical positions. He equated *conservation* with anthropocentrism – the view that only humans matter, morally speaking – and he equated *preservation* with the view that nature possessed intrinsic value and was thus morally considerable for its own sake. We elaborate on these ideas in Section 1.6. For now, it is important to note that these two philosophical commitments are in opposition to each other, and it would be highly unlikely that someone could hold both views simultaneously.

Philosopher Bryan Norton (1986) argued that this distinction is not necessary and perhaps not helpful. Norton proposed:

> to **conserve** a resource or the productive potential of a resource generating system is to use it wisely, with the goal of maintaining its future availability or productivity. To **preserve** is to protect an ecosystem or a species, to the extent possible, from the disruptions attendant upon it from human use. Armed with these definitions of activities, one could then define a **conservationist policy** as one that recommends conserving the resources and productive potentials of ecosystems in all or most cases for future consumption. A **preservationist policy** would recommend that most ecosystems not yet seriously altered by human management should be maintained in their unaltered state by excluding disruptive human activities from them. A **conservationist** would thus be an individual who, faced with concrete choices regarding resource use, usually advocates a conservationist approach. A **preservationist** is someone who, when faced with choices regarding what to do with a pristine ecosystem or area, usually advocates preservation of it.
>
> *(p. 200; emphasis in the original)*

Using Norton's definitions, it is possible for someone to be both a conservationist and a preservationist, depending upon the question being asked.

We think that environmentalists tend to prefer preservation over conservation whenever the two views come into conflict. For example, large tracts of the Canadian boreal forest have never been exploited for timber harvesting. For these undisturbed tracts, a conservationist would advocate sustainable use management, while a preservationist would advocate leaving the land untouched. We think in many cases environmentalists would prefer to leave the land untouched wherever that is possible.

As a terminological note, we will generally not make a distinction between 'conservation' and 'preservation' except where such a distinction is critical to our meaning.

1.4.4 Preference for Wild over Domesticated Populations

Plants and animals that have been bred for horticulture, agriculture, as companion animals, etc., are not typically regarded as proper targets of conservation. Although there are people and societies dedicated to the conservation and preservation of heritage breeds of livestock and rare breeds of orchids, to name a few, these goals are not part of the environmentalist agenda. Conserving wolves is a genuine environmentalist goal, but conserving the Tibetan Mastiff, or other rare breeds of dogs, is not.

1.4.5 Preference for Native over Introduced

> Each contracting Party shall, as far as possible and as appropriate, prevent the introduction of, control or eradicate those alien species which threaten ecosystems, habitats or species.

> Article 8(h) Convention on Biological Diversity

Species that have evolved in the location, habitat or ecosystem of interest are native and are worthy of significant conservation efforts. Species that evolved elsewhere and were introduced to the location of interest are not only regarded as unworthy of conservation, the environmentalist agenda often includes a goal of *eradicating* these introduced species. Preventing and eliminating species introductions is Target 9 of the Aichi Biodiversity Targets.

Deciding whether a species is native or introduced depends in part on the timeframe being considered, and sometimes on whether or not humans played a role in their introduction. The possum (*Trichosurus vulpecula*) in New Zealand has been naturalized[11] for more than 150 years, yet it is still considered a highly undesirable invasive species. Although horses evolved in North America, they were extirpated[12] about 12,000 years ago. The 'wild horses' that we have today in North America are a different species, introduced by Europeans about 600 years ago. This is an interesting example since a cursory glance at the internet would suggest that wild horses in North America are a serious target of biological conservation, but a deeper look reveals that the real target of conservation is the desire to "preserve a living symbol of America's frontier past" (Ginsburg, 2001). In fact, these horses are a major conservation headache. Every year, the US Bureau of Land Management rounds up hundreds to thousands of horses because there are too many of these 'wild' horses for the land to support – more than 12,000 too many, by recent estimates.[13] Unlike most nuisance exotic mammals, the horses are not simply shot. The BLM goes to great lengths to try to adopt out the animals and to care for those that are not successfully placed; indeed, the BLM has a policy of not selling these animals to slaughterhouses or other buyers who wish to use the animals for their hides or other parts. The New Zealand possum is not treated so kindly.

1.4.6   Preference for Historical vs. Changed Communities and Ecosystems

This ideal overlaps to some extent with 'Natural vs. Human-made' and 'Native vs. Introduced,' since prior to the rise of humans as a species everything was 'natural' and all species were 'native' (see Chapter 9). Generally, environmentalists assign moral significance to one or more historical states of biodiversity. Even where species

---

[11] Naturalized populations have escaped human cultivation and now maintain self-sustaining populations without intervention by humans. A particularly memorable example is the rose-ringed parakeets of London, England. Native to India, this naturalized population now numbers well over 30,000, with 10 major roost sites located around the city. See http://bit.ly/2qGlBQY

[12] 'Extirpated' is an ecological term meaning 'became locally extinct.'

[13] See https://on.doi.gov/2rARcTj

introductions have not resulted in native species extinctions, and so have increased species richness, as has been the case for example with many plant introductions (Sax et al., 2002, Sax and Gaines, 2003), environmentalists object to these changes. It is not that introductions are bad because the new species sometimes displace the previous species; introductions are bad wherever they take hold since they change the historical species composition of an ecosystem.[14]

1.4.7 Preference for Ecological Wholes over Individual Sentient Animals

> This brings us finally to the headaches and heartaches that are experienced by all managers of elephants. A decision has to be made before elephant damage occurs as to whether the area ... will be managed as an elephant reserve or whether the maintenance of biodiversity will be the priority.
>
> Ian John Whyte (2002, p. 83)

We will take up this idea in Section 1.6, and in earnest in Chapter 8. For now, suffice it to say that the environmentalist agenda includes the idea that sacrificing sentient (non-human) animals in order to conserve non-sentient plants, native species, or habitats is not only *acceptable*, it is *morally preferable*. An example of this would be the culling of African Elephants in Kruger National Park in South Africa, in order to conserve rare species of native plants.

1.4.8 Preference for In Situ vs. Ex Situ Conservation

Zoos, botanical gardens, and germplasms may be important *tools* in conservation biology, but the environmentalist agenda does not view such examples of ex situ conservation as a desirable *goal*. Part of conservation is to conserve the environment and biological community of which the species is a part. So, for example, in cases where the extinction

---

[14] Of course, this begs the questions of *which* historical configuration do we make normative and why choose that particular configuration over other equally 'historical' configurations? The choice is not functional (i.e. the issue is not about achieving a particular function or particular level of a particular function), nor does it seem to be justified at all on the basis of instrumental value to humans.

of a species has been prevented by maintaining it in a zoo, this can only be viewed as a temporary state, not as a solution to the conservation problem. The ultimate goal must always be reintroduction into the wild. In cases where the wild habitat no longer exists or where, for other reasons, there is no hope of reintroduction, 'extinct in the wild' means 'extinct' to the environmentalist.

I.5   TOTAL COMMITMENT VS. THE CETERIS PARIBUS ENVIRONMENTALIST

Ceteris paribus is a Latin phrase meaning 'all else being equal.' The *ceteris paribus* environmentalist might value the commitments discussed above as a matter of preference, but, given the right justification, she might be willing to compromise on certain values were the circumstances to require it. For example, she might be willing to accept certain changes in the historical species composition in a region. Or, she might decide against the culling of some sentient animals to protect an ecological whole (like a species, habitat, or ecosystem). A *ceteris paribus* environmentalist might also accept that an introduced species has been present long enough to be considered a sort of 'naturalized citizen' of the particular environment. And so on. In other words, to the *ceteris paribus* environmentalist, the environmentalist agenda represents an ideal situation, but pragmatic considerations might mean that this environmentalist is willing to give up any particular plank of the agenda for one reason or another. The total commitment environmentalist, on the other hand, is committed to the agenda in a way that admits no compromise. These environmental values are strongly held, no matter the policy consequences that follow from these values. In fact, the state of affairs that follows from these values is exactly what the total commitment environmentalist desires.

I.6   ENVIRONMENTAL ETHICS AND INTRINSIC VALUE

Environmental ethics is a subdiscipline of philosophy that grew directly out of environmentalists' concerns about human-centered thinking in ethics. The origins of the field are often traced to ecologist

Aldo Leopold [1887–1948] and his 1949 book *A Sand County Almanac,* and in particular to the concluding essay on "The Land Ethic." In that essay,[15] Leopold claimed that a move away from human-centered thinking in ethics is "an ecological necessity" for contemporary technological societies (Leopold, 1949, p. 203). As Leopold described it, a land ethic

> enlarges the boundaries of the community to include soils, waters, plants, and animals, or collectively: the land. ... A land ethic of course cannot prevent the alteration, management, and use of these "resources," but it does affirm their right to continued existence, and, at least in spots, their continued existence in a natural state.
>
> *(Leopold, 1949, p. 204)*

And in what became the best-known passage of his 1949 essay, Leopold described the core principle of a land ethic thus:

> A thing is right when it tends to preserve the integrity, stability, and beauty of the biotic community. It is wrong when it tends otherwise.
>
> *(Leopold, 1949, pp. 224–225).*

As the modern environmental movement emerged during the 1960s and 1970s, Leopold's essay appealed to a growing chorus of voices arguing that a root cause of environmental problems (perhaps *the* root cause) is human-centered thinking in ethics. Denis Hayes, the US national coordinator of the first Earth Day (held on April 22, 1970), described the goal of the event in these terms: "We hoped it would lead to a new kind of ideology, a new value system based on ecology and a reverence for life" (*New York Times*, April 16, 1990). Similarly, the authors of the first United Nations' *World Conservation Strategy*, published in 1980, wrote:

> Ultimately the behaviour of entire societies towards the biosphere must be transformed if the achievement of conservation objectives is to be assured. A new ethic, embracing plants and animals as well

---

[15] Here the page references refer to the reprinted version of the book: *A Sand County Almanac, and Sketches Here and There*: Oxford University Press, USA; 1989.

as people, is required for human societies to live in harmony with the natural world on which they depend for survival and wellbeing. The long term task of environmental education is to foster or reinforce attitudes and behaviour compatible with this new ethic.

(Allen, 1980, section 13.1)

The claim being made here is that environmental problems force us to re-examine our concept of moral value. In the Western philosophical and religious traditions, it is claimed, only human beings are thought to matter, morally speaking; but the thought was that an environmental crisis will not be avoided unless we break with tradition and acknowledge that non-human nature also has some kind of 'direct' moral standing, that non-human nature is something more than a resource or means to the ends of humans.

Among academics, scholars from a variety of disciplines took up the call for a move away from human-centered thinking in ethics. A 1967 essay by historian Lynn White Jr. [1907–1987] titled "The Historical Roots of Our Ecologic Crisis" gave classic expression of the view that our anthropocentric Christian cultural heritage is the primary cause of the environmental crisis. And in 1972 Christopher D. Stone, a legal theorist, published "Should Trees Have Standing? Toward Legal Rights for Natural Objects." After being cited in a dissenting opinion of the US Supreme Court in an important environmental case, the essay was reprinted in book form and became a classic.

The first book-length treatment of environmental problems by an academic philosopher was published in 1974 by Australian John Passmore. *Man's Responsibility for Nature* was written as a reply to White's charge that anthropocentrism tends to create environmental havoc. Around the same time, essays on environmental ethics appeared by three philosophers now regarded as founders of the field. Australian Richard Routley [1935–1996] (who later changed his name to Richard Sylvan) presented "Is There a Need for a New, an Environmental Ethic?" to the World Congress of Philosophy in 1973, the same year Norwegian Arne Naess [1912–2009] published "The Shallow and the Deep, Long-

Range Ecology Movement: A Summary" in the philosophy journal *Inquiry*, and in 1975, American Holmes Rolston III published "Is There an Ecological Ethic?" in the philosophy journal *Ethics*. These essays each called for a 'new,' non-anthropocentric ethic grounded in, or at least informed by ecological science. Discussion of related issues soon exploded. In 1979, the journal *Environmental Ethics* appeared, followed by *Environmental Values* in 1992 and *Ethics and the Environment* in 1996. The number of books published in the area is now very large, and most university departments of philosophy include a course in environmental ethics.

In this section, we present a taxonomy of views in environmental ethics that relates to the structure of this book. To set the stage for that taxonomy, however, the next subsection provides a brief overview of a basic distinction in value theory that is implicit in the call to move away from human-centered thinking in ethics.

1.6.1 Intrinsic vs. Instrumental Value

Environmentalists defending the preservation of biodiversity commonly invoke the distinction between 'intrinsic value' and 'instrumental value,' and the field of conservation biology has been defined – by some – in terms of a claim about intrinsic value. In a famous essay from 1985 titled "What is Conservation Biology?" ecologist Michael Soulé (1985) included a claim about intrinsic value as "the most fundamental" ethical or normative proposition in his definition of conservation biology:

> *Biotic diversity has intrinsic value,* irrespective of its instrumental or utilitarian value. This normative postulate is the most fundamental. In emphasizing the inherent value of nonhuman life, it distinguishes the dualist, exploitive world view from a more unitary perspective: Species have value in themselves, a value neither conferred nor revocable, but springing from a species' long evolutionary heritage and potential or even from the mere fact of its existence.
>
> *(1985, p. 731; emphasis in original)*

Soulé then refers to works by academic philosophers as evidence that "a large literature exists on this subject." In the quoted paragraph, however, Soulé does not define the term "intrinsic value" and he uses another term, "inherent value," as if he takes the two to be equivalent. In this subsection, we provide an overview of the concept of intrinsic value, and some different senses in which the term is used. In Section 1.6.2 we use the general notion of intrinsic value to categorize views in the field of environmental ethics, and in later chapters (7–11) we will refer back to some of the differing conceptions of 'intrinsic value' that we identify in this subsection.

The general notion of intrinsic value is developed in contrast to instrumental value. *Instrumental value* refers to the value things have as means to some end, purpose, or goal. To say that something has *intrinsic value*, by contrast, is to say that it somehow has value in and of itself, independently of its serving the ends, purposes, or goals of others.

This is the distinction that informs the structure of this book. In Part I we consider instrumental value arguments for preserving biodiversity. These arguments depend on claims that biodiversity promotes a variety of human ends – for instance, by contributing to ecosystem services and stability, supporting innovations in food, medicine, and other areas, and increasing humans' enjoyment of nature. We will argue that while each of these 'defenses' provides some support for biodiversity conservation, the empirical evidence that supports various claims about biodiversity's contribution to human well-being is largely incomplete, and sometimes much weaker than is generally asserted. More importantly, a defense of biodiversity conservation grounded in instrumental value can logically commit one to a variety of policies that are seemingly at odds with important parts of the environmentalist agenda.

Then, in Part II, we consider intrinsic value arguments for preserving biodiversity. These arguments are attractive to environmentalists insofar as they need not depend on factual claims about the usefulness of species and ecosystems to humans, as do the instrumental value arguments considered in Part I. We will emphasize, however, that there are significant philosophical complexities implicit in environmentalists' claims about intrinsic value, complexities that usually go unacknowledged by environmentalists, and we think that the reason is often that they have not critically engaged with these arguments.

For instance, we already noted that in his famous quote about conservation biology's commitment to the intrinsic value of species, Michael Soulé also refers to 'inherent value,' and (at least implicitly) what has come to be called 'objective intrinsic value.' In the philosophical literature, these terms refer to further distinctions within the concept of intrinsic value, and, as we will emphasize in Part II, the distinctions map onto different ontological commitments about the nature of intrinsic value.

Earlier, we said that in attributing intrinsic value to something, one is saying that it 'somehow' has value in and of itself. The further distinctions within the concept of intrinsic value are specifications of that 'somehow.' In this book, we will distinguish between the general 'concept of intrinsic value' and various particular 'conceptions of intrinsic value.' Just as the political philosopher John Rawls [1921–2002] found it helpful to distinguish between the concept of justice, which plays the same role in various political philosophers' thoughts, and those philosophers' various particular conceptions of justice (Rawls, 1971, p. 5), we find it helpful to distinguish between the concept of intrinsic value, which plays the same role in a number of environmental philosophers' thoughts, from various particular conceptions of intrinsic value.

The concept of intrinsic value appears in the work of philosophers who endorse very different conceptions of it. Some environmental philosophers, e.g. Paul Taylor [1923–2015], believe that intrinsic value would exist in nature even if there were no conscious valuers around. This is an objectivist view, according to which intrinsic value is a property of the external world that is discovered by human valuers. Other environmental philosophers, e.g. J. Baird Callicott, believe that intrinsic value is, as it were, "in the eye of the human beholder." This is a subjectivist view, according to which intrinsic value is projected by conscious valuers onto an otherwise valueless world. A third position holds that judgments about intrinsic value arise out of the interaction between human psychological faculties and certain features of the natural world. This is a *relational* conception, according to which the intrinsic value of a natural entity is 'co-constituted' by human subjects and certain natural objects. Among those who endorse a relational conception of intrinsic value, there is further disagreement regarding the nature of the subjective component and its capacity to vary among individuals or cultures. One view would be that human beings are 'hard-wired' in our judgments about intrinsic value (or at least some subset of those judgments), such that there will be convergence among different cultures in terms of the natural entities that they recognize as intrinsically valuable. Another view holds that intrinsic value judgments are influenced by culturally shared norms and values, such that members of particular societies might recognize different classes of entities as intrinsically valuable. Yet another would be that intrinsic value judgments are idiosyncratic to the individual.

In this book, we will use the following labels to distinguish among the specific conceptions of intrinsic value described in the preceding paragraph:

1. **Objective intrinsic value** =df[16] intrinsic value that exists in nature independently of human valuers.[17]

To attribute intrinsic value to something in this sense is like saying that a physical object exists in nature independently of humans'

---

[16] Philosophers commonly use '=df' to indicate 'stipulative definitions' of key terms. Such definitions establish specific meanings that, in day-to-day discourse or other contexts, they do not necessarily have. An example is Peter Singer's stipulative definition of 'sentient' as "having the capacity for suffering and/or experiencing enjoyment." Dictionaries contain other definitions of the term, including "having sensation or feeling," "being self-aware," etc. Agreeing on stipulative definitions of key terms is helpful in discussions such as the present one, where there is controversy over the nature of a key concept. In defining various varieties of intrinsic value as we do in this subsection, we do not intend to define anyone's position out of bounds. Our goal is only to provide labels for the various kinds of intrinsic value that different people have in mind.

[17] Since our audience in this book is human beings, we find it simpler to speak in terms of 'people' although, strictly speaking, these definitions should refer to 'conscious valuers' in general (since for all we know some non-humans value some things non-instrumentally).

perceiving it. Just as a stone exists whether or not anybody notices it, intrinsic value in this sense is possessed by an object whether or not anybody values it. In fact, whether or not anybody is capable of perceiving it, a stone exists (imagine that it's a stone in a cave that nobody will ever be able to visit, or in a crevice in a crater of the moon) and on this conception of intrinsic value, the value exists even if nobody could ever think about it. One of the most famous definitions of intrinsic value in this sense was given by British philosopher George Edward Moore [1873 – 1958], whose work we'll refer to later in a couple of different contexts. Moore defined 'intrinsic value' as the value that something has in virtue of its intrinsic properties, by which he meant the thing's non-relational properties.

'Relational properties' include a thing's tendency to elicit various reactions from human beings. Many champions of biodiversity think that nature's intrinsic value is relational, and specifically that nature has intrinsic value in virtue of the intrinsic valuing that it elicits in organisms such as us. A variety of views fit that description, however, so we need a general label to contrast all such views with what we're calling objective intrinsic value views. Let's call them 'non-objective' views:

2. **Non-objective intrinsic value** =df intrinsic value that is relational; it is actualized when a person values something for itself, rather than as a means to some further end.

This group has at least two members, however, which we will distinguish using the terms 'subjective' and 'relational.'

One of those members takes something to have intrinsic value if someone *in fact* values it non-instrumentally, without placing any qualifications on what properties the intrinsically valued object must have. We call this:

2.A) **Subjective intrinsic value** =df intrinsic value that is 'projected onto' nature by human valuers without the properties of the natural object placing any restraints on the valuing reaction.

This is the view of someone who believes that nothing in nature 'has' intrinsic value in and of itself, that intrinsic value is entirely 'in the eye of the beholder'; to paraphrase Shakespeare: "there is nothing intrinsically valuable in non-human nature, but human thinking makes it so" (*Hamlet*, Act 2, Scene 2). If intrinsic value is subjective in this way, then anything could 'have subjective intrinsic value' for anyone at any time, without regard to what properties the valued object has.

Some philosophers want to admit that something's having intrinsic value requires it to stand in *some* kind of relationship to a conscious valuer, but they think that the properties of the valued object in some way determine or constrain the judgments of intrinsic value that the valuer makes. We call this 'relational intrinsic value':

2.B) **Relational intrinsic value** =df intrinsic value that is actualized when a person perceives certain properties of a natural object.

This valuing reaction to the properties of the object could be:

2.B.i) 'hard-wired' into our judgments about intrinsic value, so that all normal, adult humans will tend to make the same judgments about what has intrinsic value; or

2.B.ii) influenced by culturally shared norms in ways that produce convergent judgments about intrinsic value within particular cultural groups; or

2.B.iii) idiosyncratic.

So understood, intrinsic value is a relational property – because a thing's having it depends on that thing's standing in a certain relationship to a person – but under this relational conception, (2.B.i) through (2.B.iii) describe a range of constraints that the thing's properties can place on the reactions of the person.

Later chapters will provide an opportunity for more detailed illustrations, but for now the above variations on relational intrinsic value can be illustrated as follows. Suppose (we don't believe that this is so, but for the sake of illustration, just *suppose*) that members of our species are hard-wired to have a certain kind of aesthetic response when perceiving a yawning chasm directly in front of us, and that this aesthetic response somehow amounts to valuing the chasm non-instrumentally. Were that so, then when standing on the rim of the Grand Canyon,[18] each of us would react the same way, and each of us would react by valuing the canyon intrinsically. So described, the Canyon would have intrinsic value in sense (2.B.i).

Now, suppose that we've all grown up in late twentieth-century America while being exposed to lots of nature writing, television, and film that celebrates having positive aesthetic responses to yawning chasms. Then 'we' would all have a similar response to the Canyon, and it would have intrinsic value in sense (2.B.ii). But of course a person raised in a culture that found 'wilderness' threatening would probably have a very different reaction, something akin to fear. In that case, the Canyon would still have intrinsic value, but only 'for' – meaning in virtue of its relationship to – those of 'us' who were socialized the same way.

Finally, suppose that a friend of yours has come to find the prairie plant Canadian wild rye (*Elymus canadensis*) beautiful as a result of it taking over an unkempt area in his backyard and he values it non-instrumentally for being beautiful in the way it is. Having developed this love of Canadian wild rye, your friend now begins to find stands of wheat beautiful in a way that he didn't previously. You may not know anyone else who thinks that Canadian wild rye is beautiful, but it now has intrinsic value in sense (2.B.iii), at least for – meaning in virtue of its relation to – him. The fact that your friend has generalized his reaction from one species of grass to another indicates that in valuing these grasses intrinsically, he is reacting to some set of properties of the grasses, even if his intrinsic value judgments are shared by no one else (i.e. they are idiosyncratic).

---

[18] Readers unfamiliar with the Grand Canyon can see http://bit.ly/2bsqGX4 for further information. Co-author Varner made this 270 degree panorama of the famous "yawning chasm" from a remote overlook http://bit.ly/2c0Srob.

Notice one related thing. Suppose that your friend can't say anything about what properties of the grass make him find it beautiful, and he doesn't generalize his reaction to any other species of grass that are similar in various ways to Canadian wild rye. Now his attribution of intrinsic value looks (in our terminology) more *subjective* (sense 2.A) than *relational* (sense 2.B), because it seems that he is not reacting to any specified properties of the thing that he values intrinsically. That is, his valuing the thing in question seems to bear no relation to the properties of that thing; he seems just to be projecting intrinsic value onto it. In general, the more you can articulate a set of properties that interact with a psychological disposition to produce a judgment of intrinsic value, the more the intrinsic value seems to be relational rather than subjective.[19]

The point of this initial exercise in distinctions and definitions is this. Environmentalists (and scientists) often use the term 'intrinsic value' without seeming to notice that the term can mean significantly different things. In Soulé's famous characterization of conservation biology, he seems to mean what we are calling *objective* intrinsic value. We say this because he spells out what he means by saying that "species have value in themselves, a value neither conferred nor revocable." This statement seems to be asserting that the value in question exists in nature, entirely independently of human valuers. That is certainly a stronger claim than asserting that biodiversity has *relational* intrinsic value. And of course, someone who claims that biodiversity has relational intrinsic value needs to recognize that, as we emphasized earlier, the valuing reaction can be caused by very different things, ranging from a feature of human nature to a personal idiosyncrasy.

---

[19] For what it's worth, note also that the properties of the thing that is attributed relational intrinsic value (sense 2.B) can themselves be relational properties of that object. For instance, the value of a tool (say, an electric drill) is normally thought to be exhausted by its instrumental value. But suppose that the tool in question was given to you by your father. Even after the tool quits working, you might continue to value it, intrinsically, because it was given to you by your father. This would seem to be an example of intrinsic value in sense (2.B.iii). But in this case the property of the tool, in reaction to which you value it intrinsically, is itself a relational property – that is, the tool's relationship to your father. We mention this because among philosophers, Moore's famous definition of intrinsic value mentioned above is in terms of the non-relational properties of the object.

As we noted earlier, Soulé also uses the term *inherent* value as if it is synonymous with *intrinsic* value. It is important to note, however, that *inherent* value has been used by some philosophers as a contrast term to *intrinsic* value. For instance, in his landmark book on animal rights (Regan, 1983), and in a 1981 essay, Tom Regan [1938–2017] uses the term 'intrinsic value' in Moore's sense, to refer to what we are calling objective intrinsic value;[20] but Regan reserves the term 'inherent value' for a different kind of value. Specifically, Regan defines 'inherent value' as the specific kind of value that, on his view, individuals with moral rights have: "To view [rights holders] as having inherent value is thus to view them as something different from, and something more than, mere receptacles of what has intrinsic value" (Regan, 1983, p. 236). Thus, in Regan's work, to think of an entity has having *inherent* value is to think of it as being due a certain kind of respect that, he thinks, individuals do not get in utilitarian thinking about ethics (for more on this, see Section 8.4).

We urge Soulé, and environmentalists in general, to be more clear about such key terminology when describing their value commitments. This is important because different conceptions of intrinsic value (as well as Regan's conception of inherent value) face different philosophical challenges, as we will emphasize throughout Chapters 7–11. Most generally, showing that biodiversity has objective intrinsic value – the kind Soulé has in mind – is more challenging than establishing that it has relational intrinsic value.

We think that environmentalists are tempted to invoke the concept of *objective* intrinsic value because they think it has more 'moral force.' So, for instance, suppose we are trying to show that an endangered species is worth preserving. One reason might be that it has historical significance in our culture, and that might be articulated as a claim that the species has relational intrinsic value in sense 2.B.ii. An example in North America might be the bald eagle (*Haliaeetus leucocephalus*), which is sacred in some native cultures and has been the

---

[20] Relatedly, during the early 1980s Regan was working on a book on Moore's philosophy that was published in 1986.

symbol of the United States since its earliest days. That might be a compelling reason to people immersed in American culture, but, like the value of wildness, it is culturally relative, and that makes it seem less morally compelling than claiming that the species has objective intrinsic value, which doesn't depend on it standing in some historical relationship to a human culture, or in any relationship to human beings at all. For that reason, environmentalists will be tempted to make claims about the objective intrinsic value of biodiversity, but, as we will emphasize in Part II of this book, claims about objective intrinsic value carry special argumentative burdens. A main one stems from the fact that the traditional paradigm of an entity with objective intrinsic value is a conscious human person. So anyone who claims that a species, ecosystem, or other unconventional candidate has objective intrinsic value, should be able to explain *why* others should recognize this value – he should be able to say *why* both human persons and a species or an ecosystem has objective intrinsic value.

Relatedly, we want to emphasize one more thing about the passage from Soulé's "What is Conservation Biology?" that we quoted earlier. There, Soulé describes the claim that "Biotic diversity has [objective] intrinsic value" as "a postulate." But a *postulate* is something that is *assumed* for the sake of a discussion, and environmentalists cannot assume that biodiversity has intrinsic value, of any kind, for the sake of a public debate over environmental policy. If they treat intrinsic value as an unargued assumption, then they are not engaging intellectually with others who make contrary assumptions about what has – and what *doesn't* have – intrinsic value. By learning something about how philosophers defend theories of environmental ethics (as we will describe in Part II), however, they can see how to provide arguments in support of such basic value commitments, while acknowledging the limitations or weaknesses of any particular claim that they are attempting to defend.

1.6.2   *A Taxonomy of Views in Environmental Ethics*

Positions in environmental ethics are commonly categorized according to their commitments on the question of what has intrinsic value.

Since the field emerged in response to environmentalists' call to move away from human-centered thinking in ethics, theories of environmental ethics are categorized by which types of things have intrinsic value according to each.[21] Thus, *anthropocentrism* is standardly defined as the view that only human beings' lives, interests, experiences, etc., have intrinsic value, and that all of non-human nature has only instrumental value.

As the current debate over 'animal welfare' and 'animal rights' emerged in the wake of the 1975 Peter Singer book *Animal Liberation: A New Ethics for our Treatment of Animals*, environmental philosophers adopted the term *sentientism* to refer to the view that the conscious lives of both humans and all other sentient animals have intrinsic value. The term 'sentient' sometimes carries the connotation of self-consciousness, but Singer adopted the term "as a convenient if not strictly accurate shorthand for the capacity to suffer and/or experience enjoyment" (Singer, 1975, p. 9; 1990, pp. 8–9). Conscious suffering and/or enjoyment covers a broad range of things, from pinpricks and third degree burns to the joy of cooking and aesthetic contemplation. Outside of science fiction, however, we generally do not encounter individuals who are capable of suffering and/or enjoyment of any kind who are not also capable of suffering from physical pain specifically.[22] So in the debate over animal ethics, 'sentient' is

---

[21] Traditionally, philosophers categorized ethical theories in terms of how they define right actions. Some theories define right actions and institutions in terms of their consequences. The most well-known example is utilitarianism, which refers to a family of theories each of which holds that – at least ultimately – the right thing to do is to maximize the aggregate happiness of those affected by our decisions. Other theories define what is right in non-consequentialist terms. For instance, some philosophers describe moral rights as 'trump cards' against utilitarian arguments, so that if one has a moral right to something, then a utilitarian argument is not a sufficient justification for depriving one of that thing. Both such a 'rights view' and utilitarianism will be discussed in greater detail in Chapter 8, but in this section we will focus on a different way of categorizing ethical theories that has generally been adopted by philosophers working on environmental ethics, specifically.

[22] A real-world exception is humans with congenital insensitivity to pain (CIP). People with this extremely rare congenital condition do not feel physical pain, even when they break a leg or are badly burned. They are, however, otherwise capable of the entire range of enjoyments and sufferings available to normal people. As illustrated in the documentary film *A Life Without Pain*, humans with CIP only survive with extensive support of an understanding community, so it seems unlikely that an animal with CIP would live long.

often taken to mean 'capable of feeling physical pain,' and debates over the extent of sentience among non-humans are usually conducted in terms of evidence for physical pain among non-humans.

For reasons discussed in Chapter 8 of this book, it seems unlikely that sentience extends beyond vertebrates and a few invertebrates, let alone beyond the animal kingdom. It almost certainly does not extend to aggregations of organisms – to entire species or ecosystems, for example. And so labels have developed for views that attribute intrinsic value to both non-sentient and sentient organisms, on the one hand, and to 'holistic' entities such as species and ecosystems, on the other. *Biocentric individualism* refers to the former view on intrinsic value: 'biocentric' because such an ethic is life-centered, and 'individualism' to distinguish this view from *ecoholism*, which refers to the view that environmental 'wholes' also have intrinsic value.

Within holistic environmental ethics we find it helpful to introduce one further basic distinction with regard to what has intrinsic value. Obviously, if you think that not only human beings and sentient animals, but also plants and other non-conscious organisms, as well as both species and ecosystems, all have intrinsic value, then there are going to be many trade-offs to be adjudicated, and our additional distinction dramatizes one way to eliminate the trade-offs. By *pure holism* we mean the view that *only* the wholes (species and/or ecosystems) have intrinsic value. But most holists talk about species and ecosystems counting *in addition to* some or all of the individuals that the other three types of theories are concerned with. The latter view we will refer to as *pluralistic holism*.

Although some of the rhetoric of more 'radical' environmentalists is suggestive of what we are calling *pure* holism, we think that, on reflection, almost no one is literally a pure holist. For instance, the first issue of the newsletter of the Voluntary Human Extinction Movement included the graph shown in Figure 1.1. In it, the "quality of Earth's health" is inversely proportional to the human population, such that "Earth recovers" when humans go extinct. That's suggestive of a pure holist stance, but note that VHEMT's call is for "**voluntary**

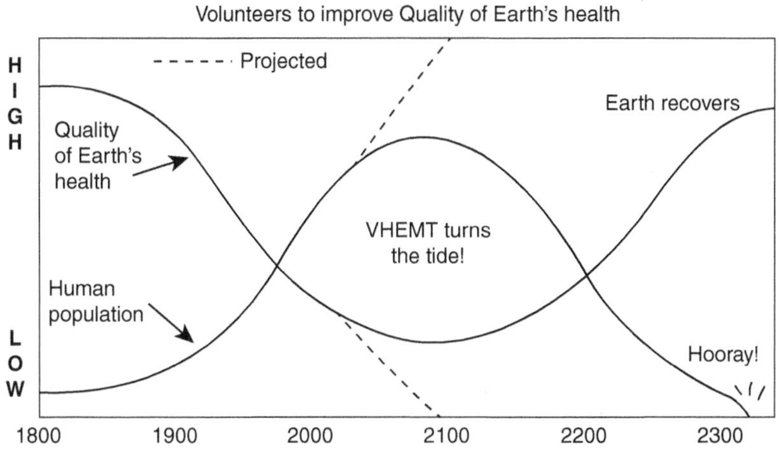

Volunteers to improve Quality of Earth's health

FIGURE 1.1 From the Voluntary Human Extinction Movement newsletter, *These Exit Times*, 1990, volume 1, number 1. (http://vhemt .org/TET1.pdf). Reproduced under Creative Commons License 3.0.

human extinction" – through individual decisions not to breed – and, in addition to "freedom of choice," that first issue of their newsletter expressed their commitments to "peace and justice," "good health and social security," and "dignity in dying," each of which expresses some kind of commitment to respecting individual humans, in addition to the "quality of Earth's health."

Similarly, sometimes a well-known author says something that, taken literally and in isolation, would imply a pure holist perspective, but it is clear from other things that they are pluralistic holists. A good example is Aldo Leopold's summary description (quoted earlier) of the land ethic as holding that "A thing is right when it tends to preserve the integrity, stability, and beauty of the biotic community. It is wrong when it tends otherwise." As Leopold's son Luna Leopold [1915–2006] emphasized in the foreword to *Aldo Leopold: The Professor* (McCabe, 1987, a collection of reminiscences published to celebrate the centennial of his birth), if the above quote is taken to be "the sole criterion on morality," then the land ethic would have various extreme implications:

> It has been suggested that Leopold's words imply that the value of an individual person would be inversely proportional to the supply of people. The words have even been interpreted to convey the idea that abortion, infanticide, war and other means for the elimination of the less fit may be unobjectionable because they are ecosystemically unobjectionable.[23]

But, Luna Leopold emphasized, to treat the oft-quoted summary statement of the land ethic as "the sole criterion on morality" does not fit with the "deep personal concern for the individual" that his father manifested in various ways (McCabe, 1987, p. viii).

We think it clear that Leopold was, in our terminology, a pluralistic holist, and that his famous quote should be understood as one 'moral precept' that he endorsed among others, including precepts referring to respectful treatment of individual humans. A collection of moral precepts is no substitute for a fully articulated moral theory, however, and those who believe that a broad range of things have intrinsic value face a significant philosophical challenge explaining how to handle situations in which claims on behalf of such diverse entities as human persons, various non-human organisms, and holistic entities such as species and ecosystems pull in different directions.

---

[23] Here Luna Leopold is probably referring to Callicott (1980, pp. 326–327 and 334) and Regan (1983, pp. 361–362).

Table 1.4 graphically displays the taxonomy of views in environmental ethics that we have described in this subsection. We noted earlier that the *concept* of intrinsic value appears in the work of philosophers who endorse very different theories of environmental ethics, e.g. J. Baird Callicott and Paul Taylor, who employ different *conceptions* of intrinsic value, conceptions that carry very different philosophical baggage. Here we add that these philosophers fall into different camps in this taxonomy: Callicott is a pluralistic holist, whereas Taylor is a biocentric individualist. Nonetheless, each employs a conception of intrinsic value in their efforts to move away from anthropocentric thinking about the environment.

It is not our purpose in this book to side with any particular view about what has intrinsic value or what sort of intrinsic value. As we will note in the concluding chapter, we authors have been partisans of different views, and we endorse different conceptions of intrinsic value. The present book is not intended to defend a particular position in these debates. Later chapters will include more detailed discussions of such debates, but our purpose in presenting those debates will be to provide environmentalists with a philosophical 'tool kit,' to sharpen our understanding of basic concepts in environmental ethics, and to deepen our understanding of the philosophical issues that are implicit in various arguments for preserving biodiversity.

I.7   THE STRUCTURE OF THIS BOOK

Why should we conserve biodiversity? Environmentalists have traditionally responded to this question along the lines of Paul and Anna Erhlich (1992, p. 219, numbers in [] denote chapters in this book that address these enumerated defenses):

> Biodiversity, the vast array of non-human organisms of our planet, should be valued for four general reasons. First, we (and many others) believe that, as the dominant species on Earth, *Homo sapiens* have an ethical, stewardship responsibility towards humanity's only known living companions in the universe

Table 1.4 *A taxonomy of views in environmental ethics, in terms of which things have intrinsic value*

	Anthropocentrism	Sentientism	Biocentric individualism	Holism (pluralistic)	Holism (pure)
Human beings?	Yes	Yes	Yes	Yes	
Sentient animals?		Yes	Yes	Yes	
Non-sentient organisms?			Yes	Yes	
Species and ecosystems?				Yes	Yes

[Chapters 7–10]. Second, as attested to by activities as diverse as gardening, making of nature films, and ecotourism, biodiversity has aesthetic values [Chapters 5 and 11]. Third, humanity has derived many direct economic values from biodiversity, including all of its food and many of its medicines and industrial products [Chapter 4]. The potential of nature's genetic library for providing more of these benefits is enormous [Chapter 3]. Fourth, and most important from an anthropocentric perspective, plants, animals, and microorganisms help to supply human beings with an array of free ecosystem services, without which civilization could not persist [Chapter 2]. These include such things as controlling the gaseous mix of the atmosphere, generating and maintaining soils, controlling pests, and running biogeochemical cycles. The present extinction episode caused by human activity seriously jeopardizes the ethical, aesthetic, direct economic and life-support values of biodiversity; it may be the single most important externality associated with human economic activity.

This book is organized around the distinction between instrumental value and intrinsic value. In Part I, we ask how far instrumental value defenses of biodiversity get us in defending the environmentalist agenda as described in Section 1.4. Instrumental value arguments for preserving biodiversity are relatively less complicated philosophically, but they are not as clearly supported by the relevant empirical evidence as environmentalists sometimes assume. Also, adopting such a defense can logically commit an environmentalist to policies that are at odds with other parts of the environmentalist agenda. And herein often lies the motivation of some environmentalists to adopt an intrinsic value defense.

In Part II, we consider the challenges implicit in taking an intrinsic value approach to defending biodiversity. These intrinsic value arguments can proceed largely independently of the complicated empirical issues that the instrumental arguments face, but there are significant conceptual issues implicit in the various conceptions of intrinsic value, and the philosophical arguments needed to support them are complex. In our experience, environmentalists commonly claim that 'nature' or ecosystems or species have intrinsic value without acknowledging various philosophical difficulties. In surveying these difficulties, we do not mean to dismiss such views; indeed, each of the coauthors of this book believes that in at least some sense, parts of non-human nature have intrinsic value. Our goal is, first, to sensitize readers to the philosophical challenges so that they can appreciate why such views are controversial and certainly not obviously correct; and second, we hope that scientists and environmentalists can in the future contribute more to philosophical discussions of those challenges.

I.8   FURTHER READING

Doherty, B. and T. Doyle (2006). Beyond Borders: Transnational Politics, Social Movements and Modern Environmentalisms, *Environmental Politics* 15(5): 697–712.

Maclaurin, J. and K. Sterelny (2008). *What is Biodiversity?* Chicago: University of Chicago Press.

Neumann, R. (2004). Moral and Discursive Geographies in the War for Biodiversity in Africa, *Political Geography* 23: 813–837.

Sarkar, S. (2005). *Biodiversity and Environmental Philosophy: An Introduction.* New York: Cambridge University Press.

Takacs, D. (1996). *The Idea of Biodiversity: Philosophies of Paradise.* Baltimore: Johns Hopkins University Press.

PART I Instrumental Value Defenses

In Part I, we examine arguments that people commonly advance as justifications for conserving biodiversity that are based on how *useful* the biodiversity is to humans. We term these *instrumental value defenses*. We focus on whether biodiversity is useful *to humans*, because this is an uncontroversial claim. The interests of humans in living healthy and fulfilling lives is undeniably morally relevant, and aspects of biodiversity that help us to do so have undeniable instrumental value. All else being equal, we ought to conserve that biodiversity, for that reason. The instrumental defenses in this part of the book turn, for the most part, on their supporting empirical evidence. That is, if we cannot show that some biodiversity is useful to us, then we have no good reason to conserve it, according to such instrumental value arguments. What's more, even if we can show that some bit of biodiversity is, in fact, useful to us, we need to show that it is *more* useful than whatever we want to do that might endanger it.

We consider these instrumental value defenses roughly in order of importance to debates about the environmentalist agenda. We start, in Chapter 2, with the argument that biodiversity is necessary to maintain ecosystem function and stability. There, we examine the empirical evidence for a relationship between biodiversity and ecosystem function. We show that there is evidence to support a positive relationship, but that the evidence may not be as strong as many people assume. We then go on to show that even if the empirical relationship between an ecosystem function and biodiversity was strong and unambiguous, the *relevance* of that evidence to actual conservation problems might still be tenuous. And finally, we show that even if the empirical evidence was strongly relevant to conservation practice, a reliance on this defense logically commits environmentalists to policies that are at odds with other parts of their agenda.

In Chapter 3 we consider the precautionary principle. This principle, and its associated precautionary defenses, are often employed by environmentalists after finding that some bit of biodiversity is either not useful, or not more useful than some land use that would involve losing it. The precautionary argument says, in effect, that although some bit of biodiversity might not seem useful now, it is uncertain how useful or important it might be in the future. Environmentalists think that this uncertainty demands that we ought to err on the side of caution and preserve the biodiversity, in case it turns out to be very useful to humans in the future. We show that the precautionary principle may be logically flawed, and in any case it is problematic to use in practice because it ignores the opportunity costs of the proposed remedy, as well as the benefits of the proposed action that is said to endanger the biodiversity.

In Chapter 4 we consider defenses based on biodiversity's contributions to food security and as a source for developing new medications. While initially attractive, this defense would seem to provide support for very little of the environmentalist agenda. These two arguments for biodiversity's usefulness apply to only a small fraction of global biodiversity. Very few species are currently used for food or medicines, and this defense provides no support for species that are known to not be useful in these respects. We then consider the option value, or the quasi-option value, of biodiversity. These are economic arguments about the *future* value of biodiversity that might eventually be discovered. Unfortunately, these defenses are deeply problematic. It seems that the arguments from agricultural and pharmaceutical value do not offer compelling reasons to conserve *biodiversity per se*. They offer reasons for conserving a small number of species, for limited periods of time, under very special economic conditions.

In Chapter 5 we consider the argument that biodiversity ought to be conserved for the value that humans receive through their enjoyment of it, broadly called nature-based tourism. We also consider the argument that biodiversity ought to be conserved because it has the power to transform the degree to which we value that biodiversity (called 'transformative value'). We show that nature-based tourism can be an important tool for helping people see value in the wilder ecosystems that are repositories of much of the biodiversity we want to conserve. However, we suggest that the defense seems unlikely to have enough positive support on its own to serve as a strong defense of the environmentalist agenda. We also suggest that biodiversity's supposed transformative value doesn't seem likely to make up for this deficiency. There exists considerable variability in human responses to nature. That variability can't be ignored or glossed over, and that variability might be a reasonable objection to these defenses.

We conclude Part I with Chapter 6, where we briefly consider how far all of these defenses get environmentalists in terms of the agenda we laid out in Chapter 1. We conclude that instrumental defenses, singly and in conjunction, get environmentalists some of the agenda, but by no means all of it. Additionally, some of these defenses, while offering support for part of the agenda, imply commitments that are at odds with other parts of the agenda. This suggests that either some of the environmentalist agenda might need to be abandoned or modified, or that instrumental defenses are not good *general* defenses for conserving biodiversity, and that environmentalists will need to look elsewhere for such general defenses.

2 Ecosystem Functioning and Stability

Each species on our planet plays a role in the healthy functioning of natural ecosystems, on which humans depend.

William H. Schlesinger (pers. comm.)

2.1 THE BASIC ARGUMENT

A common argument in favor of conserving biodiversity is that biodiversity is necessary to maintain the ecosystem services and functions on which all human societies depend. The argument goes something like this:

Premise 1: We ought to preserve the ecological background conditions on which all human societies depend.

Premise 2: All human societies rely on various products and services provided by natural ecosystems. These products and services either cannot be reproduced by human capital or would be very expensive to provide by human capital, whereas now we get these services for free.

Premise 3: The level of products and services provided by natural ecosystems decline as biodiversity declines.

Conclusion: Therefore we ought to conserve biodiversity.

In this chapter, we will not debate the anthropocentric focus articulated in the first premise of this argument. Instead, our focus will be on evaluating the empirical claims made in the subsequent premises. However, it is important to understand from the outset how this first assumption (that human interests trump non-human interests, but non-human interests might still matter) bears on the rest of the argument.

We begin with a fairly straightforward logical point. Before one can consider the value of ecosystem services or their link to biodiversity, one must first identify some focal beneficiary of those services. Without a focal beneficiary (e.g. an organism or community) the notion of an ecosystem service doesn't even make sense. Simply put, the very idea of a *service* implies that the interests of someone or something are being served in some way. Although this point may be obvious, it is surprising how frequently it is overlooked. When environmentalists appeal to an ecosystem services defense of biodiversity, it is often unclear which beneficiaries are under consideration. Even worse, there is a widespread tendency to start off by evaluating the benefits that biodiversity provides to humans, and then 'move the goalposts' by shifting to some other species whose interests should also be served. The problem with this move, however, is that any change in an ecosystem is likely to be good for some species and bad for others. There is unlikely to be any species-general ecosystem service – i.e. a service that benefits all species equally. Thus, it is important to keep the goalposts firmly anchored when considering empirical questions about the value of ecosystem services or whether those services are linked to biodiversity.

As we have noted, this chapter focuses on human needs and interests. There are several reasons for adopting this anthropocentric stance when considering an ecosystem services defense of biodiversity. First, many of the empirical studies on this topic also focus on human needs and interests. So the anthropocentric stance has considerable precedent within the relevant literature on ecosystem services. Second, this assumption is morally uncontroversial. If causing species to go extinct prevents some humans from fulfilling their basic needs, then doing so would generally be accepted as morally wrong. By comparison, the assumption that there are other entities possessing moral worth (Section 1.6.2), and whose needs and interests should therefore enter into this discussion, is much more contentious. We discuss the question of non-anthropocentric interests in Part II (see Chapters 7–11). For the purposes of this chapter, however, it is preferable to focus on the least controversial case, with humans as the focal beneficiaries. If the ecosystem services defense of biodiversity doesn't work for humans, then it probably won't work for other species either. Finally, the third reason for focusing this discussion on the needs and interests of just humans is that it allows us to set aside another thorny ethical issue: the problem of how to prioritize competing interests. To illustrate this point, suppose it turns out that humans have a moral duty to look out for the needs and interests of certain other species besides our own. For example, suppose we have a duty to conserve all sentient creatures (see Chapter 8). Presumably there will be some sentient creatures that require ecosystem services that we humans do not require. For example, octopuses are arguably sentient creatures. One species of octopus called the blanket octopus (*Tremoctopus gelatus*) uses stinging tentacles from the Portuguese man-o-war (*Physalia Phyllis*, a type of jellyfish) as a form of defense. This species of jellyfish provides a valuable service to the blanket octopus. However, stinging jellyfish tentacles are probably a *disservice* to us. The point of this example is to show how the prioritization problem makes the debate over ecosystem services extremely complex. As we shall illustrate later in this chapter, it is a serious empirical challenge to determine how biodiversity and ecosystem services are linked, even for our own species. This problem is only compounded if we have to take other species into account. Our strategy in this book is to deal with each of these issues independently. Hence, for the remainder of this discussion we shall assume, for the sake of simplicity and clarity, that the anthropocentric focus adopted in premise 1 is correct.

In this chapter, we examine how far the *empirical* claims about ecosystem functions in premises 2 and 3 carry us toward an anthropocentric rationale for biodiversity conservation. We will show that:

- Within the relevant experimental literature there is empirical support for a positive relationship between species richness and some ecosystem functions (although the support may not be as strong as people often assume).

- Nevertheless, there remain some serious questions about how meaningful those experimental findings are to real-world ecosystems and/or conservation policy.
- People who rely on this defense of biodiversity conservation would be logically committed to conclusions that are at odds with other commitments that are associated with the environmentalist agenda (as described in Section 1.4).

2.2 PRELIMINARIES

Before discussing the available empirical research, we must discuss some crucial terminology and concepts. These ideas and definitions might seem disjointed at first, but we'll bring them all together by the end of the chapter, so please bear with us.

2.2.1 Biodiversity

Although 'biodiversity' was defined broadly in Chapter 1, it is crucial to realize that, in the context of this chapter, biodiversity *most commonly* refers to 'species richness': the number of species present in the biological community of species. There is now a body of work that considers the effects of genetic diversity (the variety of alleles in a given population, and/or the relatedness between the species) and what is called 'functional diversity' (the number of functional traits represented by the species present) on the functioning of ecosystems.[1] It might turn out that these types of diversity are more important than species richness. Nevertheless, species richness has been the focus of the majority of research attention (Hendriks and Duarte, 2008), it is commonly understood by the public, and it is a common goal of conservation policy.

2.2.2 Ecosystem Functions and Services

A definition that is commonly used for ecosystem services is Gretchen Daily's (1997, p. 3): "the conditions and processes through

---

[1] For more on genetic diversity and ecosystem functioning, see Cadotte et al. (2008). For more on functional diversity and ecosystem functioning, see Petchey et al. (2004).

which natural ecosystems, and the species that make them up, sustain and fulfill human life." Among the conditions and processes Daily mentions are water purification, soil fertility, and air quality. We might also include things like crop pollination, net primary productivity (roughly the rate of biomass accumulation), breakdown of toxic substances, seed dispersal, and so on. As broadly used in the literature, 'ecosystem services' and 'ecosystem functions' mean the same things. Some researchers (e.g. Hooper et al., 2005) distinguish between 'ecosystem goods' and 'ecosystem services,' the former meaning things for which there already exists an economic market, the latter being reserved for those properties of ecosystems that have no market value and yet are important for human well-being.

Ecosystem stability can be thought of as another type of ecosystem function or ecosystem service. However, it can be more difficult to understand, and the mechanisms linking biodiversity to ecosystem stability can be quite different from those linking biodiversity to other ecosystem functions. This is a fascinating and rich area of research,[2] but for our purposes, it is enough to think of ecosystem stability as simply another type of ecosystem service or function, and leave it at that. The theoretical and practical details of the differences don't affect our main points in this chapter. See Box 2.1 for more details.

2.3 RELATIONSHIPS BETWEEN BIODIVERSITY AND ECOSYSTEM FUNCTIONING

Before getting to the effects of biodiversity on ecosystem functioning, it is important to understand that ecosystem functioning is also affected by climate, geography, and soil. In fact, a good deal is known about these other drivers of ecosystem functioning and less about the effects of biodiversity. Nevertheless, this much is clear: with no biodiversity, ecosystems don't function. Living organisms are an essential part of any functioning ecosystem. But how does the *level* of functioning change as we add or subtract species?

[2] A good entry to this literature is McCann (2000).

BOX 2.1   **Biodiversity and Ecosystem Stability**

The relationship between biodiversity and ecosystem stability has been of interest to ecologists since at least the 1950s. The balance of scientific opinion has shifted back and forth as to whether more diverse ecosystems are more 'stable.' Ecosystem stability has been defined many different ways, and some of the disagreement amongst ecologists has turned on the particular definition of choice. While the history of this disagreement is fascinating, we will not attempt to cover it here; a good starting point can be found in deLaplante and Picasso (2011).

For our purposes, we note that three types or definitions of stability have been common in the experimental literature. **Temporal stability** is when the level of some aggregate ecosystem property, typically biomass production, varies little through time. A typical experiment will vary the number of different plant or algal species, and measure biomass production at several points in time. Researchers then calculate the coefficient of variation[3] for this sample of time points as a measure of variability. The other two types of stability are defined with reference to some sort of perturbation or disturbance. **Resistance** is the ability of the ecosystem to resist changing the level of some function in the face of a disturbance. Again, most of this research has been on biomass production in grasslands. The typical disturbance has been the impact of drought. Such experiments might measure ecosystem biomass for several years, including one in which the plots experience a drought year. The most resistant plots are those where the biomass produced in a drought year varies the least from the biomass produced in a non-drought year. Finally, **Resilience** is how quickly the ecosystem recovers the level of some function after it has been altered through a disturbance.

---

[3] The coefficient of variation (CV) is estimated as the standard deviation of the sample divided by the mean of the sample. The CV is a preferred measure because it takes into account the fact that variance often increases as the mean gets larger.

BOX 2.1 **(cont.)**

A review of the literature by John Griffin and colleagues (2009) found some support for a positive biodiversity–temporal stability relationship (18 of 22 experiments), but less support for a positive biodiversity–resistance relationship (5 of 17 experiments), and only modest support for a positive biodiversity–resilience relationship (4 of 7 experiments). More studies have been added since 2009, but there have still been far fewer experiments that study the biodiversity-ecosystem stability question than those studying the biodiversity-ecosystem function question. A more recent review by Bradley Cardinale and colleagues (2013) of just the temporal stability hypothesis as it pertains to biomass production examined data from 34 studies. They concluded that:

> First, while it may be generally true that biodiversity enhances both productivity and stability, it is also true that the highest levels of productivity in a diverse community are not associated with the highest levels of stability. Thus, on average, diversity does not maximize the various aspects of ecosystem functioning we might wish to achieve in conservation and management. Second, knowing how biodiversity affects productivity gives no information about how diversity affects stability (or vice versa).
>
> *(Cardinale et al., 2013, p. 1687)*

Historically, researchers routinely referred to the six hypothetical relationships shown in Figure 2.1 (Naeem et al., 2002). Briefly, *Redundancy* is the idea that most species do similar things and so there is redundancy in function, meaning that species loss doesn't have a large effect on ecosystem functioning until the community has very few species left. *Linear* reflects the idea that all species make approximately equal contributions to ecosystem functioning and they all do different things. This means that each species that is lost from an ecosystem reduces overall functioning by the same amount. *Idiosyncratic* reflects the idea that it is difficult to predict a priori

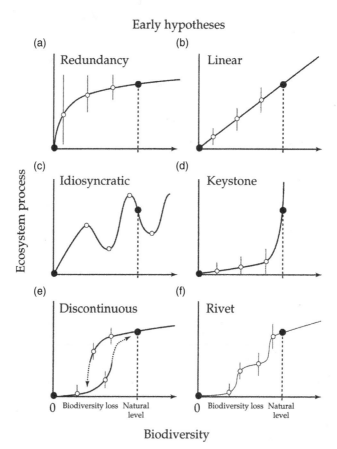

FIGURE 2.1 Reprinted from Naeem et al. (2002). Original caption: Graphical representations of early hypothetical relationships between biodiversity and ecosystem processes. These were meant primarily as heuristic devices or graphical representations of testable hypotheses representing a variety of potential mechanisms. Beyond the point at the origin (where there is no diversity and therefore no measurable processes) and the often highly predictable second point at natural levels of diversity, there was insufficient empirical and theoretical information to know under which circumstances which of the above possible relationships applied to ecosystems. Contemporary research rarely refers to these early hypotheses, although the terminology is still often in use when referring to different classes of associations. Reprinted by permission of Oxford University Press.

whether the loss of a species will result in a decrease or increase in ecosystem functioning. *Keystone* is the idea that some species, despite their relative rarity, play an important role in maintaining ecosystem functioning. The loss of that species would result in a large and rapid loss of function. *Discontinuous* reflects the idea that once a certain number of species have been lost, adding more species back in will not recover the high levels of ecosystem functioning that existed prior to the species reduction. *Rivet* is probably one of the best-known hypotheses about the relationship between species loss and ecosystem functioning. The idea was that, like rivets on an airplane, you can probably lose some, perhaps many, but once a sufficient number of rivets is lost the plane will lose some major function (e.g. a wing will fall off). Although there is a rich history of discussing the relationships shown in Figure 2.1, and *many* others (see, e.g., Schläpfer and Schmid, 1999, Naeem et al., 2002), as we will see in Section 2.5.6, the data primarily supports what is labeled 'Redundancy' in Figure 2.1.

What has become clear in the past 20 years is that not a lot can be learned about the mechanistic relationship between species richness and ecosystem functioning by just looking at the shape of the relationship in illustrations such as Figure 2.1. It turns out, for example, that species redundancy is not the only mechanism that can generate the sort of decelerating relationship seen in Figure 2.1a. A relationship of that shape is an inevitable consequence of continuing to add species into a system with finite resources (Cardinale et al., 2009). Since, as we will see, most empirical evidence supports a relationship like Figure 2.1a, and such a relationship is the inevitable consequence of finite resources, it becomes critically important to know what is the *mechanistic* relationship between species richness and ecosystem functioning. If the relationship really were mainly caused by redundancy then, in general, the loss of species might not be very important, at least as far as ecosystem functioning is concerned, because other species will be performing the same function(s).

Historically, as researchers attempted to home in on the mechanism(s) that determined the relationship between species richness and ecosystem functioning, attention turned away from the largely heuristic explanations of Figure 2.1, and toward more mechanistically grounded ideas. While ecologists identify many different mechanisms in

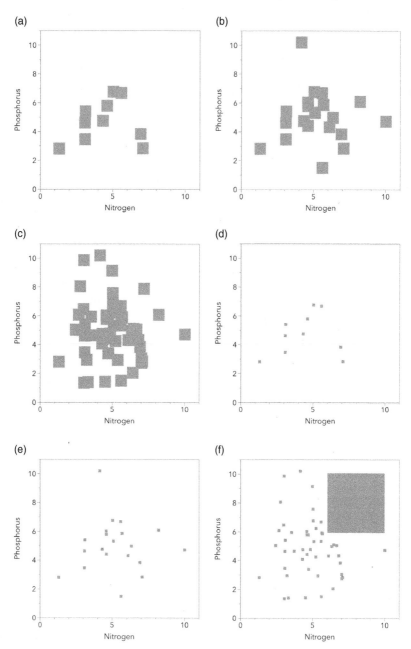

FIGURE 2.2 Each graph represents the niche space that is available to a hypothetical plant community. Each square represents the

explaining the impact of species loss on ecosystem functioning, for the most part, modern explanations fall into two categories: those that rely on species richness per se, and those that rely on species composition. Species-richness explanations encompass a number of related ideas about the way that species interact. Chief among these are: *facilitation* (sometimes called positive species interactions) and *complementarity* (and the related but more specific term *niche partitioning*). Species composition explanations suggest that the effect of biodiversity does not particularly come from the number of species per se, but from the identity of, or perhaps combinations of, particular species. Again, there are several related ideas, but the most common is called the 'sampling effect' (also known as the 'species of strong effect'). We will now discuss each type of mechanism in slightly more detail. It should become apparent that the conservation strategy that would be required in order to maintain ecosystem functioning depends very much on which mechanism(s) are in play.

2.3.1 *Facilitation*

Ecosystem functioning might increase with increasing species richness if there are *positive interactions* among the species present. One such class of positive interactions is called 'facilitation.' Facilitation occurs when the presence of some species either alleviates harsh environmental conditions or provides extra resources for the other species. A classic

---

Caption for Figure 2.2 (CONT.)
two-dimensional niche of a single species. The assumption is that the greater the niche area, the greater the total biomass production of a plant species. 2.2a depicts 10 random species that each have identical niche areas. The regions of overlap represent *redundancy* between the overlapping species in terms of use of these resources. 2.2b depicts the addition of another 10 random species (20 in total) and 2.2c depicts an additional 30 random species (for a total of 50). 2.2d and 2.2e are the same as 2.2a and 2.2b, but each species has a relatively smaller niche. 2.2f depicts the 'species of strong effect' where one species occupies most of the niche space and thus produces most of the biomass.

example of this type of interaction, from the experimental literature, is the presence of legumes (e.g. clover) in grassland ecosystems. Because legumes are able to fix atmospheric nitrogen, they tend to enhance the nutrients available to the non-leguminous species. Ecosystems with more species present are more likely to include facilitator species than ecosystems with fewer species present.

2.3.2 *Complementarity*

Complementarity is thought to result from reduced competition and niche separation that results from coevolution. If competition causes species to spread themselves out in their use of different resources (sometimes referred to as 'niche space'), then ecosystems with more species will more fully use the available resources, resulting in greater ecosystem functioning. This mechanism is depicted in Figure 2.2a–2.2c. Each square represents a unique plant species in the two dimensions of a nitrogen–phosphorus niche space. In Figure 2.2a there are 10 random species depicted and they overlap relatively little in the space they occupy. Overlap represents redundancy in resource use.[4] The total area of the graph represents the total kinds of available resources, and the total amount of gray represents the total kinds of resources that are used by the species present. In Figure 2.2b there are 20 random species and in Figure 2.2c there are 50 random species. If this mechanism were active in an ecosystem, the more species present the more total resources would get used and the higher the level of ecosystem functioning that would occur. Also, the more species we randomly assemble, the more likely it is that species will start overlapping in their resource use. If we plotted the amount of gray space in the figures against the total number of species present, the graph would form a positive saturating curve (e.g. Figure 2.1a) because eventually all of the resources would be used and any additional species would be 'totally redundant' in the sense of resource use.

---

[4] The ecological 'competitive exclusion principle' suggests that two species that highly overlap in their resource use cannot long coexist and the inferior competitor will eventually be excluded.

2.3.3 *Sampling Effect/Species of Strong Effect*

Perhaps only one or a few species actually have a relatively large effect on ecosystem functioning. This idea is depicted in Figures 2.2d through 2.2f. In Figure 2.2f you can see that one species uses a large area of the resource space, and all the other species occupy very small areas in this space. The former species is often referred to as a 'species of strong effect.' If there are such species (and we know that there are), then ecosystems containing more species in total are more likely to include these particularly impactful species compared to ecosystems containing fewer species. Otherwise, the same implications arise with this mechanism as they do with complementarity. That is, the more species present, the more kinds of resource that will get used, and hence the higher the level of ecosystem functioning achieved. The resulting graph of the amount of gray area against species number would, on average,[5] be a positive saturating curve (as in Figure 2.1a). Nevertheless, notice that, all else being equal, conservation of the one species of strong effect in Figure 2.2f preserves nearly all of the ecosystem functioning. Likewise, the loss of some or all of the remaining species would have little negative impact on that functioning.

Controversy arises in this field as to whether the sampling effect is a real ecological mechanism that operates in nature. This is because, in such experiments (see, e.g., Section 2.4.1), communities are assembled *at random* by sampling from a species pool. If communities are assembled at random, then the more samples you draw from the pool, the more likely you are to draw the species of strong effect. The argument then is that such experiments are not really demonstrating something interesting about the nature of the relationship between species richness and ecosystem functioning, they are merely demonstrating an *experimental artifact* that has come to be known in this literature as the 'sampling effect.' Ecologists do not agree about whether the sampling effect is a real ecological mechanism or an artifact (Hooper et al., 2005). The resolution

---

[5] On average, because in any single realization of this process the shape will depend strongly on when the species of strong effect enters the community.

of this disagreement has to do with whether you think that real ecological community assembly is in some sense analogous to the random assembly used in experiments (see Section 2.4.1), and ecologists do not agree whether the two processes are analogous.[6]

In any case, ecologists certainly know of some ecosystems where functioning is primarily controlled by one or a few dominant species. Soil processes, for example, such as decomposition, and carbon and nitrogen dynamics, depend much more on the dominant plant species than on the diversity of plant species (Wardle et al., 1997, Hooper and Vitousek, 1998). Regardless of that argument, if this effect is what causes the positive relationship between ecosystem functioning and biodiversity, it implies that the species of strong effect *alone* requires conservation in order to maintain the majority of ecosystem functions.

2.4   LIMITATIONS OF EXPERIMENTAL DESIGN

In the preceding section we saw that different mechanisms can cause a positive (saturating) relationship between species richness and ecosystem functioning, but different mechanisms might imply different conservation attitudes toward species richness per se. Much turns on knowing which mechanism is causing the relationship. It is relatively easy to experimentally estimate *the shape* of the species richness–ecosystem functioning relationship. It is relatively difficult to determine *the causal mechanism*. In this section we look at some of the experimental challenges confronting researchers in this field.

2.4.1   A Typical Experiment

It will help to ground our discussion if we have an example in mind. We'll use a study conducted by Maria Calderia and her colleagues (2005). [7] It is very typical of the sort of experiment that is conducted to detect an effect of species diversity on ecosystem functioning. The

---

[6] Another argument employed is that even if most of the ecosystem functioning is supplied by one or a few species, the other species are necessary for those species of strong effect to persist.

[7] For brevity, we will only present the details of the experiment that are important to our discussion. We encourage the interested reader to refer to the original paper for further details.

experiment was conducted in a Mediterranean grassland, located in central Portugal (38°46′N, 8°38′W). The researchers established 56 plots that were each 2 x 2 m (i.e. 4 m^2), which varied in the number of species they contained. The researchers used a pool of 14 species from 3 functional groups: 5 grass species, 3 nitrogen-fixing legume species, and 6 species of herbaceous plants. All species were planted as monocultures and replicated twice (28 plots), and the remaining 28 plots were assembled randomly from among the species pool in plots of 2 species (10 plots), 4 species (10 plots), 8 species (4 plots), or 14 species (4 plots). The plots were prepared by plowing them, and then covering each plot with black plastic to raise the soil temperature and hopefully kill the remaining seed bank. The plots were then sown with 8000 g of seed per plot, divided equally among the number of species in each plot. The seeding rates were adjusted based on germination tests for each species so that roughly the same number of *viable* seeds were sown for each species while maintaining overall plant density between plots of different species richness. The plots were periodically weeded to keep out unwanted plants. The plots were sown in 1996 and the total biomass (living and dead, to a depth of 5 cm above the soil) was collected from a 20 x 50 cm quadrat from each plot once in 1997, 1998, and 1999.

The results of this experiment are shown in Figure 2.3. A couple of observations will be obvious without reference to the statistical analysis. First, there is a positive but saturating relationship between species richness and biomass production. And second, in each year there are some monocultures that produce more biomass than some or all of the most species-rich plots. Both of these results are quite typical of such experiments, as we will see in what follows.

2.4.2 Incomplete Factorial Experimental Designs

A perfect experiment would allow ecologists to both determine the shape of the functioning–species richness relationship, and to answer the question: is it species richness per se that we have to maintain, or just certain species or species combinations? To understand the methodological difficulties associated with achieving these experimental

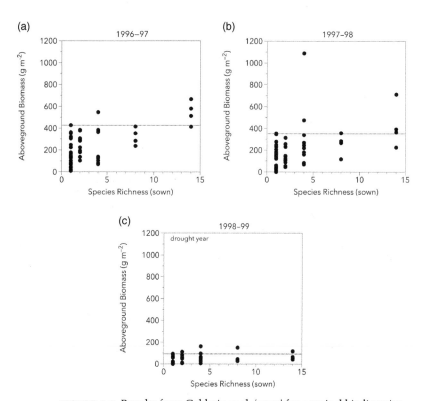

FIGURE 2.3 Results from Calderia et al. (2005) for a typical biodiversity (species richness)–ecosystem functioning experiment. The experiment was established in 1996 and ran for three years. The horizontal dashed line shows the performance of the most productive monoculture. Note that year three was a drought year. See text for further description. We are grateful to Andy Hector and Maria Calderia for providing us with the original data.

goals, let's reconsider the example experiment from Section 2.4.1. In an ideal experiment, we would plant plots of all the species in the pool as monocultures, and then all of the 2-species combinations, all of the 3-species combinations, and so on, until all combinations of species in the pool were planted. Ideally, we want to replicate each plot more than once, but let's just stick with one replicate per plot type for this example.

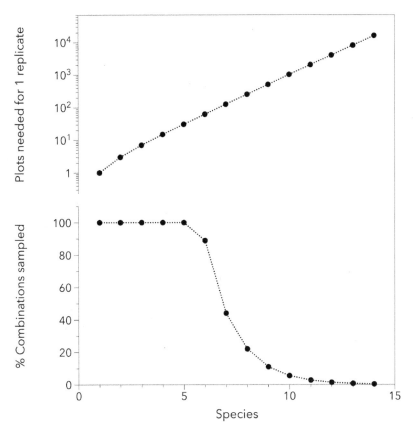

FIGURE 2.4 This top figure shows why the 'ideal' experimental design (the full factorial experiment) is infeasible for any but the most extremely species-poor communities. The number of experimental units (plots in the case of grassland experiments) increases exponentially as the number of species considered increases (note the logarithmic scale on the top Y-axis). The bottom figure shows the percentage of possible combinations that could be covered using 56 plots (see Section 2.4.1) and an incomplete factorial experimental design.

Figure 2.4 shows the number of plots needed to replicate every combination of species for species richnesses ranging in size from 1 to 14 species, as used by Calderia et al. (2005). You can see that if you only had 56 plots available as in Section 2.4.1, you could only do this ideal experiment for a species pool of 5 species; 6 species would require

63 plots and so could not be done. An experiment with 14 species would require more than 16,000 plots to construct a single replicate of every species combination. Even just doing all of the species combinations for the richness levels Calderia et al. used (1, 2, 4, 8, 14) would require 4,110 plots for one replicate.

Despite this problem, species richness–ecosystem functioning experiments are typically conducted with more than five species. How is this accomplished? It is done using something called an 'incomplete design.' This just means that all combinations of species are not represented in the experiment. The drawback to an incomplete design is that there is inevitably a loss of information. In practice, this means sacrificing something we want to know about. This is not desirable, but it is necessary.

Using an incomplete factorial design means that one can only sample a small fraction of the possible combinations of species that could be constructed from the species pool (see Figure 2.4). As the number of species in the species pool gets large, the fraction actually sampled becomes vanishingly small. This doesn't matter very much if all we want to do is estimate the shape of the relationship between functioning and species richness, but it matters a lot if we are trying to answer the question of whether richness per se matters or just the presence of a few particular species or species combinations. In order to try and answer this question, researchers employ one of a few possible statistical methods that are beyond the scope of this text.[8] For our purposes here, let us accept that such experiments can at least estimate the relative strengths of the mechanisms that might account for the results.

2.4.3   *Experiments with Extremely Depauperate Communities*

A review of species-richness–ecosystem-functioning experiments found that 93% of these experiments manipulated a single trophic level (usually plants) containing an average of just seven species

---

[8] Interested readers should see Hector et al. (2009).

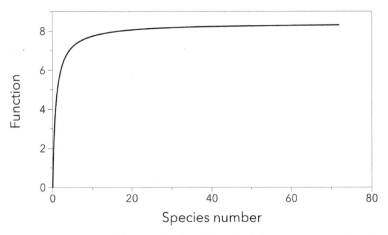

FIGURE 2.5 An example of a real species richness–ecosystem functioning relationship. This curve was estimated using data from Bell et al. (2005) from an experiment manipulating the number of bacterial species and estimating the respiration rate as a measure of functioning. Bell et al. originally fit the following equation: Functioning = a × ln(richness) + b. That equation doesn't asymptote but does decelerate. Following Cardinale et al. (2011), we fit a saturating equation to the data. One would get a very different view of the relationship between richness and functioning if one conducted an experiment with a species pool of 10 or fewer than if one used 72 species, as did Bell et al.

(Cardinale et al., 2009). Since a 4 m² plot of natural grassland might have several dozen species of plants growing in it, an experiment with only seven species would be asking about the contribution of species richness in an already *highly impoverished* community. If, as we will see in Section 2.5.6, the relationship between species richness and ecosystem functioning is saturating, then experiments that use small numbers of species are really looking at the far left-hand edge of the graph. This can be visualized in Figure 2.5. Because of the shape of the relationship, the effect of losing a species when you have 60 species present is very different than the effect when you have 6 species present. The very best[9] experiments in this area might actually use 60 species, but the vast majority do not because of the huge expense of running such experiments.

[9] See, for example, the Jena Biodiversity Experiment in Jena Germany: http://bit.ly/2cbrQDz.

2.4.4 Aspects of Community Assembly

Community assembly is the process where species from a regional pool colonize and coexist to form local communities. Real communities are assembled over time. During the assembly process species interact with each other and with the environment, and may even change the environment. The composition of species within a community often changes through time, as do the relative abundances of particular species. Soil processes also change (often quite slowly), as do the below-ground communities of fungi and bacteria which interact with the above-ground plant communities. Populations of herbivores and/or diseases can also build up to such a point that they alter the plant community membership or relative abundances. And so on. Through time the rich array of ecological interactions, environmental filters, and chance events combine to affect the diversity and abundances of species that comprise the community. Note that the vast majority of experiments in this discipline (see, e.g., Section 2.4.1) are of quite short duration relative to the generation times of the organisms used in the studies, and very short relative to the times needed for processes such as soil carbon and nitrogen to reach any sort of equilibrium. For real practical considerations, the vast majority of these experiments use communities that have recently been assembled by unnatural processes, and have not had sufficient time to resemble anything like a mature ecosystem.

2.4.5 Limitations

Experiments in this field of research are unable to examine the vast majority of inter-specific interactions when using even relatively small species pools. Most experiments use very few species compared to the communities they are meant to represent, and they investigate unnaturally assembled communities with processes that are far from equilibrium. All of these limitations mean that the experimental evidence in this discipline needs to be taken with a bit of 'perspective.' This is an issue that will come up in Section 2.7, where we consider whether the results of these experiments can be legitimately extrapolated to natural systems, or whether they should serve as a basis for conservation policy. Before doing so, however, it is important to ask what the experiments themselves show. This question will be addressed in the next section, where we focus exclusively on whether a relationship between biodiversity and ecosystem functioning has been identified just within the types of artificial experiments that we have been describing. Whether those experiments serve as an adequate gauge of natural processes is a question to be set aside until Section 2.6.

2.5   A SUMMARY OF THE EMPIRICAL EVIDENCE

Since 1990 there have been over 600 empirical studies of the biodiversity–ecosystem functioning relationship. Two major syntheses of this literature were published recently by Bradley Cardinale and colleagues (2011, 2012). Such syntheses use a statistical technique called a 'meta-analysis' that aggregates the data from various individual studies that each focused on a specific set of species in a particular context. The aim of a meta-analysis is to identify generalizations that emerge from the individual, system-specific studies (see Linquist et al., 2016). It is important to note, however, that the limitations and experimental constraints we discussed earlier don't go away; they get subsumed in the analysis and remain important caveats in the interpretation of any conclusions.

Here, for brevity, we examine in detail only the 2011 meta-analysis by Cardinale et al. All of the experiments examined by these authors pertain to 'producer species,' i.e. green plants or algal species, and they measure at least one of biomass production, nutrient uptake, or litter decomposition as their measure of ecosystem functioning. This may sound odd given our discussion of ecosystem functioning in Section 2.2.2, but nevertheless, these are in fact the most common 'ecosystem functions' that get measured in such experiments. Cardinale et al. examined the experimental support for the questions and experimental hypotheses shown below.[10] They chose these questions and hypotheses because they are the same ones that are regularly studied in this discipline. It is the answers to these questions that provide the bulk of the evidence in support of the claim that biodiversity is necessary for maintaining ecosystem functioning.

2.5.1 Does Producer Species-richness Influence the Efficiency and Productivity of Ecosystems?

In ecology, 'productivity' usually means Net Primary Production, and is the total gain in biomass per unit of area per unit of time (e.g. $kg\ m^{-2}\ yr^{-1}$). It is equal to the change in the biomass from one time to the next, plus any losses due to death and decomposition, from all the above- and below-ground plant parts. Most experiments (see, e.g., Section 2.4.1) measure only the standing biomass at the end of a year or growing season, which is used as *a proxy* for production. Cardinale et al. examined three popular hypotheses from the literature:

> *When averaged across the species in the experiments, the net effect of producer species loss is to*

H1a. ...*reduce the standing biomass of a producer community* (tissue per area or volume).

H1b. ...*reduce the efficiency by which producers assimilate inorganic resources.*[11]

H1c. ...*reduce rates of primary production* (oxygen produced per carbon dioxide sequestered per unit time).

Cardinale et al. conclude that there is overwhelming support for H1a and H1b. However, the vast majority of support for H1b comes from

---

[10] The questions and hypothesis are, for the most part, quoted directly from Cardinale et al. (2011) with the main exception being that we have used 'species richness' in place of 'diversity' as species richness is what was actually explored by the experiments examined by Cardinale et al. For ease of readability we avoid adding quotation marks in the cases of the questions and hypotheses.

[11] Most often this is about how efficient the plants are at taking up nitrogen or phosphorus. Measuring uptake rates can be very difficult so it is more common to simply measure that standing stock of the nutrient in the soil or water that remains at the time the biomass is harvested for quantification.

experiments on grassland communities and little is known about this hypothesis in other types of ecosystems. Cardinale et al. are careful to remind the reader that the tendency for standing (above-ground) producer biomass to increase with species richness does not, in and of itself, mean that species loss will decrease the productivity of ecosystems, because, as noted at the start of this subsection, standing biomass is only a proxy for Net Primary Production. They conclude that more research is needed to directly answer the question of Net Primary Production per se.

2.5.2 Does Primary Producer Richness Modify Herbivory?

If biomass production is to serve as the ecosystem function of interest, then it might turn out, as predicted, that an increase in species richness produces more biomass. However, this is not necessarily what will happen in an experimental context. Instead, it is possible that an increase in biomass simply results in higher rates of herbivory. That is, all the additional biomass that gets produced just gets eaten by the herbivores. Such a result might be undesirable from a human perspective. Cardinale et al. test the following hypothesis:

H2. *Herbivore impacts on producer biomass decline as producer richness increases.*

The idea behind this hypothesis is that species-rich plots might have a lower abundance of herbivores (fewer individuals, not necessarily fewer species) than species-poor plots or monocultures, perhaps because the species-rich plots somehow also support more natural enemies of the herbivores. Cardinale et al. conclude that H2 is not supported, although this conclusion is based on just 13 observations and, therefore, more research is needed to properly evaluate this hypothesis.

2.5.3 Does Producer Species Richness Influence the Decomposition of Litter?

Rate of decomposition is another commonly studied ecosystem function. Decomposition involves the cycling of nutrients from living plants and animals to soil bacteria and fungi and eventually to freely available forms in the soil, where they are absorbed by growing plants. In grasslands, decomposition is generally measured by placing a sample of plant material into a mesh bag (called a litter bag). The bag is then placed either on the soil surface or just below it. After a period of time, the bags are collected and an estimate is made of the amount of biomass lost. The difference provides an indication of the rate of decomposition in a given region. Cardinale et al. examined the following hypothesis:

H3. *Richness of producer species (plants or algae) accelerates decomposition, leading to lower stocks of detritus.*

Slow decomposition rates mean that the nutrients tied up in the biomass are not released quickly back into the soil, and this might act as a negative feedback mechanism that slows down biomass production in species-rich plots. Faster decomposition rates mean that nutrients cycle more quickly between producers and their available forms in the soil. Cardinale et al. conclude that the balance of evidence is consistent with a positive relationship between species richness and decomposition rate, but this is largely only true in stream ecosystems, not in grasslands or forests, and that, although statistically significant in aquatic systems, the effects are relatively small. For example, over a half a year, litter produced from more species-rich communities tend to lose just 5% more mass than the average of litter produced from monocultures. This finding suggests that the effects of biodiversity on decomposition rate are quite small and are limited to certain systems.

2.5.4   *What Mechanisms Are Responsible for Producer Species-richness Effects on Ecosystem Processes?*

So far, we have seen that greater species richness results in greater biomass production, little change in herbivory, and slightly faster rates of decomposition in aquatic habitats. As mentioned in Section 2.3, an important question is: what mechanism accounts for these effects? Cardinale et al. examined the three most commonly proposed mechanisms:

H4a. *Effects of species richness are due to niche partitioning among species.*

H4b. *Effects of species richness are due to some form of complementarity.*

H4c. *Effects of species richness are due to species-specific selection effects.*

They conclude that, with regard to these hypotheses, the literature is a "reader beware" situation since only about half of the publications that claim to identify a particular mechanism actually make any direct test of the claim. Of the actual tests of particular mechanisms, aquatic ecosystems provide support for H4b, and not for H4c. In terrestrial systems, the evidence was equally divided in favor of H4b and H4c. The authors of the meta-analysis conclude that, despite the widespread claims of researchers, there is inadequate evidence to even address H4a.

These results suggest that the mechanistic explanation of why ecosystem functioning might depend on species richness doesn't generalize across ecosystems very well, and, at least in the case terrestrial systems, the results imply that conserving specific species is more important than species richness per se, at least half the time.

2.5.5 Do Species-Rich Communities 'Out Perform' Their Most Efficient or Productive Species?

Recapping again, we have seen that, within the available experiments, greater species richness results in greater biomass production, little change in herbivory, and slightly faster rates of decomposition in certain habitats. In the last section we saw that, at least in terrestrial systems, it is fairly common for a species of strong effect (see Section 2.3.3) to be driving these results. Here, Cardinale et al. ask whether the species-rich plots (which they call 'polycultures') have higher levels of ecosystem functioning (biomass production, nutrient uptake, or decomposition rate) than plots of the most efficient or productive single species (which they call 'monocultures') *regardless* of the mechanism from Section 2.5.4. Specifically, they address three hypotheses:

H5a. *Species-rich polycultures outperform their most efficient or productive component species.*

H5b. *Species-rich polycultures capture more nutrients than their most efficient component species.*

H5c. *Litter from a species-rich mixture decomposes faster than litter from the fastest decomposing individual species.*

Cardinale et al. conclude that there is little evidence in support of any of these hypotheses. *In fact, the opposite is usually true.* That is, the biomass produced by the most efficient monoculture is usually greater than that produced by the most species-rich polyculture. You can see a specific example of this in Figure 2.3. Similarly, the concentrations of nutrients left in the soil or water of the most efficient monoculture were usually lower than the concentrations left in the most species-rich polycultures. Finally, the mass of litter remaining from the fastest decomposing species monoculture is usually less than the mass of litter remaining from the most diverse polycultures.

Taken together, the results so far suggest that, *on average*, species-rich plots produce more biomass and (sometimes) decompose more quickly than the *average* individual species, but the most rapidly growing or rapidly decomposing individual species is still better than the species-rich mixtures. A cynical interpretation of these results might suggest that so long as we conserve the best performing species, we would still retain a good deal of existing ecosystem functioning.

2.5.6 What Is the Shape of the Richness–Functioning Relationship?

Although, as we said earlier, the shape of this relationship cannot tell us much about the causal mechanisms, the general shape is still of interest to ecologists. Cardinale et al. examine the evidence for the three most commonly hypothesized shapes:

H6a. *Ecosystem processes decline linearly with species loss.*

H6b. *Ecosystem processes decline exponentially with species loss.*

H6c. *Ecosystem processes show accelerating declines with increasing species loss.*

These three hypotheses are depicted in Figures 2.1b, 2.1d, and 2.1a respectively (although recall that the labels used in Figure 2.1 are historical and don't necessarily indicate the particular mechanism responsible). Cardinale et al. conclude that the evidence supports hypothesis H6c and that this implies that ecosystem functioning saturates after some level of species richness, suggesting that some fraction of species loss results in little or no decrease in ecosystem functioning. There is little support for the other two hypotheses, although the evidence is more diverse for decomposition than it is for either biomass production or nutrient uptake. They also note that, on average, these functions only explained about 30% or less of the variation in the experimental evidence. The results of such experiments are usually very 'noisy,' as seen in Figure 2.3, for example.

2.5.7 What Fraction of Species Do We Need to Maintain Ecosystem Processes?

In many ways this is really the fundamental question of interest, but it is very difficult to address this question experimentally. In the late 1990s researchers attempted to address this question by using a survey of expert opinion (Schläpfer et al., 1999). They asked questions such as "If a grassland with 16 plant species maintains the present intensity of ecosystem processes (defined as 100%), then with how many plant species could a level of 50% be maintained?" (p. 348). From the results of this question and others like it, the general expert opinion was that 50% of the species were needed to maintain 75% of the maximum value of the ecosystem functioning. Although crude, these values give some sense as to how many species we might be able to lose before current ecosystem functioning were to be compromised.

Cardinale et al. tested the following hypothesis:

H7. *50% of species are needed to maintain processes within 75% of their maximum value.*

This is a tricky hypothesis to evaluate using a meta-analysis, as it requires some aggressive data manipulation to normalize the results across the disparate experimental evidence and some very important caveats for the interpretation of these results. We refer the interested reader to the original paper for details. Suffice it to say that Cardinale et al.'s conclusions should be taken with a healthy dose of skepticism (as they themselves admit). It is also important to note that the question posed in the original research defined 100% functioning as equivalent to that produced by 16 grassland species, consistent with the bulk of experimental studies. However, Cardinale et al. took the "75% of their maximum value" to mean 75% of the maximum *achievable* value. This is important since most experiments contained far too few species to achieve this hypothetical maximum value, so it had to be extrapolated from the fitted curves, and extrapolating beyond the range of one's data is always a risky thing to do.

Caveats and limitations aside, Cardinale et al. conclude that for the ecosystem functions of producer biomass and nutrient uptake, expert opinion *underestimated* the fraction of species required to maintain 75% of ecosystem functioning (i.e. we need more than 50% of the maximum number of species to maintain 75% of the maximum ecosystem functioning, at least in these experiments). What their analysis shows, for these two ecosystem functions, is that not surprisingly (see Section 2.4.2) most experiments used far fewer species than would be required to produce the maximum level of ecosystem functioning. Their analysis suggests that researchers needed about 3 times the number of species actually used in these experiments just to achieve 75% of maximum producer biomass, and 4 times the number of species actually used to achieve 75% of the maximum nutrient uptake.[12] For decomposition, on the other hand, Cardinale et al.'s analysis suggests that experimenters only needed about half the number of species used in their experiments to achieve 75% of the maximum decomposition rates.

Although this was an interesting academic exercise, it is not clear to us that it really says anything particularly useful about how many (what percentage of) species can safely be lost before seriously

---

[12] According to their analysis, these studies needed about 8 times and 11 times the number of species actually used just to achieve 90% of the theoretical maximum level of functioning.

compromising ecosystem functioning. Rather, to us, the meta-analysis says more about the small species pools (Section 2.4.2) used in such studies.

2.5.8 Are Diversity Effects 'Stronger' at Larger Spatial Scales and/or Longer Time Scales?

Most experiments take place in very small experimental plots and for relatively short periods of time. These considerations raise the question of whether the observed results would 'disappear' if the experiments were permitted to run for longer, or if they were conducted on much larger plots. As you might imagine, the data available for addressing this question are fairly sparse. Nevertheless, Cardinale et al. examined the following two hypotheses:

H8a. *Effects of producer species richness on biomass increase with the duration of the experiment.*

H8b. *Effects of producer species richness on biomass increase with the size of the experimental plots used in the experiment.*

If these hypotheses are supported, it suggests that such experiments *underestimate* the importance of biodiversity. Cardinale et al. conclude that the results are generally consistent with these two hypotheses, and slightly more supportive of H8a than H8b. They conclude that: (i) spatial relationships are not consistent across types of systems; (ii) where they exist, spatial relationships are weaker than temporal relationships; and (iii) there are far fewer experiments on spatial relationships than on temporal relationships. Cardinale et al. point out that neither time nor space are mechanisms that moderate species richness effects, and they conclude that:

> We caution researchers against propagating more blind-faith statements about diversity being more functionally important at larger scales until the time we can identify a solid mechanistic basis for such claims.
>
> *Cardinale et al. (2011, p. 587)*

2.5.9   Unanswered Questions

Cardinale et al. conclude that the following important questions are not actually answered by the available literature:

1. How do species-richness effects documented in experiments scale-up to real ecosystems? (see Section 2.6.2)
2. Species richness effects are significant, but are they more or less important than other forms of environmental change? (but see Hooper et al., 2012)
3. Would conservation and management of ecological functions be better achieved by focusing on genetic, species, functional, or even higher levels of diversity?
4. How does biodiversity simultaneously impact the suite of ecosystem processes that are required to optimize the multi-functionality of diverse ecosystems?

2.5.10   Conclusions from the Experimental Evidence

This section has provided a synopsis of the bulk of the experimental evidence in support of the empirical claims given in Section 2.1. Bearing in mind the limitations discussed in Section 2.4, here we discuss a few conclusions that we think can be drawn about the relationship between biodiversity and ecosystem functioning *within these sorts of artificial experimental plots*. First, the vast majority of the experimental evidence deals with ecosystem 'functions' that probably don't immediately and directly influence human flourishing. The vast majority of the experimental evidence also comes from ecosystems that people may directly care relatively little about (grasslands and aquatic algal communities). So, the relevance of this research for functions of more direct impact to humans, and in ecosystems that we might consider more important, depends upon how well the results generalize across different taxa, different habitat types, and at various spatial/temporal scales. Even for just the particular dimensions considered in the available research, several of the conclusions don't seem to generalize very well (e.g. Section 2.5.3, Section 2.5.4). Second, there is fairly strong evidence for a saturating positive relationship between species richness and both biomass production and nutrient uptake (at least in grasslands), but for terrestrial systems these results are attributable to species of strong effect at least as often as they are to complementarity. And regardless of the mechanism involved or the ecosystem of focus, the most efficient or productive species can usually outperform the most species-rich communities. It is not immediately clear to us that these results form the basis of a strong, general argument for conserving species richness per se. Others will certainly disagree with us (see, e.g., Cardinale et al., 2012) but nevertheless we hope we have at least given the reader a better understanding of how biodiversity and ecosystem functioning tend to be related within experimental conditions. In the next section we consider whether these experimental findings generalize to real-world ecosystems, and indeed whether we as environmentalists should be concerned about the loss of ecosystem functioning in the first place.

2.6 QUESTIONABLE RELEVANCE OF THE EXPERIMENTAL EVIDENCE

As we hopefully made clear in the previous section, there is strong empirical support for some aspects of the relationship between biodiversity, or at least species richness, and certain ecosystem functions as they have been operationally defined within various experimental contexts. For other dimensions of biodiversity and ecosystem functioning, the evidence is either lacking or equivocal. In this section we don't want to dwell on whether, or how, biodiversity and ecosystem functioning are related. Let us assume for the sake of argument that most experiments identify a link between the loss of biodiversity and decreases in ecosystem functioning, at least within experimental contexts. We now turn to the relevance of such results for our understanding and management of real-world ecosystems.

Great controversy was stirred up in this field when, in 1999, ecologist Shahid Naeem and colleagues published a pamphlet for the

Ecological Society of America, titled *Biodiversity and Ecosystem Functioning: Maintaining Natural Life Support Processes.*[13] The pamphlet engendered controversy because it concluded with a claim and recommendation that:

> Recent evidence demonstrates that both the magnitude and stability of ecosystem functioning are likely to be significantly altered by declines in local diversity ... the importance of ecosystem services to human welfare requires that we adopt the prudent strategy of preserving biodiversity in order to safeguard ecosystem processes vital to society.
>
> *(Naeem et al. 1999, p. 9)*

Both the claim and the recommendation were met with some harsh criticism (see deLaplante and Picasso, 2011, for a thorough treatment of this episode) for both their lack of empirical support and the rush to endorse a particular policy. Over the subsequent years, the first part of Naeem et al.'s quote has been greatly clarified (see, e.g., Section 2.5) but the link between the empirical work and its applicability to actual conservation goals and policy is still a matter of debate and uncertainty.

In this section we briefly enumerate some of the more important challenges to the claim that it is necessary to conserve biodiversity to preserve ecosystem functioning. However, we wish to make clear that conducting this kind of research is extremely difficult, expensive, time consuming, and does not fit comfortably within the current models of research funding around the world. The fact that *any* of this research is conducted is impressive indeed. The work that has been done to date sets the stage for the work to come. All that we are saying, in detailing some of the criticisms, is that it may be too early to use research on this subject as a strong mandate for conservation policy (see also Chapter 3 for an important discussion of the precautionary principle).

---

[13] http://bit.ly/2bJkzA6

2.6.1 Link between Global and Local Biodiversity Changes

Globally we have a pretty good sense that, at this point in the history of the Earth, biodiversity is declining (see Chapter 1). However, it does not automatically follow that *local* biodiversity is declining as well, because locally the loss of a species might be balanced by the immigration or introduction of other species. All of the work discussed in Section 2.5 focuses on species richness on small spatial scales. Until recently, it has been an untested assumption that local biodiversity is, in fact, declining and therefore we have to worry about a loss of ecosystem functioning. Ecologist Mark Vellend and colleagues (2013) tested this assumption by conducting a meta-analysis of 168 experiments and >16,000 non-experimental results that address local changes in biodiversity. They concluded that:

> We find no general tendency for local-scale plant species diversity to decline over the last century, calling into question the widespread use of ecosystem function experiments to argue for the importance of biodiversity conservation in nature.
>
> *(p. 19,456)*

Not only did Vellend et al. find that, *on average*, local plant biodiversity was not declining, they also found that plant diversity was just as likely to be *increasing* as it was to be decreasing. Such increases are rarely considered in research like that described in Section 2.5, but theory suggests that such increases are likely to improve ecosystem functioning. As Vellend et al. (2013) note, the results of research on the relationship between biodiversity and ecosystem functioning might have some application to activities such as grassland restoration or maybe forest management, but they conclude that:

> In more natural settings, however, experimental results with plants cannot be used as a motivation or justification for biodiversity conservation in a general way, given that local richness in these ecosystems is just as often increasing as it is decreasing. In addition, although the maintenance of larger-scale regional biodiversity is

necessary, over the long term, to maintain local biodiversity via "spatial insurance", we still do not expect global diversity loss to filter down to the local level in the foreseeable future, given the widespread increases in plant diversity at regional scales (hundreds of square kilometers) in recent history due to the spread of nonnative species.

(p. 19,458)

In other words, the evidence that more plant species result in greater biomass production (Section 2.5.1) is not a strong motivation to conserve biodiversity in general because locally, on average, we aren't losing plant species. The 'extinction problem' is a global problem, not a local problem, but the evidence is that local biodiversity, not global biodiversity, is important for maintaining ecosystem functioning.

2.6.2   *Temporal and Spatial Scales*

In Section 2.5.8 we addressed some hypotheses about the importance of temporal and spatial scales. We looked at the conclusions that could be drawn from the limited experimental data that addressed these questions. Nevertheless, the vast majority of this work has been at quite small spatial scales. Diane Srivastava and Mark Vellend (2005) point out that conservation policy is normally applied to areas from a few hectares to many hundreds or even thousands of square kilometers. At these sorts of spatial scales, there has been no work on the consequences of regional extinctions for local ecosystem functioning. Srivastava and Vellend (2005, p. 276) conclude that:

> In sum, theory suggests that when local diversity is constrained by immigration from the regional species pool, changes in regional diversity could lead to changes in ecosystem function. At present, it is unknown whether this would actually happen, even in an experimental system. Thus it is too early to derive any significant conservation implications concerning the links between regional-scale diversity and ecosystem function, although this line of inquiry seems promising.

The lack of realistic spatial and temporal scales in the experiments that comprise the vast majority of the empirical evidence might cause one to question the relevance of that literature as a basis for a general reason to conserve biodiversity.

2.6.3   Patterns of Species Loss (or Gain)

As we saw in Section 2.4.1, typical experiments construct experimental plots by randomly sampling from a species pool. So, comparing species-rich to species-poor plots in experiments is the equivalent of studying random patterns of species loss (or species gain, depending on how you look at it). However, actual patterns of species losses (or gains) are rarely completely random. Extinction depends on things such as: body size (large organisms are more at risk); population size (small populations are more at risk); sensitivity to environmental stress; home range size (large home range increases risk); trophic level (higher predators are more at risk); and degree of specialization (specialists are more at risk than generalists). If realistic patterns of species loss yield similar results to those of random species loss, then we might be better able to generalize the experimental research. Unfortunately, there is very little empirical evidence that addresses this question. Emmett Duffy and colleagues (2009) found just four empirical studies. These are shown in Table 2.1.

Notice that in three out of the four studies reviewed by Duffy et al. there was no negative effect of non-random species loss on the ecosystem function of interest, calling into question the bulk of the random species-loss studies (e.g. Section 2.5). Moreover, there are *many* possible realistic extinction sequences and these studies examined only a tiny fraction of those sequences. On the whole, it is too early to say much about the relationship between the random species-loss experiments and realistic extinction sequences. This is certainly an active area of research and Cardinale et al. (2012) list this as an important direction for future research. Nevertheless, the lack of realism in the vast majority of the experimental evidence again causes one to wonder about its relevance as a reason to conserve biodiversity.

Table 2.1 *Experiments that investigate the role of realistic patterns of species loss*

	Ref 1	Ref 2	Ref 3	Ref 4
Organism manipulated Ecosystem function	Grassland plants Productivity	Grassland plants Resistance to invasive species	Marine algae Nutrient use	Stream insects Leaf processing
Trait mediating extinction	Competitive ability	Unspecified	Unspecified	Tolerance of acidification and pollution
Change with random declining species richness	Function declines	No change	No change	No change
Change with realistic declining species richness	No change	Function declines	Function declines	Function declines
Real – Random	Weaker	Stronger	Stronger	Stronger

Source: Extracted and redrawn from Duffy et al. (2009). Ref 1: Schläpfer et al. (2005); Ref 2: Zavaleta and Hulvey (2004); Ref 3: Bracken et al. (2008); Ref 4: Jonsson et al. (2002)

2.6.4 Overly Simplified Trophic Structures

Natural ecosystems comprise: primary producers that capture solar energy and make it available to the ecosystem, herbivores, carnivores, secondary carnivores, parasites, mutalists, detrivores, etc. In other words, they have complex multitrophic structures. However, in order to construct a rigorous experiment, such multitrophic structure is usually ignored and species richness is manipulated solely within a single trophic level, most commonly grassland plants. In fact, a recent review of biodiversity–ecosystem functioning experiments found that 93% of the studies focused on a single trophic level composed of an average of just seven species (Cardinale et al., 2009). In contrast, even some of the simplest ecological communities contain hundreds of species distributed across multiple trophic levels.

In a review of extinctions in complex trophic structures, Srivastava and Vellend (2005, pp. 281–282) concluded:

> multiple extinctions at various trophic levels can affect a given ecosystem function either synergistically or antagonistically. . . . multitrophic interactions can have strong effects on the relationship between diversity and function, but the direction of these effects is highly context dependent. In practice, it will be difficult to predict such [biodiversity – ecosystem functioning] effects in all but the simplest food webs. Note that many multitrophic [biodiversity – ecosystem functioning] experiments report unexpected or idiosyncratic results. Thus multitrophic extinctions and interactions weaken the [biodiversity – ecosystem function] argument for conserving diversity in order to maintain certain levels of ecosystem [functioning].

And in a more recent review of the literature, Cardinale and colleagues (2009, p. 106) stated:

> At present, it is unclear whether such over-simplifications are justified, or alternatively, whether they have led ecologists to potentially erroneous conclusions. . . . At the very least, [what we

know about higher trophic interactions] suggests that the past focus of [experiments] on diversity within a single trophic level may be insufficient to quantitatively predict, and perhaps even qualitatively reflect, the ecological consequences of diversity loss.

The lack of realistic trophic structure in the vast majority of the experimental evidence means that the experimental evidence might have little relevance to real-world ecosystems and hence might not be a very good argument for conserving biodiversity.

2.6.5   *Unnatural Rank–Abundance Relationships*

Schwartz et al. (2000) argue that most experimental studies are biased toward finding a positive biodiversity–ecosystem functioning relationship because they are usually created by putting together equal numbers of individuals from each species (see also Section 2.4). Natural communities are not structured like this. Natural communities have one or a few species that are present in great abundance and many rare species. Figure 2.6 shows an example of a real grassland

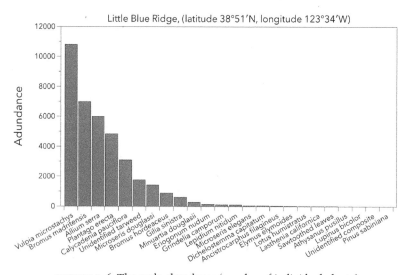

FIGURE 2.6 The rank–abundance (number of individual plants) relationship for Little Blue Ridge grassland in California. Data from Green et al. (2003).

community. In the figure we can see that the grass *Vulpia microsta-chys* (commonly called 'small fescue') comprises 30% of the community, and the 3 most abundant species comprise two-thirds of the community. By contrast, the 10 least abundant species combined comprise just 0.3% of the community. Now imagine the differences between how this community might function vs. how it might function in an experiment (see Section 2.4) where all 24 species would be equally abundant in the experimental plots.

Kevin Gaston (2008) gives a few striking examples of this with birds, e.g.: the 25% most abundant British birds species comprise 95% of the individual birds and 88% of the avian biomass. Gaston notes that although rare species may make important contributions to ecosystem functioning, "in the main the influences of common species tend individually and en masse to be substantially greater" (p. 77). Some have suggested that this criticism may not be very important (see discussion in Lawler et al., 2002, p. 304), but research suggests that, just like the relationship with species richness, the relationship between species evenness and ecosystem functioning can be either positive or negative (Hillebrand et al., 2008). Isbell et al. (2008) demonstrate this point using the same experiment that was described earlier, looking at two ecologically realistic scenarios in tall grass prairie communities.

Again, the lack of realism in the way that biodiversity–ecosystem functioning experiments are conducted causes one to question the relevance of the experimental evidence as a general reason for biodiversity conservation.

2.6.6 *Relevance*

We started this section by asking you to put aside any doubts about whether, in the available experiments, there is evidence for a positive relationship between biodiversity per se and ecosystem functioning. In this section we have considered the *relevance* of the experimental evidence for biodiversity conservation. We offered four reasons to doubt the relevance of the experimental evidence for actual conservation problems. First, we suggested that the evidence might not be relevant because, on average, local biodiversity isn't actually declining. Then we went on to question the match between the experimental conditions and the natural situations they were meant to represent, called an experiment's 'external validity.' All experimental research faces a trade-off between experimental control and external validity. Controlled experiments are needed to infer cause-and-effect relationships, and the more control one exerts in an experiment, the easier it is to find such relationships if they exist. But generally the more control one has, the less external validity one has. Specifically, we noted that most experiments are of very short duration, take place over irrelevantly small spatial areas, consider random rather than realistic species extinction patterns, and examine the role of species richness in communities that have unnatural relative abundances of species – all of which might cause one to worry that the experimental evidence is not particularly relevant to actual biodiversity conservation.

2.7 UNPALATABLE IMPLIED COMMITMENTS

Let's take stock of the last three sections before moving on. In Section 2.4 we examined the experimental difficulties in this discipline, and showed that:

1) We can only examine a small fraction of the possible number of species interactions in communities that have more than a few species;
2) Partly as a consequence of 1), experiments tend to look at very small groups of species mimicking extremely depauperate communities; and
3) The necessarily short time since the communities were experimentally assembled means that they are unlikely to exhibit the same properties and dynamics as naturally assembled communities.

In Section 2.5 we examined the evidence itself and we showed that:

4) There is strong support for a positive, but saturating, relationship between species richness and some ecosystem functions;

5) Mixtures rarely outperform monocultures of the most efficient or productive species within the mixture; and

6) At least for terrestrial systems, individual species are important in generating the relationship at least as often as is the number of species per se.

And finally, in Section 2.6 we reviewed some reasons to doubt that the evidence provided in Section 2.5 is particularly relevant to biodiversity conservation, because it generally lacks external validity.

7) On average, *local* biodiversity is not declining;

8) The short temporal and small spatial scales of the experiments do not relate to actual conservation problems;

9) The experimental evidence is based on random species loss rather than realistic patterns of loss; and

10) The experimental evidence is based on unnatural relative abundances of species.

All of this might cause one to doubt that the experimental evidence forms a convincing basis for a general defense of biodiversity conservation.

Nevertheless, in this section we would like to put aside any reservations we might have about the nature or applicability of the evidence as the basis for such a strong general defense. In this section we want to postulate both universally strong experimental evidence and that this evidence is directly relevant to our understanding of ecosystem functioning in nature. In that case, there would be strong empirical support for the argument presented at the outset of this chapter, in Section 2.1. What we want to do now is to see what follows from such a position. What kinds of policies can be justified by this defense? In particular, would such policies be consistent with the environmentalist agenda, as discussed in Chapter 1?

In this section we show that using the 'biodiversity supports ecosystem function' rationale for conserving biodiversity commits environmentalists to several conclusions that we think most would find unpalatable: that species introductions might be a good thing;

that in some cases species extinctions might be a good thing; and that the wholesale substitution of ecosystems might be a good thing.

2.7.1   Would Non-native Species Be Beneficial?

Environmentalists tend to support policies that prohibit the introduction of non-native species. They often advocate for the removal of species that have already been introduced. In this section, we argue that reliance on the relationship between biodiversity and ecosystem functioning logically commits us to policies of species introductions, where we think such introductions offer improved ecosystem functioning. Before knowing whether a species introduction would 'improve' the level of ecosystem functioning, we'd need to answer the question of how much of a function is the 'right amount?' Figure 2.1 identifies the 'natural level'[14] of biodiversity and its corresponding level of ecosystem functioning. Is that our conservation goal? The curves all go on past this point, indicating that perhaps we could achieve higher levels of functioning if we were to increase local biodiversity. Should that be our goal?

The logic of the biodiversity–ecosystem functioning defense is very much an argument about *local* biodiversity, not global biodiversity. No one is arguing that local ecosystem functioning depends on the number of species we have *on Earth*, just on the number in a particular ecosystem. And, as we showed in Section 2.6.1, local biodiversity is often increasing. It would seem that if we use the logic of the biodiversity–ecosystem functioning defense, then we have to accept that, *on average*, species introductions are a good thing because they tend to bolster ecosystem functioning. This is the very sort of argument that led Robert Soulé (1996) – the 'father' of the academic study of conservation biology – to explicitly reject the

---

[14] There are many problems with even defining what is the 'natural level,' let alone making that condition normative. See further discussion in Chapter 9.

ecosystem functioning defense. He worried that if we use this defense, then we must accept that if the same function can be accomplished by a non-native species, species introductions is a reasonable policy.

2.7.2 Would Local Extinction Be Beneficial?

At a research seminar at the University of Oxford in 2004,[15] ecologist and conservation biologist Stuart Pimm stated: "Extinction ought not to happen and human caused extinction is not natural and not right." This statement pretty clearly sums up one plank of the environmentalist agenda (Section 1.4). However, in this section, we argue that using ecosystem functioning as a defense for biodiversity conservation might, in some cases, actually logically commit us to supporting human-caused extinction (or at least extirpation[16]).

There are several ecosystem processes and measures of stability that actually decrease with diversity (see, e.g., Lawler et al., 2002, p. 302 and references therein). For example, David Wardle and colleagues (1997) have shown that, for 50 forested islands, a variety of important ecosystem functions are actually negatively correlated with biodiversity. So, if the maintenance of ecosystem functioning is our goal, then we should be willing to accept species extinctions, at least in systems where that would increase the ecosystem functioning or stability. More generally, in another recent review by Bradley Cardinale and colleagues (2012, p. 63), they point out that:

> Finally, there are instances where increased biodiversity may be deleterious. For example, although diverse assemblages of natural enemies (predators, parasitoids and pathogens) are frequently more effective in reducing the density of herbivorous pests, diverse natural enemy communities sometimes inhibit biocontrol, often because enemies attack each other through intra-guild predation. Another example relates to human health, where more diverse

---

[15] Attended by the coauthor, Jonathan Newman.
[16] Extirpation means the local extinction of a species rather than its global extinction.

pathogen populations are likely to create higher risks of infectious disease, and strains of bacteria and viruses that evolve drug resistance pose health and economic burdens to people. Such examples caution against making sweeping statements that biodiversity always brings benefits to society.

The evidence in Section 2.5 encouraged us to think of primary production as a beneficial ecosystem function. If complementarity (Section 2.3.2) is driving the relationship between species richness and resource use, and if this applies more generally than in the primary producer communities in which it is usually studied, then more herbivore species should ensure that more producer biomass is consumed. This would seem to be either an example of where biodiversity (species richness) is bad for human welfare, or where causing the (at least local) extinction of species is good for human welfare, or both.

2.7.3   Would Substituting One Ecosystem for Another Be Beneficial?

If you are able to clearly define a desired level of functioning, then it seems to us that one logical extension of this particular defense should be that we ought to manipulate biodiversity, in whatever ways are necessary, in order to achieve the desired goal. For example, suppose we have a pasture of native tall grass prairie and our goal is to maximize carbon sequestration. It may be possible to increase the carbon sequestration by introducing other species (Section 2.7.1), substituting or eliminating species (Section 2.7.2), or perhaps by just replacing the grassland with a forest ecosystem, which would store more carbon, not just in its biomass but also in the soil. If we thought any of those options would maximize ecosystem functioning, should we not consider them?

At this point in the argument, there is a tendency to want to shift the goal posts, so to speak. Environmentalists often assume that the 'natural ecosystem' and its corresponding 'natural level' of ecosystem functioning is the right goal, and that any variation in the levels of these functions or compositions of these systems represents something that is 'bad.' This line of argument rapidly degenerates into a defense of the status quo level of ecosystem functioning, or a defense of some past level of functioning, with little or no reference to the particular utility that humans may (or may not) be deriving from such functioning. The argument quickly begins to resemble a naturalistic fallacy, which we address in Chapter 9, and explicit use of the biodiversity–ecosystem functioning defense is abandoned.

An alternative response to the prospect of ecosystem substitution is to invoke another function that cannot be so easily substituted. For example, tall grass prairies are useful for maintaining populations of wild pollinator species that help pollinate nearby agricultural fields. To maximize this function we might substitute or add more additional flowering plant species to the community. Grasses are generally wind pollinated and not particularly beneficial to pollinators. Maybe we should substitute some of the grasses for plant species that are more beneficial to pollinators? And so on. We can quickly invoke dozens of functions reputedly beneficial to humans, each with its own relationship to species richness per se, and also to the particular species that would maximize each ecosystem function. In making such a decision with multiple objectives, even if we could actually identify the option that maximized human utility, it's not clear that the correct decision would be to leave the system 'as it is.' And even if such wholesale substitutions were rarely beneficial, if it were true in even one case, the ecosystem functioning defense would seem to commit us to that line of action even though it simultaneously seems to be at odds with aspects of the environmentalist agenda, to which many of us are drawn.

2.8 CONCLUSIONS

In this chapter we have made three points:

1) The empirical support for a positive relationship between biodiversity (species richness) and ecosystem functioning is not as strong as many people assume;

2) Even if the available scientific evidence strongly and unambiguously supported there being a positive relationship, there remain some serious questions about how to generalize those findings to real-world ecosystems and/or conservation policy; and

3) People who rely on this defense of biodiversity conservation would be logically committed to conclusions that are at odds with other common commitments of environmentalists (see Chapter 1).

In conclusion, while the biodiversity–ecosystem functioning argument is initially attractive, upon closer examination we conclude that the empirical claims on which it depends are weakly supported, and that some of the implications of relying on it alone would be unpalatable to many in the environmental movement. All that can be said based on the currently available research is that with no biodiversity you get no ecosystem functioning and with some biodiversity you get some positive ecosystem functioning. Beyond that the evidence is contradictory, and much of it is of questionable relevance; we have, at present, a very incomplete understanding of the relationship between biodiversity and ecosystem functioning. And given that ecosystem functioning could in some circumstances be improved by the introduction of non-native species, or the extinction of native species, exclusive reliance on this argument leads to conclusions that are at odds with the environmentalist agenda.

2.9   FURTHER READING

Cardinale, B.J. et al. (2011). The functional role of producer diversity in ecosystems. *American Journal of Botany*, 98:572–592.

(2012). Biodiversity loss and its impact on humanity. *Nature*, 486:59–67.

deLaplante, K. and Picasso, V. (2011). The biodiversity-ecosystem function debate in ecology. In: *Handbook of the Philosophy of Science. Volume 11: Philosophy of Ecology* (ed. by K. deLaplante, B. Brown, and K.A. Peacock), pp. 169–200.

Naeem, S. et al. (2009). *Biodiversity, Ecosystem Functioning, and Human Wellbeing: An Ecological and Economic Perspective.* New York: Oxford University Press.

Srivastava, D.S. and M. Vellend (2005). Biodiversity-ecosystem function research: Is it relevant to conservation? *Annual Reviews of Ecology, Evolution and Systematics*, 36:267–294.

Vellend, M. et al. (2013). Global meta-analysis reveals no net change in local-scale plant biodiversity over time. *Proceedings of the National Academy of Sciences, USA*, 110: 19456–19459.

2.10 APPENDIX: ECONOMIC VALUE OF ECOSYSTEM FUNCTIONING

We discuss the concept of 'value' more comprehensively in Chapter 7. Here it will suffice to note that, within the confines of this chapter, we are talking about value to humans. Although the issues surrounding economic valuation of nature are complex (Pearce, 1998) there are a variety of techniques available for doing so. Economics is the science of allocating scarce resources to meet the needs of humans. Given the anthropocentric focus on ecosystem services in this defense, it makes a certain amount of sense to view ecosystem functioning in economic terms. And there is certainly a precedent in this debate for doing so.

As is articulated in Premise 2 of the argument formulated at the start of this chapter, we humans get a great deal of service from ecosystems for free and these services are either irreplaceable or extremely expensive to replace. How expensive? Perhaps the best-known attempt to answer that question is a 1997 paper by Rob Costanza and colleagues (1997) published in the prestigious journal *Nature*. In that paper, Costanza et al. argue that global ecosystems provide between $16 and $54 trillion USD in annual total value, with an average of $33 trillion. These estimates far exceeded the aggregate Gross World Product at the time ($18 trillion USD). If global ecosystem services had to be replaced by human capital, we would need to triple the size of the total global economy. This is certainly not something that could be achieved in the short term (or perhaps even the long term) and therefore represents a clear reason for conserving biodiversity, or so the argument goes. This celebrated paper has been cited more than

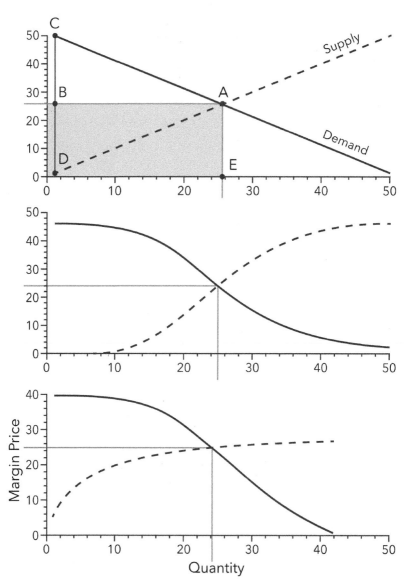

FIGURE 2.7 The 'price-quantity paradox.' Costanza et al. estimated value as the price-quantity product (the area in grey in the top graph). The consumer demand curve represents the consumers' marginal willingness to pay to obtain one unit of the good or service shown on the x-axis. So the consumers' total willingness to pay for the total quantity on the x-axis is given by the area under the demand curve. Similar logic leads us to the concept of the suppliers' willingness to accept compensation. A free

1,400 times in the academic literature alone, and has been hugely influential in conservation arguments.

The paper is, however, problematic because Costanza et al. had to use a surrogate to approximate value, and it can readily be shown that the surrogate is not a very good approximation. Several papers have been written detailing the problems with Costanza et al.'s economic analysis. One very clear, and quite succinct, paper is Robert Ayres' (1998) 'The Price-Value Paradox.' The problem comes from the way that Costanza et al. measured 'value.' In a traditional economic analysis, the value of a good or service is represented by the sum of the consumer and supplier surpluses (see Figure 2.7). This type of analysis requires detailed knowledge of the supply and demand curves, something currently lacking for most ecosystem functions. In a pinch, value can be estimated using only the consumer surplus, but lacking even the demand curves for ecosystem functions, Costanza et al. used the marginal price times the quantity (sometimes known as the 'price-quantity product') as a surrogate measure of value.

Caption for Figure 2.7 (CONT.)

market will reach an equilibrium where supply = demand, indicating both the equilibrium price and the equilibrium quantity. But notice that, for the equilibrium quantity in top graph, the consumer was willing to pay the entire area under the demand curve (CAED) but only pays the price × quantity (BAED). The area CAB indicates the amount that the consumer was willing to pay but did not have to – the consumer's surplus. Following a similar logic we arrive at the supplier's surplus (BAD). In the supplier's case, they are willing to accept the area AED in compensation for the equilibrium quantity. However, they actually receive the price × quantity (BAED). This then leaves them with the supplier's surplus of BAD. In economic analyses 'value' is measured as the consumers' surplus + the suppliers' surplus. Together, the three graphs give an example where the price-quantity product does not change, but the economic value (sum of consumer's and supplier's surpluses) is quite different across the three figures. Unless one knows the shape of the two curves, the price × quantity product may or may not be a good estimate of the actual value.

Unfortunately, the surrogate is not a very good approximation (see Figure 2.7 and Ayres [1998] for a detailed critique).

All of this is not to deny that we do get many ecosystem services for free, and this in itself might be a reasonable, general defense of biodiversity conservation. However, whether the value of these services is three times the current gross world product is debatable, and environmentalists should stop quoting this value without understanding the difficulties associated with its calculation. More fundamentally, it is not clear what quantity of many particular ecosystem functions we desire, how we should trade-off losses in one ecosystem function for gains in another ecosystem function, or how, quantitatively, all of this might be related to the quantity of biodiversity. Furthermore, if the focus is on ecosystem functioning as an economic issue (i.e. a problem of allocating scare resources), then environmentalists must accept that biodiversity conservation will certainly not always 'win.' There will be times when the economic value of conservation does not trump the economic value of not conserving. If environmentalists want to accept and use the rhetorical and philosophical power of an economic argument to justify conservation, then we must also accept that argument when it fails to justify conservation.

For further discussion on this topic, see the Special Issue of *Ecological Economics* (1998) volume 25, issue 1.

3   The Precautionary Principle

3.1   INTRODUCTION

A common statement of this defense comes from forester and wildlife manager Aldo Leopold [1887–1948]: "To keep every cog and wheel is the first precaution of intelligent tinkering" (Leopold, 1966, p. 190). Applied to species extinctions, these statements certainly seem to imply something like: when in doubt, assume that the species is valuable to us, even if we don't know why, and so conserve it. In this chapter we will consider the so-called 'precautionary principle,' or, more generally, the 'precautionary approach.'

The precautionary defense is widely used in discussions of biodiversity conservation, sometimes explicitly, many times implicitly. The precautionary approach is often touted by its proponents as an alternative to risk analysis, cost–benefit analysis, or both. The precautionary principle is meant to be applied in the face of missing information, in the face of uncertainty, or when scientific knowledge is incomplete. To quote just one example of the supposed superiority of the precautionary principle over, in this case, risk analysis, Michael Pollan (2001) stated:

> [Risk analysis] is very good at measuring what we can know – say, the weight a suspension bridge can bear – but it has trouble calculating subtler, less quantifiable risks... Whatever can't be quantified falls out of the risk analyst's equations, and so in the absence of proven, measurable harms, technologies are simply allowed to go forward.

Strictly speaking, this isn't correct: risk analysis does account for uncertainty in the calculations, as we shall see when we talk about risk analysis later in the chapter. Nevertheless, the point seems pretty clear: Pollan (and many others) hold up the precautionary principle's supposed ability to handle unknown threats of harm in a way that is superior to traditional approaches.

What we will see in this chapter is that, although attractive at face value, the precautionary principle has a variety of philosophical and practical problems associated with it, suggesting that perhaps the principle ought to be thought of as more of a slogan than a principle, in much the same way as "live free or die," the motto of the US state of New Hampshire. As a motto, "live free or die" implies that the citizens of New Hampshire highly value their liberties. As a senti-ment it is informing. As a principle on which to base decisions, though, it would be difficult at best. The people of New Hampshire have the good sense not to enshrine their state motto as the guiding principle for their legislation. We will find that the precautionary principle might best be viewed similarly.

3.2   WHAT IS A PRECAUTIONARY DEFENSE?

A precautionary defense goes something like this:

Premise 1: The loss of biodiversity (e.g. a species or ecosystem) will potentially have unknown negative consequences.

Premise 2: A particular action A could result in biodiversity loss.

Premise 3: If an action potentially has unknown negative conse-quences, then it should be avoided.

Conclusion: One should avoid A.

The justification for Premise 1 may appeal to *the potential* for biodi-versity to provide any or all of the instrumental benefits that we discuss in Part I of this book. At its heart, the precautionary defense states that some particular bit of biodiversity may be (very) useful or necessary for human welfare, for example, because it promotes eco-system services, ecological stability, or some other property that humans value directly or indirectly. However, the argument con-tinues, since we do not know with certainty the connection between biodiversity and those valued properties, the prudent course of action is to err on the side of caution and avoid biodiversity loss. Importantly, erring on the side of caution is usually taken to mean that the particular bit of biodiversity *is* useful or important, until shown otherwise. Since, on this view, it is very difficult to prove the negative (i.e. that the bit of biodiversity is entirely useless) precaution dictates avoiding any loss of biodiversity.

Premise 2 seems straightforward enough, but ideally we would like some clarity on what is meant by 'could' and 'loss.' In this context, does 'could' mean any conceivable event, no matter how remote the possibility, or only those to which we can attach a probability? Since the precautionary principle is meant to help us in the case of significant scientific uncertainty, we presume it does not mean the latter. The problems with the former view will be made clear when we discuss 'Costs, Benefits, and Alien Abduction Insurance' (Section 3.6.1) and also when we discuss 'Pascal's Wager' (Section 3.7.4). What are we to make of 'loss'? If we are thinking about species, then presumably loss means extinction, which seems pretty straightforward (but see Section 9.3.2). However, 'loss' probably needs to incorporate the idea of 'population reduction' as well if it is to really capture all of the impacts intended by the premise. If that is the case, then loss isn't an all-or-nothing event, and we'd need to come to grips with the question of how much loss would be acceptable.[1] What about ecosystems? No matter what one does to an ecosystem, the ecosystem continues to exist. It may not have the same species, or the same fluxes of energy and material, but it is still *an* ecosystem. So, presumably the idea of 'loss' also encompasses 'damage' or 'degradation' (but see Chapter 9 for discussion of why this is still problematic).

We tackle Premise 3 in more detail in Section 3.6.1. Premise 3 is key to the argument, because the conclusion does not follow from the other two premises alone. For now, we will just point out that, taken at face value, probably every action has a *potential* for *unknown*

---

[1] Notice that the same argument can also be applied if we are talking about local, rather than global, extinction. How many populations can we lose before we need to be worried?

negative consequences. Following this prescription would make it paralyzingly difficult to adopt any course of action, *including doing nothing.*

3.3   DEFINING THE PRECAUTIONARY PRINCIPLE

As Norman Myers (1993, p. 74) put it:

> In essence, the precautionary principle asserts that there is a premium on a cautious and conservative approach to human interventions in environmental sectors that are (a) unusually short on scientific understanding, and (b) unusually susceptible to significant injury, especially irreversible injury.

There are many formulations of precautionary principles (Sandin, 1999, counts 19 different statements, and there are probably more since then, see Sandin's appendix II), but perhaps the most well-known is the one used in the 1990 UN Economic Conference on Europe (later adopted verbatim as Principle 15 of the Rio Declaration[2] in 1992):

> Where there are threats of serious or irreversible damage, lack of full scientific certainty shall not be used as a reason for postponing cost-effective measures to prevent environmental degradation.

This statement is sometimes known as 'the weak precautionary principle.' It is occasionally phrased more generally as: "lack of full certainty is not a justification for preventing an action that might be harmful" (and other variants). Contrast this with the so-called strong precautionary principle:[3] "take no action unless you are certain that it will do no harm."

While there seem to be many formulations of the precautionary principle, an analysis by philosopher Neil Manson (2002) suggests that

---

[2] http://bit.ly/2qlvdC7

[3] Philosophical problems with the strong precautionary principle seem so transparent (there is no way to be *certain*) that we will not spend time discussing it. Indeed, even proponents of the principle have backed away from the strong statement. See Pereira Di Salvo and Raymond (2010) for further discussion.

they all share a common three-part structure. Manson starts out by observing that for any given *activity* that may produce an environmental *effect*, the precautionary principle is meant to provide a *remedy*. The three parts are a damage condition, a knowledge condition, and a remedy. Manson puts it like this: "If the activity meets the damage condition, and if the link between the activity and the effect meets the knowledge condition, then decision makers ought to enact the specified remedy" (p. 256). Table 3.1 provides some examples of the three parts.

The precautionary principle is such a 'grab bag' of ideas that arguments about its use are often at cross purposes. Pereira Di Salvo and Leigh Raymond (2010) conducted an extensive analysis of how the precautionary principle is used in practice. They concluded that the most common use in the literature mixes stronger and weaker elements of the precautionary principle, but broadly resembles Principle 15 of the 1992 Rio Declaration as quoted above. They suggest that the specific formulation of the principle "has become weaker over time, and that its critics formulate it more strongly than proponents" (p. 86). We will focus only on the weak version in this chapter.

3.4 WHY VS. HOW: USES OF THE PRECAUTIONARY PRINCIPLE

The precautionary principle is used in two distinctly different contexts in debates about conserving biodiversity. On the one hand, the precautionary principle is used as a philosophical defense for *why* we should conserve biodiversity, as in the argument we presented at the start of this chapter. On the other hand, the precautionary principle is used in a much more managerial sense, as a tool for making management decisions about *how* to conserve biodiversity.

Ecologist Richard Root's paper (2003) is a good example of the 'why' question. Root considers only the scientific question: does this well-studied community contain any species that are functionally redundant, such that there would be no negative consequences if the

Table 3.1 *Three elements that comprise a statement of a Precautionary Principle*

Suggested Damage Conditions	Suggested Knowledge Conditions	Suggested Remedies
1. Serious	1. Possible	1. Ban or otherwise prevent the activity
2. Harmful	2. Suspected	2. Put a moratorium on the activity
3. Catastrophic	3. Indicated by precedent	3. Postpone the activity
4. Irreversible	4. Reasonable to think	4. Encourage research alternatives to the activity
5. Such as to destroy something irreplaceable	5. Not proven *with certainty* that it is not the case	5. Try to reduce uncertainty about the causal relationship between the activity and the effect
6. Such as to reduce or eliminate biodiversity	6. Not proven *beyond the shadow of a doubt* that it is not the case	6. Search for ways to diminish the consequences of the activity
7. Such as to violate the rights of future generations	7. Not proven *beyond a reasonable doubt* that it is not the case	7. Choose an option that is reversible over one that is not

Adapted from Manson (2002), who notes that: "the generic elements and logical structure of the precautionary principle have been identified in light both of actual usage and suggested applications (as gleaned from various laws, treaties, protocols, etc.). Because these are the primary guides an outside observer has to the meaning of any term, those who object that the suggested framework cannot capture what they mean by 'the precautionary principle' are obliged to articulate what they do mean" (p. 265). The authors thank Neil Manson for copyright permission to reproduce this table.

species were extirpated?[4] He considered a species expendable if there were other species capable of performing all of the target species' significant functions. Since Root was considering only a specific herbivorous insect community, he argued that these were the significant traits that needed to be considered for a given species of insect: (1) its feeding guild (folivores, sap suckers, leaf miners, etc.); (2) its feeding tissue (roots, shoots, leaves, seeds, etc.); (3) its natural enemies (their predators, parasites, and diseases); (4) its mutualists; (5) its dispersal services (e.g. pollination, seeds, diseases); and (6) its constructions that benefit other organisms (e.g. webs, tunnels, leaf rolls, etc.). Of the 101 species of phytophagous insects that feed on goldenrod (*Salidago altissima*), 42 species, representing 17 families, are specialists that feed only on goldenrod. Root identified the gelechiid moth, *Dichomeris leuconotella*, as potentially expendable. Through extensive fieldwork at many sites over many years, Root determined that the moth was quite rare and had no measureable impact on the goldenrods. The moth's functions were highly redundant, largely due to the fact that there are five other *Dichomeris* species that also feed on goldenrod. They all form leaf rolls that are used by spiders and mites after the moths abandon them. Three of the congeneric moths have the same temporal patterns of development (phenologies). All of the plant species eaten by *D. leuconotella* are also eaten by at least one of the other three coexisting congeners. *D. leuconotella* are eaten by spiders, ants, and wasps, which all attack a wide variety of prey species. All of the parasitoids that attack *D. leuconotella* also attack other *Dichomeris* species at the same times, in the same habitats, and at the same stages of development. Root concludes, with some caveats, that the list of traits that overlap between the congeneric species is so extensive that *D. leuconotella* appears to be a good candidate for the label 'expendable,' at least in the short term. After having demonstrated, rather convincingly, that *D. leuconotella* is probably expendable, Root resists his own compelling argument and

---

[4] Extirpation is the local extinction of a species.

instead sketches out some possible changes that could arise through evolution or phenotypic plasticity that might alter our judgment in the future. He concludes (Root, 2003, p. 290):

> The case of *D. leuconotella* also illustrates how judging the expendability of species solely on the basis of their functional traits can be misleading. As is the case with *D. leuconotella*, most species are rare and perform highly redundant functions; most would produce no appreciable effects if they were removed. Although current efforts to document the importance of biodiversity for maintaining ecosystem functions and services are essential for understanding large-scale processes, I suspect that many species encountered in such investigations will be determined to play only negligible roles. To appreciate why these species with little current significance are not expendable requires that we consider the evolutionary dimension. To use Hutchinson's metaphor, it may be that our most compelling reasons for retaining species will be found in the evolutionary play rather than the ecological stage.

Although Root did not explicitly invoke the precautionary principle, his arguments about how evolution or phenotypic plasticity might alter our views of *D. leuconotella*'s expendability are very much precautionary arguments. Since this assessment was a mental exercise rather than a serious proposal to extirpate a species of phytophagous insect from the goldenrod community, Root didn't need to go any further than he did. But if this were a serious proposal, we feel pretty certain that Root would have explicitly invoked the precautionary principle as a reason for avoiding species loss.

Root's essay was part of a larger volume edited by ecologists Peter Kareiva and Simon Levin (2003), titled *The Importance of Species: Perspectives on Expendability and Triage*. In the introduction for the section that includes Root's essay, Kareiva and Levin write (p. 237):

> The most striking feature of the chapters in this section is the general reluctance to deem any species to be more or less important

than another. If ecological studies fail to find an important role for a species, then evolutionary arguments are invoked. The problem is that 'importance,' and conversely 'expendability' are value-laden terms that have implications for environmental policy. The discomfort we feel in using a word such as 'expendable' or 'redundant' with regard to any species suggests that policy regarding biodiversity (or extinctions) must be founded on general principles rather than on a case-by-case justification for each species. Or, perhaps ecologists need to admit to themselves, as well as to others, that there are ethical dimensions to the discussion that contribute to their unwillingness to deem any species expendable.

Presumably, Kareiva and Levin's argument for general principles rather than case-by-case justification is an admission that many species will not survive a case-by-case scrutiny and using general principles might get environmentalists out of having to reach the uncomfortable conclusion that a species is, indeed, expendable. The second part of the quote, we suspect, is more telling of Kareiva and Levin's true position, namely that conservation need not be, or perhaps *ought not* be, defended on the basis of the usefulness of biodiversity, but on some claim about the intrinsic value of biodiversity, a claim that we introduced in Chapter 1 and take up in detail in Part II of this book.

Quite apart from *why* we should conserve biodiversity is the argument about *how* we should do so. What management strategies are optimal for achieving the goal of conserving biodiversity? Let's look at an example of the precautionary principle used as a management strategy. Here, we briefly present a case made by conservation biologist Alison Rosser and colleagues (2005) regarding *Capra falconeri*, commonly known as the Central Asian Markhor, native to Pakistan. The markhor is a large wild goat (c. 100 kg) with impressive spiral shaped horns. The markhor was listed as 'endangered' by the IUCN (International Union for Conservation of Nature) in 1994.[5]

[5] As of 2015, the IUCN had reclassified this species' status to 'near threatened' and indicated that its numbers were increasing.

Rosser et al. used the precautionary principle as it appears in Principle 15 of the Rio Declaration (presented in the first section of this chapter) and the formulation used by CITES (The Convention on International Trade in Endangered Species of Wild Fauna and Flora, 1973), which states: "Recognizing that by virtue of the precautionary principle, in cases of uncertainty, the Parties shall act in the best interest of the conservation of the species when considering proposals for amendment of Appendices I and II."[6] Appendix I prohibits commercial international trade, and appendix II regulates international trade through a permit system. According to Rosser et al., parties to the treaty are encouraged to list species in the appendices even though international trade may not have been a driver in the species' population decline. So, CITES followed a precautionary approach by favoring regulation of all trade in the face of uncertainty about the effects of that trade on the species' conservation status, many times without any clear evidence that regulating trade would have any impact. Rosser et al. claim that this is particularly true of trophy hunting.

Trophy hunting can be extremely lucrative and has an automatic feedback to management in that, if the herd is not managed well, the quality of the trophies declines and then so does the demand for trophy hunting. Prior to its 'red list' status by the IUCN, the Torghar Conservation Project was started. Under that project, revenue from sanctioned trophy hunts was used to employ game wardens to prevent poaching. Under this program, the Torghar Hills population of markhor increased from 56 individuals in 1985 to more than 1,500 by 1999. The IUCN had approved an export quota of 6 animals in 1997 (only 2 of which came from this population). In 2002, with the population then at 1,684, the IUCN doubled the quota to 12 animals per year (4 from this population). Rosser et al. feel this is very conservative and that this population alone could sustain an annual harvest of 18 animals.

What was the 'precautionary approach' in this case? Rosser et al. argue that to answer this question requires value judgments on the

---

[6] https://www.cites.org

part of the person doing the evaluation. For those who think extractive use is always 'bad,' the decision by the IUCN to grant export quotas might have been seen as decidedly *non*-precautionary. Indeed, it could be argued that the most precautionary approach would have been to ban all exports. On the other hand, with the population seemingly recovering by 1997, and the demonstrable benefits of using the funds generated by trophy hunting to pay game wardens, it might be argued that the most precautionary approach was to support success and approve the quota application. Rosser et al. further argue that it is not always clear what course of action is precautionary, and that this decision is almost certainly context specific. They argue that automatically applying the precautionary principle to oppose trophy hunting, as they suggest that some conservation groups do, ignores the potential benefits of such hunting and, in their view, is an inappropriate use of the principle.

Clearly, in this last example, the question of whether the markhor ought to be conserved was not being questioned. What was at stake was how to go about doing so. It is not immediately obvious in this example which management strategy best fits the precautionary principle, and this seems to have as much to do with one's values as it does with the alternative outcomes. In the next section we take a look at other ways of making decisions about the environment besides the precautionary principle.

3.5 THE PRECAUTIONARY PRINCIPLE, RISK ASSESSMENT, AND COST–BENEFIT ANALYSIS

As we mentioned at the start of this chapter, many proponents of the precautionary principle see it explicitly as an alternative to either risk assessment/management[7] or cost–benefit approaches. In this section we consider these alternatives to the precautionary principle – or,

---

[7] Note that risk assessment and risk management are different parts of the same process. Risk assessment is done first, and is meant to be an entirely scientific process whereby the magnitude of the risk faced is quantified. Risk management is the value-laden process that follows risk assessment; it tries to determine what are acceptable risks and whether a proposed course of action is consistent with the acceptable risk.

more correctly, the precautionary principle *is* an alternative to these two approaches, approaches that have for many years dominated environmental policy and decision making. Before we do that, however, we need to first define 'risk' and 'uncertainty.'

In common usage, 'risk' is often understood to be synonymous with 'hazard,' but in the field of risk assessment/management, risk is the probability that the hazard will occur. The word risk is used even more generally to refer to the likelihood of a 'stochastic event.' Stochastic is the opposite of 'deterministic.' A deterministic event is one that always occurs, with probability 1. A stochastic event may or may not occur, and its probability of occurrence is the 'risk' associated with the event. So, for example, flipping a fair coin results in a stochastic, or risky, outcome of heads with probability ½ and tails with probability ½. 'Uncertainty' refers to a stochastic event where some or all of the outcomes and/or the probabilities (risks) are unknown.[8]

Why does the distinction between risk and uncertainty matter? It matters because it is under conditions of uncertainty that the precautionary principle is meant to help us. If we know all the possible outcomes of some action, and we have a good idea of their associated probabilities, then, as philosopher Jamie Whyte (2007) says, we don't need precaution because we have all the information we need to make a decision. Let's take a look at a hypothetical problem, adapted from Whyte, which will illustrate the distinction and the dilemma from a *cost–benefit* perspective.

3.5.1   Costs, Benefits, and Alien Abduction Insurance

Philosopher Elliot Sober puts the question like this: Are "we prepared to accept a small chance of great disaster in return for a high probability of a rather modest benefit"? (1986, p. 147). Of course we are, we do it all the time. As Sober points out, every time we fly, we take such a calculated risk. It is an example of the sort of informal cost–benefit

---

[8] There is a rich literature on how people perceive and respond to risks, but that is beyond the scope of this text. Interested readers might like to see Paul Slovic's (2000) *The Perception of Risk*.

analysis that we do every day. Another example of this would be alien abduction insurance. Are we willing to accept a small probably of suffering an uncompensated alien abduction in return for a certain, but rather modest cost (the price of the premium)?

Suppose that you were offered the opportunity to purchase an insurance policy, for a single payment of $19.95, to provide you with lifetime coverage against alien abduction. If you are abducted by an alien, then your beneficiary will receive $10 M. You can actually purchase this policy;[9] the question is, should you do so? Suppose your chance (lifetime risk) of being abducted by an alien is one in a thousand. Then the 'expected value' of this policy is $10,000; well worth the $19.95 purchase price.[10] But suppose that you don't know the odds of being abducted by an alien, so the risk might be considerably less (or more) than one in a thousand. What should you do? This is exactly the kind of problem where the precautionary principle is meant to be helpful. The principle, in effect, says it is "better to be safe than sorry." You really don't want to suffer an uncompensated alien abduction, so the principle says buy the insurance. As Whyte (2007) puts it: "Those who advocate precaution typically favor incurring costs now to reduce the chance of incurring greater costs in the future."

Let's unpack this example a little further. Some basic maths[11] tell us that, for the policy to have an expected value of $19.95 or more, our chances of alien abduction must be more likely than 1 in 501,253. So it would seem that on a strategy of *maximizing our net payoff*, we should forego the insurance if we think we are less likely than that to be abducted. Such a strategy might be referred to as 'risk-neutral.' We can contrast this with two alternative strategies: 'risk-prone,' and 'risk-averse.' There are so-called optimal solutions for making

---

[9] see http://www.ufo2001.com/   [10] $\$10,000,000 \times \frac{1}{1,000} = \$10,000$

[11] $\$10,000,000 \times \frac{1}{x} = \$19.95$

$$x = \frac{\$10,000,000}{\$19.95}$$
$$= 501,253.1$$

decisions under risk,[12] which can be used once a policy objective has been defined, to determine the course of action that optimizes the chances of successfully achieving the objective. Defining the policy objective is not a scientific problem, it is a value problem. What constitutes 'acceptable' risk is often a question of value, and/or a political decision that reflects the attitudes and values of the polis toward risk.

Returning to our alien abduction question, why would we contemplate abduction insurance in the first place, since it is unlikely that we would personally benefit from an insurance payoff? Basically, for the same reasons that we purchase life insurance policies: because we have financial obligations to our families or others and we wish to ensure that those obligations are met in the case of our *untimely* demise. Insurance companies are in the business of making money; they are not charities. The premiums they charge are carefully calculated so that the company's net expected payoff from selling us a policy is positive, which means that *on average*, they make money and we lose money. So why do we buy the policies? The reason is that we are 'risk-averse.' We prefer a small certain (deterministic) loss (the cost of the premium) now to a large risky (stochastic) loss in the future (*cf.* Whyte quote, above). But many people do not have life insurance policies – how come? Because they are 'risk-prone.' They prefer the large risky (stochastic) loss in the future over a small, but certain (deterministic) loss now. Why do people differ in their attitudes toward life insurance? They differ for many reasons, but two important reasons are psychology and income effects. Psychology accounts for the fact that some people are inherently more willing to gamble than others, rational argument and expected net gain calculations aside. For example, state lotteries are sometimes unkindly referred to as a 'stupidity tax' because the odds of winning are so small that the net expected payoff is effectively zero. People play the lottery anyway

---

[12] For a nice introduction see Raiffa (1968).

because they like to gamble. Nevertheless, when thinking about how a society as a whole should respond to risk, psychology is perhaps not very helpful. However, the second reason is quite important. People who can't afford life insurance don't buy life insurance. People whose monthly budget is pretty close to their monthly income need to take a risk-prone strategy to ensure that they can meet their short-term financial obligations. They take a risk and hope for the best when it comes to their long-term obligations. From society's perspective, attitudes toward risk reflect society's value judgments about acceptable and unacceptable risk.

Now, imagine that you are financially well-off; you might think to yourself that you ought to be risk-averse. You ought to buy the abduction insurance. In the previous paragraph, we contrasted risk-prone, risk-neutral, and risk-averse as if they were discreet strategies, but our attitude toward risk is really on a continuum and risk-neutral is just the point at which we switch from being risk-prone to risk-averse. So, there is really a range of risk-averse (prone) strategies, of 'risk-averse-ness' as it were, from being only slightly risk-averse to being completely risk-averse. In the case of the alien abduction insurance, if we were only slightly risk-averse, we might, for example, buy the policy if our odds of abduction were 1 in 600,000, but not less than that, even though we know that our net expected gain from doing so is negative (the policy would only be worth $16.67,[13] but we would pay $19.95). If we were completely risk-averse we would buy the policy no matter how vanishingly small the chances are of alien abduction. So long as the cost of the policy is less than the benefit paid in the event of abduction, then we would buy it. Complete risk aversion seems to be a monumentally stupid financial policy. Even the most wealthy people in the world do not buy insurance policies to cover absolutely every conceivable bad thing that could happen to them, no matter how remote the possibility. If they did, they would quickly cease to be wealthy! Nevertheless, this is what the precautionary principle

---

[13] $10,000,000 \times \frac{1}{600,000} = \$16.67$

seems to be arguing for: complete risk aversion. Complete risk aversion is an extreme value judgment. To resist this move, proponents of the principle might be tempted to fall back on the phrase "cost-effective," but to determine cost effectiveness requires a cost–benefit analysis, something the proponents also resist.

Now, let's return to the problem we posed above: should you buy the insurance policy if you don't know the odds of an alien abduction? Better safe than sorry, right? We think most people would say that in the case of abduction by aliens, you lack sufficient information to make a rational decision. Without more information you can't know whether purchasing the policy is the safe course of action or the sorry one. But the precautionary principle says: "Where there are threats of serious or irreversible damage, lack of full scientific certainty shall not be used as a reason for postponing cost-effective measures to prevent [uncompensated alien abduction]." So, the precautionary principle would seem to be telling us to buy the policy!

From a cost–benefit perspective, a problem with the precautionary principle is that it fails to consider the opportunity costs of pursuing a precautionary strategy (a theme we will return to in Section 3.7.4 on Pascal's Wager). Opportunity costs are the utility you forego by spending your money (resources) on the precautionary strategy instead of other potential benefits. For example, suppose that, worried about stocks of wild fish species, authorities adopted a precautionary policy of banning ocean fisheries. On the assumption that people will replace that protein with some other form of meat, a rough calculation[14] suggests that we would need an additional 129 million km^2 of grazing land to replace wild-caught fish with livestock. The opportunity cost of such a policy would be all of the benefits we could have gotten, including for biodiversity, from leaving the land in its current use rather than converting it for livestock. When it comes to environmental policies, regulation can often be expensive, and there is

---

[14] We get about 0.7 tons of meat per km^2 from livestock grazing, and we land about 90 million tons of marine seafood per year (Food and Agriculture Organization of the United Nations, 2013).

also the economic value of development foregone to conserve biodiversity. These costs can be substantial. As Whyte (2007) says: "It is a strange kind of caution that recommends spending such sums when the chance of success is unknown." A strategy of always gambling if the reward is greater than the wager is not a winning strategy in the long run.

Perhaps, as environmentalists, we should resist the analogy to alien abduction insurance. Most people have an intuitive sense that even if they don't know what it is, the likelihood of suffering an alien abduction is extremely low. What about the loss of biodiversity? Remember, there are two ways in which the precautionary principle might be invoked in discussions about biodiversity. In the *why* case, we are thinking about the likelihood that the particular biodiversity lost *might* have been valuable to us. The precautionary principle is not invoked to defend biodiversity with known instrumental value, it is invoked when we do not know its value. What is the likelihood of great disaster if we lose some particular bit of biodiversity? As environmentalists, we seem to have an intuition that the likelihood is high, even though we don't know what it is.

Ecologists seem less sure about this intuition, as evidenced by Root's quote (2003, p. 290). As Sober (1986) asked: "And there are so many species. How many geese that lay golden eggs are there apt to be in that number?" (pp. 175–176). And how does this intuition help us in cases like the one presented by Root, where we have good reason to believe that no great disaster would follow a species' extinction? In the *how* case, the crucial questions are about the probability of biodiversity loss arising from different possible courses of action. If we adopt action A, what is the chance that we will lose some bit of biodiversity? In both circumstances it is assumed that no one knows the associated probabilities, but that based on one's *intuitions* about the magnitudes of those probabilities, it is possible to choose the safe course of action.

In this section we have shown that the precautionary principle is meant to help us make decisions when we have insufficient information for making a rational decision using cost–benefit analysis. The precautionary principle seems to be arguing for complete risk aversion, a strategy that would lead to economic ruin because it does not take account of the probability of the hazard's occurrence. We also showed that the precautionary approach seems to disregard the opportunity costs of taking the so-called precautionary action (or imagines that there are none).

At this point, proponents of the precautionary approach might be tempted to argue that, in such cases of ignorance, all the precautionary approach implies is that we should await more information before making a decision. The trouble with this move is two-fold. First, how much information is needed before we are allowed to make a decision, recognizing that we will never be in a position of complete information? This question really does demand an answer if this move is to rescue the precautionary principle. Second, once we have enough information, what are we to do with it? Proponents of the precautionary principle resist cost–benefit analysis, so presumably they would stick to their principle and try to determine the safe option without considering the information, or the opportunity costs? These are significant problems for the precautionary principle, but they don't end there. Before looking at further problems for the precautionary principle, let's look at the other alternative approach for making decisions: ecological risk assessment.

3.5.2 Ecological Risk Assessment

Ecological Risk Assessment (ERA) is the process of evaluating the likelihood of an undesirable ecological outcome, like the loss of a population, habitat, or ecosystem, occurring as a result of some action such as a new policy, a new construction project, etc. The process involves gathering and analyzing data, assumptions, and uncertainties. There are three parts to an ERA: problem formulation, analysis, and risk characterization. Here we briefly consider these parts, and refer the interested reader to Wentsel et al. (2008) for more detailed discussion. We hope that our brief consideration of the ERA process gives the reader some understanding of the intellectual maturity and

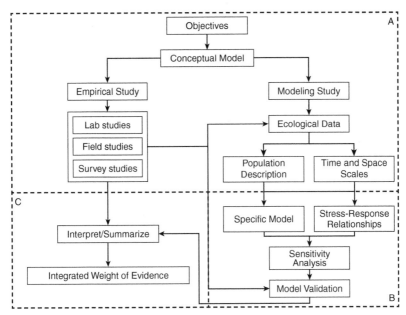

FIGURE 3.1 A schematic sketch of the work involved in Ecological Risk Assessment. (A) shows the steps involved in problem formulation, (B) shows the typical steps in analysis phase, and (C) hints at the work involved in the risk characterization phase. See text for more details. Adapted from Wentsel et al. (2008).

rigor, as well as the transparency of the approach, in contrast to how we are meant to derive sound policy from profound ignorance, as seems to be suggested by the precautionary principle.

Problem formulation (denoted by box A in Figure 3.1) involves deciding on appropriate 'end points' – i.e. the environmental values that we seek to protect. In the context of conserving biodiversity, appropriate end points might be, e.g. the persistence of key indicator species populations (i.e. species-level conservation), conservation of foodweb structure and integrity (i.e. ecosystem structure), and/or rates of nutrient cycling, water purification, etc. (i.e. ecosystem functions). Problem formulation also involves the development of a *conceptual model* where we link our actions/decisions to various environmental stressors and consider how these stressors interact with routes of exposure to the ecological effects we designated as endpoints. Finally, the problem formulation part includes a plan of analysis that describes what will be measured, what will be done with the data, what will be modeled, how the model will be developed, and how these measures and model outputs will be used to assess the impacts on the specified endpoints. The analysis part of ERA (denoted by box B in Figure 3.1) has to accomplish two goals: characterize the exposure, and characterize the ecological impacts. Exposure characterization involves quantifying how, and how often, the ecological end point comes into contact with the stressor. For example, it may be the case that our actions clearly cause the existence of a stressor (e.g. a water pollutant) but that there are few if any routes of exposure for the species in question to experience the stressor. Impact characterization can either evaluate a stressor-response (analogous to a dose-response) relationship, or provide evidence that exposure causes some observed response. When the ecological endpoint involves the persistence of a rare or endangered species, the analysis part of ERA often takes the form of a population viability analysis (PVA). A PVA seeks to provide statements of the form "species A has an X% chance of extinction following policy Y." Risk characterization (denoted by box C in Figure 3.1) estimates and interprets the risks, but also characterizes the strengths, weaknesses, assumptions, and uncertainties associated with the evaluated risk.

As we mentioned in response to Pollen's quote at the start of this chapter, it is incorrect to assume that risk assessment can only deal with measured and measurable risks. A standard practice in risk assessment is to incorporate a so-called uncertainty factor to account for places where uncertainty creeps into the calculation of risk. These uncertainty factors are not wholly scientific: there are elements of arbitrariness and value judgment inherent in choosing a value for this factor (Ritter et al., 2007), *but* where this process differs completely from applications of the precautionary principle is that uncertainty factors are *transparent*. Anyone can see how the uncertainty was incorporated and can see for themselves how sensitive the recommended decision is to the choice of the value of the factor.

The details and nuances of ERA are many, fairly technical, and beyond the scope of this book. Perhaps one of the more difficult steps comes after the risk assessment (in a stage called 'risk management'), i.e. stating what are and are not acceptable risks. ERA is not unique in the fact that such an assessment cannot be scientific. It is clearly a value-laden activity, but no more so than the precautionary principle's seeming advocacy for complete risk aversion. With ERA, at least the process is transparent and one could conceivably evaluate the sensitivity of the decision to this attitude toward risk. Gregory Biddinger et al. (2008) describe this example of a standard to be used in risk management, from the US state of Oregon, which has adopted specific regulatory language that unacceptable risk occurs when:

> There is a >10% chance that >20% of the population of the target species (the assessment endpoint) will be exposed to the stressor at levels greater than the "toxicity reference value" (the regulation is stated in terms of a hazardous substance, but one can readily reframe the statement to incorporate other types of stressors).

So the risk is deemed acceptable if the toxicity reference value[15] is exceeded, so long as this happens to less than 20% of the population.

This example shows how ERA differs from more traditional risk assessment in the context of human health. There, the health of the individual is the assessment end point. That is, traditional risk management would not deem it an acceptable risk if 15% of a human population were exposed to lethal levels of a hazardous substance. In ERA, except in the context of legally protected species, individual organisms are not our concern. Some environmental stressor may cause the death of some individuals of a (non-human) species, but as long as that mortality is *compensatory* rather than *additional*, ERA

---

[15] TRVs are estimates of levels of exposure of the ecological population that are not likely to cause any significant risk of adverse effects over a specified time period. So exceeding the TRV means that the population is likely to suffer adverse effects.

would say that we don't need to worry about it. What does that mean? It means that individuals in any population will die anyway, and, for density-dependent reasons, killing some through one route of mortality (e.g. exposure to a toxic chemical) may mean that fewer die from another route (e.g. intra-specific competition). In other words, the mortality caused by the anthropogenic stressor substitutes, or compensates, for mortality from natural causes (Biddinger et al., 2008).

In this section, we presented ERA as an alternative to the precautionary principle. ERA is a sophisticated approach to decision making that is informed by science, but is still driven by value decisions. In contrast to the precautionary principle, the value judgments in ERA are explicit and easily examined. Like cost–benefit analysis, ERA requires information in order to arrive at policy recommendations. The precautionary principle is meant to be helpful when we lack such information. We take up the problems with this claim in the next section.

3.6 FURTHER PROBLEMS FOR THE PRECAUTIONARY PRINCIPLE

We have already shown that although its proponents tout the benefits of the precautionary principle over cost–benefit analysis and risk assessment, the principle does not seem to have the intellectual maturity or rigor of these alternatives. And in seeming to argue for a strategy of complete risk aversion, the precautionary principle would commit us to an endless outlay of resources, with no basis for believing that these expenses would achieve the desired effects.

In this section, we consider some of the objections we have already raised in more detail, as well as a few we have not. We consider the following five philosophical objections that are commonly raised in response to the precautionary principle: (1) that lack of knowledge is a serious impediment to making sound decisions; (2) that failing to account for the benefits of action is a problem; (3) that the precautionary principle leads to a logical contradiction; (4) that following a precautionary policy is not without its costs (Pascal's Wager); and (5) that the various statements of the principle are desperately in need of conceptual clarity if they are to be anything more than a thin veil to hide the absence of justification in our decision making.

3.6.1 Is the Lack of Information a Problem?

Both cost–benefit analysis and ecological risk assessment take all of the available information and attempt to come to a reasoned decision about whether or not to take a particular risk. Each has methods for dealing with and incorporating uncertainty into the decision-making process (although we did not go into those methods in our presentation). If the information is available, Whyte (2007) says that you don't need 'precaution' or recklessness, or anything else: the numbers alone are sufficient. But when you lack sufficient information, the precautionary principle is meant to help you make a wise decision. Whyte says that the precautionary principle promotes the idea that a lack of information is not a serious problem for decision makers, and that wise decision makers can choose the cautious policy without knowing the likely outcomes. He sees this as a reason for abandoning the principle altogether.

Critics of Whyte, and others who characterize the precautionary principle as helpful, reply with arguments like this:

> This attack on the precautionary principle may sound plausible to some people at first, but it is not. The argument breaks down because the author [Whyte] concludes that, when the outcomes of a decision are unknown, we cannot take precautionary action. Obviously this is false – precautionary action can be as simple as "Try to learn more before deciding," or "Favor a decision that is reversible in case it turns out that you're wrong." There is ALWAYS a way to take sensible precautionary action if you have reasonable suspicion that harm is occurring or is about to occur.
> (Rachel.org [2007]: http://tinyurl.com/7utxamq)

It's not entirely clear that these seemingly common-sense actions are implied by the various statements of the precautionary principle. Even if they are indeed implied, it's still not clear that they are 'good sense' even if they are 'common sense' for many of the same reasons we have already raised as objections. As Sober (1986, p. 175) said: *"out of nothing, nothing comes ....* If you are completely ignorant of values, then you are incapable of making a rational decision."

At this point, proponents of the precautionary principle might object that they never claimed that one can make a decision if they are profoundly ignorant, only that full scientific knowledge is not necessary, or that cause-and-effect relationships don't have to be fully established. We offer a simple, real example of the dangers of such a decision-making approach. In the early-to-mid-1970s scientists had serious concerns that the Earth was rapidly cooling and perhaps getting ready to enter another ice age. There were papers in *Science*, books, news and magazine articles, and several reports from the US National Academies of Sciences, which were seriously thinking about this possibility, even though the science was unclear. In a famous popular science book of the time called *The Cooling*, by Lowell Ponte (1976), the concern is strikingly clear:

> Since the 1940s the northern half of our planet has been cooling rapidly. Already the effect in the United States is the same as if every city had been picked up by giant hands and set down more than 100 miles closer to the North Pole. If cooling continues, warned the National Academy of Sciences in 1975, we could possibly witness the beginning of the next Great Ice Age. Conceivably, we would see mass global famine in our lifetimes, perhaps even within a decade. Since 1970, half a million human beings in northern Africa and Asia have starved because of floods and droughts caused by the cooling climate.[16]

Indeed, a leading proponent of global cooling at the time was Stephen Schneider [1945–2010], who would go on to become a leading proponent of global warming. Schneider notes that he had gotten the maths wrong in trying to evaluate which was more potent, carbon dioxide, which warms the Earth, or sulfate aerosols, which cool the Earth.

---

[16] As cited in Maslin (2004), p. 27.

Schneider endorsed Ponte's book with a quote for the dust jacket. The point of this example is that were the precautionary principle around at the time, and environmentalism more politically robust, environmentalists might have invoked the principle to justify a strategy of producing *more* carbon dioxide to warm the planet and avoid the potential disaster that might come from global cooling. We don't want to make too much of this episode, as the science was clearly wrong, but it does illustrate the potential dangers of taking precautionary action when you don't know the science.[17]

3.6.2 *The Precautionary Principle Fails to Account for the Benefits of Action*

As we said earlier, many proponents of the precautionary principle view it as an alternative to traditional cost–benefit analysis. One way that this is so is that the precautionary principle does not consider the potential benefits of an action, only the potential costs. Here, we present some examples of this problem, originally developed by Brendan Moyel (2005).

Suppose that you had to select one conservation strategy for a species at risk, from two possible management strategies. Suppose further that we conducted a population viability analysis (PVA) of the species and determined that the *minimum viable population*[18] size was 500 individuals. Both strategies incur the same costs, and you have only enough money to enact one of the strategies. You have to

---

[17] As an aside, it seems pretty clear to us that one need not invoke the precautionary principle as justification for taking action to halt global warming. There is no great scientific uncertainty anymore, and there is a clear imperative to take action. Whether we should have waited this long, to be sure we had the science right, is an interesting question, and perhaps we had *enough* information to act much earlier, but climate change is easily analyzed from a cost–benefit approach (sensu The Stern Report [http://bit.ly/1PDrLtc] and its critics) or a human or ecological risk assessment approach.

[18] The Minimum Viable Population size, or MVP, is the size of the population needed for the species to have a probability of X of surviving for the next Y years. X is often taken to be 0.95 and Y is often taken to be 100 years. The MVP is a product of a Population Viability Analysis. The values 0.95 and 100 are not defined by the PVA approach, rather they are choices made by the analyst. Readers interested in learning more about PVA might be interested in Steven Beissinger and Dale McCullough's (2002) edited volume: *Population Viability Analysis* (University of Chicago Press).

employ the strategy before you can know the outcome. Suppose, mainly to keep things simple and to see the point more clearly, that each strategy can result in only one of two outcomes (expressed in terms of population sizes), but you don't have any idea of the associated probability distribution. Presented this way, we can depict the problem as a decision matrix:

	Outcome 1	Outcome 2
Strategy 1	500	500
Strategy 2	600	400

An application of the precautionary principle would argue for adopting Strategy 1, since there is no risk of the population going below the minimum viable population size. Now consider a second problem, as illustrated in the next matrix:

	Outcome 1	Outcome 2
Strategy 1	500	500
Strategy 2	1500	499

Strategy 2 again carries the threat that irreversible harm (population extirpation) will result and so the precautionary principle again recommends Strategy 1. The principle is explicitly concerned with avoiding irreversible loss; there are no provisions for weighing that loss against possible gain (otherwise we are using cost–benefit analysis). As Moyle argues, no decision rule that completely ignores potential gains will be efficient. The problem is that the cost, in this case the opportunity cost, of choosing strategy 1 is ignored by the precautionary principle. Moyle illustrates this problem with the real example of the Chatham Island Black Robin (*Petroica traversi*) in New Zealand. There were just five individuals left of this species in 1980. At this point, conservation managers adopted a bold strategy of capturing and relocating these birds to another island, a predator-free nature reserve. They also took the bold step of removing the first clutch of the year and putting those eggs into the nests of another species to cross-foster, causing the black robin females to lay a second clutch. These strategies were gambles. The researchers did not know if the strategies would work, and, as such, the precautionary principle would seem to have recommended that such invasive and risky strategies not be used. Moyle says that in reality the managers were unwilling to expend the time and resources to test these ideas first, but rather their decision making was dominated by the possible large gain from the translocation and cross-fostering strategies. It turns out that this decision may have proved correct since the population is now more than two hundred individuals – although, since there is no control or reference population, we can't be sure that a recovery wouldn't have happened anyway.

3.6.3   A Logical Contradiction: Applying the Principle to Its Proposed Remedy

In the alien abduction example given earlier, it was clear (we hope!) that an uncompensated alien abduction would be a bad outcome for you. Here, we want to look at a different example, one where the 'best' outcome is not so clear.

Many conservation organizations reject a policy of developing and using genetically modified organisms (GMOs) or genetically engineered organisms (GE; the terms are interchangeable), and they explicitly invoke a precautionary argument for doing so:

> Greenpeace opposes the release of genetically engineered (GE) crops and animals into the environment based on the precautionary principle. ... The most serious environmental threat posed by GE crops is the loss of biodiversity. Nature and traditional breeding techniques have created an incredible diversity of crops. GE crops that reproduce form a living, genetic pollution and pose unpredictable and possibly irreversible risks. Genetic pollution can spread as plants and microorganisms grow and reproduce, and could result in superweeds. ... The potentially harmful effects of GE

organisms may only be discovered when it is too late. GE organisms have been released into the environment and have landed on our dinner tables without first undergoing long-term health tests and without a clear understanding of how they will interact with other living organisms. The burden of proof that an organism is safe has not been required of biotechnology corporations such as Monsanto. Genetically engineered organisms should be subject to the precautionary principle: don't wait for disaster before taking action.

(Greenpeace website: http://bit.ly/2rasY5X)

Applying Manson's framework (Table 3.1), we can deduce from this quote, and other statements on the website, that the damage condition Greenpeace has in mind is (among others) the loss of biodiversity. The knowledge condition that links the release of GMOs and the damage condition is 'potentially,' and the remedy that Greenpeace poses (gleaned from elsewhere on their website) is either a ban or a moratorium on the use of GMOs.

There are several problems with this approach. First, the knowledge condition is a double-edged sword. On the one hand, the complaint seems to be that companies such as Monsanto cannot prove beyond (any, a shadow, a reasonable) doubt that their GMOs are safe. This would seem to invoke the precautionary principle and imply that we should adopt the stated remedy. This approach asks for a high standard to satisfy the burden of proof. On the other hand, Greenpeace may readily admit that it is up to them to make a positive case that GMOs have such negative effects, but the knowledge conditions that they must live up to are quite modest: as Manson says "they need only establish its bare possibility, or have a hunch that it is true, or point to a precedent for thinking that it is true, or have reasonable grounds for concern that it is true. They need not prove it with full scientific certainty, or prove it beyond a shadow of a doubt, or have any scientific evidence for it at all" (Manson 2002, p. 269). To invoke the precautionary principle, either approach suffices. Whether they place a high knowledge standard on the proponents of GMOs, or a low knowledge standard on themselves – or, indeed, both – hardly matters. Either method of meeting the required knowledge condition suffices to invoke the precautionary approach.

The type of precautionary principle that Greenpeace seems to be employing is something that Manson refers to as 'the catastrophic principle.' In such a use of the precautionary principle, if we can identify the effect as catastrophic and there is a mere possibility that the activity can cause that effect, then we should impose the remedy regardless of the likelihood that the activity indeed causes the effect. The problem with this argument is that we don't know that the proposed remedy itself won't have catastrophic consequences. That is, we have no reason not to apply the same argument to the proposed remedy itself. Such an argument might go something like this.

Suppose that human-caused climate change turns out to be as bad as the worst predictions suggest it may be. We could face massive disruptions to our agricultural production. Faced with famine on a global scale, humanity would convert even more wild land for agricultural production, and since loss of habitat is widely acknowledged to be one of the most significant risks of extinction, we would face an almost certain loss of biodiversity. We might need genetically modified crops to ensure agricultural production in the face of such extreme climate change, and to prevent the loss of even more biodiversity. Perhaps this scenario is not terribly likely, but we certainly can't say that there is no chance that this would happen. Indeed, all that we need to say is that there is a mere possibility that this would happen. The precautionary principle therefore tells us that we should develop GMOs.

Not developing GMOs is the activity, the effect is loss of biodiversity (due to being unable to cope with the effects of climate change), and the proposed remedy is to develop GMOs. The precautionary principle would seem to be arguing, *simultaneously*, that we should both prevent the development of GMOs and that we should develop GMOs. How is this possible, and what does it say about the usefulness of the precautionary principle? An argument that leads to a logical contradiction (i.e. to both *A* and *Not A*) is seriously flawed, and, in any case, useless.

3.6.4 Pascal's Wager and the Cost of the Precautionary Principle

The applications of the precautionary principle that we considered above, with GMOs, climate change, and biodiversity, are examples of a more generic fallacious argument known as Pascal's Wager. French mathematician Blaise Pascal [1623–1662] offered the following argument:

Premise 1: Either God exists or God does not exist.

Premise 2: If we believe in God and God exists, then we are rewarded with eternal happiness in the afterlife.

Premise 3: If we don't believe in God, and God does exist, then we will be damned to hell for all eternity.

Conclusion: Therefore, the mere possibility that God exists justifies our belief in God.

That proponents of the precautionary principle see it as a sort of Pascal's Wager is clear from their comments. According to Norman Myers (1993, p. 74):

> It's a case of: If we live as if it matters and it doesn't matter, it doesn't matter. If we live as if it doesn't matter, and it matters, then it matters.

Pascal's Wager has a well-known response, called the 'many gods' objection. The objection goes like this. Suppose that Shiva (the Hindu 'destroyer god') is a jealous and vengeful god. We can readily substitute Shiva for God in the argument above and come to the conclusion that we ought to believe in Shiva. Furthermore, if we believe in God, and God does not exist but Shiva does exist, then we will certainly suffer infinite sorrow because Shiva is a jealous and vengeful god. This means that a belief in God is not without potential cost.

The general point from this comparison with Pascal's Wager is that even if the effect of the activity is infinitely bad (i.e. catastrophic) it *does not follow* that we should adopt the suggested remedy, *unless* we know (with certainty?) that the remedy itself does not also lead to infinitely bad consequences. Unless we know this (and how can we ever know it, because of our lack of knowledge?) then we are stuck applying the precautionary principle, which leads us to the conclusion that we should both believe in God and not believe in God. This is why we said that Pascal's Wager is just a more general version of the GMO and climate change examples we gave in the last section.

What could be 'infinitely bad' about conserving biodiversity? Maybe it's not the biodiversity itself that is infinitely bad, but the cost or other social consequences of adopting the conservation strategy. At its heart, the many gods objection is about the *opportunity costs* of making (or failing to make) a decision. Conservation is not free. Every conservation decision costs money (and perhaps other resources) that could have been used on other conservation projects, perhaps on projects that are more necessary. Recall that we gave an example of the opportunity cost problem in the section on costs, benefits, and alien abductions, in the context of banning ocean fisheries.

3.6.5 Striving for Conceptual Clarity

One problem is that environmentalists have not, to our knowledge, undertaken a conceptual analysis of the precautionary principle. A conceptual analysis aims to clarify the meaning of a term by considering the circumstances in which it is appropriately (or inappropriately) used. For example, philosophers have conducted various conceptual analyses of the species concept as it is used in biology. This has resulted in the identification of various different conceptions of what a species is, some of which are associated with particular research programs in evolution or ecology (see Table 9.1). One benefit of such an analysis is that it makes it less likely for practitioners to talk past one another – for example, in cases where two parties fail to recognize that they are operating with different senses of the same term. A similar analysis of the precautionary principle should likewise help to sharpen its meaning and provide a much needed focus to this debate.

To illustrate, let us again consider the following statement of the precautionary principle: "Where there are threats of serious or irreversible damage, lack of full scientific certainty shall not be used as a reason for postponing cost-effective measures to prevent [loss of biodiversity]." Unpacking this (or any other) definition of the precautionary principle would require us to do our best to define the important terms – that is, to state as best we can the conditions for employing the relevant terms. How are we to understand 'threat,' 'damage,' 'cost-effective,' etc.? Does 'damage' simply mean 'change,' or can we be more specific? Does 'threat' mean any conceivable event, or only those to which we can attach a probability? What does 'cost-effective' mean? Are they only those actions where the net expected gain is positive, or are they any action where the cost is smaller than the possible loss (as in our alien abduction insurance example)? What does 'irreversible' mean? In some strict sense, any change to the environment is irreversible.

By itself, an objection on the grounds of conceptual clarity (or, more specifically, its absence) is not particularly compelling. After all, there are many useful concepts that have not been subjected to this kind of rigor. Nevertheless, the plea for conceptual clarity in this case seems particularly important if the precautionary principle is to be rescued from its critics. However, we fear that some environmentalists might be reluctant to undertake this kind of analysis. As Derek Turner and Lauren Hartzell (2004) note: "The more precise the formulation, the more vulnerable it is to decisive objections" (p. 451).

By way of illustration, let's look at one example of an attempt to clarify a concept from the precautionary principle, studied by Turner and Hartzell (2004): "threats of harm." In the Wingspread version of the precautionary principle, the principle is stated as:

When an activity raises *threats of harm* to human health or the environment, precautionary measures should be taken even if some cause and effect relationships are not fully established scientifically.

(p. 451)

What is a 'harm' (something we take up more fully in Chapters 7, 8, and 9) and, more importantly, what is a "threat of harm," ask Turner and Hartzell. They use the example of pesticide use, and note that no one seriously disputes that large-scale agricultural application of pesticides *can* harm the environment (although, again, see Chapter 9 for more on the notion of harm to ecosystems). But what about minor use to control weeds in a home vegetable garden? Does that use harm the environment? There might well be a way around the difficulty in defining harm, but what about the *threat* of harm? The least stringent definition might be something like: "a threat of harm arises whenever there is the slightest indication that some activity A could have a harmful effect E, given the most liberal conception of what a harm is." Given this definition, it is difficult to imagine what activity does *not* carry with it the threat of harm. Since we do not have such a great track record of always being correct about what are and are not harms, Turner and Hartzell (2004) suggest that someone might take a more rigorous view of what constitutes threats of harm: "in order for there to be a genuine threat of harm at all, there must be (a) some preliminary evidence that activity A will produce harmful effect E; and (b) some reason to think that the possible effect E would be quite harmful if it occurred" (p. 456). But as they note, this leads to the problem of defining how much preliminary evidence is necessary before we can conclude that (a) or (b) is correct. The more stringent we make this second definition, the more scientific evidence we require to activate the precautionary principle – exactly the situation that the precautionary principle is supposed to get us out of!

We could continue with attempting to achieve conceptual clarity for this or any phrase, from any version of the precautionary principle. This is a debate that continues to draw attention in the academic literature, and we won't attempt a complete review of the debate here. For now, we just note that clarifying the concepts embedded in any version of the precautionary principle is not straight forward, and is probably a major source of confusion in the larger discussion about the principle and its usefulness in environmental decision making.

In this section, we have discussed the following problems: (1) the dangers of taking action when we lack the knowledge necessary to make a wise decision; (2) that the principle is probably incoherent since it seems to lead to a logical contradiction (arguing both for and against the same proposition simultaneously); (3) that failing to account for the potential benefits of an action leads to sub-optimal solutions, perhaps even dangerous solutions; (4) that even precaution has its costs and those costs can be significant; and (5) that many of the clauses in the various statements of the precautionary principle are so lacking in conceptual clarity that it is difficult to see the justification behind supposed precautionary policies.

3.7 CONCLUSIONS

As a slogan, or motto, that expresses our desire to think about the environment first, to be careful in our decision making about the environment, and to make both the proponent of development and environmentalists responsible for bringing positive arguments to the table when making decisions about the environment, the precautionary principle is a helpful rallying cry. As a principle for forming policy, it is woefully problematic and not a reasonable substitute for either cost–benefit analysis or ecological risk assessment. It promotes the idea that we can make wise decisions when we lack the necessary information to do so. The principle itself leads to logical contradictions and so is useless. It ignores both the possible benefits of the proposed action, *and perversely*, the opportunity costs of adopting the precautionary remedy that the principle allegedly proposes. Finally, the principle is so completely lacking in conceptual clarity that it is next to useless as a policy guide. So, while at first glance we see the precautionary principle as attractive, upon closer inspection we see that it has many gaps that need filling before it, by itself, will be a useful defense of biodiversity conservation.

The precautionary principle still has its proponents, and there are active attempts to clarify the principle and rescue it from its detractors. For the purposes of this book, it is important to recognize that if we intend to use the precautionary principle as a justification for conserving biodiversity, then we need to overcome the objections raised in this chapter. That will not be easy. Many of these objections are substantive and will be difficult to overcome. Attempts to do so will certainly advance the level and quality of discussion around arguments about conserving biodiversity, far more so than vacuously repeating the precautionary defense without any appreciation of the difficulties it has to overcome.

3.8 FURTHER READING

Löfstedt, R. and Frewer, L. (eds.). 1998. *The Earthscan Reader in Risk and Modern Society*. London: Earthscan Publications Ltd.

Morris, J. (ed.). 2000. *Rethinking Risk and the Precautionary Principle*. Butterworth-Heinemann, Oxford.

Sunstein, C.R. 2002. *Risk and Reason: Safety, Law, and the Environment*. Cambridge: Cambridge University Press.

4 Agricultural and Pharmaceutical Benefits

Contemporary societies depend on a variety of agricultural and pharmaceutical products that ultimately derive from nature. Had our forbearers inherited a less biodiverse planet, presumably a significant portion of these products would not exist. Extending this line of thinking into the future, it seems that the loss of existing biodiversity threatens future agricultural and pharmaceutical prospects. After all, it would be arrogant to assume that current technologies exhaust nature's potential to improve human health and welfare. For that matter, who can predict with confidence the novel challenges facing future generations? It is therefore prudent, some would argue, to conserve as much biodiversity as possible in order to maximize the agricultural, pharmaceutical, or similar benefits to future societies.

Before discussing this line of reasoning, a few points of clarification are in order. First, it is important to note that there are two versions of the argument. One version identifies the potential *agricultural* benefits of biodiversity; the other focuses on the potential *pharmaceutical* benefits. It often goes unnoticed that 'biodiversity' refers to something different in each context. In an agricultural context, biodiversity conservation aims to mitigate threats to existing systems of food production. Common threats include (but are not limited to): pests, disease, and habitat modification due to climate change. Biodiversity conservation is important, in this context, insofar as it supplies a pool of genetic variants to buffer against unforeseeable changes. The hope is that some of those variants are predisposed to overcome pests or resist disease, or that they are pre-adapted to a future climate. Here the primary conservation target is genetic diversity *within* certain species or their close relatives. Of particular interest are the wild populations from which domesticated species are derived. Just in case something happens to those domesticated strains, the thinking goes, it might be necessary to draw upon the genetic diversity inherent in ancestral populations. Occasionally, an analogous case is made on behalf of wild species, not currently used in agriculture, that are candidates for domestication. In such cases the focus of biodiversity conservation is on those few under-utilized species, not on genetic diversity per se. These candidates for future cultivation represent only a minute fraction of the total diversity of plant species, but the basic rationale for their conservation mirrors the argument from agricultural diversity: multiple species are main-tained as a buffer against unforeseen contingencies.

In the context of pharmaceutical benefits, biodiversity conser-vation often means something different. The emphasis here is on conserving a variety of species in the hope that some portion of them will render useful bioactive compounds. In this case, the conservation focus is not on maintaining within-species genetic diversity. Nor is species diversity per se the object of value. Rather, the focus is on conserving just the few species whose bioactive compounds have yet to be identified and harvested. It is sometimes further assumed that the best way to hedge one's bets, pharmaceutically speaking, is to conserve as many species as possible. This would perhaps make sense if pharmaceutically valuable compounds were scattered ran-domly across the tree of life. In that case, options are perhaps max-imized by conserving a diversity of species. But, as we will discuss in Section 4.4, the argument from pharmaceutical benefit relies on a number of questionable assumptions. Among these is the assumption that bioactive compounds are scattered broadly among taxa, as opposed to being clustered in just a few lineages.

4.2 A PRECAUTIONARY WARNING

Before discussing these two arguments, it is useful to first identify a common defense of conservation that tends to emerge in this context. Notice that both the agricultural and the pharmaceutical arguments identify uncertainty as a reason for conservation. In the agricultural case, uncertainty takes the form of potential threats to food or to other important products. Sometimes the magnitude and likelihood of those threats are identified. For example, much is known about the effects of temperature increase on rice cultivation and the impact of ensuing shortages on available nutrition in certain Asian societies.[1] But in many other cases those threats are stated in vague and general terms. For example, conservation is sometimes identified as necessary for ensuring 'food security,' where the specific types of food and the nature of the threats are unspecified. Uncertainty takes a slightly different form in the case of the pharmaceutical argument. In this context, the health benefits potentially derived from nature are unknown. We might ask: What sorts of drugs are likely to be derived from a specific bioprospecting venture? Which ailments will be cured? These sorts of questions are very difficult to answer, even probabilistically, and so proponents of the pharmaceutical argument often invoke outcomes that are much less precisely stated.

Notice that when uncertainties are stated in such vague and general terms, the arguments from agricultural and pharmaceutical benefit are, in fact, thinly disguised versions of the precautionary defense that we critiqued in Chapter 3. This point will resurface in what follows. Well-articulated uncertainties are sometimes substituted for poorly formulated ones as the argument proceeds. As sophisticated environmentalists, whenever we seem to be slipping back into a wholly precautionary defense, we ought to stop and think about whether our invocation of this defense is subject to the same objections that were raised in Chapter 3.

4.3 IS BIODIVERSITY NECESSARY FOR FOOD?

Here's an example of the argument from agricultural benefit as it is employed by the World Wildlife Fund:[2]

---

[1] http://bit.ly/1kADY4P   [2] http://wwf.to/2escn3a

> Biodiversity is essential for ensuring food security. All of the
> world's major food crops, including corn, wheat, and soybeans,
> depend on new genetic material from the wild to remain productive
> and healthy. Breeders and farmers rely on the genetic diversity of
> crops and livestock to increase yields and to respond to changes in
> environmental conditions. Plant breeding, using wild genetic stock
> and other sources, was responsible for half the gains in agricultural
> yields in the United States from 1930 to 1980. ... Teosinte, a wild
> relative of corn discovered in Mexico during the 1960s, is resistant
> to four of the eight major diseases that kill corn in the United States.
> Had it been available to US farmers in the 1970s, losses of $1 billion
> could have been avoided when disease wiped out uniformly
> susceptible varieties. Corn is the essential ingredient in a range of
> products from animal feed to corn syrup. Thanks to Teosinte, prices
> for grain-fed meats, soft drinks, and other corn-related foods have
> been kept low. This example shows that genetic biodiversity
> protects American farmers and consumers alike.

Let's consider the intended target of conservation in this context. Here, the WWF is expressing concern about existing domesticated plants and animals and their capacity to adapt to environmental change. As was mentioned earlier, the conservation target is not species diversity per se. One does not need to maximize the number of species being conserved in order to buffer domesticated species against threatening changes. Rather, the kind of diversity being targeted by this argument is within-species genetic diversity. Conserving the wild, undomesticated ancestors of common domesticated species is being offered as one way to maintain a diverse and adaptable gene pool.

In fact, there are excellent reasons for maintaining genetic diversity within those (relatively few) domesticated species on which humans depend. Basic evolutionary theory tells us that genetically diverse populations are more adaptable to change and less prone to extinction. It is therefore not surprising that governments invest heavily in this initiative. The International Rice Research Institute in the Philippines has a collection of more than 100,000 wild rice populations and agricultural cultivars, obtained from 127 countries. That collection is held in duplicate in the United States. This strategy of ex situ conservation involves maintaining germplasms[3] – banks of seeds, in the case of plants. Many individual countries have their own germplasms, in addition to larger international stores. For example, in addition to the IRRI rice germplasm, the US Department of Agriculture also maintains their own collection of rice seeds that contains more than 53,000 populations and cultivars. China maintains its own rice germplasm, with more than 60,000 populations and cultivars, and so on. Because rice is such a globally important crop, there are many rice germplasms around the world. The same is true for any of the important plant species used for food or fodder. Table 4.1 shows the 25 most important plant species worldwide, from which humans and domesticated animals obtain 85% of all of their plant-derived calories and 70% of total calories. Note that the top five plants provide 65% of the total plant-derived calories. In the right-hand column we report the holdings from just a single germplasm for each species (remembering that many of these species are independently collected in multiple germplasms). The point is that, for plant species that are known to be agriculturally important, governments already do a fairly exhaustive job of conservation.

Some might argue that a better job could be done of conserving domesticated plant species and their associated genetic diversity, for instance, because there are gaps and vulnerabilities in our global collections. This may be true. If so, it makes sense to close these gaps and to reduce those vulnerabilities. But this is hardly an argument for conserving all of biodiversity, or even the majority of plant species. There are approximately 300,000 species of plant in the world. Table 4.1 shows that humans rely on less than 1/1000th of 1% of that diversity, and we do a decent job of conserving those species. Hence,

---

[3] As we mentioned in Chapter 1, environmentalists view ex situ conservation as a tool, but not a goal of conservation. The fact that agricultural plant species are well conserved in germplasms around the world is not likely to be convincing to someone promoting the environmentalist agenda.

Table 4.1 *Top 25 plant-based food items in the human diet*

Plant	kcal/ day	% of diet	% of veg	Cum % veg	Germplasm Accessions	Source	
Rice (Milled Equivalent)	532	19.0	23.0	23.0	108,256 | 127	http://bit.ly/JBMe1H	IRRI
Wheat	529	18.9	22.9	45.8	60,135 | ≥119	http://bit.ly/2qojanJ	USDA
Sugar Cane	198	7.1	8.6	54.4	2,617	http://bit.ly/2qo39P1	Sugarcane Breeding Institute (India)
Maize	139	5.0	6.0	60.4	28,247 | ≥130	http://bit.ly/2qojanJ	USDA
Soyabeans	105	3.8	4.5	64.9	21,875 | ≥90	http://bit.ly/2qojanJ	USDA
Potatoes	59	2.1	2.5	67.5	6,175 | ≥40	http://bit.ly/2qojanJ	USDA
Palm Oil	44	1.6	1.9	69.4	1,780	http://bit.ly/Kyl5KD	Malaysian Palm Oil Board
Cassava	43	1.5	1.9	71.2	2712	http://bit.ly/KoMAFH	IITA
Rape and Mustard Oil	37	1.3	1.6	72.8	243	http://bit.ly/JYKDTA	AAFC
Groundnuts	34	1.2	1.5	74.3	1815	http://bit.ly/KoMAFH	IITA
Sorghum	33	1.2	1.4	75.7	45,572 | ≥112	http://bit.ly/2qojanJ	USDA
Millet	32	1.1	1.4	77.1	3,270 | ≥32	http://bit.ly/2qojanJ	USDA
Sunflowerseed Oil	30	1.1	1.3	78.4	4,155 | ≥59	http://bit.ly/2qojanJ	USDA
Beans	23	0.8	1.0	79.4	17,355 | ≥101	http://bit.ly/2qojanJ	USDA
Sweet Potatoes	22	0.8	1.0	80.3	1,272 | ≥41	http://bit.ly/2qojanJ	USDA
Bananas/Plantains	18	0.6	0.8	81.1	250	http://bit.ly/KoMAFH	IITA

Table 4.1 (*cont.*)

Plant	kcal/ day	% of diet	% of veg	Cum % veg	Germplasm Accessions	Source	
Cottonseed	14	0.5	0.6	81.7	10,118 | ≥94	http://bit.ly/2qojanJ	USDA
Coconut	12	0.4	0.5	82.2	116 | 27	http://bit.ly/2pQIG29	International Coconut Genetic Resources Network
Apples	10	0.4	0.4	82.7	6,869 | ≥49	http://bit.ly/2qojanJ	USDA
Olive Oil	10	0.4	0.4	83.1	1,208 | 52	http://www.oleadb.it/	National Research Council of Italy
Onions	10	0.4	0.4	83.5	2,312 | ≥62	http://1.usa.gov/Koyynj	USDA
Oranges, Mandarines	10	0.4	0.4	84.0	1,046	http://bit.ly/LMMHP6	National Citrus Germplasm (China)
Tomatoes	9	0.3	0.4	84.4	10,364 | ≥94	http://bit.ly/2qojanJ	USDA
Barley	7	0.3	0.3	84.7	33,914 | ≥108	http://bit.ly/2qojanJ	USDA
Grapes	6	0.2	0.3	84.9	4,806 | ≥51	http://bit.ly/2qojanJ	USDA
Totals		70.3	84.9				

Shown are the top 25 plant-based food items in the human diet worldwide. The items are shown by their kcalorie content, the percentage they comprise of the diet, the percentage of the vegetables in the diet, the cumulative percentage of vegetables in the diet, the number of accessions (populations | number of countries represented by the accessions), the source website, and the organization responsible for the major germplasm (note that for most species there exists many more than a single germplasm)

IRRI = International Rice Research Institute, USDA = the United States Department of Agriculture, IITA = International Institute of Tropical Agriculture, AAFC = Agriculture and Agri Food Canada.

the argument from agricultural benefit is sound, so long as it is limited to genetic diversity within a small number of (mostly domesticated) species.

What, then, of the vast majority of species that, in all likelihood, humans will never want to eat? They are not covered by this defense. At this point in the argument, the tendency is to fall back on some form of precautionary argument. Something along the lines of:

Premise 1:   Some unknown species might potentially be an important source of food during some future food crisis.

Premise 2:   A particular action *A* could result in biodiversity loss.

Premise 3:   If an action potentially has unknown negative consequences, then it should be avoided.

Conclusion: One should avoid *A*.

Note that this argument is just another form of the one given in Chapter 3 (The Precautionary Principle), where we have substituted P1 above for P1 from Chapter 3: "The loss of biodiversity (e.g. a species or ecosystem) will potentially have unknown negative consequences." In this case the unknown negative consequence is that the potentially useful food source (species) won't be here to serve that function. This argument is vulnerable to all of the objections that we raised against the precautionary defense in Chapter 3.

Another potential strategy for defending the conservation of biodiversity on agricultural grounds is to identify other species that interact with domesticated plants and animals. If valuable domesticated species depend on a vast number of other species, it might be argued that biodiversity conservation is in fact required to maintain the target species on which we rely. For example, all known legume species enjoy an obligate mutualistic relationship with soil bacteria (*Rhizobia*). Thus, maintaining adaptable, genetically diverse legume populations requires also maintaining a diverse population of the micro-organisms on which they depend. And so on it goes, one might argue, for the conditions supporting those bacteria. By bootstrapping one's way up from the most agriculturally valuable species through the network of their ecological interdependencies, one might thus claim that the argument from agricultural benefit casts a wider net over biodiversity than we have so far imagined.

The important thing to note about this move is that much depends on the nature of those ecological connections. Specifically, how extensive are they and what is the degree of interdependence among species? One might concede that a healthy legume population requires rhizobial bacteria. But now we might ask the same question of those micro-organisms as we previously asked of species: how much of the total bacterial diversity is necessary for maintaining healthy legume populations? Again, the answer is that only a small fraction of the planet's micro-organisms enjoy a mutualistic interdependency with some agriculturally valuable species. Of course, one might argue that this example merely illustrates a more general principle – namely, that all of nature is interconnected, and so conserving the agriculturally valuable species requires, out of ecological necessity, the conservation of all biodiversity. Notice, however, that this version of the argument is no longer about agriculturally valuable species per se. There has been a subtle shift in conservation targets. We have gone from talking about genetic diversity within a few domesticated species to species diversity within some functionally integrated superorganism. If this holistic picture of nature is correct, there is no need to single out agricultural species as especially important targets of conservation. Indeed, the focal question of this chapter – the medical and industrial value of biodiversity as a basis for its conservation – becomes secondary to questions of the functional interdependency of ecosystem components. We will have more to say about this possibility in Chapter 10 (Section 10.4.3.2).

Recapping, objections to the argument from agricultural value include: (1) it's not species diversity per se that is targeted by this argument, but rather genetic diversity within a limited number of species. This target is much more modest than the ambitions of many environmentalists as described in Chapter 1; this line of argument will have limited application. (2) Certain nations already do a very good job of conserving those species on which their citizenry depends for food. (3) Many deployments of this defense are simply additional examples of the precautionary defense that we dealt with in Chapter 3.

4.4 THE ARGUMENT FROM PHARMACEUTICAL VALUE

A fairly standard defense of biodiversity conservation points to the roles of certain plants and animals in drug discovery. Consider, for example, this passage from Primack's (2002) *The Essentials of Conservation Biology*:

> Effective drugs are needed to keep people healthy, and they represent an enormous industry, with worldwide sales of around $300 billion per year. The natural world is an important source of medicines currently in use and possible future medicines. One species with great medicinal use is the rose periwinkle (*Catharanthus roseus*) from Madagascar. Two potent drugs derived from this plant are effective in treating Hodgkin's disease, leukemia, and other blood cancers. Treatment using these drugs has increased the survival rate of childhood leukemia from 10% to 90%. How many more such valuable plants will be discovered in the years ahead – and how many will go extinct before they are discovered? ...
>
> All of the 20 most frequently used pharmaceuticals in the United States are based on chemicals first identified in natural products. These drugs have a combined sales value of $6 billion per year. Twenty-five percent of the prescriptions filled in the United States contain active ingredients derived from plants, and many of the most important antibiotics, including penicillin and tetracycline, are derived from fungi and other microorganisms. ... the natural world is being actively searched for the next generation of medicines and industrial products.
>
> *(p. 104; references omitted)*

Belinda Hawkins put it more succinctly: [4]

> However, it is not an overstatement to say that if the precipitous decline of these [plant] species is not halted, it could destabilise the future of global healthcare.

On the face of it, this sounds like a powerful argument for conserving biodiversity, and it has certainly enjoyed its share of popularity. In the early-to-mid-1990s there was considerable enthusiasm for pharmaceutical value as a justification for conservation. The defense was discussed in books such as Timothy Swanson's (1998) edited volume, *Intellectual Property Rights and Biodiversity Conservation: An Interdisciplinary Analysis of the Values of Medicinal Plants*. The defense made its way into conservation textbooks and conservation classrooms, where it remains today. Despite its popularity, there are at least three groups of problems with the argument from pharmaceutical value.

First is a problem of biodiversity units. The argument targets particular entities (species, molecules, genes) and not biodiversity per se. The problem, as we explore in Section 4.4.1, is that the available evidence suggests that only a small fraction of species contain medicinally valuable compounds. So the argument from pharmaceutical benefit has, at best, limited scope.

Second, this argument is ultimately an economic argument. Thus, one must employ the tools of cost–benefit analysis to determine whether there is, in fact, a net gain to be derived from conservation in the name of pharmaceutical benefit. As we outline in Section 4.4.2, existing economic models offer little support for these ventures.

A third set of problems stems from an emphasis on the *potential* value of biodiversity in drug discovery. Some bioprospecting enthusiasts argue that since the risks to society of losing medical benefits are so large or unknown, biodiversity should be conserved as a bet-hedging strategy. This argument rests on an unspoken reliance on the

---

[4] http://tinyurl.com/2cdq5p BBC news article, January 19. 2008, "Medicinal plants 'facing threat'."

precautionary principle (see Chapter 3). In its slightly more sophisticated form, the argument rests on a problematic understanding of the economic notion of *option value*.

The remainder of this chapter will proceed by considering each of these three lines of defense in detail.

4.4.1   What Is the Conservation Target of Bioprospecting?

The search for pharmaceutically valuable compounds in nature is often called 'bioprospecting.' This practice usually involves screening tissue samples from plants, animals, or micro-organisms in search of bioactive compounds. In these cases, the target of bioprospecting is a bio-medically promising molecule that occurs in some species or a broader taxonomic group. Recent years have seen the incorporation of genetic screening techniques into this process (Li and Vederas, 2009, Zotchev et al., 2012). The 'metagenomic' approach to bioprospecting screens hundreds or even thousands of genomes in a collective soup. In this case, the targets are particular genetic sequences that are likely to produce a protein with medicinally useful applications.

Regardless of whether bioprospecting occurs at the level of species, molecules, or genes, it seems fairly obvious that the conservation targets are particular entities and not biodiversity per se. That is, pharmaceutical benefits do not arise because there are lots of different species, molecules, or genes; they arise because some (perhaps rare) individuals possess the desired properties. One might therefore object to the argument from pharmaceutical value on the grounds that it is not an argument for *biodiversity* conservation per se (Maier, 2012). However, some might regard this as a tricky attempt to dodge the spirit of this line of defense. The spirit of the argument, we think, is that although value resides in some (perhaps small) number of individual species, because there is uncertainty about which ones they are, we should preserve as much biodiversity as possible until it can be exhaustively searched. The more biodiversity that is conserved, the greater the possibilities for finding the proverbial goose that lays the golden egg. How good is this defense?

Ben-Erik van Wyk and Michael Wink's *Medicinal Plants of the World* (2004) has a 37-page appendix titled *Quick Guide to Commercialised Medical Plants*. The guide lists 785 plants or groups of plants, which at first blush suggests a broad diversity of medicinally valuable species. By extension, one might infer that if bioactive molecules are well represented in the plants that have been screened so far, this applies also to the plants that are yet to be investigated. However, the picture becomes less convincing when you realize that 734 of those plants are used only in 'traditional' or 'alternative' medicine. These are, at best, *potentially* bioactive plants or animals, assuming that traditional use is a reliable proxy for novel bioactive molecules. Of the 50 that remain, after all of the double entries[5] are removed, we are left with just 37 pharmaceutically valuable species (see list in Table 4.2). Of the 37, 23 of those claimed to be of use in 'modern medicine' are difficult to trace and/or not very widely used. Many of the species are not 'discovered from nature' in the sense usually intended when thinking about drug discovery. For example, the list contains: avocado, tomatoes, grape vines, pine trees, opium poppy, papaya trees, pineapple, garlic, marijuana, and a variety of species used frequently in horticultural practice and/or that are actually nuisance weeds in many places (e.g. Scotch broom, mistletoe). With few exceptions, the putative bioactive ingredient is also produced by a variety of other organisms and can often be produced synthetically.

Let's try to unpack Primack's claim that "All of the 20 most frequently used pharmaceuticals in the United States are based on chemicals first identified in natural products." This claim is based on an often cited book chapter by Francesca Grifo and colleagues (1997). In that chapter, Grifo et al. show that the organisms related to four of the top five drugs[6] are: the domesticated horse (*Equus caballus*), the domesticated sheep (*Ovis aires*), the bread mold (*Penicillium notatum*), and 'various mammals' which seems to be a reference to

---

[5] The same bioactive compound or very closely related compound being listed as produced by more than one species or species group.

[6] The fifth was entirely synthetic.

Table 4.2 *Pharmaceutically valuable plants*

Species	http://tinyurl.com/	Bioactive Compound(s)	Sources of Bioactive Compounds	Uses in Modern Medicine	Current Status	Used in Alternative Medicine?	Domesticated?
Acokanthera oppositifolia, Digitalis lanata, D. purpurea, D. lutea, Strophanthus gratus, S. kombe, Urginea maritina; Apocynaceae; Hyacinthcea; Scrophulariaceae	Kolxndb	Cardiac glycosides (e.g. bufadienolides, ouabain, strophanthin)	Cardiac glycosides are widely produced by a number of plants across three families, as well as several animal species	Heart disease, mainly angina	Not commonly used anymore	Y	Y
Aconitum napellus; Ranunculaceae	kecg3rk	Diterpenoid alkaloids (mainly aconitine)	Produced by members of the genus which includes >250 species	Antipyretic, analgesic	Not used	Y	Y
Allium sativum (garlic), *A. ursinum;* Alliaceae	lerb7wx	Allicin, sulfur-containing compounds: alliin, ajoene, diallyl polysulfides, vinyldithiins, S-allylcysteine	About 750 species in this genus	Various, evidence from scientific studies is weak and mixed	Not commonly used in modern medicine	Y	Y

Table 4.2 (cont.)

Species	http://tinyurl1.com/	Bioactive Compound(s)	Sources of Bioactive Compounds	Uses in Modern Medicine	Current Status	Used in Alternative Medicine?	Domesticated?
Ananas comosus (pineapple); Bromeliaceae	myv4uz6	Bromelain	8 species in the genus. May be produced by all members of the family Bromeliaceae (>3100 species)	Digestive aid	Not commonly used	N	Y
Artemisia annua; Asteraceae	mbwxy3b	Artemisinin	Can be synthetically produced or biosythesized in several genetically engineered yeast	Anti-malarial	Important	Y	Y
Atropa belladonna (deadly nightshade), *Datura stramonium*, *Duboisia myoporoides*, *Erythroxylum coca*, *Brugmansia spp.*, *Mandragora spp.*.	ny4jvhh	Tropane alkaloids (mainly atropine, cocaine, hyoscyamine, scopolamine)	Tropane alkaloids are minimally found in the *Datura* (9 species), *Mandragora* (3 species), *Brugmansia* (7 species), *Erythroxylum* (>200	Many	Important	Y	Y

Species; Family	PDB ID	Compound	Notes	Use	Usage		
Hyoscyamus niger, H. albus; Solanaceae			species), *Hyoscyamus* (10 species) genera, as well as many others in the Solanaceae family (3,000–4,000 species)				Y
Berberis vulgaris (barberry); Berberidaceae	2cg6736	Berberine	450–500 species in the genus. Berberine is found in plants of other genera as well	Alternative to Metformin in treating poly-cystic ovarian syndrome. Possible uses for several other diseases	Not commonly Used	Y	
Camptotheca acuminata; Cornaceae	muths5d	Pentacyclic quinoline alkaoids (camptothecin)	Two species in the genus. Many analogues are produced synthetically	Cancer. Two analogues are used in cancer chemotherapy: topotecan and irinotecan	Used	Y	N/A
Cannabis sativa; Cannabaceae	2ywcg2	Tetrahyrdo cannabinol	Also found in *Cannabis indica*	Sedative, analgesic, anti-emetic	Commonly used	Y	Y
Carica papaya (papaya tree)	laon42s	Papain	Papain chemical family members are found in baculovirus, eubacteria, yeast, and practically all protozoa, plants and mammals.	?	Not used	Y	Y

Table 4.2 (cont.)

Species	http://tinyurl.com/	Bioactive Compound(s)	Sources of Bioactive Compounds	Uses in Modern Medicine	Current Status	Used in Alternative Medicine?	Domesticated?
Catharanthus roseus (Madagascar periwinkle)	lhwbwzd	Monoterpene indole alkaloids	Vinblastine now largely produced by synthetic chemistry. 8 species in the genus	Extracts vinblastine and vincristine are used to treat leukemia and Hodgkin's lymphoma	First used in the 1960s, still commonly used in generic formulations	Y	Y
Centella asiatica	d2gzcx	Asiaticoside, asiatic acid, madecassic acid	2–3 species in the genus.	May have useful anti-cancer properties	?	Y	?
Chondrodendron tomentosum (curare)		Tubocuarine	3 species in the genus	Muscle relaxant	Not commonly used in modern medicine	Y	?
Claviceps purpurea	ly6pnjh	Ergot alkaoid Ergotamine	This is a fungus that grows on many species of small-grained grasses like rye. Ergotamine can be synthesized	Treat migraine attacks	Used	Y	Y

Colchicum autumnale, Gloriosa superba; Colchicaceae	yc4vvkd	Colchicine	13 species in the genus *Colchicum;* many produce cochicine. All 10 species of the genus *Gloriosa* are known to produce colchicine. May occur more widely in the >140 species in the *Colchicaceae* family. Colchicine can be made synthetically	Treat gout	Used	N	Yes but N/A
Combretum caffrum (bushwillow)	mb33hm2	Combretastatin	370 species in the genus, can be synthesized	?	No currently approved drugs	Y	?
Corydalis cava, C. solida, C. yanhusuo; Fumariaceae	mewovlw	Bulbocapnine, corydaline, aporphine alkaloids	Found in some of the other 470 species in the genus. Also found in the 8 species of the *Dicentra* genus, as well as among others of the 575 species of the *Fumariaceae* family. Can also be created synthetically.	It has been used in the treatment of muscular tremors and vestibular nystagmus	Used	Y	N/A

Table 4.2 (cont.)

Species	http://tinyurl.com/	Bioactive Compound(s)	Sources of Bioactive Compounds	Uses in Modern Medicine	Current Status	Used in Alternative Medicine?	Domesticated?
Crataegus monogyna. *C. laevigata*	dygqsek	Procyanidins	Around 200 species in the genus. Procyanidins can be found in many plants, notably apples, maritime pine bark, cinnamon, aronia fruit, cocoa beans, grape seed, grape skins	Cardiac disease	?	Y	Y
Cytisus scoparius (Scotch broom), Fabaceae	kkhgmb6	Sparteine	Can also be extracted from *Lupinus mutabilis*, among other species	Antiarrhythmic agent	Not used	Y	Y
Galanthus nivalis, *G. woronowii*, Amaryllidaceae	2hgwm6	Galanthamine	20 species in the genus. Also produced by species in related genera like *Narcissus* (50 species), *Leucojum* (2 species), and *Lycoris* (12–20 species). Is produced synthetically	Treatment for Alzheimer's disease	Used	N	Y

Lycopersicon esculentum (tomato); Solanaceae	5ogsa8	Lycopene and other carotenoids	Found in other red fruits	Antioxidant	?	Y	Y
Papaver somniferum (opium poppy); Papaveraceae		Source of many narcotics, including morphine (and its derivative heroin), thebaine, codeine, papaverine, and noscapine	The species is widely cultivated and morphine etc. can be made synthetically	Analgesic	Widely used/ important	Y	Y
Paullinia cupana (guarana); Sapindaceae	n2kz7xa	Catechin	Catechin is found in other terrestrial plants including *Uncaria rhynchophylla* and *Potentilla fragarioides*; it is also found in the green alga *Myriophyllum spicatum*.	?	Not important?	Y	Y

Table 4.2 (cont.)

Species	http://tinyurl.com/	Bioactive Compound(s)	Sources of Bioactive Compounds	Uses in Modern Medicine	Current Status	Used in Alternative Medicine?	Domesticated?
Pausinystalia johimbe; Rubicaceae	3fmpm4g	Yohimbine	20 species in the genus	Sold as prescription medicine the treatment of sexual dysfunction	?	Y	?
Persea americana (avocado); Lamiaceae	ytepk8	Oleic acid, Palmitic acid, Linoleic acid	Oleic and linoleic acids are found in many vegetable oils (e.g. olive oil, canola oil, etc.). Palmitic acid is found in palm oil, and also in meats and dairy products	?	Not commonly used in modern medicine	Y	Y
Physostigma venenosum (calabar bean); Fabaceaa	2dn58vm	Physostigmine (pyrrolidine alkaloids)	Made synthetically	Physostigmine is used to treat glaucoma, Alzheimer's disease and delayed gastric emptying	Used	N	N/A

Picea abies (spruce) and related species, *Pinus mugo*. Pinaceae	2g9zu5b	Bornylacetate, pinene, phellandrene	35 species in the *Picea* genus. Pinene is found in pine resin and the resins of many other conifers, as well as in non-coniferous plants such as big sagebrush (*Artemisia tridentata*). Phellandrene comes primarily from *Eucalyptus radiata*, as well as the oil of *Foeniculum vulgare* and *Abies balsamea*.	Primarily used in perfume and other fragances. No current modern medical uses?	Not used	Y	Y
Podophyllum hexandrum, P. peltatum; Beberidacea	1mwd4c8	Podophyllum resin with podophyllotoxin	?	Is used as a topical treatment of external genital warts	Used	Y	?
Silybum marianum (Scotch thistle); Asteraceae	kvt7rka	Silymarin	Is produced in cell culture	Possible treatment for some liver poisons	Not used	Y	N, N/A

Table 4.2 (cont.)

Species	http://tinyur l.com/	Bioactive Compound(s)	Sources of Bioactive Compounds	Uses in Modern Medicine	Current Status	Used in Alternative Medicine?	Domesticated?
Strychnos nux-vomica; Loganiaceae	jtaz6	Strychnine and brucine	The genus contains 196 species, and many plants in this genus contain strychnine	Brucine is primarily used in the regulation of high blood pressure and similar benign cardiac ailments	?	Y	Y
Styphnolobium japonicum; Fabaceae	3wlvoj3	Rutin	Rutin is found in many plants, especially the buckwheat plant *Fagopyrum tataricum*. Rutin is also found in fruits and fruit rinds, especially the citrus fruits (orange, grapefruit, lemon, and lime) and apple. Rutin is found in berries such as mulberry, ash tree fruits and cranberries	?	Not used	Y	Y

| Taxus baccata, T. brevifolia and other species; Taxaceae | 2yhd5r | Paclitaxel (taxol) | Actually produced by an edophytic fungus, not the yew tree itself. It has since been found in a number of other endophytic fungi, including those in the genera: *Nodulisporium*, *Alternaria*, *Cladosporium*, *Metarhizium*, *Aspergillus*, *Mucor*, *Chaetomella*, *Phyllosticta*, *Phomopsis*, *Pestalotiopsis*, *Phyllosticta*, *Podocarpus*, *Fusarium*, *Pestalotiopsis*, *Botryodiplodia*, *Gliocladium*, *Nigrospora*, and *Taxomyces*. Can be created entirely synthetically. | Paclitaxel is used to treat lung, ovarian, breast, head and neck cancer, and some forms of Kaposi's sarcoma | Used, important | N | Y, N/A |

Table 4.2 (cont.)

Species	http://tinyurl.com/	Bioactive Compound(s)	Sources of Bioactive Compounds	Uses in Modern Medicine	Current Status	Used in Alternative Medicine?	Domesticated?
Trachyspermum ammi; Apiaceae	36gvxw	Thymol	In addition to *T. ammi*, at least two *Moranda*, four *Origandum*, and four *Thymus* species produce thymol.	Antimicrobial, antibacterial	Not used?	N	Y
Vinca minor, V. major, Voacanga africana, V. thousarsii; Apocynaceae	2rx2p5	Vincamine and tabersonine (used in the semisynthesis of vincamine)	Produced synthetically	Supplement for vasodilation and as a nootropic	Used	Y	Yes but N/A
Viscum album (mistletoe); Viscaceae	9ucxol	Lectin, viscotoxins	?	?	?	Y	Y
Vitis vinifera (grape vine); Vitaceae	kcny6oq	Proanthocyanidins, pycnogenols	Contained in a wide variety of plants, including but not limited to: apples, maritime pine, cinnamon, aronia fruit, cocoa beans,	Blood flow, blood pressure. Recent meta-analysis of clinical studies on Pycnogenol: "Current evidence is insufficient to support	Not commonly used	Y	Y

	lgbn4gl	Saponins	grape seed, grape skin, red wines, bilberry, cranberry, black currant, green tea, black tea, cocoa beans, and oak trees	Pycnogenol(®) use for the treatment of any chronic disorder"		
Yucca filamentosa; Agavaceae		Saponins are derived from plants and marine organisms. They are found in a great many plants, including but not limited to plants in the families: Caryophyllaceae, Sapindaceae, Aceraceae, Hippocasta-naceae, Cucurbitaceae, Araliaceae		?	Y	Y

The 37 species, or groups of species, that produce bioactive compounds used in modern medicine (i.e. excluding any that are used solely in traditional or alternative medicine).

Source: Adapted with permission from Ben-Erik van Wyk and Michael Wink's *Medicinal Plants of the World* (2004).

laboratory rats and dogs used in the initial screening (Maier, 2012). In a more recent survey, David Newman and colleagues (2008) add two additional species of *Penicillium* (*P. citrnum* and *P. brevicompactum*), and the opium poppy (*Papaver somniferum*). While there are, to be sure, some actual 'wild species' on both Grifo et al.'s and Newman et al.'s lists, there are also a preponderance of domesticated species, or at least species that are not remotely of conservation concern. In Grifo et al.'s analysis, of the top 150 drugs in the USA, 86 are derived in part from some living thing, but that list of living things includes just 20 different species. Considering that some of these are domesticated animals, and some are bacterial species, which are rarely the target of conservation concern or activities,[7] this is not an entirely convincing argument for the conservation of species diversity.[8]

One twist on this argument, which seems aimed at enlarging this fairly slim list of medically important species, is to appeal to 'traditional medicines' and 'alternative medicines.' Peter Canter and colleagues (2005), referring to a World Health Organization report, say that there are approximately 50,000 'medicinal plants' or other 'folk remedies.' As Don Maier (2012, p. 202) points out, this number would seem to be more convincing, but it begs the question of efficacy: that is, "whether or not they are actually promoting human health beyond the psychological benefit of the ministrations of traditional healers who typically dispense them." We don't wish

---

[7] As Primack correctly points out, many medicinal compounds are derived from micro-organisms, but micro-organisms have never been the target of conservation activities. It is not even clear if it would be necessary, or possible, to conserve the biodiversity of micro-organisms. In many cases, particularly for bacteria, the organisms have a resting state in which they can persist for thousands of years, and become active again only when a favorable environment returns. Because of this, it is not clear that the term 'extinction' applies very often to micro-organisms. But see Griffith (2012) for an alternative view.

[8] A more recent survey by Zhu et al. (2011) comes to a similar conclusion. They surveyed 939 approved drugs and 369 pre-clinical trial drugs for their sources. It turns out that 80% of the approved drugs are concentrated in just 17 drug-prolific families, and 67% of the unapproved were drawn from just 30 families of plants. For reference, there are 620 families of plants, so approved drugs derive from <3% of plant families, and trial drugs derive from <5% of plant families.

to engage in the debate surrounding the efficacy of treatments such as alternative or traditional medicine. For now, it will suffice to say that nothing like randomized, double-blind, placebo-controlled studies[9] support the position that the vast majority of these traditional/alternative medicines are effective. The issue of efficacy matters, because the use of organisms for traditional medicine is not without its own risk to biodiversity. Many traditional medicines are harvested (often over-harvested) from the wild, with all of the attendant damage that such activities can cause. Other medicinal plants are farmed using commercial agriculture, which is often associated with negative environmental impacts. Traditional medicine has, in part, led to the endangerment of several species of rhinoceros (family *Rhinocerotidae*), the tiger (*Panthera tigris*), and Asiatic black bears (*Ursus spp.*), to name a few (Maier 2012). Hence, there is risk to biodiversity that often comes from the claim that a species provides pharmaceutical value, regardless of whether such claims are scientifically well established. Obviously, resource endangerment is not a prerequisite for using nature to produce medicine; but it is a risk, and, if conservation of biodiversity is our ultimate goal, those risks ought to be worth taking. We don't feel that such appeals to traditional medicine are particularly convincing arguments to justify the environmentalist agenda.

4.4.2 Unfavorable Economics

It is both costly and time consuming to extract useful pharmaceutical compounds from nature (for a review see Borris 2017). Not only does research and development involve considerable effort and expertise, but land preservation often comes with an opportunity cost. Regions set aside for bioprospecting can potentially be converted into other uses – e.g. agriculture or forestry – whose benefits are often more

---

[9] This is the 'gold standard' for demonstrative efficacy for medicines. Because many treatments such as 'natural health products' are not sold as medicine per se, they are not subjected to such rigorous testing standards.

immediate and tangible. Even on the rare occasion when a useful compound is identified in nature, decades of clinical testing are required before an approved drug becomes commercially available (McChesney et al., 2007). In an ideal world, perhaps, governments would shoulder these up-front costs. Arguably, only publically funded institutions are able to undertake such long-term investments. In reality, however, it is rare for adequate public funding to be allocated to such projects (Pearce, 2005). In our contemporary, largely capitalist societies, these costs are more likely to be borne by deep-pocketed corporations who license the rights to natural compounds in the expectation of realizing profit.

Thus, at its heart, the argument from pharmaceutical value is an economic argument. It says that, because of their inherent potential to yield beneficial drugs, diverse regions are worth more intact than if they were developed for other uses. Early estimates of the economic value of biodiversity reinforced this impression. Pharmacognosist[10] Norman Farnsworth [1930–2011] and colleagues (1985) estimated the value of each undiscovered medicinal species at $1.57 million, while Peter Principie (1996) went as high as $10 million. Likewise, environmental economists David Pearce [1941–2005] and Seema Purushothamon (1995) estimated an annual loss of $25 billion if 60,000 species were to go extinct. Such estimates encouraged a wave of enthusiasm for conservation in the name of human health and economic benefit. The only obstacle, it seemed, was to arrive at an equitable profit-sharing arrangement among pharmaceutical companies – responsible for screening, development, marketing, and sales – and the (often) developing countries where valuable species are located. In 1992 the Convention on Biological Diversity was drafted. This international legal framework protects the interests of developing nations and indigenous people against the threat of 'biopiracy.' With this mechanism in place, it seemed ·that the stage

---

[10] Someone who studies medicinal drugs derived from nature (typically, but not exclusively, plants).

was set for an economically viable and mutually beneficial approach to conservation.

More than twenty years later, things have not worked out as planned. It is generally recognized that the pharmaceutical and conservation benefits once projected for bioprospecting have failed to materialize (Firn, 2003). In fact, the period from 2001–2008 saw a 30% decline in the number of naturally derived products undergoing clinical study (Harvey, 2008). Aside from a few success stories (Dias et al., 2012, Newman and Cragg, 2012), the clear trend is one of corporate divestment. A variety of factors potentially explain this trend. Some analysts point to supply shortages in plant biomass, others cite inefficiencies in bio-screening technologies,[11] still others point to imperfections in existing legal frameworks. The candidate explanations are numerous and difficult to assess. However, a good place to start is with the modeling literature in environmental economics. Recent theoretical findings in this discipline offer an insightful glimpse into the challenges facing any bioprospecting venture.

Consider once again the impressive numbers assigned to individual species by Primack and other bioprospecting advocates. Looking back, we can see that they were based on an oversimplified calculation. These estimates simply multiplied the proportion of species likely to yield a novel compound by the net profit potentially derived from a successful drug. Such calculations overlook the fact that bioprospecting is a serial search process. Pharmaceutical companies start out with a range of searchable items at their disposal. Costs accumulate as one adds items to that pool. After a certain point the net benefits derived from an occasional success are outweighed by the mounting search costs. Thus, the appropriate question is not "What is the total estimated value of a given pool of species?," as economists had previously asked. Rather, the relevant

---

[11] Li and Vederas (2009).

question for a pharmaceutical company is "What is the expected benefit of adding an additional (i.e. marginal) item to an existing pool of species?"

In 1996, economist David Simpson and colleagues developed a model of bioprospecting that respects its serial nature (Simpson et al., 1996). This model assesses the value of an item according to whether its inclusion in a pool of species improves the chance of discovering a drug. The model assumes that a pharmaceutical company starts out with a particular target, such as a specific illness that it wants to treat. At its disposal is an existing pool of search items (e.g. species). The company searches through the list, paying a cost per item as it goes. The search terminates when either the last item is searched or a successful target is found. If the company wants to search for some other target that solves a different medical problem, it repeats the search through the same list of species. Importantly, value is assigned to the *marginal* species – the one that is most recently added to an existing list. The value of a marginal species depends on two factors: (1) the probability that it will yield a useful compound; and (2) the likelihood that the compound is redundant – that is, that it will be found in some other species already contained in the search pool. Redundancy is a serious threat to successful bioprospecting: a company pays all of the costs associated with search and analysis, only to find that the resulting compound has the identical pharmaceutical application to some existing drug. Redundant items are typically unmarketable. Thus, even if bioactive compounds are abundant in nature this alone does not guarantee that bioprospecting will succeed commercially.

The dynamics of this model explain why bioprospecting never seems to have motivated any serious conservation effort. A key finding is that the value of the marginal item decreases in proportion to the size of the search pool. Intuitively, the more biodiversity one has available to search, the less valuable the marginal item becomes. This means that pharmaceutical companies should never pay to conserve large pools of species. To understand why this is so, it is helpful to imagine two extreme scenarios. Suppose, on the one hand, that valuable bioactive compounds are rare in nature. Then, all of the items in a search pool will have low value because of their small chance of yielding a lead. In this case, adding a marginal item to the pool does little to increase overall value. Yet a company still absorbs the cost of conserving and potentially screening the marginal item, resulting in a net loss. At the other extreme, suppose that bioactive compounds are common in nature. In this case, everything depends on the extent to which those compounds are redundant in their pharmaceutical application. Even for modest levels of redundancy, the value of the marginal item decreases rapidly in proportion to the size of the existing pool. Thus, regardless of whether bioactive compounds are rare or plentiful, it seems that the value of a marginal item is negligible. Newly acquired items almost never add value to an already extensive search set, and thus pharmaceutical companies should not invest in adding items, such as endangered species, to their existing pool of candidates.

As the final step in their analysis, Simpson and colleagues estimated the parameters of their model from data, and found that the marginal value of an additional species is much lower than previous economists had estimated. Even under the most generous parameter settings, they estimated that the maximum value of a marginal species was $9,431. Their next calculation attempted to determine the value of a marginal unit of land in such 'biodiversity hotspots' as Ecuador. Even in one the most diverse regions of the world, the maximum marginal value of a hectare of land was just $20. This value is very low compared to the potential profits gained from forestry, agriculture, or other land uses.

As with any model, it is important to question the legitimacy of the relevant assumptions. In particular, the model assumes that all items in a search pool have an equal likelihood of yielding a 'hit.' No reasonable drug search would proceed in such haphazard fashion. This criticism was raised by economists Gordon Rausser and Arthur Small (2000). They identified numerous sources of information that would help to guide and refine the search process:

> Researchers can, and do, draw on rich bases of publicly available data describing the location and properties of plants, animals, their evolutionary history, and their survival and reproductive strategies. These data, when filtered through a model that makes sense of them, can serve to tag those creatures most likely to display economically valuable characteristics.
>
> *(p. 176)*

These authors developed an alternative search model aimed at assessing the influence of information on drug discovery. In their model, search items are ranked according to their probability of yielding a lead. High probability leads are screened first and the entire search terminates as soon as a lead is identified. Rausser and Small used their model to assign dollar values to units of land for conservation. Interestingly, they initially reported much higher land values (up to $9,177 per hectare) than when Simpson, Sedjo, and Reid (1996) performed the same calculation. Initially, it seemed that information and ranking were responsible for improving the efficiency of bioprospecting. However, a subsequent re-analysis with more accurate parameter values found that informed ranking has only minor impact on land value (Costello and Ward, 2006). It turns out that the increase in land values reported by Rausser and Small were attributable to numerous discrepancies in other parameter settings. When all things are made equal, informed ranking increases land value from between $1.23 and $1.69 per hectare to the range of $14 to $65 per hectare. This is a significant improvement, but it is still too low to promote conservation for future bioprospecting efforts (Costello and Ward, 2006). For example, for the same timeframe, that same land would have been worth approximately $530/ha if converted to grow maize.[12] Even if

---

[12] According to FAOSTAT, Ecuador produces maize in the area of this Biodiversity Hotspot, and in 2000 they achieved a yield of 1.39 metric tons per hectare, which they could sell for $380/ton.

the most favorable estimate for every parameter was chosen, the marginal conservation value could only be as high as $300 per hectare. Costello and Ward conclude (2006, p. 625):

> Our results are consistent with the empirical evidence of private-sector biodiversity protection, where bioprospecting firms have been reluctant to invest in conservation for this purpose.

In fact, the mounting costs associated with bioprospecting only become more daunting the more one looks into the details. One contributing factor is the infrequency of endemic species in nature. For example, Conservation International identifies 34 Biodiversity Hotspots around the world.[13] These 34 locations combined house 150,371 endemic plant species[14] in approximately 339 million hectares of land. This means that the densities of endemic plant species range from 0.0001–0.0047 species per hectare. Under the most species-dense estimate, one would still have to search on average more than 200 ha to find each endemic plant species.[15]

The most optimistic estimate of the probability that any endemic plant will lead to a commercial drug is 1 in 1,000, but might be as low as 1 in 40,000 (Costello and Ward, 2006). These costs start to add up quickly. Nevertheless, the search costs are small compared to the screening costs. Costello and Ward (2006) quote estimates of $4,000–$18,000 per sample when screening in bulk. Of course, once a promising compound is identified, it takes between 5 and 20 years to get it through the three phases of clinical trials required for market approval, at a cost of between $104 million and $467 million. And remember, these estimates are for the best-case scenario, looking only in the world's 34 biodiversity hotspots. The economics only become less favorable as the density of endemic plants declines.

---

[13] http://bit.ly/1Tws48c   [14] Roughly half of the plant species on Earth.

[15] 0.0047 spp/ha = 212.77 ha/spp. In the lowest density scenario, one would have to search an average 10,000 ha to find each endemic plant species.

Summarizing these results, one comes to recognize that species diversity is not in itself of value to a pharmaceutical company. Each additional item in a search pool represents an increase in cost and a potential redundancy. At the same time, pharmaceutical companies have at their disposal various synthetic means of generating novel compounds. Notwithstanding some very dramatic success stories in the field of bioprospecting, the value of such activities compared to alternative land uses (i.e. the opportunity costs) is very small and probably not a good justification for conservation.

4.4.3 Option Values

At this point in the conversation, proponents of the argument for pharmaceutical value often turn to the 'uncertain future' caveat. Sure, a given species may not possess compounds that are of current utility, but the future is uncertain. Screening techniques might improve. New problems might arise for which this species offers a unique solution. Since these possibilities cannot be ruled out, the argument goes, even currently non-bioactive species should be preserved for their so-called option value. Astute readers will recognize this as an unspoken reliance on the precautionary principle. The argument therefore inherits all of the problems associated with such a defense (see Chapter 3). In addition, the appeal to option values raises a host of special problems for this line of argument, which we will now briefly discuss.

Philosopher Donald Maier (2012) undertook a detailed analysis of the economic concept of option value as it applies to biodiversity conservation. His general conclusion is that this term is frequently misapplied by conservationists. Here, we summarize a few of his key points, focusing in particular on their relevance to the argument from pharmaceutical value.

In economics, an option value is basically the price one is willing to pay to reserve the right to consume some resource at a later point in time. A key ingredient of option value is the likelihood that it will in fact be consumed. Intuitively, the less likely it is that the good will be consumed, or the less likely that it will be desirable at some future date, the lower the option value one should pay to reserve it. In the case of biodiversity conservation, a pharmaceutical company can be thought of as setting aside a certain pool of species for later 'consumption' (i.e. screening). As we have seen, the value of reserving this option depends in part on the likelihood that the pool will contain a compound that can be developed into a profitable drug. The concept of option value makes clear a second relevant parameter: the likelihood that the drug will be in demand at some future point in time. This depends on, among other things, whether some substitute drug is developed before a company manages to screen for its equivalent. Needless to say, these probabilities are difficult (if not impossible) to estimate. It is therefore hard to imagine a clear-cut case where it is demonstrably in the economic interest of a drug company to pay an up-front cost to reserve the option of searching some pool of species at a later time. Such scenarios are certainly possible, but in reality it seems doubtful that the relevant likelihoods could be estimated with a sufficient degree of certainty to make a convincing economic case.

Perhaps a better argument can be constructed around the concept of quasi-option value. As Maier (2012) explains, quasi-option value is similar to option value in the sense that one pays an up-front cost for the right to later consume some resource which may or may not be valuable at a future point in time. However, in the case of quasi-option values, one is entirely ignorant of the relevant likelihoods. To illustrate, suppose that you have no idea about the likelihood that a given pool of species will someday yield a profitable drug. Nonetheless, you might be willing to pay an up-front cost in order to delay a decision on whether to conserve and ultimately explore it. Hopefully, your state of information will improve between now and the time when that decision needs to be made. This line of thinking seems to accord with what some people have in mind when defending biodiversity conservation in the name of pharmaceutical benefits. The probabilities that useful drugs will emerge from some sample, or be in demand if they do, are difficult (or impossible) to calculate at a given point in time. The question then comes down to this: how much should a pharmaceutical company be willing to pay in order to prolong its state of ignorance, and for how long?

As Maier notes, this framework tends to overlook the opportunity costs associated with prolonging a decision. In the case of a pharmaceutical company, opportunity costs take the form of resources that might be better invested in other modes of drug development. The magnitude of those costs will depend, in turn, on the alternative uses for the land in question. If land holders have the opportunity to convert to agriculture, for example, then the price a company would have to pay in order to forestall this decision might be significant. It is far from obvious that it will be in the economic interest of a pharmaceutical company to compensate landholders for their opportunity costs just to prolong their decision about whether bioprospecting will ultimately pay off. Also, a key factor in this equation is the period of time over which the decision is delayed. It is not rational to indefinitely prolong a decision in the vague hope that a more perfect state of information will eventually arrive. Deciding the length of this period is a crucial factor in determining whether quasi-option values outweigh the more immediate benefits of development. As mentioned earlier, in the case of estimating future pharmaceutical discoveries, the lag between discovery and production is significant (from 5–20 years). This only increases the costs associated with reserving the right to make those decisions. A further problem with the argument from quasi-option values is that this framework assumes that decisions are irreversible. For example, if a company decides not to conserve a piece of land, the pharmaceutically valuable compounds contained therein will be gone forever. In effect, this assumes an extremely high degree of endemism for pharmaceutically valuable species. In reality, the levels of endemism of plant species, even in biodiversity hotspots, are fairly low. From the perspective of a pharmaceutical company, it might not be profitable to pay for the option of conserving and eventually prospecting a region, if the species therein are not in serious danger of extinction. It would be better to wait until more efficient screening technologies or better information becomes available, and then undertake a more informed cost–benefit analysis at that time.

Finally, let us suppose, for the sake of argument, that it is rational for a company to conserve biodiversity in a certain region in order to secure the option of future bioprospecting. It is important to keep in mind just how tenuous a form of conservation this in fact is. Such protection does not extend to species or regions that are unlikely to harbor useful bioactive compounds. Nor does it offer grounds for protecting species once their useful compounds have been identified. Pharmaceutical benefits are unlike other option values that keep on giving, so to speak, if and when their value is realized. For example, suppose you pay for the option to preserve a park in the hope that it will be enjoyed recreationally in the future. If that bet pays off, then the park retains its value as long as it produces recreational benefits. The opposite is true in the case of bioprospecting. In this case, one likewise pays to conserve a region in the hope that it will become worthwhile to screen for bioactive compounds at some later time. But if that bet pays off, and screening proceeds, the region immediately begins to lose value. This is because, whenever a promising bioactive compound is discovered, the next step in drug development is for it to be artificially synthesized.[16] Once synthesized, the original source-species loses its value as far as that pharmaceutical benefit is concerned. Thus, even if one allows that some form of option value will

---

[16] Granted, there are some species whose chemical structure is perhaps too complex to admit of artificial synthesis. The Pacific yew tree (species) is a case in point. The discovery of a bioactive compound in the bark of the yew tree is perhaps the worst thing that could have happened as far as conservation of this species is concerned. Pacific Yew were driven to near extinction once a market emerged for their bark. Nor have agriculturally produced yew trees managed to keep up with demand, given their slow growth rate and the destructive implications of harvesting their bark. It should hardly come as a surprise that the discovery of pharmaceutical value in a wild species places it at risk of extinction unless that compound can be supplied by agriculture or some synthetic means.

make conservation an economically viable strategy for pharmaceutical companies, this provides, at best, tenuous protection for the species in question. The more one learns about the species in a given region, the *less* valuable they become.

4.5 CONCLUSIONS

Let us summarize the central conclusions of this chapter. We began by noting the distinction between the argument from agricultural value and the argument from pharmaceutical value. The agricultural argument typically focuses on conserving genetic diversity within a very limited number of species. It turns out that nations already do a good job of conserving, ex situ, the genetic diversity of important crops. This argument does not easily extend to conservation of large amounts of biodiversity in nature, in part because the vast majority of those wild species have little or no connection to the ones we use for food or fuel.

The argument from pharmaceutical value is an economic argument in the sense that it assumes that there is a net economic benefit for drug companies to conserve biodiversity so that it will remain available for future bioprospecting. Unfortunately, the economics are usually unfavorable. Drug companies already have access to large pools of both natural and synthetic compounds. Adding marginal items to this extensive list adds little value overall. Meanwhile, the company incurs the cost of conserving and screening those species. Matters only worsen as the amount of functionally redundant compounds within a pool of candidates increases above a very modest level. But even if the economic conditions favored conservation, this argument extends only to a few species or compounds – the ones deemed likely to harbor bioactive compounds. All the rest of nature's diversity is a source of noise in an already costly search process.

The argument that biodiversity might be worth conserving as a form of option value borders on an appeal to the precautionary principle. To take this suggestion seriously would require estimating probabilities of future drug discoveries and future markets at least 5–20 years in advance. Such projections are difficult, if not impossible. Thus, some conservationists might appeal to quasi-option values as a reason for conserving biodiversity. The idea here is that a company might pay a price up front to conserve a region so that it will have the option of bioprospecting at a later time, when it will hopefully be able to undertake a more informed cost–benefit analysis. This suggestion is fraught with problems, not the least of which is that pharmaceutical companies are in a perpetual race to be first to patent. In the time that a company sits on a biodiverse region, trying to figure out whether bioprospecting will pay off at some point, a competitor might beat them to the punch with a synthetically derived drug. Meanwhile, the biodiversity that they are paying to conserve might not even be under serious threat of extinction. For these reasons, we think that the arguments from agricultural and pharmaceutical value do not offer compelling reasons to conserve biodiversity. At most, they offer reasons for conserving a small number of species, for limited periods of time, under very special economic conditions. Presumably, this is not what environmentalists had in mind when appealing to these arguments.

4.6 FURTHER READING

Gershell, L.J. and Atkins, J.H., 2003. A brief history of novel drug discovery technologies. *Nature Reviews Drug Discovery*, 2(4), pp. 321–327.

Li, J.W.H. and Vederas, J.C., 2009. Drug discovery and natural products: end of an era or an endless frontier? *Science*, 325(5937), pp. 161–165.

McChesney, J.D., Venkataraman, S.K., and Henri, J.T., 2007. Plant natural products: back to the future or into extinction? *Phytochemistry*, 68(14), pp. 2015–2022.

Pearce, D., 2005. Paradoxes in biovidersity conservation. *World Economics*, 6: 57–69.

Polski, M., 2005. The institutional economics of biodiversity, biological materials, and bioprospecting. *Ecological Economics*, 53(4), pp.543–557.

Saslis-Lagoudakis, C.H., et al., 2012. Phylogenies reveal predictive power of traditional medicine in bioprospecting. *Proceedings of the National Academy of Sciences of the USA*, 109(39), pp.15835–15840.

5 Nature-based Tourism and Transformative Value

> Here then is the dilemma: Ought species preservationists to continue espousing nonanthropocentric reasons for species preservation, knowing full well that these reasons cannot yet be supported by a clear and rationally defensible axiology, or should they fall back on unquestioned human demand values as the full basis for the policies they recommend?
>
> Bryan Norton (1987, pp. 187)

5.1 INTRODUCTION

Nature-based tourism is an umbrella term for activities such as hiking, camping, whale watching, safaris, and so on. It encompasses the more specific term 'ecotourism,' but is less strictly defined than that term. Ecotourism has been defined by the International Union for the Conservation of Nature (IUCN) as:[1] "Environmentally responsible travel to natural areas, in order to enjoy and appreciate nature (and accompanying cultural features, both past and present) that promote conservation, have a low visitor impact and provide for beneficially active socio-economic involvement of local peoples." The IUCN definition emphasizes the sustainable and responsible character that such travel should involve if it is to be considered 'ecotourism.' As its name implies, nature-based tourism relies on having nature available for tourists to experience and enjoy. It is thus thought to be a 'win–win' situation for the environment and sustainable development, but quantitative assessment of this assumption is not common (Naidoo and Adamowicz, 2005).

Environmental economists like to talk about the 'value' of something as:

[1] www.nature.org/greenliving/what-is-ecotourism.xml

173

Total value = use value + option value + bequest value + existence value

Use value is pretty straightforward: it is the value we get from using nature (perhaps sustainably, perhaps not). Use value is often separated into two kinds: *direct use* and *indirect use*. Examples of direct use would include the agricultural and pharmaceutical uses we considered in Chapter 4, for example. Indirect use would include at least some of the ecosystem services that we considered in Chapter 2, for example. **Option value** we discussed in Chapter 4 with regard to pharmaceuticals; it is roughly your willingness to pay to secure the option of using nature in the future. **Bequest value** is your willingness to pay to secure the option for your (grand-)offspring to be able to use nature. This differs from option value only in the sense that it won't be you personally using nature in the future. **Existence value** is the *non-use* value you derive from knowing something exists in nature even though you will never use it yourself, nor will anyone you know likely ever use it. Existence value[2] comes about as close as economists get to the notion of intrinsic value that we discussed Section 1.6.1, and that we will make extensive use of in Part 2 of this book. The way economists use existence value, it is really more a form of weak anthropocentrism. Weak anthropocentrism does not attribute intrinsic value to non-human individuals, species, or ecosystems. However, it differs from strong anthropocentrism in that it embraces a much broader view of what is considered valuable to humans. For example, weak anthropocentrism would embrace the view that non-human species could be valuable for their contributions to the formation of human ideals. See Norton (1987, pp. 12–14) for further discussion. As economist Kerry Turner and colleagues (1993, p. 113) say of existence value:

> such values are taken to be entities that reflect people's preferences,
> but include concern for, sympathy with, and respect for the rights

---

[2] In the economics literature, you will find a distinction made between pure existence value, and something termed the 'warm glow of giving,' or sometimes just 'warm glow,' which was originally coined by James Andreoni (1989). For our purposes this distinction is not particularly important.

or welfare of non-human beings. These values are still anthropocentric but may include a recognition of the value of the very existence of certain species or whole ecosystems. Total economic value is then made up of actual use value plus option value plus existence value.

In this chapter we will discuss a form of indirect use value, namely recreation and ecotourism, but we will also discuss a form of value that is proposed to exist beyond any of those mentioned above: **transformative value**. Philosopher Bryan Norton (1987) distinguishes transformative value from demand values, which include all of the values listed above, and from intrinsic value. Norton's thesis is that demand values do not adequately capture the value of an object to its human valuer, because demand values do not take account of an object's power to transform those very same demand values.

5.2   DEMAND VALUE OF BIODIVERSITY

In this section we consider demand value arguments. First, we show that arguments of this type are economic in nature. We then go on to consider whether or not it is an argument about biodiversity per se, or rather about 'nature' more generally. We introduce the economic concept of 'willingness to pay' as a measure of people's preferences and consider some economic data on what, and how much, people are willing to pay for nature-based tourism. We then draw the distinction between using nature-based tourism as a *reason* to conserve biodiversity vs. as an effective *method* for conserving biodiversity. In the latter case, we note that some of the goals of nature-based tourism as an economic activity might be at odds with the goals of biodiversity conservation. And finally, we consider what all of this means in terms of a defense of the environmentalist agenda.

5.2.1   The Economic Justification

Nature-based tourism is a use value, albeit largely non-consumptive, that nature in some sense fulfills. In this sense, then, nature-based tourism as a defense of the conservation of biodiversity is an economic justification. An example of this defense in action can be seen in the writing of environmentalist Norman Myers (1996, p. 2766; references removed):

> Ecotourism. Biodiversity plays a vital part in the fast growing sector of ecotourism. Each year people taking nature related trips contribute to the national incomes of countries concerned a sum estimated to be at least $500 billion, perhaps twice as much. Much of the enjoyment of these ecotourists reflects the biodiversity they encounter.
>
> In the late 1970s, a single lion in Kenya's Amboseli Park earned $27,000 per year in tourist revenues, while an elephant herd earned $610,000 per year. In 1994, whale watching in 65 countries and dependent territories attracted 5.4 million viewers and generated tourism revenues of $504 million, with annual rates of increase of more than 10% and almost 17%, respectively. A pod of 16 Bryde's whales at Ogata in Japan would, according to very conservative estimates, earn at least $41 million from whale watchers over the next 15 years (and be left alive), whereas if killed (as a one-shot affair) they would generate only $4.3 million. In 1970, ecotourism in Costa Rica's Monteverde Cloud Forest Reserve generated revenues of $4.5 million, or $1250 per hectare – to be compared with $30–100 per hectare for land outside the reserve. Florida's coral reefs are estimated to be worth $1.6 billion a year in tourism revenues.

The above quote clearly emphasizes the economic value of biodiversity in (for lack of a better term) 'aesthetic enjoyment.' The numbers quoted by Myers are, at this point, more than 20 years old, and ecotourism has developed considerably since then.

In a more contemporary, and carefully researched, cost–benefit analysis, conservation biologist Christopher Kirkby led a team of scientists and social scientists in a study of competing land uses in the Peruvian Amazon (Kirkby et al., 2010). They found that the net present value of land devoted to ecotourism was $1,158 (USD) per hectare, which is substantially more than the value of all surrounding, competing land uses. However, it is not always the case, as we saw in Chapter 4, that the conservation value of land exceeds the opportunity costs of converting that land to some other use. For example, environmental economist Kenneth Chomitz and colleagues (2005) evaluated the value of conservation land areas in the Brazilian Atlantic Rainforest, compared alternative land uses, and found that the remaining land use in forests was worth 70% of the value of cleared land nearby.

It should be recognized that the value of any single nature-based tourism activity, at any given time, depends in part on the global supply of alternative nature-based tourism opportunities, and on the global demand for these activities. If the supply were to grow faster than the growth of tourists demanding such opportunities, then the value of each individual opportunity would tend to decline. Such a situation would threaten the economic sustainability of these activities. Nature-based tourism probably requires considerable expansion if it is going to *directly* impact biodiversity conservation, but such an expansion jeopardizes current ecological sustainability.

The nature-based tourism argument is clearly an economic argument. Sometimes the economic value of this tourism exceeds the opportunity costs, and sometimes it does not. Just as in the other cases of use value that we have examined so far in this book, the very idea that conservation of biodiversity should be seen as an economic argument is anathema to some environmentalists (see, e.g., McCauley, 2006). The very idea that we can put a price on biodiversity or that such a price should be used to make decisions about use or conservation is considered unappealing. So some environmentalists see this as a reason to reject this argument. And many of the same environmentalists find the earlier economic arguments (or anthropocentric arguments more generally) unappealing for similar reasons. As we said, there are certainly examples where biodiversity conservation, because of nature-based tourism, or some other use value, will be justified on economic grounds. The problem is that if we accept this argument in those cases, then we are logically committed to the alternative when the economic justification is found wanting. It will be worth bearing this in mind as we explore these defenses further in this chapter.

5.2.2   Biodiversity or Nature?

Accepting for the moment the argument that conserving nature for nature-based tourism makes sense as an economic argument, what is it about nature that is actually valued by these tourists? Carol Ann Kearns (2010) writing about American landscape architect Fredrick Law Olmstead [1822–1903], noted that he:

> believed in the rejuvenating powers of nature. He felt that contemplating nature's grandeur allowed man to put his life into perspective. In modern times, with increasing urbanization, people seek out local parks, open space and trails, and travel to national parks and wild places where they can enjoy nature. Birding, hiking, fishing, hunting, gardening, and other forms of recreation in nature are popular activities, and are economically important.

Is Olmstead making an argument in defense of *biodiversity*, or is it really just exposure to 'natural settings' that matters? The answer is important because it implies different conservation and management policies. For example, urban parks are often unrelated to 'natural' ecosystems that one might have found in that location were it not for the urbanization. Urban parks tend to be dominated by managed turfgrass, which in North America at least tends to be dominated by non-native, even invasive, European grasses. Another possibility is that tourists are more interested in beautiful vistas or particular charismatic species rather than biodiversity per se.

A survey conducted by the World Tourism Organization (part of the United Nations), specifically about ecotourism and what people valued, found that 46% of those surveyed ranked seeing rare species in the top two categories of importance (Table 5.1), although simply viewing wildlife or being in wilderness seems to be considerably more important. In another study by conservationist Robin Naidoo and economist Wiktor Adamowicz (Naidoo and Adamowicz, 2005), the number of bird species in parks in Uganda was found to affect their attractiveness as tourist destinations and hence the total revenue

Table 5.1 *Ecotourists' rankings of natural traits*

	Most important	Next most important	Lesser* importance	Average rank
Wildlife viewing	53	24	21	1.74
Wilderness	41	26	24	1.97
Rare species	26	21	59	2.50
Archeology	21	35	44	2.62
Indigenous people	18	1	35	2.65
Birdwatching	21	21	59	2.71
Marine/water activity	12	44	44	2.76
Botany	3	9	88	3.65
Geology	0	6	94	3.91

* Includes rankings 3, 4, and 5. Source: Tour Operator Survey, 2001.
Source: Redrawn from (World Tourism Organization, 2002). http://bit.ly/2qofgf2

generated by the park (see Figure 5.1). So, although there aren't many studies specifically looking at the value of biodiversity to nature-based tourism, there is some reason to think that such activity might provide some justification for biodiversity conservation. It is just not clear whether tourists' interest in charismatic species such as birds means that they also care about, for example, fungal biodiversity, or amphibian biodiversity.[3] A large synthesis review paper by conservationist Oliver Krüger (2005) found that having a 'flagship' species present significantly influences whether or not an ecotourism destination is likely to be economically sustainable or not.

5.2.4 People's Preferences

Conservationist Enrico Di Mini and colleagues (2013) studied tourists' willingness to pay preferences for safaris in KwaZulu-Natal, South Africa. Willingness to pay is one way that economists measure

[3] But see, for example, Cerda et al. (2013) for an interesting example of the positive existence value people attach to a species of moss on an island off Chile.

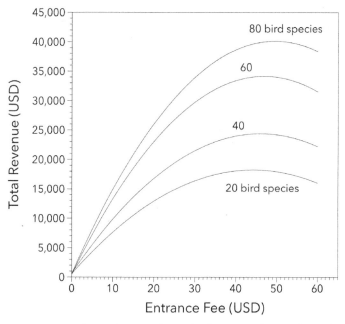

FIGURE 5.1 Redrawn from Naidoo and Adamowicz, (2005). Shows the modeled total revenue generated by parks in Uganda as it relates to the entrance fee collected and the number of bird species present in the park.

people's preferences,[4] the idea being that if you really have a preference for something then you should be willing to pay to secure that preference, and the more you are willing to pay, the more you prefer that thing or experience. Studies like this are akin to consumer marketing studies for new products.[5] Di Mini et al. produced the results shown in Figure 5.2. The results are categorized by whether the tourist was from South Africa or from some international destination, and by

---

[4] Another is your willingness to accept compensation for the loss of something or some experience. In theory, willingness to pay and willingness to accept compensation ought to be equal, but in practice they are often not. Also, economists have shown that hypothetical Willingness to Pay is often very different than actual Willingness to Pay. That is, when you ask someone how much she is hypothetically willing to pay, she often states a higher value then when you actually ask her to part with cash to secure her preference.

[5] For those interested readers, examples of the survey material are contained here: http://bit.ly/2fsvT22.

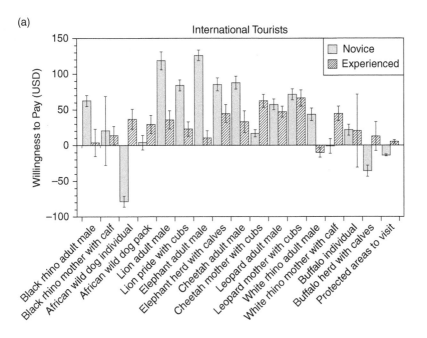

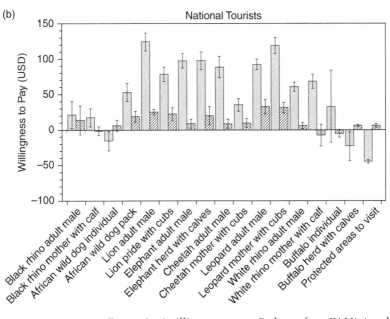

FIGURE 5.2 Ecotourists' willingness to pay. Redrawn from Di Mini et al. (2013). Shown on the y-axis is the Willingness To Pay in US dollars, by international and national tourists, to be able to see the things shown on the x-axis. Note that the IUNC has classified the black rhino as *critically endangered*; African wild dogs as *endangered*; lions, cheetahs, and elephants as *vulnerable*; leopards and white rhino as *near threatened*; and buffalo are classified as *of least concern*.

whether or not they had previous experience of African safaris. The results reveal surprising variation among tourists' willingness to pay. For example, internationally experienced tourists had a strong preference for seeing female leopards (*Panthera pardus*) with cubs and are seemingly not willing to pay to see an adult black rhino (*Diceros bicornis*) even though the latter is classified[6] by the IUCN as 'critically endangered' while the former is classified as 'near threatened.' Novice international tourists, on the other hand, are most willing to pay to see male elephants (*Loxodonta africana*) and least willing to pay to see African wild dogs (*Lycaon pictus*), even though the former is classified as vulnerable while the latter is classified as endangered. Notice too that experienced tourists are willing to pay considerably less for the experience of seeing their most desired animal than are novice tourists, which indicates that the value might be more in the novelty of the experience. Finally, notice the variation between national and international tourists in terms of which species they value and how much they value each species. It's also interesting that neither group particularly favors visiting protected areas per se, which are arguably more effective tools for the conservation of biodiversity than are individual species-based approaches.

We think that this study, and others like it, demonstrate that individual preferences for nature-based tourist activities can be variable, weak (in at least some cases), and idiosyncratic. It is also worth bearing in mind that nature-based tourists or ecotourists are probably a relatively small segment of the total tourist population, and they tend to be more affluent and more highly educated (Fennell, 2015). How such willingness to pay preference expression would play out in the broader population remains to be seen, but to us there doesn't seem to be anything approaching universal support for this position – perhaps not even majority support. This is important because the logic of the economic argument is that we should conserve biodiversity because enough people are each willing to pay enough money so

---

[6] IUCN classifications ranked in order of extinction risk: of least concern, near threatened, vulnerable, endangered, critically endangered, extinct in the wild, extinct.

that the area in question ought to be conserved rather than put to an alternative use. Certainly, there are some areas around the world where tourism clearly justifies conservation, but there will be areas where it does not, and it is an important empirical question as to whether there are enough economically sustainable tourism opportunities to make a significant impact on global biodiversity conservation.

5.2.5 Reason vs. Method

Discussions about the economic value of nature-based tourism can confuse two different issues. Sometimes this economic value is stated as a *reason* to conserve nature, and other times the value is touted as a good way to achieve conservation because tourism justifies investment in conservation. Note that the latter is not really a defense of biodiversity conservation. It assumes that conservation is a good idea, for whatever reason, and advocates tourism as a good *tool* for achieving the conservation goal. It is important not to conflate these two arguments.

In this chapter, we are primarily concerned with whether nature-based tourism is a good *reason* for conservation of biodiversity, but it is worth thinking about whether it is even a good tool for conservation. Even if it turns out to be a good reason for conservation, it might not be a good strategy if it does more harm than good. For example, in a paper that considers whether spending conservation money to promote and support community-based ecotourism is a good strategy, conservationist Agnes Kiss (2004, p. 232), of the World Bank, argues that:

> There are many examples of projects that produce revenues for local communities and improve local attitudes towards conservation, but the contribution of [community-based ecotourism] to conservation and local economic development is limited by factors such as the small areas and few people involved, limited earnings, weak linkages between biodiversity gains and commercial success, and the competitive and specialized nature of the tourism industry. Many [community-based ecotourism] projects cited as success

stories actually involve little change in existing local land and resource-use practices, provide only a modest supplement to local livelihoods, and remain dependent on external support for long periods, if not indefinitely.

More generally, although the emphasis of ecotourism is on sustainable/sensitive use of nature, supplying the market for this demand is not without its own challenges to biodiversity conservation. Table 5.2 shows the *potential* costs and benefits of tourism on the environment.

With regard to greenhouse gas (GHG) emissions (potential impact 's' in Table 5.2), Eke Eijgelaar and colleagues (Eijgelaar et al., 2010) studied the GHG emissions for the increasingly popular cruise-ship tours of Antarctica. Eijgelaar et al. showed that such tours create up to eight times the GHG emissions, per person per day, compared to other forms of international tourism trips. Ironically, these tours are explicitly based on the impacts of climate change and marketed as perhaps a last chance to see these ecosystems before they disappear due to changing climate!

Others have noted this tension between tourism and biodiversity conservation:

> Their [the tourism industry's] customary goal of quick optimum profits is in direct conflict with long-range goals of protection and conservation. This does not mean that the only, or even primary, relationship between the tourism industry and conservationists must be adversarial. But it does mean that whatever laudable, environmentally sound policies and goals the industry articulates, they will remain subsidiary to the demand for profit. Therefore, if the tourism industry becomes the principle force in the development of ecotourism, it will certainly be detrimental to long-range environmental concerns.
>
> *(Giannecchini, 1993, p. 43, as cited in Fennell, 2015)*

Table 5.2 *Potential costs and benefits of ecotourism*

Impacts of Tourism on the Environment and Biodiversity may include:

a)   Use of land and resources for accommodation, tourism facilities, and other infrastructure provision, including road networks, airports, and seaports

b)   Extraction and use of building materials (e.g. use of sand from beaches, reef limestone, and wood)

c)   Damage to or destruction of ecosystems and habitats, including deforestation, draining of wetlands, and intensified or unsustainable use of land

d)   Increased risk of erosion

e)   Disturbance of wild species, disrupting normal behavior and potentially affecting mortality and reproductive success

f)   Alterations to habitats and ecosystems

g)   Increased risk of fires

h)   Unsustainable consumption of flora and fauna by tourists (e.g. through picking of plants; or purchase of souvenirs manufactured from wildlife, in particular such endangered species as corals and turtle shells; or through unregulated hunting, shooting, and fishing)

i)   Increased risk of introduction of alien species

j)   Intensive water demand from tourism

k)   Extraction of groundwater

l)   Deterioration in water quality (freshwater, coastal waters) and sewage pollution

m)   Eutrophication of aquatic habitats

n)   Introduction of pathogens

o)   Generation, handling, and disposal of sewage and waste-water

p)   Chemical wastes, toxic substances, and pollutants

q)   Solid waste (garbage or rubbish)

r)   Contamination of land, freshwater, and seawater resources

s)   Pollution and production of greenhouse gases, resulting from travel by air, road, rail, or sea, at local, national, and global levels

t)   Noise

Table 5.2 (*cont.*)

Potential benefits of tourism on the environment and biodiversity may include:

a)   Revenue creation for the maintenance of natural resources of the area

b)   Providing alternative and supplementary ways for communities to receive revenue from biological diversity

---

Source: Articles 41, 42, and 43 of the Secretariat of the Convention on Biological Diversity (2004: http://bit.ly/2rmMOY5), Guidelines on Biodiversity and Tourism Development – International guidelines for activities related to sustainable tourism development in vulnerable terrestrial, marine, and coastal ecosystems and habitats of major importance for biological diversity and protected areas, including fragile riparian and mountain ecosystems, Secretariat of the CBD, Montreal. Modified from the UN World Tourism Organization *Tourism and Biodiversity – Achieving Common Goals Towards Sustainability.* Madrid, Spain, UNWTO (2010, Apprendix 2)

Thus, even if tourism turns out to be a reason to conserve biodiversity, it is far from clear that it is always the best way to achieve this goal.

5.2.6   Demand Value Defenses

There is no doubt that nature-based tourism provides value to some humans, and some of that value probably is attributable to biodiversity per se. Here we think about how these uses support the environmentalist agenda and what other commitments might be implied when deploying this defense.

It seems to us that the biggest weakness in this particular defense is that it is based on individual preferences. These preferences may be weak, contradictory, idiosyncratic, and, because they are individual preferences, not particularly compelling reasons to alter behavior in individuals who do not share these preferences. In common with the other instrumental values we considered in the earlier chapters, economic value will not *always* favor conservation over alternative land uses (but see Kirkby et al., 2010). We do not doubt that, at least in some cases, there would be widespread agreement about the conservation of certain regions to allow for nature-based tourism. We do, however, doubt that these cases would make up a majority of what environmentalists see as the most important conservation needs. It also seems to us that nature-based tourism, while undoubtedly a significant economic activity, applies to a relatively small fraction of the world's population and to a relatively small fraction of the world's biodiversity. As such, on its own, this defense of biodiversity conservation seems fairly weak. However, there is hope that it might be bolstered when combined with the so-called *transformative value* of biodiversity. We take this idea up in the next section.

5.3 THE TRANSFORMATIVE VALUE OF BIODIVERSITY

Transformative value is the capacity of some item to change demand value for that item, or even for other related items. The idea can be illustrated using a modified version of an example used by Norton (1987, p. 10). Suppose that Jim, a middle-aged man, loves deep sea fishing and has been hinting to his family that he would like to do this for his birthday. Jim regularly pays $200 for a day fishing trip, indicating that such a trip has a demand value to him of at least $200. On Jim's birthday his family gives him a card with a voucher inside. At first he is delighted, thinking it is the fishing trip he hinted at, but he is disappointed when he realizes that the voucher is for a whale watching trip. Jim has no interest in whales, and he tries to give the voucher to his work associates. The fact that he tries to give it away, without compensation, indicates that he places no value at all on the potential experience. His boss convinces him that not going on the trip would hurt his family's feelings, so he reluctantly agrees to go. Much to his surprise, he finds the whales to be exciting, majestic, and awe-inspiring. Without giving up his love of fishing, Jim begins to take other whale watching trips, he buys books about whales, he studies their ecology and evolution, and eventually he sets himself a goal of seeing all 78 known species of whales, in their natural habitats. Jim ultimately derives a lifetime of pleasure and personal fulfillment that he would not have had, had he fulfilled his actual preference to go fishing instead. The whale watching trip that at first had no value at all to Jim ended up having significant *transformative value* for him, causing similar opportunities in the future to have significant demand value for him. The whale watching trip altered, or *transformed*, his future demand values.

Stories such as these are probably familiar to you; indeed, you may have had such an experience yourself from some early encounter(s) with nature. There are, however, some fairly obvious objections to this defense (Jamieson, 2007). First, transformations may be positive or negative. There is no guarantee that an encounter with nature will cause the 'positive' reactions that Jim had. Nature can in fact be a scary place, full of hazards to life and limb. It can be seen as something to be tamed and controlled rather than something to preserve and cherish. For all we know, such 'negative' reactions may even be more common than the 'positive' reactions. Second, transformations are not universal. Jim was transformed by the experience of whale watching, while others only remember being cold and seasick, and wishing they hadn't come. Third, transformations can be all-consuming to the detriment of the transformed. For example, suppose Jim becomes so obsessed with whale watching that he begins to neglect his job, his family, and his friends. He spends the money he saved for his children's education on trips to far-away places to complete his life-list of whale sightings, taking unpaid leaves of absence from work to do so. Lastly, as philosopher Dale Jamieson puts it, when discussing the work on transformative value by philosopher Sahotra Sarkar (Jamieson, 2007; p. 709–710):

> 'Biodiversity is thus signally valuable because of its intellectual interest' (p. 85). This response may find a sympathetic hearing among biologists, but developers and politicians, who are also in the business of deploying transformative values, are unlikely to be moved by it. Consumer sovereignty appears to be a systemic

transformative value in Sarkar's sense, and it has led to draining swamps and building subdivisions all over the world.[7] If this is so, then the fate of endangered species may rest on which transformative value gains precedence over the others. But this is just another way of describing the conflict between biodiversity preservation and land-use change, rather than providing a principle for resolving it.

One concrete example of the supposed transformative value of nature-based tourism is seen in the work of Eijgelaar et al. (2010), which we briefly considered in Section 5.2.5. Recall that they showed that Antarctic cruise-ship tourism generated up to eight times the green-house gas emissions of other forms of international tourism. So, on the face of it, these tours would seem to exacerbate the very environmental problem that motivated the tours in the first place (climate change). However, for many years it has been argued that such tourism transforms the tourist into an 'environmental ambassador' who will become concerned not only to protect the visited region, but to support conservation efforts and organizations more broadly. Nevertheless, when Eijgelaar et al. (2010, p. 337) surveyed Antarctic cruise participants they found "no evidence for the hypothesis that the trips develop greater environmental awareness, change attitudes or encourage more sustainable future travel choices."

It is an empirical question whether or not nature-based tourism more often than not results in 'biodiversity-friendly' transformations; but this is a little-studied question. There is a fair amount of empirical evidence on the impacts of zoos and aquaria, at least on their educational impact, if not actually on their transformative value. While the evidence is somewhat mixed (Marino et al., 2010), there is at least

---

[7] Sarkar recognizes something that he terms the 'directionality problem,' which is that transformations can go in either direction, from 'good' to 'bad', or from 'bad' to 'good'. He attempts to get around this problem by allowing only transformations that he labels 'systematic.' A transformation is systematic if, according to Sarkar, "we have a generalizable account of how it acquired such value" (Maier, 2012, p. 268). But as Maier (2012, pp. 268–269) aptly points out, neoclassical economic theory and its partner, modern marketing theory, ably fulfill Sarkar's definition of 'systematic' and yet also explain why consumers might prefer subdivisions to the wetland that had to be drained to make way for them.

some positive evidence of educational value (see, e.g., Moss et al., 2015). If this 'transformative value defense' is going to convince skeptics, we are going to need some rigorous empirical evidence that the experience of biodiversity actually achieves these transformations.

Finally, philosopher Don Maier (2012) argues that the above reasons for dismissing transformative value miss the main logical point: namely, that newly acquired preferences are not necessarily worthy of satisfaction. Proponents of the transformative value view seem to be advancing the argument that biodiversity is good because it transforms our demand value views of nature itself, and that such 'nature-positive' demand values are good. But Maier argues that the preferences have to be assessed on their own merits. The way a preference comes about has nothing to do with the normative value of the preference. In other words, we can't argue that **A** is good because **A** causes us to have positive feelings about **A** (and perhaps things related to **A**). Either **A** is good, or it is not; its alleged transformative value doesn't make it good.

So, what at first seems a defense that probably resonates with many environmentalists may, on closer inspection, not be adequate to the task of mounting a strong defense of biodiversity conservation. It seems to be one of those defenses that appeal to the 'already converted,' but does not have a lot of traction more widely. And because of the idiosyncratic nature of transformative value, it could conceivably be a detriment to the environmentalist agenda.

5.4   CONCLUSIONS

In Chapter 2 we considered ecosystem functioning and services as a reason why biodiversity ought to be conserved. In Chapter 4 we considered the role of biodiversity in producing food and medicines. Some might argue that food and medicines are nothing more than specific examples of ecosystem functions and services. And it has been argued that nature-based tourism and the transformative value of nature are also just examples of ecosystem functions and services. As such, these two defenses also suffer from some of the same counterarguments we encountered in Chapter 2.

First, the empirical relationship between people's enjoyment of a nature-based holiday (or experience more generally) and the actual biodiversity present is often weak or unknown. Second, even where the relationship is strong and unambiguous, it might well be the case that people would have greater enjoyment if we manipulated the species present (e.g. species introductions or deletions). For example, there is considerable economic value in hunting holidays. Environmentalists tend to distain such holidays when they are focused on native species, particularly where those species might be in danger of extinction (locally or globally). However, in places like New Zealand, trophy hunting for red stags (*Cervus elaphus*), Arapawa rams (*Ovis aries*), chamois (*Rupicapra rupicapra*), South Pacific goats (*Capra hircus*), and other introduced mammal species[8] is both an important economic activity and an important conservation tool. Nevertheless, these two goals are clearly at odds with each other. If the population of red deer were to go locally extinct, that would be bad news for the hunting tourism industry, but good news for conservation since red deer are a significant threat to many endangered plant species. For all we know, people might get more enjoyment from New Zealand holidays if they could see, and perhaps hunt, large red stags.

Where does all this leave us? Nature-based tourism seems to us to be an important tool for cultivating positive regard for the kind of wilder ecosystems that are repositories of much of the biodiversity we want to conserve. However, the defense seems unlikely to have enough positive support on its own to serve as a justification for all of the conservation we need or want. And, as we discussed, biodiversity's supposed transformative value doesn't seem likely to rescue this deficiency. As environmentalists, we should not gloss over or ignore

[8] A few species of bats are the only native land mammals to New Zealand. As such, hunting other mammals is a key conservation tool.

the variability of human responses to nature. Perhaps this defense is not going to achieve our goals.

5.5   FURTHER READING

Fennell, D.A. 2015. *Ecotourism*, 4th edn. Abingdon, Routledge.

Norton, B. 1987. *Why Preserve Natural Variety?* Princeton, Princeton University Press.

Sarkar, S. 2005. *Biodiversity and Environmental Philosophy: An Introduction*. Cambridge, Cambridge University Press.

West, P. and J.G. Carrier. 2004. Ecotourism and Authenticity: Getting Away from It All?, *Current Anthropology* 45(4): 483–498.

6 How Far Do Instrumental Value Defenses Get Environmentalists?

In Chapters 2 through 5 we examined four broad classes of instrumental value defenses. All of these arguments start from an anthropocentric perspective: namely, that the value of biodiversity rests in its usefulness (or otherwise) to humans. Biodiversity might be valuable to us because: it contributes to ecosystem stability, functioning and services (Chapter 2); it might be valuable to us in the future for unknown or uncertain reasons (Chapter 3); it is our source of food and some medicines (Chapter 4); or it is important to us for its recreation, tourism, and transformational opportunities (Chapter 5). In this chapter we will give some thought to which parts of the environmentalist agenda gain support from these defenses and which do not.

Recall that our goal in this book is to help environmentalists sharpen our arguments for conserving biodiversity. To do this it is important to (a) understand the strengths and weaknesses of each individual defense, and (b) advance the discussion by focusing on how to fix the weaknesses in each argument, if possible. In other words, the weaknesses are fertile ground for new thinking and new evidence.

One general conclusion is important to emphasize about *all* of the instrumental value defenses put forward in the last four chapters. Just because a species or ecosystem is useful to us does not mean that it is *more useful* than the alternatives. Instrumental defenses are essentially economic arguments. They are not necessarily economic arguments in the sense of putting a specific monetary value on the outcomes of conservation efforts, although they might indeed do this. Instrumental defenses are economic arguments in the sense that they speak to the allocation of scarce resources to fulfill human interests. The logic of such an economic argument is that we should choose the option that maximizes human utility, and so a potential consequence of relying on these defenses is that conserving biodiversity will not always be the optimal solution. And where conservation is not the option that maximizes human utility, we need to be prepared to give up the conservation fight, or be prepared to show how the current analysis is incorrect. But sooner or later, we will come upon an example where conservation is simply not the option that most advances human interests, and in those cases, to be consistent, we environmentalists need to admit that the available instrumental value defenses do not support our intuitive stance.

A second general comment is that the precautionary defense is deeply problematic philosophically. However, this defense, in one guise or another, has been around since the beginning of the environmental movement and environmentalists seem loath to give it up anytime soon. At a bare minimum, environmentalists need to recognize that many people find precautionary defenses entirely unconvincing. As we pointed out in Chapter 3, there are many active research programs that are attempting to shore up precautionary defenses, but until they succeed, environmentalists should be cognizant of the limitations of this defense.

6.2 THE ECOSYSTEM FUNCTION DEFENSE

In Chapter 2 we made three points: (1) the empirical support for a positive relationship between biodiversity (specifically species richness) and ecosystem function is not as strong or as general as many people assume; (2) even if the available scientific evidence strongly and unambiguously supported there being a positive relationship, there remain some serious questions about how to generalize those findings to real-world ecosystems and/or conservation policy; and (3) people who rely on this defense of biodiversity conservation would be logically committed to conclusions that are at odds with other common commitments of environmentalists. In particular, species additions or removals should be conducted wherever they would result in improved ecosystem functioning. Similarly, non-native species would be preferred over native species if the non-native species can better perform the ecosystem function. Indeed, this defense supports a very limited number of items on the environmentalist agenda (see Table 6.1 for a summary).

6.3 THE PRECAUTIONARY DEFENSE

The precautionary defense would, on the face of it, seem to support a good deal of the environmentalist agenda (see Table 6.1 for a summary), certainly more than the ecosystem functioning defense. However, as we hope we have shown in Chapter 3, the precautionary defense is far from universally accepted. Indeed, many have argued that this approach is deeply problematic. It suggests that we can make wise decisions when we lack the necessary information to do so. The principle itself leads to a logical contradiction and so is useless. It ignores both the possible benefits of the proposed action, and the opportunity costs of adopting the precautionary remedy that the principle allegedly proposes. So while at first glance we see the precautionary principle as attractive, upon closer inspection we see that it has many gaps that need filling before it will be a useful defense of biodiversity conservation.

6.4 THE FOOD AND MEDICINE DEFENSE

In Chapter 4 we considered basing a defense on biodiversity's contribution to our food security and human health in the form of a source for developing new medications. While initially attractive, this defense would seem to provide support for precious little of the environmentalist agenda. These two targets of biodiversity's usefulness cover a very tiny fraction of global biodiversity – we use very few species for food or medicines – and this defense provides no support for species that we know are not useful to us. Attempts to expand the scope of support for biodiversity conservation offered by these uses, by considering either the option value, or the quasi-option value of

Table 6.1 *Summary comparison of the instrumental value defenses presented in Part I in comparison to the goals of the environmentalist agenda as laid out in Chapter 1*

Element of the environmentalist agenda	Ecosystem function defense	Precautionary defense	Food and medicine defense	Recreation and ecotourism defense
Section 1.4.1 Preference for preventing extinction	**Not logically applicable and not empirically supported.** There may be times when ecosystem function is improved by local extirpation	**Logically applicable but with dubious philosophical support.** Unknown consequences of an extinction justify its prevention	**Not logically applicable and not empirically supported.** Very little of global biodiversity is useful to us for food or medicine and most is already highly conserved	**Logically applicable with some empirical support.** There is some evidence that rare species are among the things people want to see. It's not clear whether this interest extends to all rare species or just the charismatic ones
Section 1.4.2 Preference for 'natural' over modified habitats	**Not logically applicable and no empirical evidence.** There probably will be times when ecosystem function is improved by human modification	**Logically applicable but with dubious philosophical support.** Unknown consequences of a modification justify not making the modification	**Not logically applicable and not empirically supported.** The search for useful compounds or new food items is not restricted to pristine habitats	**Logically applicable and empirically supported.** This is the basis for such a defense, but one could argue that in making such habits accessible to tourists, they become modified

Section 1.4.3 A preference for preservation over conservation	Not logically applicable and empirical evidence not relevant. This defense is explicitly about the instrumental value of biodiversity, which supports conservation not preservation	Not logically applicable and empirical evidence not relevant. This defense is explicitly about the instrumental value of biodiversity, which supports conservation not preservation	Not logically applicable and empirical evidence not relevant. This defense is explicitly about the instrumental value of biodiversity, which supports conservation not preservation	Not logically applicable and empirical evidence not relevant. This defense is explicitly about the instrumental value of biodiversity, which supports conservation not preservation
Section 1.4.4 Preference for wild over domesticated populations	Not logically applicable and not empirically supported. If a domesticated species can perform the function better than a wild species, then it should be conserved	Not logically applicable and with dubious philosophical support. Unknown consequences of the loss of a domesticated species justify its conservation	Not logically applicable and not empirically supported. Nearly all species useful in these ways are already domesticated, and those that are not are the targets of domestication	Logically applicable and empirically supported. This is explicitly the basis for this defense. However, it's not clear whether this interest extends to all wild populations or just the charismatic species

Table 6.1 (cont.)

Element of the environmentalist agenda	Ecosystem function defense	Precautionary defense	Food and medicine defense	Recreation and ecotourism defense
Section 1.4.5 Preference for native over introduced	**Not logically applicable and not empirically supported.** If an introduced species can perform the function better than a native species, then it should be conserved	**Logically applicable but with dubious philosophical support.** Unknown consequences of an extinction justify its prevention	**Not logically applicable and not empirically supported.** These uses do not depend upon a species' origin	**Equivocal logical application but with some empirical support.** It is not clear whether ecotourists care particularly that what they are looking at is native, so long as it is 'wild' – but some definitions of wild would imply native as well
Section 1.4.6 Preference for historical vs. change changed communities and ecosystems	**Equivocal logical application and no empirical evidence.** This defense does not seem to speak to this agenda item	**Equivocal logical applicable and with dubious philosophical support.** This defense does not seem to speak to this agenda item	**Equivocal logical application and with no empirical evidence.** This defense does not seem to speak to this agenda item	**Equivocal logical application and no empirical evidence.** This defense does not seem to speak to this agenda item

Section 1.4.7 Preference for *ecological wholes over individual sentient animals*	Logically applicable but with equivocal empirical support. The ecological whole will usually be more important to functioning than an individual sentient animal	Logically applicable but with dubious philosophical support. Unknown consequences of the loss of an ecological whole likely to be more catastrophic than the loss of an individual animal	Equivocal logical application and with no empirical evidence. This defense does not seem to speak to this agenda item	Logically applicable with some empirical support. There is some evidence that ecotourists care more about the whole wilderness than about particular sentient animals
Section 1.4.8 Preference for *in situ* vs. *ex situ* conservation	Equivocal logical application but with some empirical support. This defense does not seem to speak to this agenda item, although to actually provide an ecosystem function the conservation effort has to *eventually* become in situ	Equivocal logical application and with dubious philosophical support. This defense does not seem to speak to this agenda item	Not logically applicable and not empirically supported. The vast majority of conservation done on these species is ex situ	Logically applicable and empirically supported. This is explicitly the basis for this defense. However, it's not clear whether this interest extends to all species or just the charismatic species

biodiversity, are also deeply problematic (see Chapter 4). We think that the arguments from agricultural and pharmaceutical value do not offer compelling reasons to conserve *biodiversity per se*. At most, they offer reasons for conserving a small number of species, for limited periods of time, under very special economic conditions. Presumably, this is not what environmentalists had in mind when appealing to these arguments.

6.5   NATURE-BASED TOURISM AND TRANSFORMATIVE VALUE DEFENSES

In Chapter 5 we considered whether people's demand for nature-based tourism or the transformative value of such nature experiences were a sound basis for defending the conservation of biodiversity. There, we concluded that nature-based tourism seems to us to be an important tool for cultivating positive regard for the kind of wilder ecosystems that are repositories of much of the biodiversity we want to preserve/conserve. However, the defense seems unlikely to have enough positive support on its own to serve as a justification for all of the conservation we need or want. And as we discussed, biodiversity's supposed transformative value doesn't seem likely to address this deficiency. As environmentalists, we should not gloss over/ignore the variability of human responses to nature, and how this limits the application of this line of argument for conserving biodiversity.

6.6   CONCLUSIONS ABOUT INSTRUMENTAL VALUE DEFENSES

No single instrumental value defense gets environmentalists everything we want in terms of support for the agenda. What about the conjunction of these defenses taken together? We don't think this helps much, because individually several of these instrumental defenses have unpalatable implied commitments – commitments that are at odds with others parts of the agenda. Putting these defenses together does not alleviate these implied commitments. For example, we noted in Chapter 2 that relying on the ecosystem functioning defense implies that we should accept introduced species where those species can provide a better level (or rate) of ecosystem functioning for us, and that that observation would logically commit environmentalists to supporting such introductions. However, such a policy would conflict with the agenda item Section 1.4.5, where environmentalists prefer native to non-native species. Adding food, medicine, ecotourist, or transformative value defenses probably doesn't alleviate this problem with non-native species.

By appealing to the anthropocentric ethical stance, environmentalists are on reasonably firm philosophical grounds. The argument that biodiversity is important because it is useful to us covers a lot of biodiversity and, if applied with due deference to the limitations of the empirical evidence, these arguments provide support for biodiversity conservation. Where environmentalists tend to get into trouble is when we refuse to accept these limitations. Where the evidence of usefulness is lacking, available but unsupportive, or suggests that other actions besides conservation would better satisfy human needs and interests, environmentalists would have to admit that we don't have a good anthropocentric argument for conserving biodiversity, as unpleasant to us as that may be.

There are three general paths open to environmentalists at this point. The first is, of course, to just 'bite the bullet' and admit that while we have very good reasons for conserving some bits of biodiversity, we lack a general reason to conserve all of biodiversity. The second is to attempt to defend conservation of the parts of biodiversity that are seemingly not useful (or in fact harmful) to humans by making an appeal to biodiversity's supposed intrinsic value. That is, environmentalists might use the instrumental value arguments as clear and convincing defenses when it suits us, and fall back on a claim of intrinsic value as a sort of last resort. And finally, environmentalists might admit that our instrumental value arguments were merely a form of 'political utility' and that our true feelings were always with our claim of biodiversity's intrinsic value. In this response, the claim of intrinsic value is front and center, not a sort of 'last resort' as in number two.

Environmentalists disagree about which route to take. For example, environmentalists Lynn Maguire and James Justus (2008) argue strongly for the first approach. They argue that a reliance on any sort of intrinsic value claim is misplaced:

> (1) intrinsic value is a vaguely formulated concept and not amenable to the sort of comparative expression needed for conservation decision making, and (2) instrumental value is a much richer concept than generally appreciated, permitting a full range of values of biota to be considered in conservation decisions.
>
> *(p. 910)*

> ... Undoubtedly, arguing that instrumental value is more useful for conservation decisions than intrinsic value will not satisfy everyone. The essential tension between the emotional appeal of intrinsic value and the trade-offs required by conservation decisions is probably irreconcilable. ... But those defending conservation against competing uses and allocating scarce resources among conservation actions are better served by building their decisions on a strong foundation of instrumental value rather than on the weak concept of intrinsic value.
>
> *(p. 911)*

Maguire's and Justus' resistance to applying an intrinsic value argument is primarily pragmatic. They don't think it is useful in a world of limited resources and difficult choices. They see intrinsic value arguments as conceptually weak, and, as is evident from the rest of their paper, incapable of dealing with value trade-offs. We indirectly address these charges in the second part of the book. Rather, Maguire and Justus think the focus should be on addressing the perceived shortcomings of instrumental value defenses. In other words, keep working to address the problems we pointed out in Part I, among others (for ours was not a comprehensive treatment of the problems).

Other environmentalists disagree, and in fact think that instrumental value arguments are not only wrong, they are wrong-headed, perhaps disastrously so. Take environmentalist Doug McCauley (2006) who argues that:

> Market-based conservation strategies, as currently articulated, offer little guidance on how we are to protect the chunks of nature that conflict with our interests or preserve the perhaps far more numerous pieces of nature that neither help nor harm us. . . .
>
> To make ecosystem services the foundation of our conservation strategies is to imply – intentionally or otherwise – that nature is only worth conserving when it is, or can be made, profitable. The risk in advocating this position is that we might be taken at our word. . . .
>
> We will make more progress in the long run by appealing to people's hearts rather than to their wallets. If we oversell the message that ecosystems are important because they provide services, we will have effectively sold out on nature.
>
> (pp. 27–28)

In his paper, McCauley is arguing explicitly for environmentalists to abandon the instrumental value arguments and return to conserving nature simply for nature's sake. In Part II we take up the challenges that arise if we take this approach.

PART II   Intrinsic Value Defenses

In Part I of this book, we discussed arguments for preserving biodiversity that turn on claims about *instrumental* value – that is, the value that biodiversity has in virtue of its contributing to various human interests.[1] With the next chapter, we begin our discussion of arguments based on claims about the *intrinsic* value of biodiversity.

As described in Section 1.6, theories of environmental ethics are commonly categorized on the basis of which things have intrinsic value according to each theory. Anthropocentrism is the view that only the lives of human beings – or their experiences, interest-satisfactions, etc. – have intrinsic value. From an anthropocentric perspective, all arguments for preserving biodiversity (apart from some diversity of human beings) are instrumental value arguments. But none of the instrumental value arguments discussed in Part I supports every goal of the environmentalist agenda as described in Section 1.4. Nor does it seem that the conjunction of these instrumental value arguments gets environmentalists everything we want, because each instrumental argument carries with it some implied commitments that oppose other parts of the environmentalist agenda.

So, in this second part of the book we will focus on the non-anthropocentric varieties of environmental ethics.[2] In particular, in Chapter 8 we discuss the sentientist and biocentric individualist approaches, which argue for the intrinsic value of individual, non-human

---

[1] Things can have instrumental value by virtue of contributing to the goals of non-human entities (animals, ecosystems, etc.), but in Part I of this book we limited our consideration of instrumental value to arguments based on claims about biodiversity's contributions to *human* goals.

[2] In Section 8.5 we note that some environmental philosophers *define* 'environmental ethics' as non-anthropocentric, but for the reasons given there, we urge environmentalists not to do this.

organisms; in Chapters 9 and 10 we discuss holistic approaches, which argue for the intrinsic value of ecosystems and species; and in Chapter 11 we discuss approaches based on the intrinsic aesthetic value or beauty of biodiversity. In each case, we will again consider the extent to which the approach in question promises to support the various 'planks' in the environmentalist agenda, as we did for the various instrumental value arguments discussed in Part I. In this second part of the book, however, we will pay more attention to the *philosophical* aspects of the arguments. This contrasts with Part I where, as we noted in Sections 1.6.1 and 1.7, the strength of instrumental value arguments for preserving biodiversity depends primarily on the extent to which the available *empirical* evidence supports claims about biodiversity's contribution to various human goals.

That the fulfillment of various human interests is intrinsically valuable is quite uncontroversial – not just any human interest, to be sure, but various important human interests, such as good physical health and living a fulfilling life. So to the extent that such important human interests are served by various ecosystem functions, it is generally uncontroversial that we have a good reason to preserve biodiversity. When it comes to arguments based on non-anthropocentric intrinsic value, however, there is much that is controversial quite apart from empirical claims. To be sure, such arguments depend on certain empirical claims, some of which are still controversial, but the commitment to the intrinsic value of non-human nature is itself controversial to an extent that the commitment to the intrinsic value of humans' lives is not. In Chapters 8–11 we will emphasize why this is so.

So just as the chapters in Part I involved fairly extensive discussion of how empirical claims are evaluated in ecological science, the chapters in this second part of the book will involve fairly extensive discussion of how *philosophical* arguments are evaluated. We think that most (if not all) readers will have come to this book with a general understanding of how scientific hypotheses are formulated and tested, and thus how empirical claims are justified. Many readers, however, will have little or no background in philosophy in general, and in particular with the ways that ethical theories and principles are defended, including claims about what has intrinsic value. So, before we discuss various intrinsic value-based defenses of biodiversity preservation in Chapters 8–11, the first section of Chapter 7 provides an overview of approaches to justification in philosophical ethics. Then, Section 7.2 discusses the role of hypothetical cases and 'thought experiments' in arguments about ethics, and Section 7.3 surveys some key terminology related to claims about intrinsic value in non-human nature.

7 Methodology in Philosophical Ethics

Ethics can be studied in two fundamentally different ways. Sociologists and anthropologists study ethics, but their interest is empirical. They treat a society's thinking about ethics as a given; they seek to describe in some systematic way how a population of humans in fact think about ethics. Philosophers have traditionally taken a different approach. Rather than describing how people *in fact* think about ethics, philosophers have tried to determine how people *should* think about ethics, whether or not they do in fact think that way. In contrast to the *descriptive* approach of sociologists and anthropologists, the philosopher's approach is called *prescriptive* or *normative* ethics; it is an attempt to rationally prove that certain moral claims are true, or at least to show that we are justified in believing them.

But what justifies our belief in a particular ethical judgment, a general moral principle, or a complete theory of ethics? The following subsections describe four approaches that philosophers have historically taken, emphasizing the last two, which inform our approach in Part II of this book.

7.1.1 Appealing to God's Will

A traditional approach to justification in ethics is to appeal to God's will, but God's will can play a justificatory role in two significantly different ways. On one hand, in the major monotheistic religions it has commonly been thought that God's willing something is what *makes* it right. But this theological approach – which is sometimes called the Divine Command Theory – faces some well-known philosophical

209

difficulties. First, it has the uncomfortable implication that *anything* would be right if God happened to will it, including things that are generally regarded as obviously wrong, such as genocide, sexism, and racism. Second, it seems to trivialize God's goodness in the following way. On this view, saying that someone is good just means that they do what God wills; but then saying that *God* is good just means that God does what God wills, which doesn't sound like much of a compliment.

On the other hand, without holding that God's willing something is what *makes* it right, with the attendant problems just mentioned, a theist can still hold that God's will is a perfect *guide* to morality. This will be so if, as is commonly assumed, God is all-knowing and all-good. For then, God will know everything there is to know about ethics, and God's will can be relied upon to perfectly exemplify moral righteousness. So when God issues commandments to us, we can be confident that they are appropriate guides to morally right actions, lifestyles, and political institutions. This makes sense from a theistic perspective, but in the public sphere, relying on God's will as a guide to ethics is fraught with difficulties, for there are a variety of religions with various conceptions of God and a variety of different sacred texts. This is even true about the major monotheistic religions: Judaism, Christianity, and Islam, which recognize different scriptures, and within each of these three religions, factions disagree about how to interpret many of the same passages. Also, holy scriptures are largely silent on the various issues related to contemporary debates about biodiversity conservation.

The second approach to justifying moral beliefs by appeal to God's will also leaves a crucial, underlying question unaddressed: Why does *God* think that some things are right and others wrong? Secular philosophers have traditionally wanted a clear answer to the question of what *makes* right actions and institutions right. The first approach to justifying moral beliefs by appeal to God's will answers that question, but in an unsatisfying way, as described in the first paragraph of this subsection, and the second approach gives no answer at all. Hence, secular philosophers have taken at least three other approaches to justification in ethics.

7.1.2 *Claiming Self-evidence (Intuitionism)*

An approach that was popular in British moral philosophy during the nineteenth and early twentieth centuries is called 'intuitionism.' The idea here is that when contemplating certain ethical principles one 'just knows' that they are true, without need for argumentation or any other form of justification. A classic version of intuitionism was articulated by Sir William David Ross [1877–1971]. In *The Right and the Good*, (1930) Ross argued that there are several basic duties that are not derived from any more general principle, each of which is immediately recognized as justified by anyone with moral 'common sense.'

Among the basic duties that Ross enumerated are some general commitments that have been called 'hypernorms.' This term is used in the literature of professional ethics to refer to norms that appear to be recognized in every human society. Candidate hypernorms include: don't harm others, tell the truth, and keep your promises. Some have argued that a shared commitment to these three norms is a necessary condition for the existence of the complex social structures embodied in any human society. Obviously, however, each of these is what Ross called a prima facie duty, meaning 'on the face of it' – that is, presumed to be a duty until proven otherwise. Sometimes, the duty not to harm and the duty to tell the truth can point in opposite directions, as can keeping one's promises and avoiding harm to others.

Ross emphasized that all of the duties on his list (which included the above three) are prima facie duties, and his 1930 book popularized the use of the expression 'prima facie duty' in the literature of ethical theory. In the spirit of intuitionism, Ross insisted that when the duties on his list conflicted in particular situations, there was no deductive or systematic way to decide which duty took precedence. For if he admitted that duties could be systematized, then he would seem to be allowing that there are some other, over-arching principles that presumably play some role in justifying belief in the duties on his list; but if the other principles played such a justificatory role, then the duties on his list wouldn't be self-evident after all!

This points to the core weakness of intuitionism. The core weakness is not the claim that some moral principles are self-evident (in fact, we think there is at least one principle that is self-evident – that of universalizability, which we discuss in the following subsection). The core weakness is instead that intuitionism provides no disciplined way of deciding hard cases where self-evident but prima facie duties conflict. This is especially evident in the context of environmental ethics. As we have noted, claims about the intrinsic value of non-human animals, plants, species, and ecosystems are at the heart of the debate. But imagine an environmentalist claiming that it is 'self-evident' that an alpine valley has intrinsic value and also 'self-evident' that such intrinsic value cannot justifiably be replaced by the instrumental value of a ski resort. Paralysis will result as soon as a developer claims that it is 'self-evident' to him that the value of the valley is purely instrumental and that its instrumental value can be maximized through development. To avoid paralysis, we think that environmentalists must reject intuitionism in ethics.

7.1.3   Appealing to the Logic of Moral Discourse

Another approach to justification in ethics involves appealing to logical requirements on specifically moral judgments. The idea here is that what makes some judgment a *moral* judgment is that it is understood to be subject to certain logical requirements that distinguish it from other kinds of judgments. Two logical requirements that are commonly thought to be definitive of moral judgments are overridingness and universalizability.

'Overridingness' refers to the notion that in making a specifically *moral* judgment, one is claiming that this judgment should override other types of norms, e.g. of prudence, law, and etiquette. 'Universalizability' refers to the logical requirement to judge similar cases similarly. The requirement of universalizability is constantly invoked in discussions of ethics, if only implicitly. It is implicit when someone asks you what you think about a hypothetical case that is similar in various ways to a real one that you're discussing. If you would judge the hypothetical case differently than the real case under discussion, then your interlocutor assumes that he or she can demand an explanation of how the two cases are relevantly different. Unless you can give such an explanation, you are guilty of a logical inconsistency (this search for compliance with the universalizability requirement is often at the heart of philosophical thought experiments; see Section 7.2). Even small children are expected to understand this logical requirement when they're asked "How would you feel if Harry took your toy from you the way you just took Harry's toy from him?"

In contrast to moral judgments, judgments about prudence (about what is best for oneself) are not thought to be either universalizable or overriding: what's best for me may not be what's best for you, and moral judgments are thought to override what's best for either one of us. Some other kinds of judgments are thought to be universalizable but not overriding. For instance (at least in the common law tradition), legal judgments must treat similar cases similarly, but legal statutes are subject to 'jury nullification,' as when a jury acquits a defendant while admitting that he or she is guilty under a statute, on the grounds that the law's application in that particular case would be morally unjust. Aesthetic judgments are also generally considered universalizable, but not always overriding (for more on this, see Chapter 11[1]).

The most famous attempt to defend a moral principle by appealing to the logic of moral discourse was the German philosopher Immanuel Kant's [1724–1804] defense of 'the categorical imperative' in his 1785 book, *Groundwork of the Metaphysic of Morals* (sometimes translated as *Foundations of the Metaphysics of Morals*). Kant (1948 [1785]) claimed that there is only one categorical imperative, although in that short book (the first edition ran to only 128 pages) he

---

[1] In Chapter 11 we note that a duty to preserve great works of art is widely recognized, but at the same time it would be wrong to put such duties ahead of important duties to human beings. This suggests that sometimes, but not always, aesthetic judgments are taken to override certain norms.

gave somewhere between three and 11 different formulations of it. For instance, the two most widely discussed formulations are:

> The **universal law formulation** of Kant's categorical imperative:
> *"Act only on that maxim through which you can at the same time will that it should become a universal law"*
> (Kant, 1948 [1785], p. 88, emphasis in original).

and:

> The **respect for personhood formulation** of Kant's categorical imperative: "Act in such a way that you always treat humanity, whether in your own person or in the person of any other, never simply as a means, but always at the same time as an end"
> (Kant, 1948 [1785], pp. 89 and 96).

Although Kant repeatedly emphasized that there is only *one* categorical imperative, which can be expressed in various equivalent ways (see, e.g., Kant, 1948 [1785], pp. 88 and 103), numerous commentators have claimed that the above two formulations in fact have different implications. For present purposes, we will illustrate Kant's claim that the categorical imperative follows from the logic of moral discourse by focusing on the first of the above formulations.

The universal law formulation of the categorical imperative can be understood as applying the logical principle of universalizability to what Kant called 'a maxim.' In contemporary English, the noun 'maxim' is generally used to refer to a short, pointed statement of some general truth or practical advice, such as "Actions speak louder than words." Kant had something very specific in mind, however. By a 'maxim,' he appears to have meant an explicitly stated rule of the form: *in order to achieve a specified goal, I will act a specified way, whenever specified circumstances obtain.* Kant believed that moral agents are always acting on such a maxim when they freely choose to perform a given action. Our maxims might only be implicit most of the time, but Kant's idea was that in order to be permissible, it must be possible to achieve the specified goal by acting on the maxim in a world in which *everyone* is acting on the same maxim (i.e. trying to achieve the specified goal by acting in the specified way under the specified circumstances). Given Kant's understanding that moral agents are always acting on maxims when they freely choose their actions, the universal law formulation of the categorical imperative expresses the principle of universalizability that is at the core of people's shared conception of moral judgment.

It's easy to see why many maxims would fail to be universalizable in the above way. Consider this one, for instance:

GOAL: In order to be able to read a book at my leisure,
ACTION: I will take it from the library without checking it out and
never return it,
CIRCUMSTANCES: Whenever I want to be able to read a book that
the library has.

If everybody was acting on that maxim, then it would be impossible to achieve your goal by acting on it.

What turns out to be more difficult is deciding how to determine, in a non-arbitrary way, what maxim one is acting on. Consider, for instance, this modification of the above maxim:

GOAL: In order to be able to read a book at my leisure,
ACTION: I will take it from the library without checking it out and
never return it,
CIRCUMSTANCES: Whenever it is 11:00 a.m. on July 16, 2015, and I
am in the city of Guelph, and my name is Sylvie
Mason.

Standing at the library door on the specified date and time, Sylvie could indeed achieve her goal by acting on this modified maxim in a world in which everyone else was simultaneously acting on it. Indeed, given that there's no one else in Guelph with her name at the time, everyone will have done what they would have done had they been acting according to the same maxim when the heist was effected at 11:00! If one can choose to describe the goal and circumstances of one's maxim so specifically, then any action could be described so that the agent could indeed achieve his or her goal by acting on it in a world where everybody else was acting on it.

On the other hand, actions that seem perfectly fine, morally speaking, would seem to be immoral according to Kant's test, depending on how the agent's maxim is stated. Consider this maxim:

GOAL: In order to relax and meet up with friends,
ACTION: I will go to the porch at Duddley's Draw,[2]
CIRCUMSTANCES: Whenever it is 5:00 p.m. on a Friday.

If everybody went to the same porch at the same time, then nobody would be able to relax or even find their friends. Perhaps the agent's intention is better expressed with this maxim:

GOAL: In order to relax and meet up with friends,
ACTION: I will go to an agreed upon location at an agreed upon time,
CIRCUMSTANCES: Whenever such an agreement has been made and it is that time.

Here, as in the case of the book heist, the issue is how to properly formulate the maxim on which an agent is 'really' acting. Kant scholars have extensively debated how to do this in a way that prevents 'rigging' the maxim so that it is universalizable when the underlying intention seems clearly immoral, while allowing for what seem like morally permissible actions.

Kant was an arch-opponent of utilitarianism, or 'the greatest happiness principle,' but in the late twentieth century R.M. (Richard Mervyn) Hare [1919–2002] argued that Kant's approach – seeking a general moral principle from the logical requirements on moral discourse – actually implies utilitarianism. We have more to say about utilitarianism in Chapter 8. Here we will focus on why Hare thought that the principle of maximizing aggregate happiness follows from the logical requirements on moral judgments.

---

[2] A bar across the street from Texas A&M University, where co-author Gary Varner is occasionally found.

Hare (1981) claimed that moral judgments have both of the logical properties described at the beginning of this subsection – universalizability and overridingness – plus a third, which he called 'prescriptivity.' The latter is a complex property, but Hare's argument for utilitarianism can be explained succinctly in terms of the familiar 'golden rule,'[3] which Hare believed gave common-sense expression to the three logical requirements, taken together. Hare claimed that if you truly adopted the perspective of the golden rule, then you would choose as if you had to experience all of the effects of your actions on others. But then, he argued, you would choose to maximize aggregate happiness across everyone affected by your actions, just as in real life you choose to maximize your own happiness across the various phases of your life, thinking it worth sacrificing some of your own happiness during some phases in order to increase your happiness during other phases. In this way, Hare claimed, utilitarianism emerges as a basic ethical commitment from the logical requirements on moral judgments as expressed in the golden rule.[4]

The examples of Kant and Hare illustrate how some philosophers have thought that a moral principle can be derived from studying the logic of moral discourse, although those two philosophers disagreed about what moral principle follows. It is important to note, however, that neither Kant nor Hare believed that logic alone will decide any interesting, more specific questions. Hare was very clear about this, emphasizing that the logic of moral discourse entails the principle of utility, but also that what the principle of utility implies in practice depends on what the facts are, including a lot of general information on human nature and the human condition. In the *Groundwork of the Metaphysics of Morals* Kant did sometimes write as if every substantive question in ethics could be decided via logic

---

[3] Roughly: "Do unto others as you would have them do unto you," although numerous variations on this formulation are found in the Hebrew, Christian, and Islamic scriptures, as well as in Confusianism, Buddhism, Hinduism, Jainism, and Zoroastrianism (see Varner, 2012, pp. 75–76).

[4] A more detailed, but still accessible account of how Hare's argument was supposed to work can be found in Varner 2012, chapter 2.

alone, but he also said that "to expound the whole of ethics . . . requires anthropology" (Kant, 1948 [1785], p. 79). That this means facts about human nature and the human condition is clear from his later works in ethics (especially his two volume *Metaphysics of Morals*, which was published in 1797).

Among contemporary philosophers, there is near unanimity that no substantive ethical judgments follow from the logical requirements on moral judgment alone. Few would follow Hare in thinking that even a general principle like utilitarianism follows, and many would say that Kant's work on the categorical imperative is really an exploration of the requirement to judge similar cases similarly, rather than a more substantive principle. However, the claim that universalizability is a logical feature of all genuinely moral judgments is uncontroversial, among both philosophers and the general public. This is the crucial lesson we take away from the attempt to ground ethics in the logic of moral discourse, and the requirement of universalizability is implicitly at work in the final method of justification in philosophical ethics that we will discuss.

7.1.4   *The Method of Reflective Equilibrium*

People usually have at least two levels of moral beliefs: *principles or rules* on the one hand, and *intuitive judgments about particular cases* on the other. Examples of the former would include 'Killing people is wrong,' 'Justice requires that people get what they deserve,' and the principle of universalizability, as discussed in the preceding subsection.[5] Sometimes people deduce moral judgments about particular cases by reasoning from such general moral norms to a conclusion about a particular case, for example: "Killing people is wrong, and abortion kills a person, so it was wrong of you to have an abortion." Other times, however, people 'just feel' that something is right or wrong without deducing it from a general rule or principle. Such

---

[5] Some philosophers draw a specific distinction between moral rules and moral principles, as did Marcus Singer in *Generalization in Ethics* (1961, pp. 327–328). We will use the terms more loosely, using 'rules' to refer to less general norms than 'principles.'

'snap judgments' are what we mean by 'intuitions about particular cases,' as when someone reacts to a specific situation with a moral judgment without necessarily relating their judgment about that particular case to whatever general moral norms they also endorse.

The method of reflective equilibrium refers to the process of bringing our intuitive judgments about specific cases into some kind of rational harmony with whatever moral rules and principles we endorse. This is called a 'coherentist' approach to justifying moral beliefs. A coherentist holds that what justifies one in holding a belief is not its being proven true, but its being part of a coherent set of beliefs. Coherentism contrasts with 'foundationalism,' which is the view that what justifies a belief is its being an inference from some belief(s) that one knows with certainty to be true.

In the method of reflective equilibrium, one repeatedly examines the consistency of one's beliefs, making adjustments at one or both levels, until they are all in harmony with each other. The American political philosopher John Rawls [1921–2002] coined the term 'reflective equilibrium' to refer to the state in which one's moral beliefs at both levels cohere with one another (Rawls, 1971, p. 20). In reality, of course, most of us have some beliefs at one level or another (intuitions about particular cases on the one hand, and moral rules and principles on the other) that don't cohere with all of the others. But the idea behind the method of reflective equilibrium is that you are rationally justified in holding your moral beliefs *to the extent that* you approximate Rawls' ideal of reflective equilibrium.

It is important to note that in the method of reflective equilibrium, adjustments are made *at both* levels. So, for instance, someone might qualify the simple moral rule about killing that we mentioned above to make it consistent with their intuitive reaction to the execution of someone who was convicted of brutally murdering a number of people by revising it to read: "It is wrong to kill *innocent* people." Other times, however, a person's intuitive judgment about a particular case may change after they reflect on its consistency with the general moral norms that they endorse. So, for instance, someone might decide that they shouldn't stick to their immediate, intuitive reaction that an elective abortion was justified, because it doesn't cohere with their belief that "It is wrong to kill innocent people." Intuitive reactions aren't always easy to change, but the idea behind the method of reflective equilibrium is that if we can achieve consistency by adjusting certain of our intuitive reactions to fit our general moral norms, then we are justified in 'training ourselves' not to have those intuitive reactions.

Our point in the preceding example is not to argue against elective abortion. After all, a person could make their intuitive reactions to the permissibility of both elective abortion and capital punishment consistent with their norms regarding killing human beings by abandoning the simple rule, "It is wrong to kill innocent people" and endorsing a set of interrelated rules, such as:

1. "It is wrong to kill people unjustly";
2. "One kills unjustly only if one deprives another person of something that they have a right to";
3. "A person duly convicted of murder has forfeited their right to life"; and
4. "A person has a right to use your body for survival only if you have expressly granted them that right."

This is (roughly) a move that American philosopher Judith Jarvis Thomson makes in her famous essay, "A Defense of Abortion" (Thomson, 1976, p. 57).

Note how the principle of universalizability, which we mentioned in Sections 7.2.2 and 7.2.3, is implicit in the method of reflective equilibrium. For if one were not required to judge similar cases similarly, then when it is pointed out that someone believes both that "It is wrong to kill people" and that convicted murderers should be executed, the person could reply: "I just happen to believe both things, and I don't need to be able to explain how they are consistent." That the commitment to universalizability is implicit in the method is hardly surprising, however, if it is indeed a logical requirement on all moral judgments. For that reason, the method of reflective equilibrium is a natural approach to justifying our moral beliefs.

There is an obvious problem with the method, however, a problem that Hare pointed out in a 1973 review of Rawls' *A Theory of Justice*. Hare (1973a, b) argued that the method of reflective equilibrium is fundamentally flawed, because our intuitive moral judgments are, at least in the beginning, a product of the moral education we receive as children. Hare argued that unless we have independent reasons for believing that the intuitions inculcated in us during that education were sound, or that some of the intuitions that we have subsequently acquired are themselves sound, the method of reflective equilibrium provides no rational support for a principle or theory. If Hare is correct, then it would seem that the method of reflective equilibrium can serve as an exercise in values clarification, but it can't prove that a moral judgment, a general moral principle, or an ethical theory is *true*.

We share Hare's misgiving about using the method of reflective equilibrium to justify our moral beliefs, but we will nevertheless employ it in this book for three reasons. First, almost everyone *in fact* relies on it. That is certainly true of moral philosophers. Even Hare goes to great lengths in his work to show how his version of utilitarianism does not have a variety of counter-intuitive implications that philosophers commonly charge utilitarianism with having. And in day-to-day debates about ethics, non-philosophers also employ it. Consider, for instance, the following example:

> Two friends, Eric and Teresa, are discussing same-sex marriage at a coffee house across the street from their college's campus. Eric says that it just seems wrong to him. He hears people describing it as necessary to achieve 'marriage equality,' but, Eric says, "It seems like asking for special favors or a *new* right, a right to a new thing that is *same-sex* marriage." Teresa reminds Eric that interracial marriage was controversial during the Civil Rights Era, and she points out that then many Americans thought that interracial marriage was unnatural and thus something 'new' that went beyond what they understood marriage to be. "I know that you

don't have any problem with interracial marriage among heterosexuals," Teresa says, "so how is the situation today with regard to same-sex marriage different?"[6]

They never give it a fancy label, but clearly Teresa and Eric are using the method of reflective equilibrium, and in terms of the method, we can imagine how the conversation might continue from there. Eric might, of course, abandon his intuitive judgment about same-sex marriage thus eliminating the apparent inconsistency in his judgment about the two cases. Or Eric might stick to his intuition that calling for a right to same-sex marriage is calling for a new right whereas calling for a right to interracial marriage among heterosexuals was not, by claiming something about the function of marriage being procreation. Then Teresa might ask Eric his view of marriage among heterosexual couples where one or both of the partners is physically incapable of reproduction, and so on.

Our second reason for using the method of reflective equilibrium in this book is that, as Norman Daniels emphasizes in his *Stanford Encyclopedia of Philosophy* entry on the method: "The method of reflective equilibrium has been advocated as a coherence account of *justification* (as contrasted with an account of *truth*)" (Daniels, 2013, section 1, emphasis added). As we noted above, the method of reflective equilibrium is a natural outgrowth of the logical requirement of universalizability, and, as such, striving for reflective equilibrium expresses a commitment to rationality in ethics, even if we admit that achieving reflective equilibrium would not guarantee the truth of our moral beliefs.

Finally, as we noted in Section 7.2.3, Hare believed that he could develop a complete moral theory without relying on the method of reflective equilibrium, because he thought that the principle of utility follows directly from a set of logical requirements on moral judgments, and that by combining the principle of utility with certain facts about humanity and the human condition he could generate a complete ethical theory. We noted there, however, that few philosophers think

---

[6] This example was suggested to us by Linda Radzik, a philosopher at Texas A&M.

that Hare's argument succeeds. We have also noted that there are extensive limitations on both appeals to self-evidence and appeals to logical requirements in establishing the truth of moral judgments, principles, and theories. In particular, we noted that only the principle of universalizability enjoys anything close to universal acceptance as a self-evident moral principle, and appeals to the logic of moral discourse seem unlikely to yield conclusions about difficult issues without significant supplementation. Given that the method of reflective equilibrium is in fact almost universally employed by moral philosophers, and given that non-philosophers often instinctively employ the method in day-to-day debates about ethics, we think it reasonable to rely on this coherentist approach to *justifying* our moral beliefs, even though we share Hare's concern about basing claims to moral *truth* on it.

7.1.5 Our Methodology in This Book

In this section, we have described how various methods of justification have been used by philosophers writing on ethics. For the reasons we have given, we doubt that appeals to God's will, to the self-evidence of certain moral judgments, or to the logic of moral discourse are viable approaches to ethical theory in general, and to controversial issues in environmental ethics specifically.

The method of reflective equilibrium is almost universally used by contemporary philosophers, and it is implicitly used by everyday people in everyday discussions of ethics. Although we believe that this method is flawed as an approach to *proving* that a moral judgment, principle, or theory is *true* on foundationalist grounds, we think that it is a reasonable approach to *justifying beliefs* in ethics on coherentist grounds. So, in this book we will freely employ the method of reflective equilibrium, and, with it, the logical requirement of universalizability.

7.2 THE ROLE OF 'THOUGHT EXPERIMENTS'

In the next chapter, we will discuss how the sentientist and biocentric individualist approaches to environmental ethics have been developed using the principle of universalizability and the method of reflective equilibrium. First, however, we want to say something about the role that *hypothetical* cases, or 'thought experiments,' play in ethical theory in general and environmental ethics in particular.

In academic philosophy, a very famous thought experiment is 'the trolley case,' which was first discussed by British philosopher Phillippa Foot [1920–2010] in a 1967 essay. In her original version of the trolley case, you are the driver of a trolley whose brakes have just failed and you see that five workers on the tracks just ahead will be killed by the runaway trolley unless you steer it onto a side track where just one worker will be killed. Most people say that the right thing to do is steer the trolley off the main track. But when asked about a variant on the case, where you are a bystander on a bridge and the only way to stop the trolley from killing five people is to push a very large man off the bridge onto the tracks where the trolley will kill him but be stopped in the process, most people say that it would be wrong to push the man off the bridge to his death. Some philosophers have made a cottage industry of analyzing people's reactions to these and further variations, with some arguing, for instance, that differing intuitions about the above two cases reflect a higher-level belief that killing someone is morally worse than letting someone die, or that there is a morally significant distinction between causing harm as a 'side effect' of bringing about a good result and 'directly intending' a harm as a means to a good result.[7]

For our purposes in this book, a detailed discussion of trolley cases is unnecessary. We mention them only because newcomers to philosophical ethics sometimes find such unrealistic cases irrelevant or off-putting, but the point of proposing such hypothetical cases is not to be realistic. The point is to control precisely the details of the cases to which people are responding, the way a scientist controls precisely the variables of a laboratory experiment. For that reason, one of us has proposed to understand such thought experiments as 'strictly hypothetical cases':

---

[7] Note that some philosophers and psychologists have criticized the use of such thought experiments on the grounds that people's reactions to them are affected by nuances in how the cases are presented, including such things as the very order in which they are presented. See, for instance, Schwitzgebel and Cushman (2012) and Sinnott-Armstrong (2008).

> To treat a case as 'strictly hypothetical' is to assume that, unless
> uncertainty about some things is stipulated in the description of it,
> everything there is to know about the case is included in the
> statement of facts, and we know both that this is the case and all of
> the stated facts with absolute certainty.
>
> *(Varner, 2012, p. 32)*

So, when presented with variations on the trolley cases described above, students almost always ask for more details that they think would affect their judgment, e.g. "Why can't people on the tracks get out of the way?," "Is anyone on the tracks a loved one of mine?," etc. By understanding a case as *strictly hypothetical*, however, we can precisely control what 'variables' are affecting our intuitive responses.

This can be illustrated using what is called 'the last man' case in environmental ethics. The first version of it (and the label) are from a 1973 conference paper by the Australian philosopher Richard Routley (who later changed his name to Richard Sylvan [1935–1996]):

> The last man (or person) surviving the collapse of the world system
> lays about him, eliminating, as far as he can, every living thing,
> animal or plant (but painlessly if you like, as at the best abattoirs).
>
> *(Routley, 1973, p. 207; parentheticals in original)*

Routley expected his readers to share his intuitive judgment that the last man's action is wrong. Since its wrongness could not be explained in terms of its effects on other people – including reducing the instrumental value that nature would have for future people – however, he intended the thought experiment to convince his readers to embrace a general principle to the effect that non-human nature has intrinsic value.

Note the parenthetical statement at the end of Sylvan's version. Presumably he added it in an attempt to convince his readers that their general moral principles about what has intrinsic value must extend it beyond sentient animals, and a sentientist might claim that what the last person does is wrong because it causes suffering to animals. But that still doesn't fine-tune the case specifically enough, since an animal rightist might hold that a painless but premature death harms an animal independently of what it might suffer in the process. And a utilitarian could argue that the last man's removing species of sentient animals from the world decreases its value in the future, independently of the world's instrumental value to future humans.

So, others have redescribed the thought experiment, fine-tuning it in an attempt to ensure that if you share the intuition that what the last man does is wrong, then you should believe that non-sentient nature has intrinsic value. For instance, in their introduction to an anthology of work in environmental ethics, Elizabeth Willott and David Schmidtz described the last man case thus:

> You are the last human being. You shall soon die. When you are
> gone, the only life remaining will be plants, microbes,
> invertebrates. For some reason, the following thought runs through
> your head: Before I die, it sure would be nice to destroy the last
> remaining Redwood. Just for fun.
>
> *(Schmidtz and Willott, 2002, p. xiii)*

Note that in this version, the last person doesn't set about eliminating any sentient beings;[8] all that he or she does before dying is kill the last member of a plant species.

This still leaves open the question of whether it is the individual tree or the species it represents that has intrinsic value, but the above variations on the last man case suffice to illustrate how the proponent of a particular position in environmental ethics can use what we are calling 'strictly hypothetical cases' to argue for specific positions on questions like "What has intrinsic value?" In both laboratory science and philosophers' thought experiments, the object is to go back to "the real world" eventually, but with a refined theory in hand. When

---

[8] They stipulate that aside from the last man, there are only "plants, microbes, [and] invertebrates" on the planet, and we think that they intend us to assume, as is widely believed, that invertebrate animals are not sentient. For a discussion of the scope of sentience in the animal kingdom, see Section 8.3.

treated as 'strictly hypothetical cases,' as defined above, however, thought experiments abstract from the myriad messy details that characterize real-world situations (just like the experiments on diversity and ecosystem function described in Chapter 2). This should make us hesitant to think that this mode of argumentation can settle all real-world issues. Thought experiments are useful, however, for sharpening our beliefs about what are the morally salient features of the situations we encounter. And this is how they figure into defenses of various positions about intrinsic value in nature that will be considered in Chapters 8 through 11.

7.3   SOME CONCEPTUAL AND TERMINOLOGICAL ISSUES

Before turning to detailed consideration of such arguments in the next three chapters, we conclude this chapter by discussing some fundamental concepts in ethical theory and some related, specialized terminology. A first thing to note is that, in addition to endorsing a norm about which things have non-instrumental value, a complete system of ethical norms would probably have to include some norms establishing priorities. Especially when the sphere of moral consideration is broadened to include non-human animals, plants, species, and ecosystems (as in a version of pluralistic holism), there are bound to be conflicting values, and some basis is needed for deciding which values to protect in situations where it is impossible to protect them all. Even in an anthropocentric theory, however, priorities will need to be established among the wide variety of interests that humans have. So, for instance, satisfying a human's interest in living a fulfilling life would presumably be given priority over a human's interest in a trivial pursuit. Thus, in addition to norms specifying which things have intrinsic value, a complete set of moral norms will include some that establish priorities among various things that have intrinsic value.

A related terminological point is that many philosophers draw a distinction between *moral considerability* and *moral significance*. The standard version of this distinction was introduced in an early essay by Kenneth Goodpaster (1978). In this usage, while 'moral considerability' is an all-or-nothing thing – something either does or doesn't deserve to be considered in our ethical deliberations – certain things should be attributed relatively greater 'moral significance' in our deliberations. Goodpaster said that:

> We should not expect that the criterion for having 'moral standing' at all will be the same as the criterion for adjudicating competing claims to priority among beings that merit that standing.
>
> *(Goodpaster, 1978, p. 311)*

Accordingly, animal ethicists have commonly claimed that while sentience is a criterion for being morally considerable, various cognitive capacities are relevant to handling various conflicts of interests among sentient beings. Similarly, a pluralistic holist (see Section 1.6.2 and also Chapter 10) might claim that there are various grounds for basic moral standing while holding that the various cognitive capacities that humans and some other animals have give their lives some kind of special moral significance in comparison to those of plants, species, and ecosystems.

A term that relates to moral considerability and moral significance, as Goodpaster described them, is *moral standing*. This term hasn't acquired a specific meaning in the writings of environmental philosophers. Sometimes it is used in the non-comparative way that 'moral considerability' is standardly used, while other times it is used in the comparative way that 'moral significance' is standardly used. The term 'standing' was used by Christopher D. Stone (1972) in his famous essay, *Should Trees Have Standing?* Stone was working in a specifically legal context, however, arguing that courts should recognize legal rights for natural entities such as streams, species, forests, and ecosystems, including the right to be recognized as plaintiffs in lawsuits. In such a legal context, 'standing' does have a standard meaning. Specifically, at law an entity has legal standing if and only if it can be named as a plaintiff or a defendant in a lawsuit. Having the legal power to bring a lawsuit does not ensure success, so "Standing . . .

does not concern [the] ultimate merits of substantive claims involved in the action" (Black et al., 1990, p. 1405). As such, the legal notion of standing is more analogous to the notion of moral considerability than to that of moral significance.

Another distinction commonly made is between *moral agents* and *moral patients*. The idea here is that the set of beings that are capable of thinking about ethics and modifying their behavior accordingly – the moral *agents* – is a proper subset[9] of those whose intrinsic value, or interests, moral agents should take into consideration – the moral *patients*. It is generally thought that only normal adult human beings are moral agents, although some ethologists believe that there are at least analogs of morality among some non-human animals. Even anthropocentrists about intrinsic value will generally acknowledge this distinction, since various humans – e.g. babies and the criminally insane – are not held morally accountable for their actions.

Without the ability to contemplate the morality of one's actions, an individual can have a variety of cognitive capacities that various philosophers have thought to be morally significant. One cluster of such capacities is often referred to with the general term *preferences*. By 'preferences' here are meant all of the conscious desires, plans, projects, etc., that one has for the future, both immediate (e.g. the desire to get a drink of water) and remote (e.g. to finish college). One version of utilitarianism is referred to as 'preference utilitarianism' because it understands happiness as some kind of integrated satisfaction of one's preferences. The term 'integrated' points to complications involved in deciding how relatively important various preferences are to an individual's happiness.

A related term that has figured prominently in some debates in environmental ethics is *interests*. The term is generally used to refer to needs or desires, the satisfaction of which benefits the individual in question. We say 'individual' because many environmental philosophers have thought that the needs or desires that define an entity's

---

[9] That is, all moral agents are also moral patients, but some moral patients are not also moral agents.

moral interests cannot meaningfully be attributed to holistic entities such as species and ecosystems (this is discussed in Chapter 9, especially Section 9.3). Some philosophers have held that having interests in this sense requires consciousness (see, for instance, the discussion of Singer on this point in Section 8.3), while others (notably the biocentric individualists discussed in Section 8.7) claim that interests include various biologically based needs, the satisfaction of which benefits an organism even if it is incapable of conscious suffering or enjoyment, let alone the thinking that figures into preferences.

Finally, the word *person* is often given a stipulative definition by philosophers. In day-to-day speech, 'person' often just means 'member of our species' and thus functions as the singular of 'people.'[10] But in literature, film, and common sense, it also has another meaning in which it typically picks out certain cognitive abilities. For instance, in science fiction, when characters debate the 'personhood' of a space alien or an android, the focus isn't on species membership, but on various abilities that the alien or android has – typically, cognitive capacities such as sentience, self-awareness, the ability to consciously plan for the future, and so on. Similarly, in popular debates about abortion, the question "Is the fetus a person?" would never arise if 'person' meant 'member of our species' in that context.[11]

Dictionaries usually acknowledge that the term has at least one other, different sense. This third sense differs from the first two in that rather than being descriptive (describing an entity as being a member of a species or as having certain cognitive capacities), it is used *prescriptively* or *normatively*. In the law, for instance, governments and corporations are said to be 'persons' and the point of this usage is to

---

[10] On this point, note that 'people' does have a plural: 'peoples'. In that usage, however, 'people' is singular, referring to a community or cultural unit, and 'peoples' refers to a plurality of those units.

[11] Sometimes in that debate, the parties find themselves at odds over the questions "when does life begin?" and "when does personhood begin?" Those who argue that fetuses are alive, and therefore morally significant, are maybe taking a position somewhat akin to biocentric individualism, while those who argue that fetuses may be alive, but they are not persons and therefore not morally considerable, seem to be taking a position somewhat akin to sentientism.

ascribe to them certain legal rights, powers, and duties. Similarly, when the 'personhood' of a fetus is discussed in the context of the abortion issue, the focus is often on what kinds of legal and/or moral rights fetuses should or shouldn't be acknowledged to have. Generally, in this normative sense of the word, calling something a 'person' means that it deserves some kind of special treatment or respect.

In philosophical writing, the term is usually used in a mixed sense, in which the philosopher offers a stipulative definition of the 'person' as an entity that deserves a certain kind of respect or treatment *because* it has certain cognitive capacities. Such a definition is always stipulative, but a virtue of defining 'personhood' in this combined descriptive/normative way is that it draws attention to an inference in need of defense, namely: *"Why* should having certain cognitive capacities qualify an entity for some kind of special treatment or respect?"

Although much could be said about various philosophers' conceptions of personhood, debates about personhood have not figured prominently in the literature of environmental ethics. Given environmental philosophers' tendency toward holism, this is not surprising. For while various animal ethicists have argued that certain non-human animals qualify as persons, both in the descriptive sense of having certain cognitive capacities and in the prescriptive sense of deserving certain special kinds of respect because they have those capacities, few holists have applied the concept of personhood to species or ecosystems, because they seem unlikely to qualify as persons in the descriptive sense. Occasionally, holists will argue for ascribing legal rights or powers to species or ecosystems. A famous example is Stone's *Should Trees Have Standing?* (1972), which argued for extending some legal rights to holistic entities. Stone compared his proposal to the now accepted attributions of legal rights to corporations, however, which he acknowledged to be a 'legal fiction,' because corporations lack the cognitive capacities that normally figure into the descriptive aspect of personhood. Similarly, non-sentient organisms, ecosystems, and species are generally not regarded as having anything like the cognitive capacities that constitute the descriptive aspect of a philosopher's stipulative definition of a 'person.' So while it is important to understand that 'person' has a specialized use in philosophical ethics, we will not have any more to say about it for purposes of this book.

7.4   CONCLUSIONS

In this chapter we have provided a general introduction to methodology in philosophical ethics and introduced some of the terminology that is commonly used by ethicists. Our game plan in the next three chapters is to survey the principal philosophical debates concerning the main alternatives to anthropocentrism that we outlined in Section 1.6.2).

Chapter 8 focuses on sentientism – the view that all and only the lives of conscious individuals have intrinsic value – and treats more briefly biocentric individualism – the view that all living organisms have intrinsic value. Chapters 9 and 10 focus on holism – the view that holistic entities such as species and ecosystems have intrinsic value, in addition to or instead of individual living organisms.

Chapter 11 turns to the view that biodiversity has aesthetic intrinsic value, and in Chapter 12 we consider how well, on the whole, non-anthropocentric claims about intrinsic value support environmentalists' push to preserve biodiversity.

7.5   FURTHER READING

Blackburn S. 2003. *Ethics: A Very Short Introduction.* Oxford: Oxford University Press.

Rachels, J. and Rachels, S. 2014. *The Elements of Moral Philosophy.* 8th edn. New York: McGraw-Hill Education.

8 Extensionism in Environmental Ethics

In this chapter, we discuss sentientist and biocentric individualist approaches to environmental ethics. As we said in Section 1.6.2, *sentientism* is the view that what has intrinsic value is the conscious lives of both humans and all other sentient animals (where 'sentient' means 'capable of conscious suffering and/or enjoyment'); and *biocentric individualism* is the view that it is the lives of all living organisms (whether sentient or not) that have intrinsic value. In environmental ethics, these approaches to thinking about value in non-human nature are commonly labeled 'extensionism,' because they extend familiar ways of thinking about ethics in relation to our fellow human beings to broader categories of individuals. The basic strategy of extensionist ethics is to argue that certain widely shared moral beliefs require us, in light of the principle of universalizability, to extend moral consideration to various non-humans.

We will focus primarily on sentientism for several reasons. First, the case for extending moral consideration to sentient non-human animals is generally thought to be more compelling than that for extending consideration to non-sentient organisms. Indeed, in modern, affluent societies it is almost universally believed that we have at least *some* moral obligations to individual vertebrate animals that we encounter in various contexts, while few believe that we have moral obligations to individual plants, let alone unicellular organisms. Second, the challenges that environmental philosophers have posed to sentientism are roughly the same ones they have posed to biocentric individualism, so a close look at the former will allow us to describe the latter more briefly. In both cases, the challenge is to show

how the practical implications of a theory that does not extend moral consideration to holistic entities such as species and ecosystems can jibe with the environmentalist agenda as described in Section 1.4. For instance, critics have charged that sentientists should support some large-scale interventions in natural systems that environmentalists find abhorrent, such as removing large predators, and oppose some interventions that environmentalists support, including hunting for wildlife population control and maintaining ecosystems that have already lost their large predators.

Our approach in this chapter, then, will be to begin by describing the two main varieties of sentientist ethics, which involves looking at how philosophers make the distinction between 'animal welfare' and 'animal rights.' We will then describe in greater detail the challenges that environmental philosophers have posed for sentientism as a practical approach to environmental ethics, and consider some responses that sentientists have made. We will describe much more briefly analogous problems posed for biocentric individualism and possible responses. The final section of this chapter will emphasize how sentientism and biocentric individualism both grow out of traditions in ethical theory that environmental holists (whose views we consider in the next two chapters) believe we need to 'get beyond' in order to adequately address the environmentalist agenda.

8.2   THE ANIMAL WELFARE/ANIMAL RIGHTS DISTINCTION

The two most widely discussed sentientist approaches to ethics are so-called animal welfare and animal rights views, as they are reflected in the work of philosophers Peter Singer and Tom Regan [1938—2017], respectively. In this section, we begin by comparing a popular and political understanding of the animal welfare/animal rights distinction with the way philosophers draw the distinction. In Section 8.3 and Section 8.4, we will describe how the classic philosophical defenses these two views get in Singer's and Regan's work reflect a fundamental divide in ethical theory between *utilitarianism* (or *consequentialism* more generally) and *deontological ethics*.

It is worth noting that a variety of other approaches to thinking about animals and ethics have been explored, especially in more recent work. For instance, Martha Nussbaum (2004) has advocated extending to animals 'the capabilities approach' that she and economist Amartya Sen previously used to evaluate international development programs and the justice of political systems. A prominent virtue theorist, Rosalind Hursthouse (2011), has argued that the welfare and rights approaches are incomplete because each 'picks up on' only one of the traditionally recognized moral virtues. And animal ethicist Bernard Rollin has in several places described 'a new social ethic' that seems to be emerging in contemporary affluent societies, an ethic with roots in the teleological views of Aristotle (see Rollin, 1981, 1995, and part I of 1999). Philosophical discussions of animal ethics since the early 1980s have been dominated, however, by the positions carved out by Singer and Regan in their classic works, and the problems environmental ethicists see for sentientism have been couched in terms of their views. Hence, they will be our focus in this chapter.[1]

In the popular media, the distinction between 'animal welfare' and 'animal rights' is usually portrayed as follows. Animal rights advocates are radicals who are bent on abolishing many currently accepted practices involving animals, and they are willing to use illegal means, even terrorist tactics, to that end. They are also represented as driven by emotional attachments to animals rather than by reason, and as being poorly informed about the nature of the animals for which they advocate. 'Animal welfare' has been promoted as a contrast term by many scientists, veterinarians, agriculturalists, and others who want to express their commitment to ethical treatment of animals while simultaneously distancing themselves from what they see as the radical agenda of animal rights advocates. Not surprisingly, then, in the curricula of colleges of veterinary medicine and agriculture, animal welfarists are

---

[1] With permission of Oxford University Press, some material here and later in this chapter is reused from Gary Varner, "Environmental Ethics, Hunting, and the Place of Animals" in Tom L. Beauchamp and R.G. Frey, eds., *The Oxford Handbook of Animal Ethics* (2011), pp. 855–876.

commonly understood as 'us,' manning the ramparts against 'them,' the dangerous, anti-science animal rights lunatics.

Philosophers' conception of the distinction is not based on *any* of the above views. First, both animal welfare views and animal rights views are represented as reasoned applications of traditional ethical theories. Specifically, 'animal welfare' refers to evaluating our treatment of animals in utilitarian terms, whereas 'animal rights' refers to views that attribute individual moral rights to animals, where those rights are conceived of as 'trump cards against utilitarian arguments,' or at least as strong demands of some kind.

Further, as we will stress in Section 8.6, neither animal welfare views nor animal rights views so conceived are necessarily committed to the complete abolition of practices such as hunting or endangered species programs, although some particular animal rights philosophers – notably Tom Regan – have called for the complete abolition of such practices. Here we should also emphasize that neither of these views is necessarily committed to employing illegal means, let alone terrorist tactics, to achieve its endorsed goals (see Singer, 1990, pp. xi– xiii, Regan, 2004, Singer, 2004).

8.3   SINGER'S UTILITARIAN SENTIENTISM

Outside of academic philosophy, Peter Singer is best known for his opposition to intensive animal agriculture (so-called factory farming) and invasive research on animals, and for his support of physician-assisted suicide and active euthanasia in a range of circumstances, including severely disabled newborns. Within academic philosophy, he is known as a leading proponent of utilitarianism in ethics, and for following utilitarian arguments to their logical conclusions. In his vastly popular book, *Animal Liberation* (first published in 1975), however, he avoided giving explicitly utilitarian arguments. This was because he wanted his criticisms of animal agriculture and experimentation on animals to reach the widest possible audience. There he did freely use the method of reflective equilibrium that we described in Section 7.2.4, and he implicitly relied on the principle of universalizability that we described in Section 7.2.3. Elsewhere, Singer has argued for relying on a complex form of utilitarianism that is difficult to describe in detail without more space than we have here.[2] So, in this section we will give a simplified summary of Singer's utilitarian position, but one that suffices to prepare us to consider how a utilitarian might respond to the charges that environmental philosophers have leveled against sentientism.

In *Animal Liberation*, Singer used the method of reflective equilibrium in defense of sentientism. His defense involved first clarifying what he took to be a moral belief that all of his readers would share: that in some sense "all humans are equal." He noted that this expresses a moral principle rather than a statement of fact, since obviously humans are in fact not equal in size, shape, strength, intelligence, social and economic advantage, or even their capacity for moral judgment. Instead, Singer suggested, what we really mean by "all humans are equal" is that they all deserve "equal consideration of their *interests*."

Assuming that's correct, the next question is what does it mean to 'have interests'? At this point Singer gave a simple argument that fits the method of reflective equilibrium. This simple argument illustrates what we said about the variety of contexts in which this method gets used. In the following passage, Singer is not using it to defend a particular moral judgment or a general moral principle (as we illustrated in Section 7.2.4), but rather a definition of a key term:

> The capacity for suffering and enjoyment is *a prerequisite for having interests at all*, a condition that must be satisfied before we can speak of interests in a meaningful way. It would be nonsense to say that it was not in the interests of a stone to be kicked along the road by a schoolboy. A stone does not have

[2] A good overview of Singer's type of utilitarianism is his *Practical Ethics*, 3rd edn. (2011). Detailed consideration of some finer points, raised by critics and addressed by Singer, can be found in Jamieson (1999) and Schaler (2009). More recently, Singer has co-authored a book on Sidgwick (Lazari-Radek and Singer, 2014) that further refines his views about how to defend utilitarianism.

interests because it cannot suffer. Nothing that we can do to it could possibly make any difference to its welfare. The capacity for suffering and enjoyment is, however, not only necessary, but also sufficient for us to say that a being has interests – at an absolute minimum, an interest in not suffering. A mouse, for example, does have an interest in not being kicked along the road, because it will suffer if it is."

(Singer, 1990, pp. 7–8, emphasis in original)

In this passage Singer didn't refer to the method of reflective equilibrium, but his argument clearly fits our description of the method in Section 7.2.4. He was confident that his readers would agree on two intuitive judgments:

Intuitive judgment #1 = A stone does *not* have an interest in not being kicked down the road.

Intuitive judgment #2 = A mouse *does* have an interest in not being kicked down the road.

And he presents an account of necessary and sufficient conditions for having interests that explains our different intuitive judgments in the two cases:

Account of what it means to 'have interests' = The capacity for suffering and/or enjoyment is both necessary and sufficient for having interests.

Having clarified both what our commitment to human moral equality really means and the meaning of the key term 'interests,' Singer went on to argue that consistency requires us to be sentientists about moral equality. That is, our reasons for thinking that 'all humans are equal' commit us to thinking that all sentient animals are equal in the very same way.

Singer's argument is very simple, but, if sound,[3] it entails sentientism about intrinsic value, and a page later he drew the

---

[3] In formal logic, an argument is said to be 'sound' if and only if both (1) its premises are all true, and (2) its form is such that it is impossible for the premises to be all true without the conclusion also being true.

conclusion by introducing a stipulative definition of the term 'sentience':

> So the limit of sentience (using the term as a convenient if not strictly accurate shorthand for the capacity to suffer and/or experience enjoyment) is the only defensible boundary of concern for the interests of others.
>
> *(Singer, 1990, pp. 8–9)*

We call this a 'stipulative definition' because the term 'sentient' is used with different meanings in various contexts. Etymologically, the word refers to consciousness of something or other, or even just perception of, or reactivity to, the surrounding environment. This is why Singer described the term as "a convenient if not strictly accurate shorthand for the capacity to suffer and/or experience enjoyment."

Later philosophers added the suffix to turn the word 'sentient' into the '-ism' label that we have been using for the family of theories that find intrinsic value only in the experiences of conscious beings. John Rodman appears to have first used the term 'sentientism' this way in a review of Singer's *Animal Liberation*, when he criticized Singer for not extending moral consideration to more of nature than just sentient animals:

> In the end, Singer achieves "an expansion of our moral horizons" just far enough to include most animals ... The rest of nature is left in a state of thinghood, having no intrinsic worth, acquiring instrumental value only as resources for the well-being of an elite of sentient beings. Homocentrist rationalism has widened out into a kind of zoöcentrist sentientism.
>
> *(Rodman, 1977, p. 91)*

Like Rodman, some philosophers use the term *derisively* to mean a view that "*arbitrarily* favors sentients over nonsentients" (Linzey, 1998, p. 311; emphasis in original).[4] Many philosophers, including

---

[4] Linzey there claims to have coined the term in 1980, but Rodman's essay appeared three years earlier.

Singer, are glad to 'own' the term, however, insisting, as Singer does in the above argument, that sentience is the only *non-arbitrary* cut-off for morally significant interests.

Assuming that sentience as defined by Singer is the cut-off, how far do conscious suffering and/or enjoyment extend? As we noted in Section 1.6.2, in debates over animal ethics it is commonly assumed that an organism that is capable of conscious suffering or enjoyment of any kind will also be capable of experiencing physical *pain*, and so the debate over the extent of sentience among non-humans is usually conducted in terms of evidence for physical pain, specifically. Early in *Animal Liberation*, Singer notes that:

> We cannot directly experience anyone else's pain, whether that "anyone" is our best friend or a stray dog. Pain is a state of consciousness, a "mental event," and as such it can never be observed. ... Pain is something that we feel, and we can only infer that others are feeling it from various external indications.
>
> *(Singer, 1990, p. 10)*[5]

He then argues that a variety of comparisons between normal human beings and various animals support the conclusion that some animals feel pain. With regard to non-human mammals and birds, specifically, he notes that they share "the central features of our nervous systems" that support consciousness of pain in humans, they behave similarly to us "in circumstances in which we would feel pain," and they display similar physiological responses (blood pressure, heart rate, pupil dilation, etc.) to what would be painful stimuli for us (Singer, 1990, p. 11). Later in the book, he argues that although their nervous systems are different in some important ways from ours, both fish and reptiles (by which he presumably means all herpetofauna, or 'herps') "share the basic structure of centrally organized nerve pathways" and behave in ways that would be indicative of pain in mammals and birds (Singer,

---

[5] A minority of philosophers do deny that each of us has such 'privileged access' to their own mental states. For discussion of the variety of ways in which self-knowledge is thought to be distinctive, see Gertler (2015).

1990, p. 172), and he advocates giving "the benefit of the doubt" to crustaceans (Singer, 1990, p. 174).

Singer's approach is typical of both philosophers and scientists who have addressed the question of how far consciousness of pain extends among non-human animals. Given that conscious pain cannot be directly observed (except by the individual suffering it), an 'argument by analogy' is used to establish a *probability* that members of a given species can feel pain. Such arguments have the following basic form:

Premise 1:   We know that both humans and animals of species X have properties $a, b, c, \ldots$, and n.

Premise 2:   We know that humans suffer conscious pain under various circumstances.

Conclusion: So it is probable that animals of species X also suffer conscious pain under various circumstances.

This argument is stronger or weaker – the probability that animals of species X also feel pain is higher or lower – as a function of how relevant to pain perception are the analogies (similarities) cited in the first premise.[6] So, for instance, since we know that hairs play no role in human perception of pain, citing the fact that both humans and other mammals have hair would not strengthen the argument that other mammals feel pain. But since we know that certain kinds of behavioral and physiological reactions are associated with pain in humans, and that certain parts of our nervous systems support our perceptions of pain, citing the fact that members of another species are similar to us in those ways strengthens the argument for pain in that species.

---

[6] In footnote #2 (this chapter), we noted that in formal logic, an argument is said to be 'sound' only if its form is such that it is impossible for the premises all to be true without the conclusion also being true. When one makes an argument by analogy, however, one is not making such a strong claim. That is, the premises of such an argument being true does not *ensure* that the conclusion is also true; the claim is only that the premises being true makes it more or less *probable* that the conclusion is also true. This is the general difference between *deductive* arguments and *inductive* arguments as described in any textbook on formal logic.

Among philosophers and scientists studying the issue, a general consensus has emerged that, on balance, the available evidence makes it very probable that all vertebrate animals can feel pain, while the case for thinking that invertebrates (with the exception of cephalopods) can feel pain is significantly weaker. Certainly there is not unanimity on this, but for the sake of discussing sentientism's adequacy as an environmental ethic in the remainder of this chapter, we will assume that all and only vertebrate animals are sentient. (For a thorough overview of 'the standard argument by analogy' with regard to sentience, see Varner, 2012, chapter 5.)

We noted above that, in *Animal Liberation*, Singer did not explicitly adopt utilitarianism as a moral principle. Instead, he formulated his arguments against certain widely accepted practices in terms of 'speciesism,' which he defined as "a prejudice or attitude of bias in favor of the interests of members of one's own species and against those of members of other species" (Singer, 1990, p. 6). He noted that racism and sexism seem objectionable because they display an analogous prejudice or bias, and by arguing that much agriculture, medical research, etc., rests on an attitude of 'speciesism' he could convince readers to oppose them, without having to convince readers to accept utilitarianism specifically. Although he credited philosopher Richard Ryder with coining the term, Singer's use of it in *Animal Liberation* is responsible for its currency in contemporary discussions of animal ethics. Singer argued that speciesism is reflected in many widely accepted practices, including animal agriculture, medical research, etc. Implicitly relying on the method of reflective equilibrium, he argued that because we would not think it permissible to inflict a given amount of suffering on a human being for the sake of having meat to eat and medical advances, consistency demands that we not think it permissible to inflict a similar amount of suffering on sentient animals for the same purpose. He concluded that "Most human beings are speciesists," because they are willing to "sacrifice ... the most important interests of members of other species in order to promote the most trivial interests of our own species" (Singer, 1990, p. 9).

A related qualification is sometimes overlooked by people who have read nothing by Singer other than *Animal Liberation*. There, without using the specific language that we introduced in Section 7.4, Singer did note that "the rejection of speciesism does not imply that all lives are of equal worth" (1990, p. 20). That is, he acknowledged that it would *not* be speciesist to think that while the capacity to feel pain gives all sentient animals moral considerability, having certain cognitive capacities bestows special moral *significance* on the members of some species. In several other publications, Singer has himself argued that certain cognitive capacities distinguish normal human beings from members of other sentient species in morally . relevant ways, and in those other publications, he uses the term 'person' in the special sense that we described in Section 7.4 to mark that special moral significance that humans' lives normally have in contrast to many non-human animals. In those publications, Singer has argued in several different ways that from a utilitarian perspective, persons' cognitive capacities make them not 'replaceable' in a way that animals lacking those cognitive capacities are 'replaceable.' For an overview of his various arguments to this conclusion, see Varner (2012), section 9.4.

8.4 REGAN'S RIGHTS-BASED (DEONTOLOGICAL) SENTIENTISM

In traditional ethical theory, a fundamental distinction is drawn between consequentialist theories and deontological theories. The distinction has to do with what distinguishes right from wrong according to the theory in question. What *consequentialist* theories have in common is that according to such theories, rightness is a function of the consequences of the action or institution in question. As a utilitarian, Singer's type of sentientism is a form of consequentialism, because rightness is a function of an action's or institution's effects on aggregate happiness. In contrast, what *deontological* theories have in common is a commitment to rightness being a function of something other than consequences. Just as there are non-utilitarian versions of consequentialism, rights-based theories are only one form of deontology. A particularly famous version of deontology is Kant's theory that is based on the categorical imperative as described in Section 7.2.3. When environmental philosophers have critiqued sentientism, however, they have had in mind the rights-based sentientism of Tom Regan (1983).

Regan's central claim is that moral rights function as what we might call a 'trump card' against utilitarian arguments, and that various animals have the same cognitive capacities that qualify human beings as rights holders. In a card game, if spades are designated as the 'trump' suit, then no matter how strong is your hand consisting only of hearts, clubs, and diamonds (imagine that you have: 10♡, J♧, J♢, K♡, K♧), if anyone has a spade of any value (imagine just 2♤), then their hand beats yours. Moral rights are commonly said to function this way against consequentialist arguments, so that no matter how good the aggregated consequences would be (your hand of cards), if doing something would violate someone's moral right (their 2♤) then it would be wrong.

Rights theorists have traditionally argued that a proper respect for human rights requires this kind of non-consequentialist thinking, at least where rights are at stake. Authors in the human rights tradition have usually enumerated a list of specific rights that individuals have, and they have evaluated a nation's human rights record in terms of how well or poorly its legal system protects those rights. A well-known example is the 'Universal Declaration of Human Rights,' which the United Nations adopted in 1948 as "a common standard of achievement for all peoples and all nations."[7] Its 30 articles include many specific claims, such as:

> Everyone has the right to life, liberty and security of person. (Article 3)
> Everyone has the right to leave any country, including his own, and to return to his country. (Article 13)
> Men and women of full age, without any limitation due to race, nationality or religion, have the right to marry and to found a family. (Article 16)

---

[7] http://bit.ly/2foV7h6

> Everyone has the right to freedom of thought, conscience and religion; this right includes freedom to change his religion or belief, and freedom, either alone or in community with others and in public or private, to manifest his religion or belief in teaching, practice, worship and observance. (Article 18)
>
> Everyone has the right to take part in the government of his country, directly or through freely chosen representatives ... [and] Everyone has the right of equal access to public service in his country. (Article 21)
>
> Everyone has the right to education. Education shall be free, at least in the elementary and fundamental stages. (Article 26)

Of course, such claims still call for interpretation. For instance: does the "right to life" block executions of duly convicted murderers, and does the right to marry extend to same-sex couples? And the longer the list of rights one endorses, the greater is the likelihood of conflicts among them. For instance, how far can people go in publicly opposing interracial marriage (which is allowed by Article 16) based on their religious beliefs (as might be suggested by Article 18)? So a complete theory of human rights would need to include ways to address such conflicts of rights and such interpretational issues.

Unlike authors in the human rights tradition, in his work on animal rights, Tom Regan adopts a very general account of what it means to 'have moral rights.' Rather than enumerate various specific rights that individuals have, as advocates of human rights commonly do, Regan characterizes 'having rights' as an all-or-nothing condition. On his view, to say that individuals 'have rights' is to say that they are due a special form of respect as individuals, the cash value of which is that if individuals 'have rights,' then we cannot justify harming them on the grounds that doing so will maximize aggregate happiness. In this way, Regan conceives of moral rights as 'trump cards' against utilitarian arguments, and this makes Regan's animal rights view fundamentally different from the kind of utilitarian animal welfare view described in the preceding section.

Before we describe Regan's view any further, this is a good place to emphasize that the word 'right' is used in a variety of ways. On one hand, it is used as an *adjective*, as in the expression 'the right thing to do.' On the other hand, it can be used as a *noun* to refer to 'a thing' that an individual can 'possess,' as in 'Everyone has the right to freedom of thought, conscience and religion.' This is important to note, because people commonly slide from talking about there being right and wrong ways of acting toward animals into saying that 'animals have rights,' where by 'have rights' they mean only that animals are morally considerable, that moral agents should consider their interests in deciding what would be the morally best action. Even Peter Singer does this, at least in popular presentations. As we said earlier, Singer is a thoroughgoing utilitarian, yet in *Animal Liberation* he refers to 'rights' more than a dozen times in the first two pages.

So in the **weakest sense** of 'having rights', saying that "Sophie has rights" is just equivalent to saying: *Sophie is morally considerable* (or, it matters, morally speaking, how we treat Sophie, or Sophie has more than instrumental value, etc.). By contrast, saying that "Sophie has rights" in **Regan's all-or-nothing sense** is saying something much stronger, that: *It would be wrong to harm Sophie on utilitarian grounds.* Furthermore, when human rights theorists go on to enumerate lists of rights to specific things, as in the UN Declaration of Human Rights, the enumerated rights are commonly distinguished into 'claim rights,' 'liberty rights,' and 'negative rights.' Each of these categories of rights is correlated with a category of duties. Consider, for instance, the right to a free elementary education described in Article 26 of the Declaration. Understood as a **claim right**, "Sophie has a right to a free elementary education" means that *certain others have a duty to provide Sophie with an education.* Understood as a **liberty right**, it means that *Sophie has no duty not to seek an education.* And understood as a **negative right** it means that *others have a duty not to interfere with Sophie in her pursuit of an education.* These three senses of 'rights' are not necessarily mutually exclusive. It might, in fact, be the case that Sophie has all three senses of the "right to an education," but note that each sense puts different duties and constraints on the actions of certain agents. All this illustrates that rights are easily asserted, but require clarity if we are to properly evaluate the assertion and to understand its implications for our future behavior.[8]

As we noted earlier, the rights enumerated on lists like the UN's Declaration can conflict, and spelling out in detail how to understand rights such as those on the UN's list is an important part of the interpretive work that needs to be done. About Regan's theory of *animal* rights, however, we noted that he does not enumerate any more specific rights that animals have beyond the general, all-or-nothing sense of having a 'trump card' against utilitarian arguments. Presumably this is because animals do not exercise rights in a political system the way humans do when we carry passports, get married, run for elected office, go to school, and so on. For Regan, to say that animals 'have moral rights' means just that they deserve the kind of respect for them as individuals that is captured by saying that they each have 'a trump card against utilitarian arguments.'

Nevertheless, Regan recognizes that there will be cases where it is impossible to avoid harming *everyone*, and in such cases the affected individuals' undifferentiated right not to be harmed on utilitarian grounds will somehow have to be weighed against each other. Given that rights are trump cards against utilitarian arguments, however, Regan recognizes that non-utilitarian principles are needed to decide whose rights to override in such cases where it is impossible not to override some individuals' rights. Given the focus on individuals, Regan argues that the principles should reflect a focus on the *magnitude* of harm to the various individuals affected, rather than the aggregated impact on a collection of individuals, which is the focus in utilitarian reasoning.

Obviously, some general conception of harm is needed to determine how significantly an individual is harmed. Regan adopts a sentientist criterion of harm, according to which an individual is harmed

---

[8] A classic, and widely reprinted account of the relationships between rights and duties was given by jurist Wesley Hohfeld in *Fundamental Legal Conceptions* (New Haven: Yale University Press, 1919), pp. 35–64. Hohfeld emphasized that two additional concepts, of "powers" and "immunities," are very important in legal contexts, where a legal agent can change the array of rights, duties, and powers that various individuals have.

to the extent that his or her capacity to form and satisfy desires is diminished. However little conscious suffering is involved, death completely eliminates this capacity, and for this reason Regan holds that death is the greatest harm that can befall a sentient individual, even if it is accompanied by no suffering whatsoever. On the other hand, Regan holds that the harm that death is to a normal, adult human being is non-comparably worse than the death of any non-human animal. The reason is that although humans and animals share the capacity to form various kinds of desires (for food, drink, sex, rest, warmth, etc.), the cognitive capacities of normal humans allow them to also form more long-term, complicated desires: to raise a family, to succeed professionally, and so on.

With this understanding of varying degrees of harm in hand, Regan defends two different principles, one to govern cases where all of the affected individuals would be harmed to a similar degree, and another to govern cases involving what he describes as 'non-comparable harms.' Regan does not offer a formula for categorizing pairs of harms as comparable or not, but he thinks that various examples are clear: "untimely death, for example, is a prima facie greater harm than a temporary loss of freedom ... [and t]he untimely death of a woman in the prime of her life is prima facie a greater harm than the death of her senile mother" (Regan, 1983, p. 303). If such non-comparable harms are involved, Regan argues, then what he calls *the worse-off principle* expresses the form of special respect that is due to individuals who have moral rights. This principle requires us to avoid harming what he calls 'the worse-off individual.' This is the individual or individuals who will, under one available option, be harmed to a significantly greater degree if their rights are overridden than any individual will be harmed under the other available options if their rights are overridden. Regan emphasizes that where this principle applies, the numbers involved do not matter, and thus the implications of his rights view are profoundly anti-utilitarian, as illustrated by situation A in Box 8.1. Of the two available options in situation A, the first would involve harming just one individual, but in a way (–10) that is

BOX 8.1 **Understanding Regan's Two Principles**

The worse-off principle:
- Applies where the harms involved are 'non-comparable,' and
- Requires us to avoid harming the 'worse-off individual.'

The mini-ride principle:
- Applies where comparable harms are involved, and
- Requires that we override the rights of the few rather than the many.

"**The worse-off individual**" refers to the individual (or individuals) under a given option who would suffer a harm that is non-comparably worse than the harm that anyone would suffer under the alternative option.

These principles' application can be illustrated using the chart in Table 8.1. Assume that: (a) each '–10' and each '–1' represents the harm that one individual would suffer if that option were chosen in the given situation, and (b) a '–10' harm is non-comparably worse than a '–1' harm.

For each situation, ask yourself: (1) Which principle would apply? (2) Which option would it require you to choose in that situation? And (3) If the worse-off principle applies, then who is (are) the worse-off individual(s)? See main text for answers to these questions.

Table 8.1 *Four hypothetical situations. In each cell, each number represents a person, the magnitude of the number represents the harm suffered by that person under the options available.*

	Option #1	Option #2
Situation A (worse-off principle applies, choose option #2)	–10	–1 –1 –1 –1 –1 –1 –1 –1 –1 –1 –1 –1 –1 –1 –1 –1 –1 –1 –1 –1 –1 –1 –1 –1 –1 –1 –1 –1 –1 –1 –1 –1 –1 –1 –1 –1 –1 –1 –1 –1 –1 –1 –1 –1 –1 –1 –1 –1 –1 –1

BOX 8.1   (**cont.**)

Table 8.1 (*cont.*)

	Option #1	Option #2
Situation B (mini-ride principle applies, choose option #1)	-1 -1 -1 -1 -1 -1 -1 -1 -1 -1	-1 -1 -1 -1 -1 -1 -1 -1 -1 -1 -1 -1 -1 -1 -1 -1 -1 -1 -1 -1 -1 -1 -1 -1 -1 -1 -1 -1 -1 -1 -1 -1 -1 -1 -1 -1 -1 -1 -1 -1 -1 -1 -1 -1 -1 -1 -1 -1 -1 -1
Situation C (mini-ride principle applies, choose option #1)	-10 -10 -10 -10 -10 -10 -10 -10 -10 -10	-10 -10 -10 -10 -10 -10 -10 -10 -10 -10 -10 -10 -10 -10 -10 -10 -10 -10 -10 -10 -10 -10 -10 -10 -10 -10 -10 -10 -10 -10 -10 -10 -10 -10 -10 -10 -10 -10 -10 -10 -10 -10 -10 -10 -10 -10 -10 -10 -10 -10
Situation D (worse-off principle applies, choose option #2)	-1 -1 -1 -1 -1 -1 -1 -1 -1 -1 -1 -1 -1 -1 -1 -1 -1 -10 -1 -1 -1 -1 -1 -1 -1 -1 -1 -1 -1 -1 -1 -1 -1 -1 -1 -1 -1 -1 -1 -1 -1 -1 -1 -1 -1 -1 -1 -1 -1 -1	-1 -1 -1 -1 -1 -1 -1 -1 -1 -1 -1 -1 -1 -1 -1 -1 -1 -1 -1 -1 -1 -1 -1 -1 -1 -1 -1 -1 -1 -1 -1 -1 -1 -1 -1 -1 -1 -1 -1 -1 -1 -1 -1 -1 -1

non-comparably worse than the harm that any individual would suffer under the second option (–1). In situation A, a utilitarian would choose option #1 and harm the one (–10) in order to avoid what would be a larger harm in the aggregate under option #2 (–50).

It is the worse-off principle that leads Regan to call for the total abolition of slaughter-based agriculture. For he argues that death in the prime of its life – even a painless death – causes a harm to each of the animals involved that is non-comparably worse than the harm that any human would suffer as a result of abolishing animal agriculture. Regan assumes that humans can thrive on vegetarian diets, and although that has been questioned, most would agree on that today, with the caveat that more restrictive, vegan diets may need supplementation with certain micronutrients (Craig, 2009). Regan considers a number of other objections, including that families dependent on the meat industry could be dramatically affected (Regan, 1983, pp. 338–347), but for purposes of discussing environmentalist criticisms of his rights view, these details need not concern us. Here we just want to explain Regan's rights-based view in sufficient detail to allow us to consider its implications for the environmentalist agenda.

It is important to emphasize, however, that Regan does argue that human beings would be justified in killing non-human animals for food if this were the only way to survive. This follows from his worse-off principle for the following reasons. As we noted above, his conception of harm leads Regan to the conclusion that the death of a normal, adult human being is a non-comparably worse harm than the death of any non-human animal. Thus, if option #1 under situation A in Box 8.1 represents a human being dying for want of food, and option #2 represents the animals that would need to die to keep him alive, then the worse-off principle implies that the human should kill the animals to stay alive. Thus, Regan concludes that when humans have no option other than eating meat to survive, they are justified in doing so; but since he assumes that humans in contemporary developed nations can thrive without eating meat, he concludes that "commercial animal farming as we know it" is not justified (Regan, 1983, pp. 351–353).

Where the harms involved are all comparable, however, Regan endorses a *mini-ride principle*, according to which "we ought to choose to override the rights of the few in preference to overriding the rights of the many." Regan recognizes that, where it applies, this principle has similar implications to utilitarianism, but he claims that its justification is non-utilitarian, that it instead expresses a commitment to "showing equal respect for equal rights of all the individuals involved" (Regan, 1983, p. 305). Thus, in situation B of Box 8.1, in the trade-off between harming ten individuals under option #1 and harming 50 under option #2, respect for individual rights requires harming the few rather than the many, but only because the harms involved are all comparable. This is the same conclusion the utilitarian would reach in situation B (because an aggregate harm of –10 is better than an aggregate harm of –50).

Notice that even if profound harms are involved, the mini-ride principle will still apply, as long as the harms involved are comparable, so in situation C in Box 8.1 avoiding overriding the rights of the many would require choosing option #1. And note that if various individuals under a given option would suffer non-comparable harms, as in situation D, then the worse-off principle would apply, requiring us to avoid harming the worse-off individual, namely the one individual suffering a –10 harm under option #1.

This brief summary of his rights view ignores many qualifications and complications that Regan discusses in his 400-plus-page book, but it suffices to set up a discussion of how an animal rightist might respond to the charges that environmental philosophers have posed for sentientism.

8.5   THE PRACTICAL CHARGES AGAINST SENTIENTISM

Early in the history of environmental ethics as a subdiscipline of academic philosophy, some philosophers thought of a sentientist ethic as being a helpful first step on the way to an environmental ethic that would find intrinsic value in non-conscious natural entities. Indeed, in two early essays, the animal rights theorist Tom Regan himself described sentientism this way. In his "Feinberg on What Sorts of Beings Can Have Rights" (Regan, 1976) Regan questioned Joel Feinberg's theory that only desiring beings can have moral rights.

Then, in his "The Nature and Possibility of an Environmental Ethic" Regan defined an environmental ethic as one that holds that "the class of those beings which have moral standing includes but is larger than the class of conscious beings," and he concluded that sentientism is "not an environmental ethic," but "'on the way to becoming' such an ethic" (Regan, 1981, p. 20).

By the mid-1980s, however, it became widely assumed among environmental ethicists that following sentientist ethics to its logical conclusion would not lead to sound environmental policy. In 1980, J. Baird Callicott gave a paradigmatic statement of this claim. His "Animal Liberation and Environmental Ethics: A Triangular Affair," (Callicott, 1980) has probably been more widely reprinted in anthologies on environmental ethics than any other essay besides Leopold's "The Land Ethic." There, Callicott gave as reasons for divorcing environmental ethics from sentientism the following claims falling under five headings.

(1) **Hunting to control overpopulation:** Callicott emphasized that environmental ethics would require hunting of animals when necessary "to protect the local environment, taken as a whole," implying that animal liberationists must oppose all hunting.

(2) **Predators:** He said that, from an environmental perspective, large predators that kill other sentient animals are "critically important members of the biotic community," whereas animal liberationists should see them as "merciless, wanton, and incorrigible murderers."

(3) **Endangered species** : Here, Callicott made two claims:

(3A) Non-sentient organisms have no moral standing according to sentientism, and therefore "humane herdspersons" might allow sheep to graze on plants that are "overwhelmingly important to the stability, integrity, and beauty of biotic communities" (Callicott, 1980, p. 320).

(3B) Additionally, while environmentalists place special value on members of endangered species, from an animal liberation perspective, individuals with similar levels of sentience are of equivalent value, even if one is a member of an endangered species while the other's species is plentiful (Callicott, 1980, pp. 326–327).

(4) *Vegetarianism*: Callicott also argued that because vegetarian diets can feed people more efficiently, the conversion to vegetarianism that animal liberationists call for would likely lead to catastrophic human overpopulation (Callicott, 1980, p. 335).

(5) *Liberating domesticated animals*: Finally, he thought that the so-called liberation of domesticated animals would lead to four potential outcomes:

(5A) They would "become abruptly extinct" because they could not survive on their own.

(5B) Some would survive but, as with feral horses, would adversely affect their environments.

(5C) With slaughter banned, populations of domesticated animals would mushroom, consuming enormous resources and greatly increasing human society's ecological footprint.

(5D) On the other hand, if we cease to allow domesticated animals to breed, Callicott claimed that "there is surely some irony in an outcome in which the beneficiaries of a humane extension of conscience are destroyed in the process of being saved" (Callicott, 1980, p. 331).

In the decade following Callicott's famous essay, various environmental philosophers expressed how such objections came to be seen as driving a deep wedge between environmentalism and sentientism.

For instance, in a 1984 essay, Mark Sagoff extended Callicott's amorous metaphor by titling an essay "Animal Liberation and Environmental Ethics: Bad Marriage, Quick Divorce." Sagoff wrote:

> Environmentalists cannot be animal liberationists. Animal liberationists cannot be environmentalists. ... moral obligations to nature cannot be enlightened or explained – one cannot even take the first step – by appealing to the rights of animals.
>
> *(Sagoff, 1984, pp. 304, 306)*

Eric Katz later advised businesses engaged in animal research to blunt the criticisms of animal rights activists by siding with environmentalists:

> I suggest that the adoption by business of a more conscious environmentalism can serve as a defense against the animal liberation movement. This strategy may seem paradoxical: how

can business defend its use of animals by advocating the protection of the environment? But the paradox disappears once we see that animal liberation and environmentalism are incompatible practical moral doctrines.

(Katz, 1991, p. 224)

And even the pragmatist Bryan Norton, whose work has stressed how the implications of environmental holism and anthropocentrism – at least 'weak' anthropocentrism (as described in Section 5.1) – converge, said flatly in a 1991 book that "equal rights" for non-human animals would be environmentally unsound because "It can never be 'fair' by human standards to kill 10 percent of an elk population because it exceeds the capacity of its range" (Norton, 1994, p. 223).

One more charge has been leveled at sentientism by environmental philosophers, one that doesn't fit neatly into any of the five on Callicott's list:

(6) ***Intervening in wild systems***: Sentientists should favor intervening in wild nature for the benefit of animals in ways and to degrees that environmentalists find abhorrent.

Below is a classic statement of this concern from Sagoff's 1984 essay. He offered the following parody of sentientism as a guide to environmental policy. It is a parody, but a parody exaggerates aspects of a work to make them more obvious and that is what Sagoff is doing here:

One may modestly propose the conversion of national wilderness areas, especially national parks, into farms in order to replace violent wild areas with more humane and managed environments. Starving deer in the woods might be adopted as pets. They might be fed in kennels; animals that once wandered the wilds in misery might get fat in feedlots instead. Birds that now kill earthworms may repair instead to birdhouses stocked with food, including textured soybean protein that looks and smells like worms. And to protect the brutes from cold, their dens could be heated, or shelters provided for the all too many who will otherwise freeze. The list of obligations is long, but for that reason it is more, not less compelling. The welfare of all animals is in human hands. Society must attend not solely to the needs of domestic animals, for they are in a privileged class, but to the needs of all animals, especially those which, without help, would die miserably in the wild.

(Sagoff, 1984, p. 303–304)

Sagoff describes large-scale interventions in wild nature that are intended to reduce animal suffering. These include removing wild predators (Callicott's charge #2), but also feeding wildlife on a scale that environmentalists find abhorrent, and generally substituting artificial environments for wild ones, which environmentalists also find abhorrent.

In this section, we have provided an overview of what we characterize as 'the practical charges against sentientism.' We use the qualifier 'practical,' because some environmental philosophers define 'an environmental ethic' – or at least 'an adequate' or 'truly' environmental ethic – so that no version of sentientism could possibly qualify. For instance, in his 1981 essay referred to above, Regan defined an environmental ethic as one that holds that both sentient beings and some non-conscious beings have objective intrinsic value.

The so-called last-man cases described in Section 7.3 have been used to argue that an 'adequate' environmental ethic must attribute intrinsic value to entities such as species and ecosystems. Suppose, we are asked, that the last human being on earth destroys a rare plant, a species, or an entire ecosystem, without affecting any sentient beings. While environmentalists typically want to say that this action of the last man would be wrong, a sentientist would seem to be committed to either reaching the opposite conclusion, on the grounds that the last human's mere whim suffices to justify the action, or to denying that there is any moral issue at all, because – in this strictly hypothetical case – no other sentient beings' interests are at stake. So, if an adequate environmental ethic must match the intuitions that environmentalists have about intrinsic value, then it looks like sentientism is inadequate in a deep way.

We urge environmentalists not to identify 'a truly environmental ethic' with holism, however. For if we *define* 'an environmental ethic' as one that reflects the intuitive value commitments of environmentalists, without reference to what arguments can be given for and against having those value commitments, we will reduce environmental ethics to a kind of moral anthropology, an exercise in descriptive ethics with no critical role. Although one of the functions of philosophical discussion is values clarification, or helping people to better identify what their values are, ultimately we want to know what their values *should be*. In environmental ethics, we want rational arguments in favor of and against various positions on what has intrinsic value, what public policies *should be*, and so on. If sentientism had the suite of practical implications that Callicott alleged in his "Triangular Affair" paper, that would be a substantive argument against it. But defining 'an environmental ethic' as a version of holism begs a central philosophical question that should be up for debate, namely: What does and does not possess intrinsic value?

8.6 CAN SENTIENTISTS RESPOND TO THE PRACTICAL CHARGES?

In this section, we describe a variety of ways in which sentientists might respond to the practical charges enumerated in the preceding section. We first deal very briefly with charges #4 and #5, which we do not think pose serious challenges. In the remainder of this section we will consider in more detail approaches to responding to #1 through #3, and to #6.

Regarding #4, it is certainly an oversimplification to say that a conversion to universal vegetarianism would lead to a dramatic increase in the human population, because modern human populations are not primarily limited by their food supplies. That may well have been so in the past, but at least since the twentieth century, the significance of the so-called demographic transition in population growth has been recognized. This refers to the fact that nations' population growth rates transition from well above replacement level to at or below replacement level as the role of children in supporting a family changes with the affluence typically afforded by modernization. So, in agrarian or poverty-stricken societies, children are a vital labor resource who play a significant role supporting their families. In such societies, children are a net benefit to the family, and because child mortality rates are higher, large families are necessary to ensure that children play that supportive role. In modern, affluent societies, by contrast, children can't contribute to supporting the family to the same extent (due to child labor laws), the average cost of rearing a child has vastly increased, and child mortality rates typically are lower. For those reasons, couples exercise more restraint and smaller families are the norm. In modern, affluent societies, then, an increase in the food supply will not automatically result in an increase in the human population, and some environmentalists argue for switching to vegetarian diets because more people can be fed on less acreage than on an omnivorous diet, which would reduce humans' environmental footprint.

Regarding Callicott's charge #5, which concerns the various scenarios under which the 'liberation' of domesticated animals might occur, Edward Johnson (1981, p. 267) pointed out in an early response to Callicott's essay that any wholesale liberation of domesticated animals would almost certainly take the final form imagined by Callicott: #5(D), i.e. forced sterility or some other end to their reproduction. In his statement of the charge, Callicott (1980, p. 331) said that "there is surely some irony in an outcome in which the beneficiaries of a humane extension of conscience are destroyed in the process of being saved." In his response, Johnson emphasized that from the individualist perspective of sentientism, "it is not the species that is being liberated, but the individual members of the species." Presently existing individuals of domesticated species or breeds are not destroyed in the process described in #5(D). Callicott's charge could be reformulated in terms of the loss to the aggregate happiness of the world that would result if future generations of domesticated animals do not come into existence, but the moral status of future generations is a topic of extensive and complex philosophical debate, including with regard to the moral status of future generations of *humans*. There is no consensus among contemporary philosophers as to whether and how the interests of future generations should count in our deliberations: some claim that the loss of any possible future generation is a real moral loss, whereas others claim that we need only consider the interests of whatever future generations will come into existence regardless of what policies we adopt in the present.[9]

So, we think that the last two of the five practical challenges to sentientism articulated in Callicott's famous essay pose no serious challenge to using sentientism as a basis for environmental policy. Thus, it's not surprising that the philosophers we quoted in Section 8.3 as echoing Callicott's criticisms of sentientism all focused on ##1–3: hunting for wildlife population control, the removal of large predators, and the relative significance of members of endangered species; and on the sixth charge that we added: a general concern with intervening in nature in ways that reduce wildness. We turn to these three points in the next three subsections.

8.6.1   Sentientism and Hunting for Wildlife Population Control

In his famous 1980 essay, Callicott described this charge by saying that, according to the Leopold land ethic (which he characterized as "the exemplary type" of an environmental ethic: Callicott, 1980, p. 311):

> to hunt and kill a white-tailed deer in certain districts may not only be ethically permissible, it might actually be a moral requirement, necessary to protect the local environment, taken as a whole, from the disintegrating effects of a cervid population explosion.
>
> *(Callicott, 1980, p. 320)*

---

[9] See, e.g., http://stanford.io/2fssQqB.

In North America, white-tailed deer are an environmental problem because they are large herbivores that reproduce quickly and tend to overpopulate their range in so-called irruptions. The effects on regional vegetation can be profound, with wide-ranging effects on a variety of species.

Two famous examples that occupied Leopold's attention during his life were the irruptions of mule deer (*Odocoileus hemionus*) on the Kaibab Plateau along the North Rim of the Grand Canyon during the 1920s, and that of white-tailed deer (*O. virginianus*) in Wisconsin during the 1940s. In her professional biography of Leopold, *Thinking Like a Mountain: Aldo Leopold and the Evolution of an Ecological Attitude Toward Deer, Wolves and Forests* (1974), historian Susan Flader described how Leopold observed from afar the overpopulation of mule deer on the Kaibab during the mid-1920s after wolves (*Canis lupus*) were exterminated there, and then advocated for significant reduction of the Wisconsin herd during the early 1940s.

Leopold summarized events on the Kaibab in the lower diagram in Figure 8.1, and compared the situation in Wisconsin as he understood it. On the Kaibab, Leopold believed, the deer population had overshot the carrying capacity of its range so badly that 60% of the herd starved to death across two winters, and the future carrying capacity of the range was reduced to less than half of what it would have been had culling been used, beginning in 1918, to prevent the overshoot of the carrying capacity. In Wisconsin, Leopold predicted that a similar collapse of carrying capacity would occur if the herd was not reduced dramatically, and he successfully campaigned for a 1943 deer harvest that was at that time the largest in state history.

Leopold believed that in both cases, the problem was caused by removal of the deer herds' most significant natural predator, the wolf. We will consider sentientist perspectives on large natural predators in the next subsection, but for present purposes, what could a sentientist say in response to the general charge that they cannot endorse the use of hunting in situations where it appears to be 'necessary' to prevent the kind of ecosystemic changes that Leopold saw in Wisconsin and on the Kaibab?

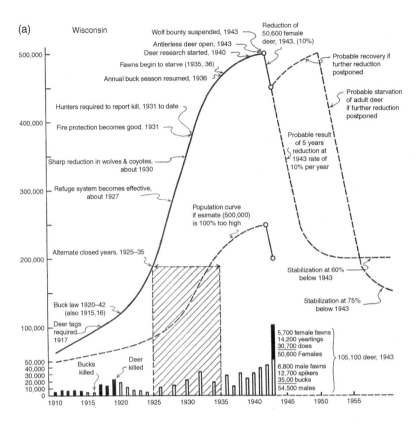

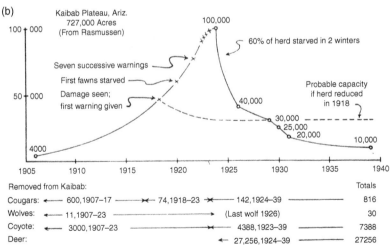

FIGURE 8.1 Figures from Aldo Leopold, as reproduced in Flader (1974).
Courtesy of the Aldo Leopold Foundation, www.aldoleopold.org

One response would be to say that contraception could substitute for hunting for this purpose. Research on wildlife contraception has been conducted since the 1950s and contraception is now routinely used to limit zoo populations of various animals. Field trials have successfully applied various contraceptive agents to various species, including white-tailed deer and horses, but at present there are few larger-scale applications to wildlife in situ. Part of the reason is that there is little political weight behind developing large-scale, economical approaches to controlling populations of commonly hunted game animals. On that note, in 2013 American researcher Allen Rutberg suggested that stakeholder groups and government agencies were actively discouraging research on deer contraception in order to keep hunting and deer management "synonymous" in the public eye (Rutberg, 2013, p. S40). On the other hand, by 2013 a long-term study using the PZP antigen in African elephants (*Loxodonta africana*) had proven effective in limiting the population of one South African reserve, and without the adverse effects on behavior and social structure that had been observed in earlier approaches (Druce et al., 2011). The elephant program is expensive, but current public opinion supports it as a non-lethal alternative for this 'charismatic' species. We conclude that for the near future, contraception will not be an effective and economical alternative for more widespread and less 'charismatic' species such as white-tailed deer. Contraception may be used in suburban areas or parks where hunting will not be tolerated, but it will not replace hunting for such a species in the large majority of its range.[10]

We believe, however, that a sentientist need not call for the abolition of hunting as a means of wildlife population control. In particular, utilitarian sentientists like Singer could base an argument for lethal

---

[10] As Rutberg himself puts it: "No one, except for hard-core hunting opponents, is suggesting contraception to control deer in the Wyoming hills; there, the values consensus for deer as usable wildlife remains largely intact. Nor are many proposing the use of contraception to control grey kangaroos (*Marcropus giganteus*) in the Australian outback, which are killed on a large scale for commercial purposes. Rather, contraception is advanced as a solution in the urban centers and their suburban fringes where the status of deer and kangaroos is ambiguous and contested" (Rutberg, 2013, p. S42).

population control of some wildlife species on Leopold's analysis of the Kaibab and Wisconsin irruptions in Figure 8.1. Note that in both of Leopold's diagrams, the carrying capacity of the deer range is represented as being reduced significantly as a result of an overpopulation event. This means that if the overshoot of carrying capacity had been avoided, then a larger number of healthy deer could have lived on the range into the future. If the object is the utilitarian goal of maximizing the aggregate happiness of deer on the range, then the deaths of deer eliminated to preserve carrying capacity could be more than outweighed by the larger population that culling would allow in the future.

Designing the cull so that unnecessary suffering is minimized would further improve the picture in utilitarian terms. Perhaps ironically, this could be done by reducing the 'sporting' aspect of hunting. For instance, the use of bait stations is generally regarded as unsportsmanlike hunting, but to the extent that bait stations near blinds make it easier for hunters to kill deer quickly and cleanly with a single shot, that would minimize associated suffering and improve the cull from a utilitarian perspective.

What about from an animal *rights* perspective? The response we've just imagined to this first charge hinges on the aggregative, utilitarian approach to ethical thinking championed by Peter Singer. But remember that Tom Regan characterizes moral rights as 'trump cards' against such utilitarian reasoning. And this is precisely why Regan himself seems to oppose all hunting of overpopulated animals:

> Put affirmatively, the goal of wildlife managers should be to defend wild animals in the possession of their rights, providing them with the opportunity to live their own life, by their own lights, as best they can, spared that human predation that goes by the name of "sport." ... If, in reply we are told that [this] will not minimize the total amount of suffering wild animals will suffer over time, our reply should be that this cannot be the overarching goal of wildlife management, once we take the rights of animals seriously.
>
> *(Regan, 1983, p. 357)*

Here Regan emphasizes that the rationale for controlling wildlife populations by hunting is utilitarian, and that if the animals have rights, then we can't justify killing them on utilitarian grounds.

If a sentientist who endorses moral rights for animals cannot endorse using hunting to prevent overpopulation on the grounds that it maximizes the aggregate happiness of the herd by maintaining long-term carrying capacity, there may still be ways that a rights-based sentientist could endorse hunting under such circumstances, however. One way is by questioning the assumption that there is a moral difference between killing and knowingly allowing avoidable deaths. It is widely believed that the act of killing (actively causing someone's death) is morally worse than knowingly allowing an avoidable death. This belief appears to be behind common intuitions about medical ethics and giving to international aid programs. Doctors who don't condone active euthanasia or physician-assisted suicide – both of which could be construed as killing – sometimes knowingly allow the death of a patient whose life could be prolonged by starting a medical intervention like artificial respiration.

Regan's rights view reflects this widely shared intuition insofar as he resists applying his worse-off principle to situations like Leopold described on the Kaibab and in Wisconsin. As a rights theorist, he articulates the relative significance of killing by denying that we violate the rights of deer who die because we do not cull to prevent overpopulation (Regan, 1983, p. 357). Note that if Regan instead agreed that our knowingly allowing preventable deaths violates the rights of the animals that die as a result, then his mini-ride principle could imply that we should cull. This can be illustrated using situation C in Box 8.1, by assuming that each of the '-10's under option #2 represents the death of a deer during the period of time that the herd overshoots its carrying capacity and as a result reduces future carry capacity, and that each of the '-10's under option #1 represents the death of a deer during the same period of years if we prevent the overshoot of carrying capacity. That is, assuming that fewer deer die when the overpopulation event is prevented than when it is allowed to occur, then if allowed-but-preventable deaths violate the animals' rights, then the mini-ride principle calls for culling in such a situation.

So although Regan himself does not endorse hunting to prevent more deaths from starvation, a rights-based sentientist could endorse it, e.g. by holding moral agents accountable for rights violations when they knowing allow preventable deaths, as well as when they actively kill individuals.[11] How plausible a rights-based sentientist can make her reply to the first charge is a topic of ongoing debate, as is the plausibility of the utilitarian response that we described above.

In addition, there are many complications beyond what has been discussed in this brief subsection. For instance, species differ widely with regard to how quickly their populations expand and contract, and with regard to how likely overpopulation events are to degrade the carrying capacity of their ranges. Our goal in this subsection has only been to emphasize that it would be premature to dismiss sentientist approaches to ethics as a guide to environmental policy based solely on the claim that they cannot support hunting in situations where wildlife overpopulation threatens ecosystem carrying capacity.[12] Of course, ecosystems support diverse populations of animals other than the 'target' species, and we will have something to say about this complication in Section 8.6.3. First, however, we briefly discuss the charge that sentientists somehow undervalue members of endangered species.

8.6.2 Sentientism and the Value of Members of Endangered Species

We noted that in his famous "Triangular Affair" paper, Callicott articulated this practical charge against sentientism in two different ways:

---

[11] We note that while utilitarians commonly question the legitimacy of the moral distinction between killing and letting die, rights theorists more often maintain that there is a significant moral difference. For an overview of positions on doing vs. allowing harm, see Howard-Snyder (2011).

[12] For more on such complications and a particularly sympathetic treatment of sentientists' ability to respond to this first charge, see Varner (2011).

(3A) Nonsentient organisms have no moral standing according to sentientism, and therefore "humane herdspersons" might allow sheep to graze on plants that are "overwhelmingly important to the stability, integrity, and beauty of biotic communities."

(Callicott, 1980, p 320)

(3B) Additionally, while environmentalists place special value on members of endangered species, from an animal liberation perspective individuals with similar levels of sentience are of equivalent value, even if one is a member of an endangered species while the other's species is plentiful.

(Callicott, 1980, pp. 326–327)

Regarding the first of these, if the plants in question were accurately described as "overwhelmingly important to the stability, integrity, and beauty of biotic communities," then they would have enormous *instrumental* value from a sentientist perspective. Of course, in Chapter 2 we critically assessed parallel arguments about humanity's dependence on biodiversity for ecosystem function and stability, and the same caveats would apply when discussing biodiversity's instrumental value for other sentient animals. But clearly the same strategy is open to a sentientist in response to charge (3A) above.

Charge (3B) is more philosophical in nature: here the objection to sentientism seems to be that it is a mistake not to attribute *more intrinsic value* to the lives of members of endangered species than to the lives of members of common species that are similarly sentient. So, for instance, the California condor (*Gymnogyps californianus*) is listed by the IUCN as critically endangered, while the turkey vulture (*Cathartes aura*) is a common, plentiful bird in North America. The species are both members of the New World vulture family *Cathartidae* and presumably the individuals of each species are similarly sentient – that is, equally capable of conscious suffering and enjoyment, with neither species distinguished from the other in terms of cognitive capacities that sentientists might value differentially as described in Section 7.4. The environmentalist's objection to sentientism seems to be that the rarity of individuals from a given species augments the intrinsic value of members of that species.

When understood as such a philosophical claim about intrinsic value, many sentientists feel it unnecessary to respond to this objection. In his famous essay, Callicott expressed the objection by saying that the value of an individual "is inversely proportional to the population of the species," adding, provocatively: "Environmentalists, however reluctantly and painfully, do not omit to apply the same logic to their own kind" (Callicott, 1980, p. 326). To many people, such a claim about the value of human life seems highly counter-intuitive, and this is what sparked Luna Leopold's reaction to the 'pure holist' interpretation of his father's 'land ethic' that we described in Section 1.6.2 (and to which we will return in Section 10.2). As extensions of the traditional utilitarian and rights-based thinking about humans, animal welfarists and animal rightists have a similar response regarding the intrinsic value of individual animals' lives. In that vein, Regan reacted to Callicott's provocative statement of this objection by saying that such a view about the value of individual lives "might be fairly dubbed 'environmental facism'" (Regan, 1983, p. 362).

8.6.3 Sentientism and Large-scale Interventions in Natural Systems

Finally, what about charges #2 and #6: that sentientists should support removal of predators and other large-scale interventions in natural systems that environmentalists would find abhorrent? One reason for not removing predators, specifically, is suggested by a statement that Aldo Leopold made about wolves. As we described in Section 8.6.1, Leopold believed that the ecosystem-disrupting irruptions of deer on the Kaibab and in Wisconsin occurred after humans removed wolves from those ecosystems. He claimed that deer populations could only be precisely controlled by wolves:

> Hunting is a crude, slow, and inaccurate tool, which needs to be supplemented by a precision instrument. The natural aggregation

of lions and other predators on an overstocked range, and their natural dispersion from an understocked one, is the only precision instrument known to deer management.

(Quoted in Flader, 1974, p. 176)

Today, this claim seems too strong, because contemporary wildlife censusing techniques and zone-sensitive hunting permit systems allow wildlife managers to more precisely control the effects of human hunting. But having constant pressure from wolves can influence an ecosystem in ways that modern human hunting, which is typically sporadic (annual or semi-annual), cannot. And ecologists have known about predator–prey population cycles since at least the 1920s. Because predators cannot instantaneously adjust their numbers in the face of changing prey populations, time lags in predator responses are destabilizing to the predator–prey system as a whole (see, e.g., May, 1973).

The reintroduction of wolves (*Canis lupus*) to Yellowstone National Park in the 1990s has been held up as a striking illustration of the many subtle ways that natural predators like wolves influence their ecosystems. Wolves were locally extinct in the area by the mid-1920s. Without the pressure of wolf predation, the area's elk (*Cervus canadensis*) population increased dramatically, so that by 1960 it was about twice the estimated carrying capacity of the range (Leopold et al., 1963, p. 40).[13] By the time wolves were reintroduced to the park in

---

[13] This led Park Service personnel to conduct a highly controversial cull of 4,283 elk during the winter of 1961–1962. A special advisory board to the Secretary of the Interior was appointed to recommend strategies in a report titled "Wildlife Management in the National Parks," but under the influence of the board's chair, A. Starker Leopold – one of Aldo Leopold's sons – the report made more sweeping recommendations that have played an important role in debates over the management of US national parks ever since. The board found that the Park Service had been justified in removing upwards of 50% of the herd, because such a population reduction was necessary to stop degradation of the park ecosystem, and sport hunting would have been both inconsistent with the basic mission of the national parks and unable to accomplish the needed reduction during autumn when elk are widely scattered in the park (Leopold et al., 1963, p. 40). More broadly, the so-called Leopold Report recommended an extensive program of research on ecological relationships within the parks, coupled with active management of park ecosystems aimed at restoring them to pre-Columbian conditions, including restoring locally extinct species of natural predators.

the mid-1990s, however, it was also clear that increased browsing by elk had had widespread, adverse effects on reproduction of several deciduous tree species, particularly aspen and willow. Since wolf reintroduction, a number of studies have documented these tree species' recovery, but the effects of wolf extirpation were much more widespread. For example, the affected tree species play a role in stabilizing riparian areas, and this is thought to have contributed to the return of beaver colonies in the area. Beaver in turn modify riparian areas in ways that affect the diversity and abundance of numerous species, including amphibians, reptiles, and fish. Furthermore, the return of willow trees has been correlated with increased richness and abundance of six songbird species that depend on them, and it has been suggested that scavenger birds (e.g. eagles, ravens, and magpies) may also be benefiting from wolf-killed carcasses (Ripple and Beschta, 2012, p. 211).

These 'cascading' effects of the wolf's reintroduction to Yellowstone illustrate how complex the effects of removing a predator from an ecosystem can be. From a sentientist perspective, the removal of the wolf might initially be portrayed as choosing to have fewer animals of one sentient species, the wolf, which could be compensated for by somewhat increasing the population of their prey, the elk. And the kinds of severe population irruptions of the elk could in principle be compensated for by regularly scheduled 'therapeutic hunts,' informed by modern censusing and using zone-sensitive permits. In order to ensure that this is the sole trade-off in sentientist terms, however, we would have to also make sure that the elk population was not inhibiting tree reproduction in the ways described above. For according to the assumption we made in Section 8.3, the animals mentioned in the preceding paragraph that benefited from wolf reintroduction – beaver, birds, fish, and herpetofauna (reptiles and amphibians) – are all sentient; and this means that in removing wolves from an ecosystem, one may also be unintentionally reducing the numbers of many species of sentient animals.

Sentientists commonly cite such unintended side effects as a reason for avoiding large interventions in natural ecosystems. For instance, Singer says:

> I would not, in principle, rule out the idea that we should intervene in nature to reduce the suffering of animals, but our record of interfering in ecological systems is not good. Unless we have reason to think that we can reduce animal suffering not only in the immediate instance in front of us, but over the long term, we should not be doing it.
>
> *(Singer, 2009, p. 461)*

Here, he assumes that we will agree that human interventions in natural systems commonly have unanticipated side effects, and his argument is that interventions designed to reduce the suffering of wild animals are for this reason likely to backfire by ultimately causing more suffering rather than less. But Singer also suggests that in devoting resources to such interventions in natural ecosystems, we are also making a questionable trade-off. For "Where the lives of both humans and animals are at risk, we may do more good by helping the humans" (Singer, 2009, p. 461); that is, given that society has limited resources to devote to improving the lot of sentient animals, until the suffering of *human* animals is addressed better than it presently is, a greater reduction in aggregate suffering would be achieved by devoting resources to reducing human suffering. Implicit in this argument is the common sentientist claim, discussed in Sections 7.3 and 8.3, that although both humans and all sentient animals have moral considerability, human lives generally have greater moral *significance* than those of other sentient animals.

A variation on this trade-offs-based response is found in philosopher Steve Sapontzis' (1987) *Morals, Reason, and Animals*. Instead of pointing to the trade-off between devoting resources to reducing the suffering of wild animals and reducing the suffering of humans, however, Sapontzis points to the trade-off between devoting resources to reducing the suffering of *domesticated animals* rather than that of *wild* ones. He argues that:

other than by preventing predation by animals under our control (e.g. pets), it seems likely that for the foreseeable future, animal rights activists will do better by directing their organized efforts on behalf of animals toward alleviating the unjustified suffering humans cause animals than by attempting to prevent predation among animals.

(Sapontzis, 1987, p. 247)

That is, humans exercise extensive and very predictable control over the conditions in which animals live on farms, in research laboratories, etc., whereas interventions on behalf of wild animals involve all kinds of factors beyond our precise control (as illustrated by the Yellowstone wolf example). So, while leaving open the possibility that more effective, precise control over the lives of wild animals will someday be possible, Sapontzis argues that, at present, far more suffering among non-human animals could be alleviated by devoting available resources to addressing issues associated with domesticated animals rather than wild ones.

A markedly different response is suggested by an aspect of Regan's rights view that was discussed at the end of Section 8.6.1. There, we emphasized that Regan holds that we do not violate animals' rights when we let nature take its course, but only when we actively intervene. Similarly, he holds that non-human predators do not violate the rights of animals that they kill, because they are not moral agents like us (Regan, 1983, p. 96 and section 5.2). So Regan could consistently hold that interventions on behalf of wild animals that appear to improve their welfare are just not called for under his rights-based version of sentientism. As he put it in a passage we quoted earlier, "minimiz[ing] the total amount of suffering wild animals suffer over time ... cannot be the overarching goal of wildlife management, once we take the rights of animals seriously" (Regan, 1983, p. 357). In this regard, remember that Regan does not attribute specific kinds of rights such as *claim* rights to animals the way many theorists of human rights attribute them to humans.

The adequacy of the responses that we have considered to the charge that sentientists should support large-scale interventions in natural ecosystems that environmentalists would abhor is an active area of debate among animal ethicists and environmental philosophers. In this subsection, our aim has again been only to emphasize that sentientists have various ways of responding to the charges commonly lodged against them by environmentalists.

8.7   BIOCENTRIC INDIVIDUALISM AND ENVIRONMENTAL ETHICS

In this chapter, we have focused on sentientism as an 'extensionist' approach to environmental ethics, and another example of extensionism is biocentric individualism. As defined in Chapter 1, this is the view that all individual living organisms have intrinsic value, but not ecosystems or species per se. Of the four categories of environmental ethic defined in Section 1.6.2, biocentric individualism has been the minority view for three reasons.

First, environmental philosophers have questioned whether biocentric individualists can adequately account for the special value of endangered species. Second, and more fundamentally, the sheer number of non-conscious organisms that surround us makes this view more challenging to defend than the more modest expansions of the moral community that sentientist views advocate. In Section 8.3 and Section 8.4, we emphasized how sentientist views use the method of reflective equilibrium to argue that other conscious animals have some kind of intrinsic moral value, and in the case of the most widely discussed versions of sentientism, this value is expressed in terms of avoiding suffering or getting satisfactions of various kinds. Biocentric individualism calls for a much more radical extension, to *all living organisms*, whether sentient or not, and a primary philosophical challenge for biocentric individualists is how to defend the claim that all of the non-conscious organisms that surround us have intrinsic value. As described in Section 8.3 and Section 8.4, traditional versions of utilitarianism and rights views can readily be extended to include conscious animals, but those theories share a commitment to the intrinsic value of individuals' conscious experiences.

Third, a related challenge for a biocentric individualist is to defend principles of relative moral significance that somehow justify a conscious organism like one of us in living at the expense of literally *billions* of other organisms. In a famous early example of biocentric individualism, philosopher and medical doctor Albert Schweitzer [1875–1965] was content to say that "Whenever I in any way sacrifice or injure life, I am not within the sphere of the ethical" (Schweitzer, 1955, p. 325), but contemporary biocentric individualists have defended various principles that would justify our existence at the expense of so many non-conscious organisms. Examples of some detailed attempts to address these three challenges can be found in Paul Taylor's *Respect for Nature* (1986), Gary Varner's *In Nature's Interests?* (1998), and Nicolas Agar's *Life's Intrinsic Value* (2001).

8.8 BEYOND 'THE CLASSICAL MODERNIST PARADIGM'?

Precisely because the tactic of expanding the realm of intrinsic value to larger and larger sets of individual organisms leads to the diverse philosophical and practical challenges that are raised against sentientism and biocentric individualism, many environmental philosophers have called for abandoning what is sometimes called 'the classical modernist paradigm' of ethics. The label is due to Kenneth Goodpaster and has been used by J. Baird Callicott to characterize how he thinks that the ecoholism of Aldo Leopold diverges from extensionist thinking about ethics as discussed in this chapter. Before turning to Callicott's interpretation of Leopold, however, in the next chapter we describe attempts to use the extensionist strategy to argue that environmental wholes such as species and ecosystems have intrinsic value or some kind of moral standing.

8.9 FURTHER READING

Varner, Gary. 2011. "Environmental Ethics, Hunting, and the Place of Animals." In Tom L. Beauchamp and R.G. Frey, eds., *The Oxford Handbook of Animal Ethics* (New York: Oxford University Press), pp. 855–876.

9 Ecoholism: Do Ecological Wholes Have Intrinsic Value?

9.1 INTRODUCTION

In this chapter we begin to examine the claim of many environmentalists that ecological wholes – things like species and ecosystems – have intrinsic value, a view called 'ecoholism.' This position is often expressed along the lines of the following quote from the Norfolk Biodiversity Partnership[1]: "Biodiversity has intrinsic value, and many people argue that all species have the right to exist." Is this true? If so, it provides a powerful reason for conserving biodiversity because it says nothing about the usefulness of biodiversity. If someone or something has *intrinsic moral* value, then there are constraints on the way that we (moral agents) may behave toward it, regardless of whether or not it is useful to us. This is a *very* different claim than the ones that were investigated in the first part of this book. Those claims, which appealed to *instrumental* values, could be evaluated according to data: Does the available evidence in fact suggest that biodiversity conservation is instrumental in achieving some desired goal? Claims of intrinsic value, by contrast, must be evaluated in light of the philosophical methods we examined in Chapter 7. All claims require a defense. It's not enough to simply assert that ecosystems have intrinsic value; one has to offer a defense if such a statement is to be taken seriously. In this chapter we discuss approaches to defending the claim that species and ecosystems have intrinsic value.

In Section 9.3 we will examine the *extensionist* approach that we referred to briefly at the end of the preceding chapter. This approach to ecoholism argues for extending something like the notion

[1] http://bit.ly/2cdaJpV

of interests or welfare/well-being from individual organisms to holistic entities like ecosystems and species. As we will see, it is very difficult to defend ecoholism via this extensionist approach.

In Chapter 10 we will examine an alternative to the extensionist approach to defending ecoholism. This alternative approach has been presented by philosopher J. Baird Callicott as rejecting the extensionist approach that we discuss in this chapter in favor of a 'communitarian' approach to ethics. Callicott has presented this alternative approach to justifying ecoholism as an interpretation of ecologist Aldo Leopold's famous 'land ethic,' and Callicott's writings on Leopold have been both widely discussed by philosophers and widely read by scientists.

9.2   SOME NON-STARTERS AND COMMON PROBLEMS

Before we begin our discussion of the extensionist approach to ecoholism, however, we first need to address some moves that are regularly attempted by people trying to defend ecoholism. We argue that these moves should be rejected as non-starters, because they either commit a logical fallacy (the naturalistic fallacy, the fallacy of composition, or an origin fallacy), they slip back and forth between holism and reductionism, or they rely on rarity per se.

9.2.1   *The Naturalistic Fallacy and Specifying What Is 'Natural'*

As we noted in Section 1.4.2, a preference for 'natural' over modified habitats is an important plank in the environmentalist agenda, but when one attempts to assign moral significance to a state of the environment because it is the 'natural state', one is in danger of committing the naturalistic fallacy. The naturalistic fallacy is committed when one attempts to assign moral significance to the 'natural state' of the environment. Sometimes the appeal to nature as normative is obvious, other times less so. Consider this use of the move from David Ehrenfeld's (1978) book *The Arrogance of Humanism*:

> This non-humanistic value of communities and species is the
> simplest of all to state: they should be conserved because they exist
> and because this existence is itself but the present expression of a
> continuing historical process of immense antiquity and majesty.
> Long standing existence in Nature is deemed to carry with it the
> unimpeachable right to continued existence.
>
> *(pp. 207–208)*

From the observation that a species has continued to exist and its current existence results from a long historical process, Ehrenfeld derives an ethical conclusion that the species *ought* to continue to exist and that we (moral agents) have some obligation to ensure that it does.[2]

The term 'naturalistic fallacy' is sometimes used as a catchphrase for several related problems and issues. The first is called the is–ought gap. This problem arguably dates back to Plato's consideration of the idea that 'might makes right' in *The Republic*. The is–ought gap was given its more contemporary formulation in the mid-1700s by Scottish philosopher David Hume [1711–1776]. It is the position that it is not possible to derive an 'ought statement' solely from 'is statements' – i.e. that statements about what *is* the case do not logically entail statements about what *ought* to be the case. Related to Hume's is–ought gap is English philosopher George Edward Moore's [1873–1958] 'open question.' In the early 1900s, Moore described this as the problem of defining a moral quality like 'goodness' in terms of a natural quality. He argued that any attempt to equate morality with a set of natural properties X will always fail, because the question "*Why* is X good?" is left open by any such definition. Moore went on to specifically define the 'naturalistic fallacy' as an attempt to equate morality with naturalism, which is the position that moral value can be equated with some set of natural properties. This is a fertile area for discussion, but is beyond the scope of

---

[2] In deontological ethics (above, and see Section 8.4), certain types of moral rights are viewed as generating moral duties on the part of moral agents. In these cases, rights and duties can be seen as different sides of the same coin. We think it is this sort of 'right' that Ehrenfeld is claiming for a species' right to continued existence.

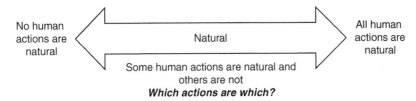

FIGURE 9.1 How do human activities fit with nature?

this book. For now, we will simply say that just because an ecosystem has properties **A, B, C, . . ., N** when the system is not influenced by human beings, we cannot validly infer that that ecosystem *ought* to have properties **A, B, C, . . ., N**. Those properties (and/or others) might be our *preferences*, but they are not our moral imperatives.

There are various active philosophical research programs aimed at closing the is–ought gap, or answering Moore's open question. But even supposing that these problems could be satisfactorily overcome, ecoholism faces a rather serious unresolved conceptual issue regarding the role of human beings in nature. Many environmentalists view a state of nature without human beings (sometimes called 'pristine') as intrinsically valuable. On this view, the standard of nature to which we ought to aspire is one untouched by human hands. But there is a problem with this claim, in that we have a fairly poor understanding of what 'nature' means. Our confusion about what nature means can be seen in our understanding of the relationship between humans and nature. Figure 9.1 illustrates the conceptual problem.

At one end of this spectrum is the position that all human actions are natural.[3] This view sees everything that operates within the laws of nature as 'natural.' Whatever humans do, we do in conformity with the laws of nature. Of course, if this extreme view were

---

[3] In an essay titled "Can and Ought We to Follow Nature?" Holmes Rolston III (1979) refers to this end of the spectrum as the "absolute sense" of following nature. The other end of the spectrum he refers to as the "artefactual sense" of following nature, and all of the possibilities in between these two ends he refers to as the "relative sense" of following nature. Rolston distinguishes the relative sense into four specific types of relative sense: the homeostatic sense, the imitative ethical sense, the axiological sense, and the tutorial sense.

widely understood to be correct, then all ecosystems are pristine in this sense. This seems a fairly trivial sense of the meaning of the word 'natural.' It is saying that only supernatural things are not natural. At the other end of this spectrum is the idea that humans alter the course of nature, and that our mental capacities in some sense exempt us from some of the forces of nature. This position is the view that when we act with deliberate intent, we are subverting nature and so all of these actions are unnatural. The problem with this view is that, if true, even actions that are intended to 'help nature' – such as conservation efforts, habitat restoration, etc. – are unnatural, and so if 'unnatural' is understood normatively, to imply that some action is wrong, then we *ought not* do these things. A third view, intermediate between the previous two, would be that not all deliberate actions are unnatural, only those that in some sense are not 'in accordance with nature'; that is, when we work *with* nature, our actions are natural, but when we work *against* nature, our actions are not natural. That is all well and good, but absent a rational, non-arbitrary way of distinguishing *which* of our actions work with nature, and which work against nature, this middle position does not really help us to categorize our actions. How much human influence, and what type of influence, can an ecosystem have before it is said to be unnatural? There are few, if any, ecosystems on Earth that humans have not influenced in at least some minor way.[4] In "Can and Ought We to Follow Nature?" Holmes Rolston III (1979, p. 28) sums it up thus:

> I am forced, of course, to concede that there are gaps in this account of nature. I do not find nature meaningful everywhere, or beautiful, or valuable, or educational; and I am moved to horror by malaria, intestinal parasites, and genetic deformities. My concept of the good is not coextensive with the natural, but it does greatly overlap it; and I find my estimates steadily enlarging that overlap.

---

[4] Subglacial lakes in Antarctica seem like good candidates for the title 'completely pristine' since they formed and have been isolated from the remainder of Earth's ecosystems longer than the species *Homo sapiens* has existed.

So, the conceptual problem for ecoholists is to give a non-arbitrary account of how we are to understand which of our actions are natural and which are not. Absent such an account, it is difficult to see how anyone can treat nature as a normative concept.

The problems discussed in this subsection may not be beyond the wit of environmentalists to resolve, but such solutions will require deep engagement and extensive critical thinking. As environmentalists, we do ourselves no favors by playing the naturalism card without recognizing the challenges involved.

9.2.2 The Fallacy of Composition

The fallacy of composition is a logical fallacy. It occurs when a characteristic that is observed in the parts of a whole is attributed to the whole itself. When thinking about ecoholism, it is tempting to point to arguments that have been offered by sentientists and/or biocentric individualists for the intrinsic value of individual organisms and argue that biological wholes like species and ecosystems have intrinsic value because they are made up of intrinsically valuable individuals. The argument seems to be this:

Premise 1:   Individual plants and animals have intrinsic value.
Premise 2:   Ecosystems are collections of individual plants and animals.
Conclusion: Therefore ecosystems also have intrinsic value.

There are times when a whole has a property because its parts have that property, but this is not always true, for obviously the following is a fallacious argument:

Premise 1:   Atoms are not visible with the naked eye.
Premise 2:   Blades of grass are collections of atoms.
Conclusion: Therefore blades of grass are not visible with the naked eye.

So from the fact that many, most, or even all of a collection's parts have a certain property, it does not follow, logically speaking, that the collection has that same property. It may be true that a lawn looks green because the individual blades of grass are all green, but that follows from additional facts about light, vision, and human color perception that don't apply at the atomic level. An explanation of why lawns look green would be incomplete without an explanation of why/how the blades' looking green ensures that the lawn looks green. By the same token, someone who attributes intrinsic value to a collection of organisms such as a species or an ecosystem owes us an argument about why/how its constituent individual organisms having intrinsic value ensures the whole's having intrinsic value.

9.2.3   Origin Fallacies

There are two related kinds of origin fallacy that sometimes arise in discussions about ecoholism. Both fallacies appeal to the idea that ecological wholes (species or ecosystems) somehow 'give rise' to individual organisms. Both fallacies are committed by the following argument:

Premise 1:   Individual organisms have intrinsic value.

Premise 2:   Individual organisms can only exist if the species (ecosystem) exists.

Conclusion: Therefore species (ecosystems) have intrinsic value because they give rise to individuals that have intrinsic value.

The first and most obvious fallacy committed by this line of reasoning is often described as the 'genetic' fallacy. The fact that some process gave rise to a morally good or bad outcome does not make that process morally good or bad. For example, let's agree that the dropping of atomic bombs on Japan during World War II was a morally bad outcome. Research on nuclear physics 'gave rise' to this outcome. It does not follow that research on nuclear physics is morally bad.

But there is a second, perhaps less obvious fallacy in this line of reasoning: it assumes that species or ecosystems 'give rise' in some sense to organisms. It is especially hard to see how a species could be considered to have this causal capacity. Species are usually thought of as sets or classes that contain individual organisms as their members. It is a straightforward error to suppose that a set (of any kind) gives rise to its members. Individual organisms beget other organisms. They are not somehow forged into existence by the category to which they belong. It is slightly more comprehensible to say that an ecosystem 'gives rise' to individual organisms. This is because most individual organisms cannot produce all the energy and nutrients required for their survival. Instead, they rely on the products of other organisms. In this sense their existence depends on the ecosystem to which they belong. But to argue that an ecosystem has intrinsic value from the fact that it in this way gives rise to individual organisms that have intrinsic value is to commit the genetic fallacy.

As with the fallacy of composition, the genetic fallacy is a reminder to us that any demonstration that biodiversity has intrinsic value must rest on the characteristics of biodiversity, and not on the characteristics of individual organisms. That these ecological wholes are useful or necessary for the continued existence of the individual organism demonstrates only that they are *instrumentally valuable*, not that they are *intrinsically valuable*.

9.2.4 Holism and Reductionism 'Slippage'

In arguments about ecoholism, one has to watch out for slippage between two independent claims: (1) that ecological wholes such as species or ecosystems have intrinsic value, and (2) that individual organisms (maybe just sentient organisms) have intrinsic value. It is not uncommon for defenses of ecoholism to slip back to the level of the individual, often without acknowledgment. This seems to be particularly common when the topic involves what is 'good' or 'bad' for the ecological whole in question. For example, imagine an oil spill in a local lake. Is that bad for the lake? Individuals of some species will do better either because they are more tolerant of oil pollution, or because their competitors, predators, diseases, etc., are particularly vulnerable to oil pollution. The temptation is to add up the individuals affected negatively and compare this to the individuals affected positively. This is not a truly *holist* view, however, for it reduces what is good for the lake to the sum (aggregate) of what is good for the individuals. For the same reason that arguments fail when they commit the fallacy of composition and the genetic fallacy, so too does this approach. For something (e.g. an oil spill) to be good or bad for a lake, it has to be beneficial or detrimental to the lake per se. We would have to evaluate our moral obligations (assuming we have any) to individuals *and* ecological wholes, and these obligations might very well conflict. Indeed, if ecoholism is to be believed, we might well be obligated to do something for the good of the lake that is clearly detrimental to many of the individuals that reside in the lake.

9.2.5   Rarity Per Se

Environmentalists commonly claim that *rare* species and/or ecosystems are more valuable (i.e. have more *intrinsic* value) than common ecological wholes. It is not difficult to imagine circumstances in which rare species or ecosystems are more *valuable to us* than common ones, but it is much more difficult to see how this can be the case for intrinsic value.

A related problem for some versions of ecoholism is that rarity is not a property of *species* in the first place. It is generally acknowledged that every species is unique. In fact, this is part of the reason why environmentalists abhor extinction: when a species disappears, it is gone for good. It follows from their uniqueness that no one species is more or less rare than any other. The sentence "Riverine rabbits (*Bunolagus monticularis*) are rare" doesn't describe a property of the species, per se. Rather, it refers to the abundance of individual members within this species. This matters, because ecoholists argue that species can possess intrinsic value above and beyond the value of their members. But if rarity is a property of individuals, not species, then rarity cannot enhance the intrinsic value of a species whose members are rare.

A further problem arises from the fact that rarity per se is not usually considered a morally relevant property in its own right. According to English philosopher Alastair Gunn [1946–2011], rarity is an intensifier of value (1984). Rare paintings are not valuable because they are rare; they are valuable, and their rarity intensifies that value (see Gunn, 1980, for further discussion). Rarity intensifies, for both the better and the worse. Encountering a Riverine rabbit is rare, and presumably good, but encountering small pox is also rare, and we probably don't value that. Yet the rareness of the encounter with the Riverine rabbit intensifies our reaction to it. And ideally we would prefer it if the Riverine rabbit were not rare; we allegedly value their continued existence, which suggests we value their *commonness*. As Gunn summarizes (1980, p. 34):

> To the extent that having rights, or having value, depends on the possession of certain qualities, rarity cannot be the basis for special claims of right or ascriptions of value, because rarity is not a quality.

9.3   EXTENSIONIST DEFENSES OF ECOHOLISM

With our survey of some moves that we believe should be rejected as non-starters for various reasons complete, we take up the extensionist approach that was referred to briefly at the end of the preceding chapter. We emphasize this approach as much as we do here, because we think that many environmentalists find it intuitively appealing.

In Chapter 8, we discussed in detail philosophers' attempts to extend moral considerability from humans to sentient animals by arguing that various psychological states that make human lives intrinsically valuable are also found in various animals. We ended that chapter by briefly describing how biocentric individualists attempt to extend moral consideration to individual, non-sentient living organisms. They do so by arguing for the moral significance of 'biological interests' that are based in the needs or natural tendencies of all living organisms (sentient or not). One approach to ecoholism is to make an analogous move with regard to ecosystems and/or species, and so, in the next subsection, we say more about the challenges facing biocentric individualist positions.

9.3.1 Problems for Biocentric Individualism

A good way to begin is by discussing one reason why biocentric individualism is a minority position in environmental ethics. In Section 8.7 we said that extensionist arguments for the moral considerability of non-conscious organisms are less persuasive than sentientist arguments for extending moral consideration to sentient animals, but we didn't say *why*. A main reason has to do with the distinction between pleasures and desires on the one hand, and needs on the other.

Utilitarians have traditionally defined the 'happiness' that they are committed to maximizing either in terms of getting pleasure and avoiding pain (this is referred to as a *hedonistic* conception of happiness), or in terms of some kind of harmonious satisfaction of one's 'desires,' broadly construed (this is referred to as a *preference* conception of happiness). In this broad sense, the term 'desires' denotes what are variously referred to as 'wants,' 'likes,' 'preferences,' 'plans,' 'projects,' etc. Deontologists, too, have commonly emphasized desires broadly construed in describing what it is that individuals have rights to and/or how individuals exercise their autonomy.[5] For these reasons, the utilitarian and deontological approaches to ethics can be extended to recognize sentient animals as morally considerable: all one has to do is show that certain animals have some of these familiar mental states. People are easily convinced that – at least other things being equal – conscious experiences of desire satisfaction add value to a life, while conscious experiences of pain detract from the value of a life. And it is plausible, given our common phylogenetic ancestry and shared neural architectures, that other animals besides humans also have these experiences.

---

[5] Although we do not discuss them in this book, some deontologists as well as some consequentialists endorse 'objective list' views of well-being, according to which what is good for an individual in various ways is independent of what they in fact desire.

This relatively easy argument isn't open to the defender of bio-centric individualism, however, who needs to argue for the intrinsic value of organisms that are, presumably, *non-sentient*, including invertebrates as well as all organisms outside of the animal kingdom. (On the presumptive scope of sentience in the animal kingdom, see Section 8.3.) As we noted in Section 8.7, a common move made by biocentric individualists is to argue that all living organisms have what we might call *biological interests* that are based in the needs or natural tendencies that they have as living organisms. In this vein, various biocentric individualists argue that for individual organisms, these 'needs or natural interests' can be defined in terms of their species' evolutionary history.[6] Hereafter, we call these *evolved interests*. These interests of an organism of a given species are determined (at least in part) by the adaptations that its ancestors acquired as a result of natural selection. On such a view, most birds have an evolved interest in being able to fly and so do most winged insects, even though the former are sentient while the latter presumably are not; and on such a view, plants have evolved interests in getting certain amounts of carbon dioxide, water, etc., from their environments.

This argument for biocentric individualism appears to get some traction from the idea that *we* are members of a species with evolved interests. On the view just described, human beings have an evolved interest in (say) being able to move bipedally, in consuming vitamin C, in caring for our offspring, etc. Moreover, as authors favoring this kind of view often point out, various psychological capacities that we value morally are the product of our species' evolutionary history. These might include our capacity for empathy and cooperation, or the ability to anticipate the consequences of our actions. Such considerations have led a number of environmental philosophers to find plausible the claim that individual organisms' morally significant interests can be grounded in their evolved interests.[7]

---

[6] Examples include Goodpaster (1978), Taylor (1986), Varner (1998), and Agar (2001).

[7] Although note that such an argument leans strongly toward committing an origin fallacy (see Section 9.2.3).

However, this line of argument begins to look much less appealing once we take a closer look at the list of traits for which our ancestors have been selected. It is almost certain, for example, that humans were selected during the Upper Paleolithic to consume as much red meat as they were able to obtain. The physical evidence for this claim is found not only in the archeological record, where one sees a prevalence of technologies specialized for hunting, but also in our dental structure and our digestive systems. Indeed, cognitive anthropologist Terrance Deacon (1998) argues that the transition to a diet rich in meat facilitated rapid growth of the human brain, ultimately giving rise to a cooperative social system and the capacity for symbolic communication. Some of these claims are more controversial than others, but for the sake of argument, let's take them at face value. It should be clear that no such facts about our evolutionary history bear on the question of whether meat consumption is ethically justified. Meat consumption is certainly an evolved interest that we inherited from our ancestors, but the fact that this activity shaped many of our traits, even our psychology, does not suffice to show that it is a good thing, morally speaking, for modern humans to eat diets rich in meat.

The philosopher Jay Odenbaugh (2015) raises a similar objection to recent attempts to ground human ethical principles in biological interests. He points out that, like chimpanzees and other primates, our ancestors almost certainly engaged in war-like conflict, where other groups were decimated in the acquisition of resources. It is plausible that humans' disposition to xenophobia was favored by selection during this time. It would follow that xenophobia is an evolved interest for humans. But this would in no way provide an ethical justification for xenophobia and the actions that it often inspires. Although this topic deserves a more detailed analysis than we can provide here, it is generally considered a mistake to align ethically relevant interests with evolved biological interests.

Returning to the topic of ecoholism, this strategy of defining the morally relevant interests of species or ecosystems in terms of their evolved interests is problematic for an even more basic reason:

ecological wholes probably don't possess evolved interests in the first place. It is important to consider species and ecosystems separately here, because the reasons that they are thought to lack biological interests differ in the two cases. The important thing to keep in mind is that, on the view we are considering, in order for some entity **E** to have activity **F** as an evolved interest, the ancestors of **E** must have been naturally selected to **F**. Let us consider first why this requirement causes problems for species. In order for selection to act at a given level, entities at that level must possess heritable phenotypic differences that impact their likelihood of survival and reproduction. Without going into details, biologists recognize that genes, biological individuals, and sometimes groups of organisms satisfy these conditions (Sober and Wilson, 1998). But things start to get murky when it comes to species. What does it mean for one species to 'survive' or 'reproduce' more readily than another? Some propose that 'survival' at the species level can be defined as resistance to extinction. Likewise, species-level 'reproduction' can be defined as speciation (the splitting of one species into two). Hence, a given trait might conceivably be selected for at the species level if it contributes to one or both of these properties.

So it is at least logically coherent that species might possess evolved interests. The problem is that such traits are very unlikely to evolve. Species-level selection is considered a weak force for a very simple reason: the rate at which species 'reproduce' (speciate) is grindingly slow compared to the rate at which genes, individuals, and even groups replicate. So, consider some trait that might otherwise be favored by species-level selection. For example, it has been proposed that species with a large geographic range are more extinction-resistant and prone to speciation than species with small geographic ranges (Grantham, 1995). So, species-level selection might favor traits that increase geographic range, all things being equal. The problem is that there are several 'forces' that potentially derail this process, and which tend to be much more potent than species-level selection. One such force is random mutation. With each generation there is a likelihood that a mutation will occur in the genes that code for a given trait. Over time, those mutations accumulate, causing the trait to physically degrade. The only way to avoid degradation is when harmful mutations are purged by selection. However, speciation is thought to be a rare occurrence. So the period between species-level selection events tends to be very long. This means that any trait that happens to be favored only by species-level selection is in danger of being lost. A second opposing force is selection at lower levels. Suppose, for example, that increasing the geographical range of a species entails the expansion of the mating territory of each individual organism, but this expansion might be individually disadvantageous, perhaps because they increase the energetic costs of defense beyond the benefits gained (e.g. Schoener, 1983). In this case, selection at the individual level opposes selection at the species level. But since individual selection occurs every genera-tion, and speciation occurs only very rarely (perhaps thousands to millions of generations), most biologists view species-level selection as an exceptionally weak 'force' in nature. For the same reasons, species are not likely to possess evolved interests.

When it comes to ecosystems, it is not even clear what it would mean for such entities to possess an evolved interest (Lewontin, 1970). [8] Again, recall that an evolved interest is defined in relation to traits that are produced or maintained by natural selection at some level. Also recall that selection requires heritable traits that make a difference to fitness. It is hard to even imagine how an ecosystem might satisfy these conditions. Ecosystems do not form heritable linages, where the traits of some ancestor are passed on to descendants. Nor do entire ecosys-tems differ in their 'fitness' or reproductive potential (whatever that might mean). Hence, ecosystems cannot have evolved interests in the way that biological individuals do, because ecosystems are not proper units of selection.

---

[8] For an historical perspective on this subject, see Joel Hagen's *An Entangled Bank: The Origins of Ecosystem Ecology* (1992, Rutgers University Press) particularly chapter 8: Evolutionary Heresies.

Perhaps the ecoholist might opt for an even weaker sense of 'interest.' They might, for instance, define an 'existential interest' as some property that an entity requires in order to continue existing in a particular form. For example, suppose that you construct a toy house out of Lego blocks. Removing or modifying too many individual blocks eventually disrupts the form of that entity until it no longer exists as a toy house. In this (attenuated) sense, the house has an 'interest' in remaining intact because its existence as a house depends on it. We do not endorse this view, but for the sake of argument, suppose that some kind of existential interest could be legitimately assigned to ecosystems. Then, as Elliott Sober noted in his essay "Philosophical Problems for Environmentalism," ecosystems will have interests, "but only in the sense that automobiles, garbage dumps, and buildings do too" (Sober, 1986, p. 184). In other words, this claim simply puts off the question of which sorts of existential interest matter, morally speaking. Presumably no one would say that merely needing something in order to avoid going out of existence defines an 'interest' in any morally significant sense.

In the following subsection we explore in greater detail how ecoholists pursuing this extensionist strategy sometimes describe the 'needs' or 'interests' of ecosystems and the problems that arise from such attempts to define the good of an ecosystem.

9.3.2 Problems with the Intrinsic Value of Ecosystems and Species

As we said in the previous subsection, for ecological wholes to have interests in a morally relevant sense, the ecoholist must both (1) identify interests that belong to *the ecosystem* or *species*, rather than the individual organisms that comprise them, and (2) explain why the satisfaction of those interests is good from a moral point of view. We have explored a variety of theoretical reasons for thinking that species rarely satisfy (1), and that ecosystems never do. These arguments were based on the same notion of an evolved interest that biocentric individualists have employed in their writings. For argument's sake, we now set aside these theoretical concerns and look more closely at a specific kind of interest that environmentalists often assign to ecosystems, namely, an interest in its 'health.'

Our first problem, and by no means a trivial one for the ecosystem health move, is that it involves the substantial ontological[9] premise that ecosystems are objectively real entities that exist in nature. This means that they can be "found and identified instead of being defined and delimited" (Jax, 2006, p. 243). Philosopher Robert Garcia, along with this book's co-author, ecologist Jonathan Newman, take up this question in their recent paper "Is it Possible to Care for Ecosystems?" (Garcia and Newman, 2016). Garcia and Newman note that this 'independent existence' claim runs into initial trouble in that there isn't a single agreed-upon definition of an ecosystem (see Jax, 2006, p. 246). Instead, there is a rich diversity of possible definitions, many of which are explicitly antirealist. That is, the authors of the concept expressly admit that the ecosystems they have in mind are merely useful mental constructs rather than mind-independent natural entities. For the minority of ecosystem concepts where the authors adopt an expressly realist stance, ecologist Kurt Jax notes that the realism claim overreaches the empirical evidence, and, in any case, is based on rather speculative metaphysical assumptions (Jax, 2007, p. 244). If ecosystems are not real physical entities, how can they be healthy or not? *What* is healthy or unhealthy? And if ecosystems are *arbitrary constructs*, what reason is there to suppose that it matters whether or not they are 'healthy,' assuming a non-arbitrary definition of health could be specified?

One might be tempted to dismiss this problem by arguing that ecosystems can be more or less healthy even if they are arbitrarily defined. The ecosystem would then have an *operational definition*. Let us grant this move for the sake of argument. The next hurdle is the definition of ecosystem health itself. What is it? Ecosystem health

---

[9] 'Ontology' is the study of 'being.' It is the study of what entities, or kinds of entities, exist in nature. P. Bricker, "Ontological Commitment," The Stanford Encyclopedia of Philosophy (Winter 2014 Edition), E.N. Zalta (ed.), http://stanford.io/2ekRpqw.

is an appealing concept, as it invokes thoughts of human health, for which we have an intuitive understanding of what it means to be 'healthy.' It sounds plausible to say that health is a morally good thing for a living organism. Hugh Lehman (2000, p. 309) put it like this:

> In general, health of a human being is a physiological and mental condition that, barring accidents, will enable the human being to live long, reproduce (with a suitable other person), and live well in a range of ways that are open to human beings to live ... Further, healthy humans can live largely free of pain ... Barring accident, the person will retain these capacities for extended periods of time falling within a normal range.

Translating this (or something like it) so that it is suitable for ecosystems, however, is fraught with difficulty, and we now turn our attention to this problem.

There exist many definitions of ecosystem health, some vague, some specific. Many of the facets or dimensions of ecosystem health included in these definitions have been discussed by others as important indicators, even when the term 'ecosystem health' has not explicitly been used. We should also point out that the concept is often controversial, no matter how it is defined. Nevertheless, let's look at some attempts to define the concept.[10]

Common characteristics of an *unhealthy* ecosystem are said to include: reduced energy throughput, reduced nutrient cycling, reduced capacity to cope with stress, or a reduced level of organization and complexity (Lehman, 2000). One classic definition posits that an ecosystem is healthy if it is stable and sustainable, i.e. "if it is active and maintains its organization and autonomy over time and is resilient to stress" (Costanza et al., 1992, p. 9). Some suggest that an appropriate measure of ecosystem health is the departure from some

---

[10] Some authors draw a distinction between the 'health' and the 'integrity' of ecosystems, but many of these authors define an ecosystem as having integrity when it is *both* healthy and retains its 'original' complement of species, so that an ecosystem with integrity is also healthy.

preferred, usually 'natural' state. Others suggest we can measure an ecosystem's health as the system's ability to continue to provide the kind of ecosystem services that we discussed in Chapter 2.

These definitions, and others like them, fall into two categories: (1) instrumental value, and (2) the 'naturalness' of particular ecological characteristics. The ability of the ecosystem to continue to provide ecosystem services, for example, speaks to its instrumental value for people, and is not an argument for ecosystems possessing independent interests and intrinsic value. It is merely a retreat to the arguments used in Part I of this book. As we noted in Chapter 6, such arguments provide support for the conservation of *some* species and ecosystems, but not all, and would seem to commit us to policies that are at odds with other parts of the environmentalist agenda.

The argument that the closer an ecosystem is to its natural state, the healthier it is, is vulnerable to two objections related to (a) the naturalistic fallacy, and (b) the arbitrary choice of the particular historic configuration. The naturalistic fallacy, as we explained in Section 9.2.1, is the fallacy of inferring from the bare fact that something *is* the case that it *ought* to be that way. The problem of historic configuration is this: Ecosystems change with time; they are neither created nor destroyed[11] (despite the common rhetoric in the environmental movement). If we think that an ecosystem's natural state has normative value, then what do we mean by its natural state? We might mean 'before modern man' (i.e. about 20,000 years ago). We might mean 'before *homo sapiens*' (about 200,000 years ago). Maybe we mean before the entire hominid lineage comes into existence (about 2,000,000 years ago). Suppose we were talking about the ecosystem(s) depicted in Leopold's *Sand County Almanac* (Leopold, 1949). Twenty thousand years ago, the area now known as the sand counties of Wisconsin were under a glacier; 200,000 years ago the sand counties were just

---

[11] Whether ecosystems can be 'created' or 'destroyed' depends first and foremost on whether one takes a realist or an antirealist stance toward their existence. If one takes a realist stance, then it depends on which of the several definitions one accepts. See Jax (2007) and Garcia and Newman (2016) for further discussion.

coming to the end of an interglacial period, but the flora and fauna of the ecosystem would have been very different than they are today. Whichever reference time we choose would be an arbitrary choice. Why not 2,000 years ago, or 200, or 20? Once again, if the choice is arbitrary, what reason is there to suppose that it is morally relevant? Let's set the sticky problem of the timeframe aside for a moment and turn our attention to the 'natural configuration' of the ecosystem.

What is the natural state or natural configuration of an ecosystem? Some have argued that the natural state is defined as either the pool size or magnitude of fluxes for energy and/or material in the system. For example, how much carbon is sequestered in the soil of some particular terrestrial ecosystem (pool size)? How rapidly is recalcitrant carbon metabolized in the soil (flux)? Ecologists Svenja Belaoussoff and Peter Kevan (2003, p. 2060), speaking specifically about ecosystem health, have argued that when species abundances within a functional group follow a log normal distribution[12], then the ecosystem is in its natural (healthy) state:

> Pollinator communities from fields unaffected by the insecticide showed a log normal distribution of diversity and abundance but those fields affected did not. This suggests that the former fields could be considered healthier than the latter, disturbed, fields. The diversity and abundance pattern of pollinator communities in insecticide sprayed fields became log normal (or healthy) after the use of insecticide ceased.

Such claims are vulnerable to objections that they commit the naturalistic fallacy (as we discussed in Section 9.2.1) or that whether or not these conditions hold, they are not morally relevant (recall the difference between evolved interests and morally significant interests that we raised earlier for the biocentric individualist). Here we want to explore one further objection: that the choice of the reference condition is arbitrary, and if it is arbitrary, so the argument goes, then deviations from

---

[12] This is referring to the statistical shape of the rank–abundance (also called species–abundance) curves such as that shown in Figure 2.6.

the reference condition are also arbitrary. For example, Belaoussoff and Kevan's claim is based on an ecosystem *at equilibrium*. Why that particular point in time? Why not some seral[13] stage of earlier succession? Log normality of the species–abundance relationship is only theoretically a property of a functional group (see Chapter 2). But the problem is that functional groups are not obviously identifiable groups. Belaoussoff and Kevan attempt to get around this problem by defining the functional group as the group of species whose species–abundance relationship is log normal, but admit that (a) the distribution might not be log normal because the functional group has been disturbed (the very thing they are trying to detect), or (b) that there can be situations in undisturbed ecosystems where the species–abundance distribution deviates from log normality. We can certainly see how an ecosystem in equilibrium might be a human preference as a preferred state of nature, but it is more difficult to see how ecosystems might have an interest in being in one particular configuration or another.

In order for us to argue that ecosystems have intrinsic value, we have to show that ecosystems have interests, independent of the interests of the individual organisms that comprise the ecosystem, and we have to show that those interests are morally relevant, which usually means that the ecosystem suffers if those interests are not respected. In this section we have given reasons to think that (i) it doesn't seem possible to define an ecosystem in a non-arbitrary way, and so even if we could show that ecosystems have independent interests, it's not clear *to what* those interests would attach. We then set aside the sticky problem of identity, and explored ecosystem health as a means of understanding what might interest an ecosystem. We provided reasons to think that (ii) such definitions are either merely assertions of instrumental value to humans,[14] or that

---

[13] 'Seral' or 'sere' is a term that means a stage of ecological succession.

[14] Note that it is entirely reasonable to define *ecosystem health* from an anthropocentric viewpoint, in any way that we like or find useful. Used in this way the term is unproblematic, and many people do use it this way. The objection that we are noting refers to attempts to make those definitions normative, or attempts to derive entirely non-anthropocentric definitions of the term.

characteristics asserted to be indicative of ecosystem health are either unsubstantiated examples of the naturalistic fallacy, or they are arbitrary and hence not examples of meaningful independent interests. Finally, we don't think that, even if all of these problems can be overcome, it will be possible to show that such interests are morally relevant, at least not when compared to the interests of clearly morally relevant human beings. As this book's co-author Gary Varner (1991) said:

> If it is plausible to say that ecosystems (or biotic communities as such) are directly morally considerable – and that is a very big *if* – it must be for a very different reason than is usually given for saying that individual human beings are directly morally considerable.
>
> *(p. 179)*

So perhaps ecosystems are the wrong ecological whole in which to locate intrinsic value. What about species?

It often comes as a surprise to non-biologists to learn that species are not well-defined units. According to philosopher and historian John Wilkins (2009), up to 26 different species concepts have been employed at one time or another. If competing species concepts classify organisms differently, and if there is no way to decide among the alternatives, then it might appear as if species don't exist in any objective sense. At least, one might question whether species are sufficiently robust to possess interests.

In fact, we do not think that this issue is quite so murky. The individuation of species is not as arbitrary as the individuation of ecosystems. To see this, consider that there are four dominant species concepts currently employed by conservation biologists (Frankham et al., 2012). These are summarized briefly in Table 9.1. It is certainly true that these definitions can result in conflicting implications for conservation policy (Frankham et al., 2012). For instance, the number of species in a given region increases by 49% if one switches from the Biological Species Concept to the Phylogenetic Species Concept, since the latter classifies species at a finer level of grain (Agapow et al.,

Table 9.1 A summary of the four dominant species concepts used in conservation biology

Concept	Definition	Reference[1]	Main objections
Taxonomic Species Concept	A species is whatever a competent taxonomist chooses to call a species.	Mayden, 1997	Not really a definition, this practice generates disagreement among experts and provides no principle for resolving disputes.
Biological Species Concept	A group of actually or potentially interbreeding individuals that is reproductively isolated from other such groups.	Mayr, 1942	Empirically unwieldy, since reproductive potential is difficult to establish. Vague boundaries, since reproductive barriers are semi-permeable – as in hybridizing species. Limited scope, since most species are asexual and do not form reproductive populations.
Evolutionary Species Concept	A species is a distinct lineage of organisms capable of evolving independently from other such lineages.	Wiley, 1978	Vague boundaries, since it is unclear how much differentiation is necessary or sufficient for speciation.
Phylogenetic Species Concept	A species is the smallest diagnosable cluster of organisms that descend from the same ancestor.	Cracraft, 1983	Vague boundaries, since many different ancestral lineages can exist within a given reproductive population (e.g. siblings).

[1] All references cited in Frankham et al. (2012)

Source: adapted partly from Frankham et al. (2012)

2004). However, despite such conflicts, there remains substantial agreement among the four definitions. For instance, physically discrete populations with no possibility for horizontal (intra-generational) genetic transmission always qualify as distinct species. Likewise, all definitions agree that members of the same, randomly interbreeding population qualify as the same species (Frankham et al., 2012). A large number of biological populations satisfy these conditions. In these cases, questions about species boundaries tend not to arise.

However, individuation issues do emerge at the intersection between closely related populations. For example, the members of closely related species often interbreed or hybridize to produce fertile offspring. Such events are arguably more common than biologists have traditionally assumed. For instance, in Eugene McCarthy's mammoth *Handbook of Avian Hybrids of the World* (2006), he reports >750 inter-specific crosses that are categorized as 'natural hybridization reported,' >500 crosses that are categorized as 'extensive natural hybridization reported,' and >250 crosses that are categorized as 'ongoing natural hybridization reported.' Many of these cases have not been evaluated for fertility of the offspring, but McCarthy reports that of those that have been evaluated, >600 show at least low or partial fertility. Inter-specific hybridization is not unique to birds. There are plenty of examples of mammals, plants, and amphibians that hybridize too. In these cases, it is impossible to say whether one is looking at a single continuous species, two overlapping species, or perhaps three interbreeding species. Different available definitions will yield competing answers, and there appears to be no principled way to decide among them. A similar individuation problem occurs in the case of so-called subspecies. Conservationists often use this label as if subspecies were an objective (non-arbitrary) biological category. But in fact there is no agreed amount of genetic distance distinguishing subspecies from populations. It would appear that the subspecies designation is just as arbitrary as the classification of ecosystems.

Why should any of this matter to the ecoholist? It matters if many of the entities that conservationists hope to protect turn out to be subspecies or hybrids as opposed to proper species. One well-known example in North America is the Florida Panther (*Puma concolor coryi*). Protected under the US Endangered Species Act, which defines a species as any genetically distinct population,[15] this 'species' was on the verge of extinction by 1995. With an estimated population size of 26 individuals, many suffered genetic abnormalities due to severe inbreeding. With little hope of staving off extinction, conservation managers embarked on a controversial strategy to increase the genetic diversity by translocating eight female Texas Panthers (*Puma concolor stanleyana*). By 2010, a large genetic study comparing samples from the late 1970s through 2009 showed that this Texas–Florida 'hybrid' had completely replaced the Florida Panther and showed no genetic abnormalities (Johnson et al., 2010).

The translocation strategy was controversial, in part, because it raised the question: *just what are we trying to conserve?* If the answer is the genetically distinct population, then the strategy could not hope to work. On the other hand, if the goal was to conserve a population of large mammalian predator in the Florida landscape, then this was the only strategy that could work. After the controversial strategy was enacted, the picture became muddier still. The species *Puma concolor* ranges throughout North and South America, from the Yukon to the Straits of Magellan. The species is commonly known as the cougar, puma, panther, mountain lion, catamount, or mountain cat. Through the 1990s, there were some 32 recognized subspecies of *Puma concolor*, with 17 in North America, and many were (and still are) the target of conservation concern. Then, in 2000, wildlife biologist Melanie Culver and her colleagues studied the mitochondrial DNA from samples collected all over the species' range, but were able to resolve only six

---

[15] See, e.g., http://bit.ly/2crfZHT.

subspecies, including only one from the entirety of North America (Culver et al., 2000). The US Fish and Wildlife Service continues to list the Florida Panther as endangered, affording it protection under the US Endangered Species Act, although the listing has more to do with the Act itself than it does with any biological evidence.

The Florida Panther example illustrates a number of points. First, the conservation problem was not, and often is not, about conserving species per se. Note that the *species* as a whole is not threatened – the IUCN classifies it as 'of least concern.' Nor is the North American Cougar subspecies (*Puma concolor couguar*) of conservation concern, except in Florida.[16] Second, if many conservation targets are not species, but subspecies or other genetically distinct populations, how do we justify the alleged intrinsic value of these groups? As in the case of ecosystems, the problem of individuation allows for irresolvable disagreements about the status of the entity in question. One could choose to lump the Florida Panther together with neighboring populations and the resulting ecological whole is in good shape. But if one divides the meta-population into distinct subspecies, and views each individual population as an intrinsically valuable unit, then suddenly the loss of this population seems significant. Without a principled way to resolve these individuation issues, individual populations are apparently not sufficiently robust to possess interests and, therefore, are not an appropriate bearer of intrinsic value – at least, not as the ecoholist understands it.

9.4 CONCLUSIONS

In this chapter we have discussed various issues that arise for the extensionist approach to defending ecoholism. In the next chapter, we turn to the most widely discussed alternative approach to defending ecoholism, an approach championed in numerous publications in both philosophical and scientific venues by philosopher J. Baird Callicott, who presents his defense of ecoholism as an interpretation

---

[16] http://bit.ly/2cBxcsr

of Aldo Leopold's thinking about 'the land ethic,' which many defenders of biodiversity see as the paradigm case of an ecoholist environmental ethic.

9.5   FURTHER READING

Agar, Nicholas (2001). *Life's Intrinsic Value: Science, Ethics, and Nature*. New York; Columbia University Press.

Taylor, Paul W. (1986). *Respect for Nature. A Theory of Environmental Ethics*. Princeton, NJ: Princeton University Press.

Varner, Gary E. (1998). *In Nature's Interests? Interests, Animal Rights, and Environmental Ethics*. New York: Oxford University Press.

10 Ecoholism 2: Callicott on the Leopold Land Ethic

In Chapter 9, we examined the possibilities for defending an ecoholist ethical theory using the extensionist approach from Chapter 8. There we found that such an approach seems implausible. If ecological wholes, like species and ecosystems, have intrinsic value, that claim will have to be defended in some other way. In this chapter we examine the version of ecoholism that ecologist Aldo Leopold [1887–1947] labeled "the land ethic."

We suspect that many readers of this book have at least a passing familiarity with Leopold and his nature writings. However, we also suspect that fewer readers will be familiar with the serious philosophical program that attempts to reconstruct a rational, defensible, and persuasive ecoholist theory from Leopold's nature writings. The non-philosophical reader may well wonder why we devote an entire chapter to an ethical theory attributed to an arguably outdated ecologist. We do so because Leopold's writings have had an outsized influence on modern environmentalists. Leopold's 1949 book, *A Sand County Almanac*, is seemingly treated as 'scripture' by some environmentalists, and his essay from the end of the book, "The Land Ethic," is almost certainly the single most influential and widely reprinted essay on environmental ethics. The breadth and depth of his influence is also evident from the fact that the authors of arguably the leading graduate-level textbook on conservation biology describe Leopold's land ethic as "the most biologically sensible and comprehensive of any approach to nature" and state that it "should serve as the philosophical basis of most decisions affecting biodiversity" (Groom et al., 2006, p. 12).

In this chapter, we focus on the work that philosopher J. Baird Callicott has done, across three decades, trying to reconstruct a systematic ethical theory from Leopold's *Sand County Almanac*. To understand that reconstruction, we begin in Section 10.1 by looking at sections of the raw material: some of Leopold's own pithy, but somewhat cryptic, statements about ethics. We then briefly discuss Leopold's life, because Leopold implied that his decades of experience as a forester and wildlife manager informed his thinking about the land ethic.

In Section 10.2 we briefly describe an early (1980) essay of Callicott's on Leopold that elicited some vehement objections to ecoholism from a range of writers. Then, in Section 10.3, we describe in greater detail the more nuanced interpretation of Leopold's land ethic that Callicott has defended in a number of later essays. In Section 10.4 we consider a variety of objections to Callicott's later interpretation of Leopold. And finally, in Section 10.5, we ask: Where does reading Leopold get us? From our critical discussion of Callicott on Leopold, we conclude that, philosophically speaking, Leopold's land ethic is weakly supported, and, practically speaking, we think that *A Sand County Almanac* itself provides precious little guidance.

10.1   LEOPOLD'S LIFE AND STYLE OF WRITING

Leopold's nature writing is celebrated on a par with that of John Muir [1838–1914] and Henry David Thoreau [1817–1862]. As commentators have noted, Leopold's style involves packing a lot of meaning into a sentence or a paragraph, by using evocative language while leaving much of the meaning implicit. This elliptical style of writing produces many memorable quotes that have ended up on web pages[1] and office doors. Consider this one about wildlands:

> [A]ll conservation of wildness is self-defeating, for to cherish we must see and fondle, and when enough have seen and fondled, there is no wilderness left to cherish.
>
> *(Leopold, 1949, p. 101)*

---

[1] See, e.g., http://bit.ly/2boLmlA

In this passage, Leopold's meaning seems clear enough, and we can easily understand what he is conveying that is not explicit in the sentence. Consider this paraphrasing:

> An area only becomes designated as a park, a national monument, or wilderness if some people love it and can garner more general support for its designation. Designating an area as such a special place calls to it attention of the broader public, however, and in the long run, those who campaigned for its designation will find that the qualities that inspired their campaign are, with increased visitation, lost. A number of Americans have therefore had an ironic reaction of sadness when, at the end of his term, a President has designated some favorite area of theirs a new national monument.[2] For designation as a monument ensures that visitation to the area will balloon in coming years, as a special color on highway maps draws the attention of thousands of people who would never have visited the area had it not received special designation.

Obviously this much longer, more explicitly worded version of Leopold's elliptical expression of the same thought would never be widely quoted!

But when Leopold writes about ethics, his tendency to use evocative language and leave a lot unsaid can lead to confusion. In fact, *Sand County* is something of a Rorschach blot, with everyone from a founder of Earth First! (Dave Foreman) to a former head of Texas A&M's Department of Rangeland Ecology and Management (Joseph Schuster) thinking that they see their own philosophy of land management expressed in Leopold's writings (Varner, 1998, p. 128).

Leopold's famous summary statement of 'the land ethic' is evocative and makes for a pithy quote:

[2] In the United States, National Parks are created by Congress, but under the Antiquities Act of 1906 (16USC431–433), a President can create a National Monument with the stroke of a pen. In recent decades, every outgoing president has used this authority to designate several new National Monuments during his last months in office.

Land Ethic Statement #1: "A thing is right when it tends to preserve the integrity, stability, and beauty of the biotic community."

(Leopold, 1949, pp. 224–225)

Any attempt to spell out what is implicit or only suggested by it will be debatable, however, because elsewhere in *Sand County* Leopold summarizes the land ethic differently. For instance, on the same page Leopold writes:

Land Ethic Statement #2: "The evolution of a land ethic is an intellectual as well as an emotional process. . . . I think it is a truism that as the ethical frontier advances from the individual to the community, its intellectual content increases."

(Leopold, 1949, p. 225)

And a page before:

Land Ethic Statement #3: "It is inconceivable to me that an ethical relation to land [a land ethic] can exist without love, respect, and admiration for land, and a high regard for its value. By value, I of course mean value in the philosophical sense."

(Leopold, 1949, p. 223)

And, back in the first four pages of the essay are these statements:

Land Ethic Statement #4: "An ethic, ecologically, is a limitation on freedom of action in the struggle for existence. An ethic, philosophically, is a differentiation of social from anti-social conduct. These are two definitions of one thing. The thing has its origin in the tendency of interdependent individuals or groups to evolve modes of co-operation."

(Leopold, 1949, p. 202)

Land Ethic Statement #5: "The extension of ethics to this third element in [the] human environment [the land ethic] is, if I read the evidence correctly, an evolutionary possibility and an ecological necessity."

(Leopold, 1949, p. 203)

Land Ethic Statement #6: "An ethic may be regarded as a mode of guidance for meeting ecological situations so new or intricate, or involving such deferred reactions, that the path of social expediency is not discernible to the average individual. Animal instincts are modes of guidance for the individual in meeting such situations. Ethics are possibly a kind of community instinct in-the-making."

(Leopold, 1949, p. 203)

Land Ethic Statement #7: "In short, a land ethic changes the role of *Homo sapiens* from conqueror of the land-community to plain member and citizen of it. It implies respect for his fellow-members, and also respect for the community as such."

(Leopold, 1949, p. 204)

These are each memorable quotes, and one has the sense that they collectively say something, but it is no easy task to explain how all seven of these very different statements about "the land ethic" and about ethics in general, fit together into a single, coherent ethical theory.

The philosopher who has published most widely on Leopold, and whose interpretation of Leopold's thinking about ethics has been influential, is J. Baird Callicott. In the early 1970s, Callicott was teaching at the University of Wisconsin – Stevens Point,[3] which is about 100 miles upstream on the Wisconsin River from the 'shack' where the essays in part one of *A Sand County Almanac* are all set.[4] In the early 1970s Callicott offered the first college course on environmental ethics, and in subsequent decades he became friends with Leopold's children, who continued to own the shack property. When the journal *Environmental Ethics* was founded a few years later, Callicott started publishing on Leopold and one of his earliest essays drew a great deal of attention (and

---

[3] J. Baird Callicott retired as University Distinguished Research Professor and Regents Professor of Philosophy at the University of North Texas in 2015.

[4] Part one of the book, titled *A Sand County Almanac*, comprises 12 essays titled by the months of the year. Part two, titled *Essays Here and There*, comprises vignettes about important experiences that Leopold had around the country during his professional work. The final part, which culminates with "The Land Ethic," is titled *The Upshot* and Leopold describes the essays in that part as being concerned with "philosophical questions" (Leopold, 1949, p. viii).

criticism). We will spend the bulk of this chapter describing Callicott's interpretation of Leopold on ethics, but first we should say a little about Aldo Leopold's life, because in the Foreword Leopold hints that various episodes in his professional life contributed to his mature land-management philosophy (Leopold, 1949, pp. vii–viii). Those already familiar with Leopold could skip ahead to Section 10.2.

Leopold was born in Burlington, Iowa, along the Mississippi River in 1887. The outdoors and hunting and fishing played a large role in his youth, and, after attending an east-coast boarding school, he entered the newly created Yale School of Forestry. Leopold graduated with a master's degree in forestry in 1909. From there, he became a forest assistant in the newly created Apache National Forest. He subsequently rose to the second-highest position in the Southwestern District of the US Forest Service before moving to the Forest Service's Forest Products Laboratory on the University of Wisconsin–Madison campus in 1924. By the time he moved to Madison, Leopold had developed a national reputation as a wildlife manager, and in 1933 he became a professor with a newly created 'Collegiate Professorship in Game Management' that had been created expressly to make Leopold a professor at the University of Wisconsin–Madison (Meine, 1988, pp. 299–300 and 307). *A Sand County Almanac* was published the year after Leopold's death in 1948.

During his time with the Forest Service in Arizona and New Mexico, Leopold successfully campaigned for reducing populations of wolves and mountain lions, using economic arguments and the 'wise use' philosophy of the Forest Service and the Yale School of Forestry.[5] With wolves and mountain lions mostly removed from southwestern forests, however, the famous irruption of deer on the Kaibab Plateau north of the Grand Canyon, which we described in Section 8.6.1, occurred during the late 1920s, and by the time he was writing *Sand*

---

[5] When Leopold entered the Forest Service, it was headed by Gifford Pinchot [1865–1946], who advocated a kind of anthropocentric utilitarianism, i.e. managing natural resources for maximum sustainable yield. The Yale School of Forestry was created with an endowment from Pinchot's parents.

County Leopold was arguing for retaining large predators for the sake of land 'health.'

Leopold was also a pioneer in ecological restoration. *Sand County* contains a monthly 'almanac' of activities around the 'shack' along the Wisconsin River, about a 55 mile drive from Madison, which he bought in 1935 to serve as a hunting camp. There, with his family, some of the first efforts at ecological restoration occurred. They painstakingly restored a worked-out corn field in front of the shack to a prairie representative of those that existed in the upper midwestern US in pre-Columbian times, and on other areas around the shack they planted trees representative of central Wisconsin woodlands. Later, Leopold was involved in the Madison arboretum's extensive effort to re-create examples of each of the distinctive biomes that were present in pre-Columbian times in what would become the state of Wisconsin.

By the time he died in 1948 (of a heart of attack, while fighting a fire on a neighboring property to the shack), Leopold was a celebrated figure in conservation circles, as documented in Susan Flader's (1974) and Curt Meine's (1988) biographies of Leopold. *A Sand County Almanac* sold fairly well when it was published the next year by Oxford University Press, but its fame grew immensely after a trade paperback edition was issued in 1966, including some additional essays from another book he had envisioned finishing one day. Amid the nascent modern environmental movement, sales skyrocketed, and, as Curt Meine puts it, Leopold is now "firmly established as a major figure in conservation history, philosophy, and practice, often mentioned in the same breath as Henry David Thoreau and John Muir" (Meine, 1988, p. 525).

10.2   CALLICOTT'S "TRIANGULAR AFFAIR" PAPER

One of Callicott's first essays on Leopold (Callicott, 1980) was published under the title: "Animal Liberation: A Triangular Affair." This is the same essay from which we extracted a list of "Practical Charges against Sentientism" in Section 8.5. The essay became well-known for having articulated a range of practical challenges for 'animal liberation' views from an environmentalist perspective, but here our focus will be on the interpretation of Leopold's land ethic that Callicott gave in this early essay. The vehement reactions that various people had to his description of Leopold's ethical thinking in "A Triangular Affair" also contributed to it being widely discussed and reprinted. Other than Leopold's "The Land Ethic," probably no single essay has done more to shape discussion of ecoholism in the philosophical literature. In a way, this is unfortunate, for, as we will see in the next section, the "Triangular Affair" piece presents an incomplete version of Callicott's interpretation of Leopold on ethics, and Callicott's later writings present a more nuanced reading of Leopold that blunts a number of the vehement objections to the land ethic that were made in response to Callicott's reconstruction of it in this paper.[6]

Before describing what Callicott said in the paper, we want to emphasize that when writing *A Triangular Affair*, Callicott's goal was to draw philosophers' attention to Leopold's environmental ethics. As he put it in the introduction to a 1989 anthology of his work, "'Animal Liberation: A Triangular Affair' ... *was intended to provoke controversy* and provoke controversy it has" (Callicott, 1989, p. 6; emphasis added). As we will see in Section 10.3, according to Callicott's later interpretation of Leopold, 'the land ethic' is intended to be just one of several components of a complete ethical theory. As we understand it, in writing the "Triangular Affair" piece, Callicott was emphasizing some radical implications that the holistic land ethic *could* have, if it operated in isolation from the other elements of Leopold's complete ethical theory. In fact, as we note later in this section (see n.8),

---

[6] In a preface to a reprinting of the "Triangular Affair," in an anthology edited by Robert Elliott, Callicott significantly distanced himself from several aspects of this essay. He writes: "I wrote 'A Triangular Affair' to sharply distinguish environmental ethics from animal liberation/rights when the former seemed to be overshadowed by the latter. Back in the late 1970s and early 1980s, when the piece was conceived and composed, many people seemed to conflate the two. In my youthful zeal to draw attention to the then unheralded Leopold land ethic, I made a few remarks that in retrospect appear irresponsible." Callicott goes on to clearly state that he "no longer think[s] the land ethic is misanthropic," that "we do in fact have duties and obligations ... to domestic animals," and that "a vegetarian diet is indicated by the land ethic, no less than by the animal welfare ethics" (Callicott, 1995, p. 29).

Callicott sometimes appears to have chosen his words carefully in the essay so as to avoid attributing certain ideas to Leopold.

The triangle metaphor in the subtitle of the essay reflects Callicott's concern to emphasize the *theoretical* differences that he sees between the land ethic on the one hand and both sentientist views and anthropocentrism on the other.[7] He emphasizes two theoretical differences. First, the latter two are individualistic, they have both "located moral value in individuals and set out certain metaphysical reasons for including some individuals and excluding others." Second, the land ethic "locates ultimate value in the 'biotic community' and assigns differential moral value to the constitutive individuals relative to that standard," and he adds that "[t]his is perhaps the most fundamental theoretical difference between environmental ethics and the ethics of animal liberation" (Callicott, 1980, p. 337).

Callicott explains that by 'animal liberation' he is referring to both of the approaches that we described in Chapter 8: the utilitarian approach that stresses equal consideration of the interests of all sentient animals, and the animal rights approach that seeks to extend equal respect for individuals' rights. Those views, he says, share with traditional anthropocentric ethics (which he labels "moral humanism") a commitment to the "equal moral worth" of individuals; the animal liberation movement just seeks to include a larger number of individuals in the moral community. Callicott emphasizes that by contrast, Leopold's statement of the fundamental principle of the land ethic – "A thing is right when it tends to preserve the integrity, stability and beauty of the biotic community" – makes "the good of the biotic *community* ... the ultimate measure of the moral value, the rightness or wrongness, of actions" (Callicott, 1980, p. 320; emphasis in original).

The land ethic manifestly does not accord equal moral worth to each and every member of the biotic community; the moral worth

---

[7] In a footnote (1980, pp. 318–319, note #21), Callicott says that he thinks that biocentric individualist views share the same modern ethical theoretical foundations as sentientism and traditional modern anthropocentric ethics.

of individuals (including, n.b., human individuals) is relative, to be assessed in accordance with the particular relation of each to the collective entity which Leopold called "land."

(Callicott, 1980, p. 327)

"In every case," Callicott says of the land ethic, "the effect upon ecological systems is the decisive factor in the determination of the ethical quality of actions" (1980, p. 320).

On the practical side, in Section 8.5 we described the anti-environmental implications that Callicott thinks sentientist views have in contrast to the land ethic. In the "Triangular Affair" essay, he also describes implications of the land ethic for the treatment of *humans*, and it was these statements that led to vehement objections from a range of authors. Callicott's descriptions of these implications come in two contexts.

The first is when he observes that if environmentalists' moral thinking parallels the fundamental principle of the land ethic as stated by Leopold (#1 of the seven listed at the beginning of this chapter), then that would explain "what otherwise might appear to be [some] gratuitous misanthropy" in the environmentalist literature:

The biospheric perspective does not exempt *Homo sapiens* from moral evaluation in relation to the well-being of the community of nature taken as a whole. The preciousness of individual deer, as of any other specimen, is inversely proportional to the population of the species. Environmentalists, however reluctantly and painfully, do not omit to apply the same logic to their own kind.[8] As omnivores, the population of human beings should, perhaps, be roughly twice that of bears, allowing for differences of size. ... If the land ethic were only a means of managing nature for the sake of man, ... then man would be considered as having an ultimate value essentially different from that of his 'resources.' The extent of

---

[8] Here is one of the places that we alluded to in the second paragraph of this section, where Callicott chooses his words carefully. Note that he does not say that *Leopold* thinks this; rather, he says that "environmentalists" do.

misanthropy in modern environmentalism thus may be taken as a measure of the degree to which it is biocentric.

(p. 326)

He then refers to this statement in the Edward Abbey (1927–1989) book *Desert Solitaire*: "I prefer not to kill animals. I'm a humanist; I'd rather kill a man than a snake" (Abby, 1968, p. 20). In the same paragraph Callicott mentions Garrett Hardin's suggestion, in "The Economics of Wilderness" (1969), to limit access to wilderness areas by 'merit' and to proscribe all rescue efforts when wilderness visitors are injured or lost (Callicott, 1980, p. 326).

The second context in which Callicott described implications of the land ethic that shocked various critics comes when he notes that the holism of Leopold's land ethic has an historical antecedent in the ancient Greek philosopher Plato [429?–347 BCE]. There he lists various policies that Plato endorsed in his late dialogue *The Republic*. Callicott describes Plato as:

> shrink[ing] from nothing so long as it seems to him to be in the interest of the community. Among the apparently inhuman recommendations that he makes to better the community are a program of eugenics involving a phony lottery ... requiring infanticide for a child whose only offense was being born without the sanction of the state ... the destruction of the pair bond and nuclear family ... the utter abolition of private property ... [and] radically restricting the practice of medicine to the dressing of wounds and the curing of seasonal maladies on the principle that the infirm and chronically ill not only lead miserable lives but contribute nothing to the good of the community.
>
> (Callicott, 1980, p. 328)

In a similar vein, he later mentions that among "tribal peoples in the past ... population was routinely optimized by sexual continency, abortion, infanticide, and stylized warfare" (1980, p. 334).

A range of people responded very negatively to Callicott's essay, many focusing their criticisms on Callicott's seeming endorsement of such implications of a holistic land ethic. An example that we mentioned earlier in this book (Section 8.6.2) is Tom Regan's characterization of the Leopold land ethic as "environmental fascism," because it would generally subordinate individual rights to the good of a community (Regan, 1983, pp. 361–363). As a specific example, Regan describes a hypothetical choice between killing a human and saving a rare plant that is important to ecosystem functioning, which may be an implicit reference to Callicott's statement (quoted above) that "the moral worth of individuals (including, n.b., human individuals) is relative, to be assessed in accordance with the particular relation of each to the collective entity which Leopold called 'land.'"

As a result of Callicott's 1980 article, other philosophers suggested that the Leopold land ethic implied draconian conclusions. For instance, in a 1984 article, William Aiken reckoned that all modern agriculture would be prohibited by the land ethic, and he wondered if killing off most of the contemporary human population would be called for: "In fact, massive human die backs would be good. Is it our duty to cause them? Is it our species' duty, relative to the whole, to eliminate 90 percent of our numbers?" (Aiken, 1984, p. 269). And in a 1985 article, Marti Kheel wrote that "the 'holists,' such as Callicott and Leopold, may be compared to totalitarians, with their insistence on the subordination of the individual to the greater good of the whole" (Kheel, 1985, p. 138).[9]

Regan and the others quoted above seemed to agree with Callicott's interpretation of the land ethic in his 1980 essay. That is, they do not question that Callicott was accurately interpreting Leopold's ethics; instead, they see themselves as criticizing Leopold's way of thinking. Others, however, have explicitly disagreed with Callicott's interpretation of Leopold. A striking example of this

---

[9] The quoted passages from Regan, Aiken, and Kheel were all published prior to Callicott's "Conceptual Foundations of the Land Ethic," which we discuss in the following subsection. Similar objections were published later by Frederick Ferré (1996, p. 18) and Kristin Shrader-Frechette (1996, p. 63).

second response to Callicott's early paper came from Leopold's own son, Luna Leopold [1915–2006]. In the foreword that he wrote to a book of essays celebrating the centennial of his father's birth, he wrote the following, which focuses on his father's concern for and valuing of individual humans, suggesting that a complete reconstruction of his father's ethical theory would not be purely holistic, or not holistic in the way that Callicott described it in his "Triangular Affair" essay:

> It has been suggested that [my father's] words imply that the value of an individual person would be inversely proportional to the supply of people. The words have even been interpreted to convey the idea that abortion, infanticide, war and other means for the elimination of the less fit may be unobjectionable because they are ecosystemically unobjectionable.
>
> These extreme extrapolations pay no heed to Leopold's deep concern for his aging mother. They do not reflect the fact that he always avoided putting anyone in an uncomfortable or embarrassing position. Never would he talk down to a person and he treated people in menial positions with the same consideration and courtesy as he would the most exalted.
>
> Rather than interpreting the concept of the land ethic as an indication of disregard for the individual in favor of the species or the ecosystem, my view is quite different. I see the concept as an outgrowth and extension of his deep personal concern for the individual. Accepting the idea that the cooperations and competitions in the human society are eased and facilitated by concern for others, he saw that the same consideration extended to other parts of the ecosystem and would tend to add integrity, beauty, and stability to the whole.
>
> *(Leopold, 1987, p. viii)*

In the first paragraph, his choice of examples seems to reflect Callicott's insinuation that a holist should endorse Plato's views and the practices that Callicott attributed to "tribal peoples in the past." In the remaining paragraphs, however, Luna stresses that his father Aldo exhibited great respect for human individuals, and he suggests that his father's ethical thinking – including its holistic component – somehow grew out of more traditional ethical thinking about our fellow human beings. In subsequent work, when Callicott went about revising his interpretation of the land ethic, he took pains to explain how he thought that Leopold's land ethic could incorporate both concern for the biotic community (holism) and respect for individuals, and how it could indeed grow out of more traditional ethical thinking about our fellow human beings.

10.3 CALLICOTT'S LATER INTERPRETATION OF LEOPOLD

In response to criticisms of his 1980 article, Callicott has presented a refined interpretation of Leopold that has four elements. He has emphasized different elements in various publications that we will draw on in this section, but ever since his controversial "Triangular Affair" paper, he has held that these four elements form a unified and coherent ethical theory. The elements in the order that we will review them in this section are:

1) An over-arching commitment to communitarianism in ethics;
2) A response to the charge of ecofascism based on an account of ethics evolving by a series of "accretions," with a pair of "second-order principles";
3) A Humean moral psychology; and
4) A Darwinian account of the evolution of ethical thinking.

As we will emphasize at the end of this section, Callicott's later interpretation makes sense of all seven of the quotations from Leopold that we listed as illustrations of Leopold's elliptical style of writing. However, his later interpretation faces various objections that we will describe in Section 10.4.

10.3.1 Communitarianism in Ethics

We noted that in his earlier interpretation of Leopold's thinking about ethics, Callicott (1980) stated that modern ethical theory is individualistic – that is, focuses on effects on individuals – whereas the Leopold land ethic focuses (or focuses also) on the biotic community. There Callicott compared Leopold's approach to ethics to that of the ancient Greek philosopher Plato, who seemed to think that the value of individuals is a function of their contributions to the community. In his later work on Leopold, Callicott has instead compared Leopold's general approach to ethical thinking to a fairly recent school of thought called communitarianism.

Communitarianism is a broad term that was originally applied to authors who reacted to John Rawls' *A Theory of Justice* (1971) by arguing that the primary role of government should not be to ensure that individuals compete fairly for resources. Communitarians, by contrast, emphasize how essential the connection with a community is to being human, sometimes echoing Aristotle's famous claim that "man is by nature a political animal" (Aristotle, *Politics* 1253a).[10] Callicott uses the term "communitarianism" in several essays to describe how he thinks that Leopold's approach to ethics departs from a paradigm of moral thinking that underlies the extensionist approach.

In one of his most widely reprinted essays, "The Conceptual Foundations of the Land Ethic" (1987), Callicott characterizes Leopold as a communitarian who rejects what he calls "the classical modern paradigm" of ethical thinking. Callicott takes that label from an essay by Kenneth Goodpaster titled "From Egoism to Environmentalism" (Goodpaster, 1979). In that essay, Goodpaster argued that the main traditions of modern ethical theory – including both the utilitarian and deontological traditions that we described in Chapter 8 – all conceive of morality as essentially opposed to egoism,[11] but as at the same time having a "tendency to form morality from the rib of egoism" (Goodpaster, 1979, p. 25). That is, Goodpaster said, both traditions think that "the only way to conceptualize and psychologically

---

[10] The "1253a" refers to the standard pagination used in scholarly references to Aristotle's work (the Bekker pagination). We used the Benjamin Jowett translation of *Politics* (Aristotle [n.d.] 1941), where the quoted language occurs on p. 1129.

[11] See Shaver, Robert, "Egoism," The Stanford Encyclopedia of Philosophy (Spring 2015 Edition), Edward N. Zalta (ed.), http://plato.stanford.edu/archives/spr2015/entries/egoism/.

explain the moral sentiment is in terms of extending self-interest to include other bearers of the sentiment" (1979, p. 25). And by making our thinking about ourselves as conscious individuals the paradigm case of what has intrinsic value, Goodpaster argues, these traditional modern approaches to ethical thinking are biased against the kind of holistic ethic that environmentalists seek.

Callicott agrees with Goodpaster. He characterizes both sentientism and biocentric individualism as growing out of this 'classical modern paradigm':

> The contemporary animal liberation/rights, and reverence-for-life-principle ethics are, at bottom, simply direct applications of the modern classical paradigm of moral argument. But this standard modern model of ethical theory provides no possibility whatever for the moral consideration of wholes – of threatened *populations* of animals and plants, or of endemic, rare, or endangered *species* or of biotic *communities*, or most expansively, of the *biosphere* in its totality – since wholes per se have no psychological experience of any kind. Because mainstream modern moral theory has been "psychocentric," it has been radically and intractably individualistic or "atomistic" in its fundamental theoretical orientation.
>
> *(Callicott, 1987, pp. 197–198)*

In contrast, Callicott notes, the moral thinking of the ancient Greeks (like Plato, whom he had quoted in his earlier, "Triangular Affair" piece) started from a very different conception of the self. Rather than thinking of moral agents as (so to speak) atomic individuals, a moral agent is always and essentially part of a human *community*.

Callicott goes on to argue that Leopold's emphasis on "The Community Concept," which is the title of one of the sections of his essay "The Land Ethic," evinces a similar type of communitarianism when Leopold writes:

All ethics so far evolved rest upon a single premise: that the
individual is a member of a community of interdependent parts. His
instincts prompt him to compete for his place in that community,
but his ethics prompt him also to co-operate (perhaps in order that
there may be a place to compete for). The land ethic simply enlarges
the boundaries of the community to include soils, water, plants, and
animals, or collectively: the land.

(Leopold, 1949, pp. 203–204)

According to Callicott, the title of the next section of Leopold's essay,
"The Ecological Conscience," signals Leopold's belief that as humans
come to understand themselves as members of a *biotic* community,
our moral thinking acquires a new layer that reflects the appropriately
different obligations that are (as he puts it) "generated" by membership in such different types of community. In various places, Callicott
describes a variety of such obligation-generating communities that
humans have inhabited over time, including the small, nomadic
groups in which early humans lived, modern local human communities, as well as what he calls a "mixed community" of humans and
domesticated animals, and, finally, the modern, global human
community.

Relatedly, in an essay titled "Animal Liberation and the Land
Ethic: Back Together Again," Callicott (1988) claimed that his later
interpretation of the land ethic would also lend legitimacy to some of
the concerns raised by advocates of animal welfare and animal rights.
In that essay he referred to the work of philosopher Mary Midgley. In
her book *Animals and Why They Matter* (1978), Midgley argues that
contemporary human nature has been shaped by associations with
non-human animals, because, since the first domestications of animals millennia ago, humans have normally lived in what she
describes as "mixed communities" of both fellow-humans and domesticated animals. She argues that these human–animal relationships
are mediated by a common-sense recognition on our part that these
animals have feelings and that we owe them some kind of moral

consideration in light of the close relationship of mutual dependence that we share. In his "Back Together Again" paper, Callicott argues that this means that domesticated animals have been part of *human* communities ever since the earliest of the "accretions" that Leopold refers to.[12] And that means that some form of respect is owed them, a form that is, he claims, probably violated by contemporary, intensive animal agriculture.

In Section 10.4, we will consider a range of objections to Callicott's interpretation of Leopold, including some issues for his use of communitarianism, but first we wish to finish laying out the elements of Callicott's interpretation.

10.3.2   Ethical 'Accretions' and 'Second-order Principles'

In response to charges that Leopold's land ethic is draconian or eco-fascist in its implications, Callicott emphasizes that Leopold saw the land ethic as an *addition to*, rather than a replacement for, more traditional ethics. As we noted at the beginning of this chapter, Leopold writes very compactly, often building a lot into a paragraph or a sentence, or, Callicott adds, into his choice of a specific word. An example of the latter, according to Callicott, is Leopold's choice of the word "accretions" to describe the extension of ethical consideration to broader communities over time in this passage from early in "The Land Ethic":

> The first ethics dealt with the relation between individuals; the Mosaic Decalogue [the Ten Commandments] is an example. Later accretions dealt with the relation between the individual and society. The Golden Rule tries to integrate the individual to society; democracy to integrate social organization to the individual.
>
> *(Leopold, 1949, pp. 202–203)*

---

[12] Callicott does not note this, but various prohibitions on cruelty to animals were incorporated into the Torah (the five books of Moses), which also contains The Mosaic Decalogue (the Ten Commandments), which Leopold gives as an example of the first "accretion."

When Leopold then describes a new ethic – a *land* ethic – as being the natural next step, he is implicitly describing the land ethic as another accretion. The significance of Leopold's word choice is this. Describing something as an "accretion" implies that it is a layer that is added to the outside of a pre-formed object. Unlike the metaphor of an 'expanding circle' of moral consideration, Callicott points out, describing the land ethic as the latest *accretion* suggests that earlier-evolved ethics remain in place and operative after the addition of a land ethic.

This idea plays a central role in Callicott's response to critics who characterized the Leopold land ethic as "draconian" or "ecofascist." In the following passage from his 1987 paper "The Conceptual Foundations of the Land Ethic," Callicott describes duties "correlative to" older systems of ethics as generally taking priority over duties "correlative to" newer systems:

> The biosocial development of morality does not grow in extent like an expanding balloon, leaving no trace of its previous boundaries, so much as like the circumference of a tree. Each emergent, and larger, social unit is layered over the more primitive, and intimate, ones.
>
> Moreover, as a general rule, the duties correlative to the inner social circles to which we belong eclipse those correlative to the rings farther from the heartwood when conflicts arise. . . . Family obligations in general come before nationalistic duties and humanitarian obligations in general come before environmental duties. The land ethic, therefore, is not draconian or fascist. It does not cancel human morality.
>
> *(Callicott, 1987, pp. 207–208)*

Although Leopold seems to refer to just three accretions in his discussion of "The Ethical Sequence," Callicott's language suggests that there may be a larger number of earlier ethics. For instance, in a 1994 article he writes: "At once, each of us is a member of a family, a civic society, a nation state, the global village, 'mixed communities' (that include domestic animals), and local, regional, and global biotic communities" (Callicott, 1994, p. 173).

This prioritization of earlier accretions allows Callicott to respond to the critics discussed at the end of the previous section by claiming that, in each of the cases where the land ethic, operating by itself, would seem to have a draconian or ecofascist implication, the land ethic's implications are "preempted" by the implications of some older, more "inner social circle." Consider, for instance, the passage by Leopold's son Luna that we quoted in Section 10.2. As we noted there, Luna Leopold seems to be questioning the emphasis on holism that Callicott played up in his "Triangular Affair" paper. Luna then adds examples of how important it was to his father Aldo to treat other individual humans with respect. Luna concludes: "These will support my conviction that the concept of the land ethic was an outgrowth and extension of his deep concern for the individual not a repudiation of the importance of the individual" (Leopold, 1987, p. viii). On Callicott's revised reconstruction of Leopold's thinking, the land ethic is an "accretion" to our ethical thinking that leaves previously evolved ethical systems operative. Those previously evolved accretions would include traditional ways of thinking about how to respect our fellow human beings as individuals. Luna does not describe Aldo as adhering to any particular traditional human-regarding ethics, but those could include rights theories, virtue theories, etc. In respecting his fellow humans as Luna describes, Aldo can be understood as operating according to an earlier, human-oriented accretion, while thinking that the land ethic has a role to play in land-management decisions.

Of course, if Callicott/Leopold endorsed the view that duties associated with earlier accretions *always* trump those associated with later ones, that would threaten to trivialize the land ethic. Consider, for instance, an environmentalist considering how to vote on a referendum to preserve the spotted owl by halting the logging of old-growth forests in the northwestern United States, and suppose that the environmentalist has a brother whose family depends on logging jobs that would be lost if the ban passes. If duties correlative to older accretions always trump those correlative to more recent accretions, then the environmentalist would be obligated to vote against the ban in support of his brother rather than vote to save the spotted owl.[13]

In the above passage from his "Conceptual Foundations" essay, however, Callicott adds that:

> The land ethic may, however, as with any new accretion, demand choices which affect, in turn, the demands of the more interior social ethical circles. Taxes and the military draft may conflict with family-level obligations. While the land ethic, certainly, does not cancel human morality, neither does it leave it unaffected.
>
> *(Callicott, 1987, p. 208)*

As he put it in another essay, "the outer orbits of our various moral spheres exert a gravitational tug on the inner ones" and "in principle" it may be possible "to assign priorities and relative weights and thus to resolve such conflicts in a systematic way" (Callicott, 1988, p. 169). The implication of the gravitational metaphor seems clear: Callicott is saying that within each accretion, some duties are 'weightier' than others, and that in some situations, a duty generated by an 'outer orbit' of moral concern should influence our moral judgment more than a 'low mass' duty generated by an 'inner orbit,' just as Jupiter affects the orbit of Mars more than Mars' own tiny moons.

In later publications, Callicott has articulated two "second-order principles" that he argues should govern our thinking about duties generated by different accretions. His idea is that within a given ethical accretion, certain principles apply, and these would establish priorities if only duties generated by that accretion were in issue. When principles from different accretions come into conflict, however, then these two second-order principles would prioritize among those conflicting first-order principles. Here is how he

---

[13] This case comes from Varner (1991, p. 176).

introduces them in an essay titled "Holistic Environmental Ethics and the Problem of Ecofascism":

> The first second-order principle (SOP-1) is that obligations generated by membership in more venerable and intimate communities take precedence over those generated in more recently emerged and impersonal communities. . . . The second second-order principle (SOP-2) is that stronger interests (for lack of a better word) generate duties that take precedence over duties generated by weaker interests.
>
> *(Callicott, 1999, p. 73)*

In the same essay, Callicott gives two examples of cases in which he thinks that it is clear that SOP-2 applies, because a "stronger interest" is at stake. The first concerns a conflict between obligations generated by one's membership in a nation-state and those generated by one's membership in a family. Callicott discusses this case because he thinks that his readers will agree that it is clear what should be done, but also because he thinks our intuitive judgment about the case can be understood as an application of his SOP-2. He describes a case made famous by the existentialist philosopher Jean-Paul Sartre in which a man, during World War II, has to choose between joining the French resistance and staying home with his mother. In Callicott's description of the case,

> The very existence of France as a transorganismic entity is threatened. The young man's mother has a weaker interest at stake, for, as Sartre reports, his going off – and maybe getting killed – would plunge her into "despair." His mother being plunged into despair would be terrible, but not nearly as terrible as the destruction of France would be if not enough young men fought on her behalf. So the resolution of this man's dilemma is clear; he should give priority to the first-order principle, Serve Thy Country.
>
> *(Callicott, 1999, pp. 73–74)*

Callicott sees this as an application of his SOP-2 to resolve a conflict of duties generated by more traditional moral communities: the family and the nation. Callicott then describes a version of the spotted owl case that we described earlier. This is a case in which duties generated by membership in a family or some larger *human* community conflict with those generated by membership in the *biotic* community. Here Callicott thinks that environmentalist readers will agree that it is clear what should be done in the case, and he thinks that intuitive judgment about the case can be understood as another application of his SOP-2:

> The spotted owl is threatened with preventable anthropogenic
> extinction – threatened with biocide, in a word – and the old-growth
> forest biotic communities of the Pacific North-west are threatened
> with destruction. These threats are the environmental-ethical
> equivalent of genocide and holocaust. The loggers, on the other
> hand, are threatened with economic losses, for which they can be
> compensated dollar for dollar. More important to the loggers, I am
> told, their lifestyle is threatened. But livelihood and lifestyle, for
> both of which adequate substitutes can be found, is a lesser interest
> than life itself. If we faced the choice of cutting down millions of
> four-hundred-year-old trees or cutting down thousands of forty-
> year-old loggers, our duties to the loggers would take precedence by
> SOP-1, nor would SOP-1 be countermanded by SOP-2. But that is
> not the choice we face. The choice is between cutting down four-
> hundred-year-old trees, rendering the spotted owl extinct, and
> destroying the old-growth forest biotic community on the one hand,
> and displacing forest workers in an economy that is already
> displacing them through automation and raw-log exports to Japan
> and other foreign markets. And the old-growth lifestyle is doomed,
> in any case, to self-destruct, for it will come to an end with the
> "final solution" to the old-growth forest question, if the jack-booted
> timber barons (who disingenuously blame the spotted owl for the
> economic insecurity of loggers and other workers in the timber

industry) continue to have their way. With SOP-2 supplementing
SOP-1, the indication of the land ethic is crystal clear.

(Callicott, 1999, p. 75)

In both of the described cases, Callicott thinks that there is clearly a
'stronger interest' at stake in the larger, less intimate community,
which triggers the application of SOP-2.[14]

Callicott's choice of examples also suggests how Leopold's land
ethic can be seen as an outgrowth of more traditional thinking about
ethics. For, as we noted above, Callicott thinks that the first example,
which concerns conflicting duties to a member of one's family and to
one's collective nation-state, is governed by the same two second-
order principles as the second example, which concerns conflicting
duties to one's fellow human beings and a land-ethical duty.

As with his communitarianism, we will consider some objections to Callicott's use of SOP-1 and SOP-2 in Section 10.4, but in the
following subsection we first describe the third element in Callicott's
later, more nuanced interpretation of Leopold. In his later writings on
Leopold, Callicott claims that Leopold's thinking about ethics is best
understood as combining the views of Scottish philosopher David
Hume [1711–1776] with Charles Darwin's group selection account
of the evolution of moral norms.

10.3.3   Humean Moral Psychology

For our purposes, it will suffice to say just two things about Hume's
views. The first is that, as Hume famously put it: "Reason is, and
ought only to be the slave of the passions, and can never pretend to any
other office than to serve and obey them" (Hume, 1978 [1739–1740],
p. 415). That metaphorical language reflects Hume's commitment to
empiricism – the view that all knowledge is ultimately derived from
experience (and also, usually, concepts). In contrast to empiricists,
rationalists hold that some significant amount of knowledge does

---

[14] Callicott included the same statements of SOP-1 and SOP-2, and the two quoted examples,
in his entry "The Land Ethic" in Jamieson (2008).

not depend on experience. Kant was a rationalist with regard to ethics, as we saw in Section 7.1.3, at least if he believed that various moral duties can be derived from the logic of moral discourse alone. Hume, by contrast, held that our concepts of right and wrong, and our knowledge of moral duties, are always based on experience.[15]

Specifically, Hume held that our judgments about right and wrong are a sort of generalization about our sympathetic reactions to some range of cases. As Alan Carter describes it:

> Sympathy leads us to take into account not just our own happiness or suffering, but that of others too – in particular those we most "associate" with. We come to judge a person's character in terms of qualities that, for example, promote the happiness or minimize the suffering of those close to us. So, because of our sympathy for others, we admire those qualities. Hence, we assess a person's character in their light. We praise people insofar as they possess these qualities, and we criticize them to the extent that they lack them or possess characteristics that lead to others' suffering. Hence, according to Hume, sympathy is the ultimate foundation of our moral judgments.
>
> *(Carter, 2000, p. 7)*

For Hume, then, the judgment that some category of action is morally good (or bad, right or wrong, etc.) is a generalization from the sympathetic reactions of people in general or, what comes to the same thing, the sympathetic reaction of a disinterested observer.

The second thing to note about Hume's moral psychology is that, according to Callicott, Hume believed that our sympathies extend to communities as such, and this committed Hume to a form of holism. In support of this claim, Callicott cites the

---

[15] Moreover (although we did not discuss this in Section 7.1.3), Kant thought that an action could be done "from the motive of duty," by which he seemed to mean that it would somehow be motivated by reason without regard to any desire or purpose of the agent. Hume, by contrast, held that reason alone cannot give one a motive for acting one way or another, only our 'passions' can. In the case of moral judgment, Hume thought that the motive that produces action is a 'sentiment of approval' or 'sentiment of disapproval'.

following reference to 'the interests of society' from Hume's *An Inquiry Concerning the Principles of Morals*:

> [W]e must renounce the theory which accounts for every moral sentiment by the principle of self-love. We must adopt a more public affection, and allow that the interests of society are not, even on their own account, entirely indifferent to us. Usefulness is only a tendency to a certain end; and it is a contradiction in terms that anything pleases as a means to an end where the end itself no wise affects us. If usefulness, therefore, be a source of moral sentiment, and if this usefulness be not always considered with a reference to self, it follows that everything which contributes to the happiness of society recommends itself directly to our approbation and good will. Here is a principle which accounts, in great part, for the origin of morality: and what need we seek for abstruse and remote systems when there occurs one so obvious and natural?
>
> *(1957 [1751], p. 47)*

Callicott concludes that, for Hume, "We care ... for our communities *per se*, over and above their individual members – for our families *per se*, for our country, and for mankind" (Callicott, 1988, p. 168). This claim about Hume's moral psychology plays a crucial role in Callicott's interpretation of Leopold on the emergence of the holistic land ethic. As we will see in the next section, Callicott argues that as ecology and the environmental sciences lead us to see ourselves as members of a biotic community, our natural 'public affection' begins to operate toward the biotic community.[16]

---

[16] Beginning with his earliest publications on Leopold, Callicott has embraced the view that intrinsic value is (as we characterized it in Section 1.6.1) *non-objective*. That is, he says that "there can be no value apart from an evaluator," but he adds that "things may ... nonetheless be valued for themselves as well as for the contribution they might make to the realization of our (or someone's) interests" (Callicott, 1980, p. 325). Thus, Humean moral psychology leaves room for claims about *intrinsic* value, but in terms of the different meanings or definitions of 'intrinsic value' that we surveyed in Chapter 1, Callicott's Humean reconstruction of Leopold's ethics commits him to thinking of intrinsic value as "non-objective." It is not clear to us, however, whether Callicott reads Leopold (or Hume) as thinking of

Again, we will discuss some objections to Callicott's use of Hume's moral psychology in Section 10.4.4.

10.3.4 A Darwinian Account of the Evolution of Ethics

Turning now to Darwin, although Leopold does not mention him by name in "The Land Ethic," Callicott believes that Darwin's account of the evolution of morality is implicit in the first three paragraphs of the essay. After proposing his theory of biological evolution in *On the Origin of Species by Means of Natural Selection* (Darwin, 2003 [1859]), Darwin addressed questions about human evolution in his *The Descent of Man* (Darwin, 1904 [1871]).

Darwin hypothesized that our 'moral instincts' are the recently evolved addition to a more basic (i.e. ancestral) set of self-regarding instincts, shared by humans and other species. Darwin proposed that those instincts remain with us today. However, he claimed that basic instincts are often suppressed, in humans, by overriding moral instincts because the latter are psychologically enduring. For instance, a violent outburst of anger is followed by a prolonged sense of guilt, the anticipation of which helps to curb angry outbursts on subsequent occasions. These moral instincts were thought to have evolved by competition among ancestral human groups. As Darwin himself puts it:

> It must not be forgotten that although a high standard of morality gives but a slight or no advantage to each individual man and his children over the other men of the same tribe, yet that an increase in the number of well-endowed men and an advancement in the standard of morality will certainly give an immense advantage to one tribe over another. A tribe including many members who, from possessing in a high degree the spirit of patriotism, fidelity, obedience, courage, and sympathy, were always ready to aid one another, and to sacrifice themselves for the common good, would be victorious over most other tribes; and this would be natural

intrinsic value as being "subjective" or as being "relational" (for these distinctions, see Section 1.6.1).

selection. At all times throughout the world tribes have supplanted other tribes; and as morality is one important element in their success, the standard of morality and the number of well-endowed men will thus everywhere tend to rise and increase.

(Darwin, 1904 [1871], p. 166)

Although Darwin does not use the term, contemporary readers will recognize this as an account of natural selection acting on differences among groups – or *group selection*, as it is often called.

Darwin's idea, as summarized by Callicott, is that at first, "Bonds of affection and sympathy between parents and offspring permitted the formation of small, closely kin social groups." Then, as Callicott puts it:

> Should the parental and filial affections bonding family members chance to extend to less closely related individuals, that would permit an enlargement of the family group. And should the newly extended community more successfully defend itself and/or more efficiently provision itself, the inclusive fitness of its members severally would be increased, Darwin reasoned. Thus, the more diffuse familial affections, which Darwin (echoing Hume . . .) calls the "social sentiments," would be spread throughout a population.
>
> *(Callicott, 1987, pp. 190–191)*

Callicott assumes that Darwin relies on Humean moral psychology, because Darwin quotes Hume on sympathetic identification with others during his discussion of the emergence of altruism in *The Descent of Man* (Darwin, 1904 [1871], p. 109).

According to Callicott, this Darwinian view of the emergence of norms led Leopold to the following generalization: "we may expect to find that the scope and specific content of ethics will reflect both the perceived boundaries and actual structure or organization of a cooperative community or society. *Ethics and society or community are correlative*" (Callicott, 1987, p. 191; emphasis in original). Thus, according to Callicott, Leopold thought that a *land* ethic would be the next step in the evolution of human moral thinking, as we enter an age of what Callicott at one point describes as "universal ecological literacy" (Callicott, 1987, p. 194).

In the opening paragraphs of "The Land Ethic," Leopold observes that across recorded history, "ethical criteria have been extended to many fields of conduct, with corresponding shrinkages in those judged by expediency alone" (Leopold, 1949, p. 202). Then he implicitly invokes Darwin's view of the evolution of our moral thinking when he writes:

> This extension of ethics, so far studied only by philosophers, is actually a process in ecological evolution. Its sequences may be described in ecological as well as in philosophical terms. An ethic, ecologically, is a limitation on freedom of action in the struggle for existence. An ethic, philosophically, is a differentiation of social from anti-social conduct. These are two definitions of the same thing. The thing has its origin in the tendency of interdependent individuals or groups to evolved modes of co-operation. . . . All ethics so far evolved rest upon a single premise: that the individual is a member of a community of interdependent parts.
>
> (Leopold, 1949, pp. 202–303)

Leopold then observes that "There is as yet no ethic dealing with man's relation to land and to the animals and plants which grow upon it," and concludes that "The extension of ethics to this third element in [the] human environment is, if I read the evidence correctly, an evolutionary possibility and an ecological necessity" (1949, p. 203). It is an 'evolutionary possibility' under a Darwinian understanding of the evolution of ethical thinking. Elsewhere, Leopold describes how twentieth century technologies were allowing unprecedentedly widespread and speedy changes to the ecological communities on which humans depend, and presumably this is why he says that by the twentieth century, a land ethic had become an "ecological necessity."

We can now summarize Callicott's reconstruction of how and why Leopold thought that a 'land ethic' would be a natural next step in the evolution of human thinking about ethics as follows:

1) Ethics is based, as Hume thought, on sympathetic feelings toward others and feelings toward the communities of which one sees oneself as a member.

2) If Hume was correct, then our concept of moral standing will reflect our understanding of the boundaries and structures of the communities to which we view ourselves as belonging.

3) According to Darwin, over the course of human prehistory, natural selection was likely to have favored groups whose members were inclined to sympathize and cooperate with one another.

4) If Darwin was correct, then this might explain why there has been an expansion of the spheres of moral concern exhibited by human societies over the centuries.

5) Ecological science, Callicott thinks, represents us as members of a cooperative biotic or *land* community.

6) Therefore, a holistic land *ethic* will be the next step in progressively wider spheres of moral concern; it will naturally emerge along with "universal ecological literacy."

Relying as he does on Hume's moral psychology, Callicott notices that Hume would seem to have a problem with this account of how moral duties to broader communities and their non-human members could arise.

For as we noted in Section 9.2.1, Hume held that you cannot get from 'is' to 'ought.' Callicott devoted a 1982 essay to clarifying how Hume could, after all, endorse an argument like the above. Callicott first presents the following argument:

> (1) Cigarette smoking is deleterious to health. (2) Your health is something toward which as a matter of fact you have a positive attitude (as today we would say; a warm sentiment or passion, as Hume, more colorfully, would put it). (3) Therefore, you ought not smoke cigarettes.
>
> *(Callicott, 1982, pp. 168–169)*

Recall that, as an empiricist, Hume treats moral statements as generalizations about the operation of natural human sentiments. So the 'ought' conclusion follows from the premises in the same way that a statement of fact would – namely, "Therefore, it is true that you will generally have a sentiment of disapprobation toward the effects of smoking on your health."

Callicott then formulates an analogous argument illustrating how ecological science can generate a conclusion about societal-level prudence (enlightened anthropocentrism, if you will):

> (1) The biological sciences including ecology have disclosed (a) that organic nature is systemically integrated, (b) that mankind is a nonprivileged member of the organic continuum, and (c) that therefore environmental abuse threatens human life, health, and happiness. (2) We human beings share a common *interest* in human life, health, and happiness. (3) Therefore, we ought not violate the integrity and stability of the natural environment by loading it with hazardous wastes or by extirpating species, upon which its vital functions depend, or by any other insults or dislocations.
>
> *(Callicott, 1982, p. 170)*

Then Callicott formulates an argument to the conclusion that it matters, morally speaking, how we treat our 'fellow citizens' of the biotic community (this is, in effect, an argument for extending our understanding of which individuals have moral standing):

> (1) we (i.e., all psychologically normal people) are endowed with certain moral sentiments (sympathy, concern, respect, and so on) for our fellows, especially for our kin; (2) modern biology treats *Homo sapiens* (a) as, like all other living species, a product of the process of organic evolution; and hence, (b) people are literally kin (because of common ancestry) to all other contemporary forms of life; (3) therefore, if so enlightened, we should feel and thus behave . . . toward other living things in ways similar to the way we feel and thus behave toward our human kin.
>
> *(Callicott, 1982, p. 172)*

Callicott emphasizes that the land ethic makes the biotic community *per se* morally considerable, and he says that from a Humean perspective, an argument to this conclusion draws an analogy between human communities and biotic communities:

> (1) we all generally have a positive attitude toward the community or society to which we belong; and (2) science has now discovered that the natural environment is a community or society to which we belong, no less than to the human global village ... (3) [so] we ought to "preserve the integrity, stability, and beauty of the biotic community."
>
> *(Callicott, 1982, pp. 173–174)*

Callicott concludes:

> If Hume's analysis is essentially correct, ecology and the environmental sciences *can* thus directly change our values: *what* we value, not *how* we value. They do not, in other words, change our inherited capacity for moral discrimination and response, nor do they change the specific profile of our human moral sentiments or passions (these change, if they change at all, only through an evolutionary process, i.e., through random variation, natural selection, etc.). Rather, ecology changes our values by changing our *concepts* of the world and of ourselves in relation to the world. It reveals new relations among objects which, once revealed, stir our ancient centers of moral feeling.
>
> *(Callicott, 1982, p. 174)*

Callicott points out that opponents of abortion similarly use information to trigger sentimental reactions in their audience:

> [They] present medical evidence to show that a fetus only five months after conception has all the outward physical features, circulatory and nervous systems, and internal organs of a human being. They wish us to conclude that the fetus is a proper object of those of our moral sympathies which are naturally excited by human beings, especially by human infants.
>
> *(Callicott, 1982, p. 171)*

He goes on to say that Leopold is doing the same thing in the first part of *A Sand County Almanac*, the 'sketches' of activities human and otherwise around the Leopold shack:

> Leopold makes use of an analogous ploy in the "Shack Sketches" of *A Sand County Almanac* when he represents other animals anthropomorphically: amorous woodcocks sky dancing, mouse engineers fretting, bird dogs patiently educating their smell-deficient masters in the fine art of olfactory discrimination, etc., etc. Leopold's anthropomorphism is always restrained by and confined to the theological facts of the animal behavior he describes. The mouse engineer is not equipped with a transit, nor does the woodcock present his lady with an engagement ring. Unlike Kenneth Grahame in *Wind in the Willows*, Leopold does not dress his animals in morning coats and sit them at table for tea and biscuits. Nonetheless, Leopold tries to excite our sympathy and fellow feeling by portraying animal behavior as in many ways similar to our own and as motivated by similar psychological experiences.
>
> (Callicott, 1982, p. 171–172)

This concludes our description of the four elements of Callicott's later interpretation of Leopold. In Box 10.1, we point out how the four elements shed light on Leopold's language in the seven quotations from the opening and closing paragraphs of "The Land Ethic" that we used at the start of this chapter to illustrate how pithy but somewhat cryptic his nature writings are.

10.4 SOME OBJECTIONS TO CALLICOTT'S INTERPRETATION OF LEOPOLD

In this section, we discuss some objections to the various elements of Callicott's later interpretation of Leopold and his land ethic, grouping the issues under four headings: (a) the normative status of the interpretation, (b) some issues with SOP-1 and SOP-2, (c) Callicott's and Leopold's appeal to group selection, and (d) the historical accuracy of Callicott's understanding of Hume's moral psychology.

BOX 10.1   **How Callicott's Interpretation Illuminates Leopold's Elliptical Prose**

We can now say how all seven of the quotations from Leopold's essay "The Land Ethic" that we listed at the beginning of this chapter relate to the four elements of Callicott's later interpretation of Leopold on ethics. The first element, communitarianism, holds that humans are essentially communal animals. On Callicott's reading of him, Leopold's references to *"the biotic community"* in the first and last quotations reflect his commitment to communitarianism:

> **Land Ethic Statement #1:** "A thing is right when it tends to preserve the integrity, stability, and beauty of the biotic community." (Leopold, 1949, pp. 224–225)

> **Land Ethic Statement #7:** "In short, a land ethic changes the role of *Homo sapiens* from conqueror of the land-community to plain member and citizen of it. It implies respect for his fellow-members, and also respect for the community as such." (Leopold, 1949, p. 204)

According to the second element of Callicott's interpretation, which is Hume's moral psychology, moral judgments are grounded in natural, in-born human 'sentiments,' but those sentiments' activity can be affected by our changing understanding of the communities we are members of. On Callicott's reading of Leopold, this explains his statements that 'love' for land is necessary, along with some 'intellectual content,' for a land ethic to take hold of our thinking:

> **Land Ethic Statement #2:** "The evolution of a land ethic is an intellectual as well as an emotional process. . . . I think it is a truism that as the ethical frontier advances from the individual to the community, its intellectual content increases." (Leopold, 1949, p. 225)

> **Land Ethic Statement #3:** "It is inconceivable to me that an ethical relation to land [a land ethic] can exist without love, respect, and admiration for land, and a high regard for its value. By value, I of course mean value in the philosophical sense." (Leopold, 1949, p. 223)

The references to the evolution of the land ethic involving an 'intellectual' process are suggestive of Callicott's account of how

BOX 10.1 **(cont.)**

spreading 'ecological literacy' (an intellectual process) will trigger our natural sentiments' expression toward non-human individuals and the biotic community. And the references to "love" and "an emotional process" reflect the Humean view that ethics is based on 'sentiments' and cannot arise from reason alone. Relatedly, in Statement #7 above, describing *Homo sapiens* as a "plain member and citizen" of the biotic community is the kind of anthropomorphism that Callicott says that Leopold uses to encourage the shift in intellectual framing that causes Hume's natural sentiments to be active toward non-human organisms and the biotic community. Finally, while Statement #1 expresses the holistic dimension of the land ethic that arises when humans' natural sentiments are extended from human communities to the biotic community with the emergence of "universal ecological literacy," statement #7 adds that the land ethic "implies respect for his fellow-members, and also respect for the community as such," which reflects the view that earlier "accretions" to morality remain operative.

10.4.1 *The Normative Status of the Interpretation*

First, we want to note a concern about the normative status of Callicott's interpretation of Leopold. Callicott offers his reconstruction of Leopold's moral thinking as an interpretation of Leopold's view on ethics, as an explanation of what Leopold is saying. One can explain what someone else is saying without agreeing with them, however, as when an historian reconstructs the ethical reasoning of the Nazis during the Third Reich. So Callicott could be read as explaining what Leopold was saying, without meaning to give an argument in support of Leopold's view. But Callicott certainly seems supportive of Leopold's views, and of environmentalists' views in general, and he began his "Triangular Affair" paper by saying that "environmental ethics ... can be defined ostensively by using Leopold's land ethic as the exemplary type" (Callicott, 1980, p.

311). Furthermore, Callicott titled the 1989 collection of his essays on the land ethic: In **Defense** of the Land Ethic.

Obviously Callicott is trying to show how the writings of a non-philosopher – writings that have inspired a wide variety of environmentalists, land managers, foresters, etc. – can be understood to be reflecting some important traditions in moral philosophy: the communitarian view of human nature as essentially social, the moral psychology of Hume, and Darwin's attempt to square ethical norms with evolution under natural selection. But there is a danger of lapsing into a simple appeal to authority here. 'Appeal to authority' is the logical fallacy of concluding that something is true simply because an authority figure said it. As Norva Y. S. Lo (Yeuk Sze Lo) puts it: "Whether the land ethic as re-presented by Callicott (or, for that matter, any other applied ethic) is an adequate ethical position, however, depends not merely on whether it has some prominent figures as its historical predecessors" (Lo, 2001a, p. 331).

Relatedly, we worry about environmentalists appealing to authority when they quote Leopold's *A Sand County Almanac*. As we noted in the opening paragraph of this chapter, environmentalists sometimes treat *Sand County* as 'scripture,' as if to say, "Leopold said it, I believe it, and that settles it." As we will note in the rest of this section, there are various problems with Callicott's reconstruction of Leopold's land ethic, and given how elliptically stated it is in Leopold's *Sand County*, the land ethic is hardly an unambiguous and practical guide for environmentalists.

10.4.2   Some Issues with SOP-1 and SOP-2

Callicott claims that communitarianism is an over-arching approach to ethics that ties Leopold's talk of 'accretions' and the two second-order principles that Callicott proposes into a single theory. It does seem that a communitarian could hold that, as humans came to be organized into larger and larger social organizations that are 'nested' within each other (e.g. a family, a local community, a nation-state, and a 'global village'), they would have recognized different sets of principles as appropriate to those different kinds of communities. That does seem to match Leopold's description of the development of ethical thinking via accretions in the passages that we quoted from "The Land Ethic" in Section 10.3.4.

What of the two second-order principles that Callicott proposes for adjudicating conflicts among the principles governing different accretions and communities? SOP-1 does seem communitarian in spirit. For someone who grounds moral thinking in community membership, it might seem plausible to rank duties associated with older, more closely knit communities over those associated with larger and less closely knit communities.

But what of SOP-2? In a carefully argued critical overview of Callicott's writings about the land ethic from his 1980 "Triangular Affair" piece thru 2001, Lo describes the problem thus:

> unlike SOP-1, SOP-2 does not employ the 'vocabulary of community' at all ... Hence, SOP-2, as it stands, is a quite independent thesis from the communitarianism advocated by Callicott to found the land ethic. Indeed, if SOP-2 can be "derived" from anything, an obvious candidate is Peter Singer's utilitarian egalitarianism, which proposes equal consideration for equal interests, a position which Callicott constantly attacks and distances from his own communitarianism.
>
> *(Lo, 2001a, p. 349)*

As we noted in our discussions of the concept of interests in the work of Singer (Section 8.3) and in extensionist attempts to ground ecoholism (Section 9.3.1), attempts to extend the concept of 'interests' to include non-sentient individual organisms, and holistic entities such as species and ecosystems, face a number of philosophical challenges. Presumably that is why Callicott inserted this parenthetical aside into his formulation of SOP-2: "stronger interests (for lack of a better word) generate duties that take precedence." Callicott is right to be concerned about invoking this concept, since he takes pains to distance his/Leopold's thinking about ethics from the anthropocentric and sentientist ethics that have dominated modern moral theory. For it is in those theoretical frameworks that the concept of 'interests' plays a large role.

In addition to noting the strangeness of Callicott's appeal to 'interests' in SOP-2, Lo argues that Callicott's second-order principles would require a kind of sacrifice analogous to one that Callicott takes Singer's ethics to task for requiring. In various places, including "Animal Liberation and Environmental Ethics: Back Together Again," Callicott claims that Singer's utilitarian egalitarianism implies very different (and less plausible) conclusions than Callicott's communitarian approach. Specifically, he trusts that readers will find implausible Singer's argument that:

> he has failed in his duty because he does not donate the greatest portion of his modest income to help alleviate the suffering of starving people living halfway around the world, even though to do so would impoverish not only himself, but his own children.
>
> (Callicott, 1988, p. 167)

Lo argues that Callicott's own SOP-2 would require a similar, if less severe sacrifice, "because the interest in not starving to death is stronger than the interest in being educated" (Lo, 2001a, p. 353). That is, affluent people like Callicott and Singer would be required – by Callicott's later interpretation of the Leopold land ethic – to send the money that they would spend on their children's educations to famine relief instead. Lo concludes that in developing his response to the charge of ecofascism, Callicott has *significantly undermined* the environment-favoring implications that can be claimed for the Leopold land ethic.

10.4.3   Callicott/Leopold on the Evolution of Morality

We have seen that, in his reconstruction of Leopold's land ethic, Callicott appeals to several biological concepts which he seems to regard as decisive. He invokes a Darwinian account of between-group selection to defend a psychological thesis about humans' affinity for fellow community members. He further proposes that insights from the science of ecology reveal that humans are part of an inclusive community, comprised of various species of plant and animal. The idea, it seems, is that a gradual appreciation of these scientific 'truths' will naturally motivate everyone to sympathize and cooperate with non-human community members.

Of course, the sciences of evolution and ecology have advanced considerably since the days of Darwin and Leopold. The status of group selection has been particularly controversial, with many evolutionary biologists denying its plausibility. The notion of an ecological community, also, has been one of the more contested concepts in ecology. In this subsection we briefly review some of these debates and consider their potential impact on Callicott's reconstruction of the land ethic.

10.4.3.1 Group Selection

The idea that certain traits evolve 'for the good of the group' came under scientific scrutiny beginning in 1966, with the publication of G.C. Williams' *Adaptation and Natural Selection*. Williams [1926–2010] argued that altruistic traits cannot be maintained by natural selection acting over the long term. Before considering his argument, it is important to avoid a common terminological confusion. In biology, the terms 'altruistic' and 'selfish' have different meanings than they do in common English. Ordinarily, to describe an act as altruistic means that it was performed with the intention of benefiting someone else. Likewise, an act is said to be selfish if is intended to promote only the interests of the person who performs it. In biology, however, altruism and selfishness have nothing to do with intentions or motives, and everything to do with the effects of a trait on the reproductive fitness of the organism possessing the trait. A trait is *biologically altruistic* if it tends to reduce the reproductive fitness of its bearer while simultaneously increasing the reproductive fitness of other (unrelated) organisms. Likewise, a trait is *biologically selfish* if it primarily tends to promote the reproductive fitness of its bearer or immediate kin. These biological definitions make no claim about psychological motive. Indeed, an organism doesn't require a brain to qualify as biologically altruistic. Even a virus particle can be altruistic, biologically speaking, if it decreases its own reproductive fitness in order to promote that of its host.

Williams (1966) argued that biological altruism is unlikely to evolve, or if it does, it is unlikely to persist over an evolutionary timeframe. He imagined a group of altruistic organisms, each one sacrificing its own fitness to promote the fitness of non-kin. Eventually, Williams notes, a selfish mutant is bound to arise which lacks the altruistic trait. This individual will receive all of the reproductive benefits offered by its altruistic cohort, while at the same time making no fitness sacrifice. Over successive generations, the proportion of selfish individuals will increase more rapidly than the altruists thanks to this fitness advantage. Eventually, Williams argued, the altruistic group will become 'subverted' by the selfish mutant's offspring.

Williams' argument was so elegant and seemingly compelling that, among evolutionary biologists, group selection rapidly fell into disfavor. Indeed, it became anathema to describe a trait as being 'good for the group' – let alone good for the species or community. However, in recent decades, the concept of group selection has undergone something of a renaissance. This has been thanks, in part, to the theoretical work of biologist David Sloan Wilson and philosopher Elliott Sober. As we will now explain, however, this revised version of group selection (more accurately described as 'multi-level selection') is much more nuanced than the naïve claims that Williams criticized.

Theoretical discussions of this topic tend to be rather technical, steeped in mathematical models which are beyond the scope of this book to explore.[17] However, one important development in this field has been a greater appreciation for the role of assortative interactions. Sober and Wilson (1998) point out that many organisms are capable of choosing to associate with certain individuals while excluding others from the group. Even the lowly bacterium is capable of cooperating

---

[17] See e.g. Gardner (2015a, 2015b) and Goodnight (2015).

selectively with similarly disposed group members (Diggle et al., 2007). Groups of altruistic individuals thus have various means at their disposal for excluding selfish variants from their midst. This is a very different scenario from the one that Williams imagined, where selfish mutants were the unavoidable beneficiaries of altruistic behavior. According to Sober and Wilson (1998), such indiscriminate altruism is biologically unrealistic.

In addition to assortative interactions, Sober and Wilson identify several other factors capable of mitigating the strength of within-group selection while enhancing the strength of between-group selection. One such factor is culture. From a biological perspective, culture can be seen as a mechanism of epigenetic inheritance by which traits are passed down over generations. Cultural transmission has the added feature of allowing for 'horizontal' transmission of traits to non-kin. One potential result of horizontal transmission is a group whose members are phenotypically similar to one another, despite genetic differences, and which differ phenotypically from other, culturally distinct groups. Culture therefore has the capacity for dampening genetic variation within groups while accentuating variation among groups. Such conditions are potentially conducive to between-group selection, *provided that it is not counter-acted by selection at some lower level.*

A few things should be clear from this brief discussion of multilevel selection theory. First, the theory that has grown up in the wake of Williams' (1966) criticism is, in a sense, more temperate than the naïve version of group selection that preceded it. It was once considered acceptable to speak vaguely about traits being good for the group, or the species, or even the ecosystem – as if these amounted to the same thing. Biologists are now careful to specify the precise level at which selection is thought to occur. This is important, in part, because for selection to occur at a given level, one should expect to find mechanisms for assortative interaction at that level. Otherwise, a subversion process is bound to kick in. A corollary of this realization is that as a group becomes larger and more disparate in its membership, it becomes more difficult to police assortative interactions. This is one reason why many biologists who nowadays might entertain the possibility of *between*-group selection wouldn't countenance selection at the levels of species or ecosystems. Such collectives are too diffusely aggregated to qualify as credible units of selection. A second feature of modern multi-level selection theory is that *within*-group selection doesn't drop out of the picture. Specifically, one needs to consider not only the potential benefits that a trait might bestow on a group, but also the fitness costs to the individual group member. Despite recognizing a place for between-group selection in nature, biologists continue to view selection at lower levels (acting on the individual organism or the genetic variant) as more influential.

Turning to Callicott/Leopold, one is reminded of the less refined version of group selection theory that Williams and his followers criticized. For one thing, Callicott assumes that between-group selection among ancestral humans is likely to have selected for an open-ended psychological mechanism – one that is indiscriminate about the inclusion of other organisms into the group. A population of humans who possessed such a mechanism would be exceedingly vulnerable to the subversion problem. On the contrary, one would predict that selection among groups of ancestral humans would have resulted in a tendency to be highly discriminating in our cooperative tendencies. This is sometimes described as the "darker side" of group selection theory. On a Darwinian model of inter-group competition, nature should have supplied us not only with positive sentiments toward in-group members, but also more hostile sentiments toward other groups. Of course, Callicott would encourage us to expand our sense of community as far as possible beyond the immediate in-group. Presumably, this is the role that he assigns to the scientific concept of an ecological community. We will turn to that topic momentarily. The main point to emphasize at this stage is that it would be naïve to think that between-group selection, even if it has been a constructive force in human evolution, has equipped us only with positive sentiments toward others.

Before turning to Callicott's presentation of the community concept in ecology, it is important to highlight another issue that evolutionary biologists are bound to raise. Notice that Callicott's discussion of human evolution, like Darwin's, is entirely speculative. So far, we have been entertaining hypotheses about how between-group selection *might* have shaped the human mind. No evidence has been provided by Callicott that between-group selection has *in fact* shaped our psychological evolution. Evolutionary biologists are cautious not to place too much stock in these sorts of adaptationist 'just so' stories. Such hypotheses are all too easy to generate from the armchair, but all too difficult to test empirically.

10.4.3.2 The Community Concept in Ecology

Readers who are even moderately familiar with the science of ecology and its history will appreciate that there is no straightforward answer to the question *what is an ecological community?* The discipline has changed considerably over the decades since Leopold developed his ideas. Frederic Clements [1874–1945] was an influential American ecologist in the decades prior to the publication of *Sand County*. Based on his work on ecological succession, Clements was led to the view that ecological communities were highly integrated assemblages of plants and animals. Clements often drew parallels between the organisms in a community and the vital organs in an individual – thus giving rise to the idea of the community as a literal superorganism.

It would be an understatement to say that ecologists have since rejected the superorganism view of ecological communities. The discipline of paleoecology informs us that individual species come and go from communities on a geological time scale (Kricher, 1998). Some ecologists go so far as to defend the extreme antithesis of Clements' view: regarding communities as *weakly* integrated, such that individual species come and go with only minimal impact on each other's survival. This 'open ended' view of ecological communities dates back at least to the work of American ecologist Henry Gleason [1882–1975] (1926), and has garnered renewed interest with the 'ecological neutral theory' of ecologists Stephen Hubble (2001) and Graham Bell (2001). Today, most ecologists recognize these as opposite ends of a conti- nuum (Rosindell et al., 2011). Real biological communities probably land somewhere in the middle, between a high degree of interdepen- dence and complete neutrality.

But let us stop for a moment and ask, what if Clements had been right? That is, what would it mean for Callicott's commu- nitarian ethic if ecological communities really were integrated superorganisms? As Callicott would have it, humans are biologi- cally disposed to extend their moral sentiments to members of the same *social* community. This is the psychological framework that we supposedly inherit from our group-selected ancestors. Callicott imagines that, once we realize that we belong to a superorganismic community, our moral sentiments will naturally follow suit. But this assumes that people will fail to distinguish between the social communities in which we evolved and the ecological communities of which we are supposedly a part. Undeniably, these are two very different types of communities. A human community is unified by cooperative social interactions among people. An ecological com- munity is unified, *if at all*, by various sorts of local biotic interac- tions such as mutualism, competition, predation, and parasitism. It is quite a leap to suppose that a psychological mechanism that has evolved to be sensitive to cooperative social relationships among humans will easily recognize ecological relationships as morally belonging to the same category. We must be cautious not to be overly swayed by the ecologists' metaphorical use of language (see also Larson, 2011).

But let us follow Callicott in blurring our eyes to this distinction. There is a deeper implication that follows from the Clementsonian view of communities that some environmentalists are bound to find unpalatable. Even Clements didn't suppose that all of the organisms on earth comprise a single, unified community. For Clements, ecological superorganisms had sharp boundaries. We cannot assume that, if such communities were to exist in nature, our evolved psychological mechanisms will also be blind to this fact. Recall from the previous discussion of between-group selection that there is a 'dark' side to our evolved moral sentiments (assuming for the moment that the Darwinian story is true). Just as humans can be expected to sympathize with fellow community members, they should be apathetic *or even hostile* to non-community members. According to the Clementsonian picture, people living in different parts of the earth belong to different ecological communities that are each defined by sharp boundaries. So, a person living in the Canadian Arctic shouldn't have the slightest concern about the ecological communities existing in the Amazon or Australia. We suspect that most environmentalists would be rather uncomfortable with this implication – we certainly are. Somewhat ironically, Callicott's story about our group-selected moral psychology, when combined with a superorganismic view of ecological communities, entails an extreme form of moral parochialism.

Of course, Clements' view about the interconnectedness of ecological communities has not been borne out by the march of ecological science. Perhaps Callicott would be tempted to avoid the unsavory implication just mentioned by adopting an updated conception of ecological communities. We will close this section by considering what such a proposal might look like.

In fact, it is difficult to translate the contemporary scientific conception of ecological communities into terms that Callicott would find amenable. Part of the problem is that ecological communities are defined as *locally interacting* assemblages of plants and animals. External factors that influence the composition of community 'from the outside,' as it were, are described as regional. So, strictly speaking, it makes no sense to say that the boundary of an ecological community can be expanded outward to include an ever more encompassing range of species and processes. The more one takes such regional influences into account, *the less* one is talking about ecological communities in the strict sense of the term.

This perhaps sounds like just a semantic point about the restrictive meaning of 'community' in contemporary ecology. In fact, there is an important theoretical consideration guiding ecologists' use of this term. Earlier, we noted that ecologists disagree about the extent to which local interactions between species determine the composition of ecological communities. Perhaps the closest thing to a consensus among ecologists is that interactions are *scale dependent* (Kneitel and Chase, 2004, Ricklefs, 2008, Chase and Myers, 2011). If one draws a narrow boundary around an assemblage of plants and animals, then it is likely that local interactions among species will have an influence on community membership. As one broadens the geographical boundaries, beyond the local community to the surrounding region or metacommunity, other factors start to become more influential than species interactions. At a medium spatial scale, the assemblage of species in a given region will be determined more by factors like speciation, migration, and extinction and less by ecological relationships. Interactions among species matter even less to the composition of a biological assemblage when one gets to a broad spatial scale, like an entire continent. At this level, macro-evolutionary processes such as geology and climate determine species composition.

Again, all of this is far from uncontroversial (see Chase and Myers, 2011, for a discussion). But let us take this picture at face value and consider the implications for a communitarian land ethic. We have suggested that there is (roughly) an inverse relationship between the geographic scale of an ecological assemblage and the degree to which its component species are interconnected. The further out one goes in drawing the boundary around an ecological assemblage, the less the species matter *to one another*. This should come as no surprise. After all, every species is limited to some degree in its spatial distribution. The problem, however, is that according to the communitarian picture, people should care morally about the species with which they interact. It would therefore seem that moral parochialism is an unavoidable consequence of communitarianism, even on a less 'bounded' understanding of ecological communities.

To drive home the significance of this implication, it is perhaps helpful to bring things back around to human communities. It is a truism about human psychology that we tend to consider our immediate friends and neighbors as more morally significant than people who live on the other side of the world. This is a point that Peter Singer, for example, often laments in his work on utilitarianism: that people find it all too easy to turn a blind eye to the suffering of people with whom they find it difficult to identify. To overcome this moral failing, we tend to think, requires a certain amount of rational thought. One must stop to appreciate the fact that there is no principled basis for morally disregarding people who belong to remote social communities. In the human case, at least, most people would consider it a bad thing to allow our group-selected sentiments to be the guide of our moral compass.

A similar implication holds for an ethic that is grounded in ecological communities. Regardless of whether they are thought of as superorganisms or more loosely defined aggregations, the strengths of community interactions are insignificant at large spatial scales. The communitarian vision would have us extending moral consideration only to the organisms with which we interact on a local or regional scale. Perhaps in ecology, as in society, it isn't entirely palatable to base moral duties on the strength of community relationships.

10.4.4 The Historical Accuracy of Callicott's Interpretation of Hume

A final problem for Callicott's work on Leopold is that some philosophers have claimed that Callicott misinterprets Hume when he says that Hume recognizes a moral concern on the part of human moral agents for their society or community *as such*. One of the coauthors of this book asserted this in a brief comment (Varner, 1991) and later supplied some defense of the assertion (Varner, 1998, pp. 12–16). A much more thorough discussion of this issue has since been provided by philosophers Alan Carter (2000), Y.S. Lo (2001b), and Jennifer

Welchman (2009). A detailed consideration of this issue of historical accuracy would take us too far afield, but the basic issue is this.

As we explained earlier, Hume grounds knowledge of moral duties in moral agents' sympathetic reactions to various treatments of our fellow human beings. But sympathy can only operate for other sentient beings. And thus while Hume could recognize duties *to* individual humans and sentient animals, Hume is committed to a reductionist account of the interests or well-being of a community of sentient individuals[18] (compare the concern about "reductionist slippage" in Section 9.2.4). Thus, Hume would not recognize duties to communities as such, but that is precisely what Callicott emphasizes as the unique feature of the Leopold land ethic. In short, as Lo puts it:[19]

> "public interest" is, for Hume, simply the interests of "strangers" all taken together. And these strangers are individual persons who are strange to oneself, not a strange entity over and above individual strangers ... Callicott has not provided adequate textual support from Hume's [works on ethics] for his own holism.
>
> *(Lo, 2001b, pp. 117 and 116).*

10.5   WHERE DOES READING LEOPOLD GET US?

We began this chapter by noting the outsized influence that Aldo Leopold has had on the environmentalist community, and that a leading graduate-level textbook on conservation biology describes his land ethic as "the most biologically sensible and comprehensive of any approach to nature" and says that it "should serve as the philosophical basis of most decisions affecting biodiversity" (Groom

---

[18] In his discussion of this issue, Varner points out that Darwin – whom Callicott characterizes as adopting Hume's moral psychology along with the concern for communities as such that Callicott attributes to Hume – himself adopts an explicitly reductionist conception of the welfare of a human community (Varner, 1998, pp. 15–16).

[19] We should note, however, that Carter (2000, sections V–XII), Lo (2006), and Welchman (2009, sections 2 through 4) each describe ways of basing a *kind* of land ethic on a careful re-examination of the role of reason and 'artificial virtues' (ones not grounded in our 'natural' sympathetic reactions) in Hume's ethics.

et al., 2006, p. 12). Based on our survey of Callicott's philosophical 'reconstruction' of Leopold's land ethic, we disagree.

In Section 10.4.3 we identified serious objections to Callicott's use of Darwin – in particular, Callicott's misunderstanding of the ability of group selection to give rise in humans to positive sentiments toward the community as such (or even other groups of humans!). We also objected to Callicott's equivocation in his use of the term 'community,' slipping from social community to ecological community, as if the two were even remotely equivalent. These are two critical planks of Callicott's reconstruction, and such biological misunderstandings hardly recommend the land ethic as a "biologically sensible" approach to ethics.

In Section 10.4.2 we noted that, in response to a charge of ecofascism, Callicott invokes SOP-1: "obligations generated by membership in more venerable and intimate communities take precedence over those generated in more recently emerged and impersonal communities." Invoked by itself, SOP-1 seriously compromises the environmental implications of the land ethic. To avoid this, Callicott needs SOP-2: "stronger interests (for lack of a better word) generate duties that take precedence over duties generated by weaker interests." But it is very difficult to see how Callicott's appeal to communitarianism in ethics functions to justify SOP-2. We also noted, in Section 10.4.4, that Callicott's understanding of Hume's moral psychology seems to be historically inaccurate.

Here we add that we don't find that the land ethic – either as reconstructed by Callicott in his work interpreting Leopold, or as articulated by Leopold himself in *A Sand County Almanac* – actually provides any detailed practical guidance.

Regarding Callicott's interpretation, we think that a key problem lies in SOP-2. As we saw in Section 10.3.2, the SOP-2 that Callicott posits as governing conflicts of duty generated by different ethical 'accretions' appeals to the notion of a 'stronger interest' without providing any general way of ranking the 'interests' at stake in various cases. Callicott gives a couple of examples where he thinks that our intuitive judgment will match his – cases where he thinks it is clear that a 'stronger interest' is at stake in the duty related to a more recent accretion like the land ethic. But citing a couple of cases about which the author and his readers' intuitions might be the same does not count as applying the method of reflective equilibrium as described in Section 7.1.4. A thorough attempt to apply that method would involve looking at a range of particular cases, and then formulating a principle that somehow explains how to distinguish the cases in which there is a 'stronger interest' at stake from those in which there is not. As we noted in Section 10.4.3, Callicott isn't even comfortable (for good reason) with using the concept of 'interests' in his statement of SOP-2. So we have to conclude that Callicott's interpretation of Leopold's land ethic remains incomplete as a practical guide to ethics in general, and to biodiversity policy specifically.

Regarding the text of *A Sand County Almanac* itself, we believe that the following summarizes all the practical guidance that Leopold offered in the book, based on his experiences during his career in forestry and game management.[20]

When Leopold arrived in the southwest with a master's degree in Forestry from Yale, he was confident about land managers' ability to thoroughly understand ecosystems and their ability to tweak ecosystems to get just the results they desired. This is why he had no qualms about advocating predator extermination during his time in the southwest: he was confident that wildlife managers could get human hunters to replace predation by wolves and mountain lions while leaving the forest ecosystem otherwise unchanged. By the time he left for Madison, however, he had noticed problems with southwestern watersheds, which he detailed in a 1923 paper that was never published during his lifetime ("Some Fundamentals of Conservation in the Southwest" was first published posthumously in the first volume of *Environmental Ethics*; Leopold, 1979). In that paper,

---

[20] This summary is adapted from Varner (1998, pp. 131–133), and the five numbered points below are reproduced from there.

Leopold cited evidence from "old timers" in the area that 90% of the watersheds studied were significantly degraded, while tree ring data indicated that the climate had been stable during the period. Leopold concluded that grazing had disturbed plant communities that had previously anchored stream banks.

Shortly after Leopold left for Madison, the famous irruption of deer on the Kaibab Plateau above the Grand Canyon that we referred to in Section 8.6.1 occurred, with over 50% of the herd said to have starved to death during two winters.[21] By the time he was writing *Sand County* in the 1940s, Leopold was involved in a pitched battle over how to manage Wisconsin's then-overpopulated deer herd, attempting to prevent a similar episode. By then, he had become convinced that:

1) We do not (and probably cannot) know enough to tinker precisely with ecosystems, designing them to get just the outcomes we want.[22]

That is why he concluded that "The conqueror role is eventually self-defeating" (Leopold, 1949, p. 204), and that while "The ordinary citizen today assumes that science knows what makes the community clock tick; the scientist is equally sure that he does not. He knows that the biotic mechanism is so complex that its workings may never be fully understood" (Leopold, 1949, p. 205).

From his experiences with southwestern watersheds Leopold also concluded that:

2) Regions vary in resilience, in the amount of human modification they can sustain without losing their long-term fecundity.

In *Sand County* Leopold emphasized that while some regions of the earth, for example Western Europe and Japan, had had their aboriginal biota completely replaced without losing their general fecundity, southwestern watersheds were becoming severely impoverished

---

[21] See Figure 8.1, the bottom half of which reproduces Leopold's 1943 graph from Flader (1974, p. 203). But see also Daniel Botkin's (1990, pp. 76–80) skepticism about Leopold's reconstruction of population figures during the Kaibab irruption.

[22] A sentiment still largely shared by ecologists, but we have certainly gotten better at managing ecosystems.

after only 50 years of the grazing that was introduced by Europeans. "Biotas seem to differ in their capacity to sustain violent conversion" (p. 218), he concluded. In the section of "The Land Ethic" titled "The Land Pyramid," he observes that land "is not merely soil; it is a fountain of energy flowing through a circuit of soils, plants, and animals" (p. 216) and "the native plants and animals kept the energy circuit open; others may or may not" (p. 218). He concluded that:

3) In all regions, the original, naturally evolved biota maintain long-term fecundity; introduced species may or may not.

And so:

4) In more fragile regions, a greater effort should be made to adopt agricultural and landscaping practices which mimic or approximate the original, naturally evolved ecosystems of the region.

Finally:

5) In all regions, samples of the original biota (including all native species) should be preserved.

Leopold's changed view of wolves, in particular, reflected the skepticism that he had developed about humans' ability to manipulate ecosystems with precision. As he put it in his "Report to American Wildlife Institute on the Utah and Oregon Wildlife Units" in 1941: "The natural aggregation of lions and other predators on an overstocked range, and their natural dispersion from an understocked one, is the only precision instrument known to deer management" (quoted in Flader, 1974, p. 176).

We think that statements ##2–5 above are good general advice with regard to the value of biodiversity and how to preserve it. But the advice reflects considerations of instrumental value of biodiversity in supporting ecosystem services, rather than an ecoholist appeal to the intrinsic value of species and ecosystems. And as far as practical guidance goes, statements ##2–5 are of the 'be sure to pay heed to this in deciding on a general conservation strategy' variety, rather than principles that give much substantive, practical guidance to policy makers.

We conclude both that (i) *considered philosophically*, as an intrinsic value-based rationale to conserve biodiversity, the Leopold land ethic as reconstructed by Callicott is weak, and (ii) *considered pragmatically*, as a substantive, action-guiding set of principles, it represents only some high-level concerns that should be kept in mind when deciding whether, where, when, and how to preserve biodiversity.

10.6 FURTHER READING

In this chapter we have concentrated on Callicott's interpretation of Leopold as an ecoholist, because that has been the most widely read and discussed interpretation. For an alternative, the reader should see either of the following works by Bryan Norton, who reads Leopold as a pragmatist who believed that the implications of ecoholism and a kind of enlightened anthropocentrism converge in practice. Readers interested in Leopold's development as a scientist should see his professional biography by Flader (1974).

Flader, S.L. (1974). *Thinking Like a Mountain: Aldo Leopold and the Evolution of an Ecological Attitude Toward Deer, Wolves, And Forests*. Columbia, MO: University of Missouri Press.

Lo, Y.S. (2001). "The land ethic and Callicott's ethical system (1980–2001): An overview and critique." *Inquiry*, 44, 331–358.

Millstein, Roberta L. (2015). "Re-examining the Darwinian basis for Aldo Leopold's Land Ethic," *Ethics, Policy & Environment*, 18, 301–317.

Norton, Bryan G. (1987). "The Constancy of Leopold's Land Ethic." *Conservation Biology* 2: 93–102.

Norton, Bryan G. (1991). "Aldo Leopold and the Search for an Integrated Theory of Environmental Management." In Bryan Norton, *Toward Unity Among Environmentalists*. Oxford: Oxford University Press, pp. 39–60.

Ouderkirk, W. and Hill, J. eds. (2002) *Land, Value, Community: Callicott and Environmental Philosophy*. Albany: State University of New York Press.

Should Biodiversity Be Conserved for Its Aesthetic Value?

II.I INTRODUCTION

The previous four chapters considered whether conservation goals are supported by intrinsic value arguments. We found that extensionist arguments provide strong support for conserving sentient animals and possibly the habitats on which they depend. However, these arguments do not extend to non-sentient organisms and ecological wholes. Unfortunately, a communitarian argument fares no better as a defense of ecoholism. Where, then, does this leave us with respect to the environmentalist agenda? The first part of this book found that instrumental value defenses provide only partial support for environmentalism. This shortcoming motivated the exploration of intrinsic value arguments as, potentially, a source of more comprehensive justification. Now, after a careful consideration of those arguments and their limitations, it seems that elements of the environmentalist agenda continue to lack rational support.

Some environmentalists who find themselves in this predicament turn to aesthetic-value defenses of conservation. They argue that certain organisms, species, and ecosystems ought to be conserved just because they are beautiful. This idea has prima facie appeal for at least two reasons. First, beauty is a strong motivator for those who appreciate it. Environmental organizations often capitalize on this fact, presenting endangered species and habitats in the most appealing light possible. By the same token, emphasizing the more grotesque features of an industrial project is an effective way to rally opposition against it. Indeed, much of the 'discourse' over environmental issues already happens at an aesthetic level. If aesthetic values could be made explicit and treated systematically by a philosophical theory, then perhaps the promotion of natural beauty could become a central plank of conservation policy.

A second reason why some environmentalists are drawn to aesthetic value is because of its historical influence. Aldo Leopold's canonical formulation of the land ethic – "A thing is right when it tends to preserve the integrity, stability, and beauty of the biotic community" – seems to place beauty on a par with stability and integrity. Contemporary environmentalists such as Paul and Anne Ehrlich (1992) also identify aesthetic value as an important reason to conserve biodiversity (see, e.g., quote at the start of Section 1.7). But the most impressive example of aesthetic justification occurred during the nineteenth century, with the establishment of National Parks at Yosemite and Yellowstone. Efforts began in 1860 when Thomas Star King, a prominent Unitarian minister, published a series of travel letters describing the natural beauty of Yosemite and the impending threat of settlement. These letters prompted Frederick Law Olmstead to visit Yosemite in 1863 and he soon joined the campaign for its conservation. Olmstead is reported to have employed artists and photographers to depict the natural beauty of Yosemite, whose work he then presented to Congress alongside scientific findings of the Geological Survey of California (Huth, 1948). In 1864, a bill was passed establishing a land grant to partially protect the Yosemite Valley, with Olmstead appointed as its chief commissioner. Olmstead continued to emphasize the aesthetic qualities of Yosemite, arguing that the preservation of scenic beauty was the "primary reason for its existence" (Hargrove, 1992). Examples such as this remind us that aesthetic value ought to be given serious philosophical consideration as a reason to conserve biodiversity. Philosopher J. Baird Callicott goes so far as to proclaim that, "In the conservation and resource management arena, natural aesthetics has, indeed, been much more influential historically than environmental ethics" (Callicott, 2008, p. 106).

However, despite these prima facie considerations, both professional philosophers and environmentalists have paid relatively little attention to the aesthetic values that are found in nature. Simple disciplinary inertia might account for the philosophers' oversight. The field of aesthetics, a fairly small philosophical subdiscipline to begin with, has focused primarily on human artifacts (painting, music, literature, etc.) in lieu of naturally occurring objects (Hepburn, 1966). This focus has only started to shift during the last few decades with the emergence of environmental aesthetics as a research program (Carlson and Lintott, 2008). Nonetheless, even within this field, relatively little attention has been paid to the link between aesthetics and conservation. Philosophers have been much more interested in the question, *What makes some natural object or scene beautiful?* than in the question, *Should species or ecosystems be conserved simply because they are beautiful?*

When it comes to the majority of environmentalists, a very different explanation for their neglect of aesthetic value seems likely. Judgments about beauty are commonly regarded as nothing more than an expression of personal preference. For example, we can easily imagine someone who prefers the sight of a large dam over a freely flowing river – perhaps because she has specialized interests in hydroelectric engineering. It is difficult to explain why, despite such individual preferences, the unobstructed river is in fact more beautiful. The temptation, rather, is to label all such judgments 'subjective' under the platitude that beauty lies in the eye of the beholder.

Most philosophers reject this subjectivist account of beauty for reasons that will be considered momentarily. However, the popularity of this attitude seems to have dissuaded some thinkers from seriously entertaining aesthetic arguments for conservation. As philosopher T. J. Diffey observes:

> One of the reasons why the beauty of an area may not be a sufficient
> reason to protect it against the building of power stations,
> motorways, airports, and the like, I believe, is the popular
> philosophical belief that beauty is merely a matter of personal
> liking. I do not mean that professional philosophers think this;

rather it is a popular philosophical belief that ... is now entrenched within our mass consciousness.

(Diffey, 2000, p 141)

According to Diffey, this popular attitude prevents aesthetic values from being publically raised during policy debates. A central tenet of modern democracy, he notes, is that individual preferences have no moral claim on the majority. In other words, we are free to pursue our individual preferences, within reason, but we cannot demand of society that they be satisfied – especially when doing so imposes an economic burden (see also Smith, 2000). Hence, if aesthetic value is regarded (accurately or not) as the mere expression of a personal preference, this would undermine its currency as a *legitimate* public concern. As Diffey asks: "Why should my preference for wild heathland be expected to carry any greater weight with a judicial tribunal than my liking, say, for strawberry ice cream?"

Diffey recommends that environmentalists would do better, strategically, to avoid aesthetic value arguments and focus instead on instrumental benefits. However, the problem with this suggestion, as we have seen in Part I, is that instrumental value arguments do not provide comprehensive support for the environmentalist agenda.

In response to Diffey, it might be argued that he is underestimating the potential influence of aesthetic value on policy decisions. There are historical examples (like the establishment of Yosemite and Yellowstone) where aesthetic considerations have influenced public debate. It might be true that, in recent years, popular attitudes have shifted toward a more subjectivist understanding of aesthetic judgment. However, if this attitude is indeed mistaken, then the appropriate response is to combat this misconception rather than to abide it.

Why, then, do most philosophers reject the platitude that beauty is merely in the eye of the beholder? It is important to clarify the meaning of this phrase. It means that judgments about aesthetic value tend to vary from one individual to the next, and, more importantly, that there is no rational way to resolve such disagreements. This is why judgments about beauty are regarded as merely the expression of a personal preference. Preferences tend to vary among individuals, as is demonstrated by our idiosyncratic tastes for certain types of food or entertainment. Moreover, we tend to think that everyone is 'entitled' to his or her own preferences, so that it would be nothing short of a *conceptual* mistake to tell someone that they really ought to prefer something which they decidedly do not enjoy. If judgments about beauty are nothing more than the expression of personal preference, this would imply that there is no rational basis for resolving aesthetic disagreement.

Now, it is hard to deny that people prefer different species and ecosystems. Our example of the hydroelectric engineer was meant to acknowledge this variation. The pertinent question, however, is whether the aesthetic *value* of those habitats, or any object, consists in nothing more than individual preferences. In other words, is beauty *merely* in the eye of the beholder? Or are there general standards of beauty that transcend the preferences of a given individual?

At this stage, it is perhaps important to remind the reader of our earlier distinction between different forms of intrinsic value. Recall that intrinsic value need not be a mind-independent property that exists 'out there' in the world, as what we defined in Section 1.6.1 as 'objective intrinsic value.' Intrinsic value can also be relational, in the sense that it arises out of an interaction between subject and object. A fairly general form of relational value involves the triggering of psychological dispositions that are common across human cultures. A less general form of relational value triggers psychological dispositions that are shared by members of a particular culture. The most limited form of intrinsic value is idiosyncratic to an individual. The subjectivist view, that beauty lies merely in the eye of the beholder, assumes that idiosyncratic intrinsic value is the only plausible account of aesthetic value.

Let's consider why many philosophers disagree with this claim. Perhaps the most influential objection appeals to the way aesthetic concerns are commonly discussed in our daily lives. It is generally considered reasonable to challenge an aesthetic judgment – to argue that it is mistaken – in a way that it would be unreasonable to challenge a judgment of personal preference. This practice suggests that aesthetic judgments make a claim to authority (they command assent or agreement) in a way that would make no sense if they were merely expressions of individual preference. To illustrate, consider the following two judgments.

> **Judgment of individual preference:** Sally and Jim are eating ice cream. Jim is enjoying strawberry flavor and Sally, his friend, is enjoying chocolate. Jim turns to Sally and says, "Strawberry tastes better than chocolate."
> **Aesthetic judgment**: Felicity and Sean are visiting an art gallery. They enter a wing exhibiting several works by the post-impressionist painter Paul Gauguin. After careful inspection of the work, Felicity turns to Sean and says, "Gaugin's work has no business being presented in this gallery. It is simply not impressive artwork."

The difference between these two judgments can be illustrated by imagining how disagreement would proceed. Suppose, for example, that Sally disagrees with Jim about his preference for strawberry ice cream. She might inquire whether his opinion is well informed: "have you *tried* chocolate lately? Have you tried it from *this* shop?" However, were Jim to insist that strawberry ice cream tastes better than chocolate, there would be no reasonable grounds on which Sally could disagree. That is, there is no sense in which she could insist that his judgment is mistaken. Jim is, as they say, entitled to his opinion.

Now consider the disagreement between Sean and Felicity. Notice that Felicity isn't merely claiming that she doesn't enjoy the work of Gaugin. Rather, she is making a normative judgment about the value of his work. We might interpret her as saying that anyone who considers carefully the work of Gaugin ought not to find it aesthetically valuable. Once again, Sean might inquire into whether

her judgment is well informed. This might involve asking whether Felicity is familiar with the historical and cultural context in which Gaugin's work is situated. Has she familiarized herself with the received standards, in other words, according to which this kind of work is appropriately judged? If Felicity is indeed familiar with the standards for judging the relevant genre of artwork, but she persists in her judgment that Gaugin's work lacks aesthetic value, it is perfectly reasonable for Sean to insist that her judgment is mistaken. Felicity "just doesn't get it," one might say.

The fact that most people find it sensible to debate the accuracy of aesthetic judgments suggests that we as a society adhere to certain shared standards. As mentioned earlier, some of those standards might emerge out of cultural traditions, like a particular genre of painting or music. Other aesthetic standards might be shared more broadly across cultures. According to E.O. Wilson's Biophilia Hypothesis (1984) most humans share an affinity for diverse and unmodified habitats. Similar ideas have been explored in greater detail under the banner of prospect-refuge theory (Appleton, 1988, 1996). More recently, philosopher Stephen Davies (2012) has identified a number of animal attributes for which most humans, arguably, share an evolved appreciation. A review of these evolutionary accounts of aesthetic value would take us beyond the scope of this chapter. The central point is that while some aesthetic judgments might turn out to be merely idiosyncratic, many others are grounded in values that are culturally and, perhaps, biologically shared (see also Stokes, 2007, Dutton, 2009).

This discussion has brought us to the edge of a very challenging philosophical topic. It is not our current aim to develop a positive account of the intersubjective validity of aesthetic judgment. Our more modest goal has been to challenge the popular view that all aesthetic judgment boils down to the mere expression of personal preference. We have suggested that some environmentalists shy away from aesthetic value as a justification for conservation not because they see aesthetic value as illegitimate, but rather because the general public equates aesthetic judgment with an expression of personal preference. We have explained how this amounts to an extreme view, in the sense that it disregards alternative forms of relational intrinsic value. We have also noted that the way in which people tend to discuss aesthetic value differs markedly from their discussion of personal preference. This tendency alone seems to indicate the existence of shared aesthetic standards. Some of those standards might arise out of particular cultural traditions. Others might be common to most members of our species. Taken together, these considerations suggest that aesthetic value ought not to be dismissed out of hand merely as the expression of an idiosyncratic preference. The remainder of this chapter will explore philosophical arguments for why aesthetic value might serve as a basis for conserving the kinds of entities (e.g. species, ecosystems, and other biological entities) that environmentalists aim to protect.

11.2 RUSSOW, SOBER, AND THE DUTY TO CONSERVE ARTWORK

Two of the earliest attempts to draw a link between environmentalism and aesthetic value were presented independently by philosophers who publish primarily in other fields. Lilly-Marlene Russow has contributed mostly to the field of bioethics, and Elliott Sober is a renowned philosopher of science. This perhaps explains why their work has a different focus than most papers in environmental aesthetics. For example, neither philosopher attempts to give an account of what makes certain natural objects beautiful. Instead, their goal is to make sense of the intrinsic values that environmentalists claim to locate in ecological wholes, such as species and ecosystems. Drawing on many of the same arguments that were outlined in Chapters 9 and 10, both Russow (1981) and Sober (1986) find it implausible that ecological wholes have moral considerability (see Section 7.3). Instead, they argue that certain environmental goals are more convincingly grounded in aesthetic value and the duty to conserve beautiful objects.

Russow and Sober identify three factors that are thought to enhance the value of a species or ecosystem: rarity, historical origin, and context. They then argue that these factors cannot plausibly be associated with moral value, but that they are quite easily understood as factors contributing to aesthetic value. Let's consider each factor individually.

11.2.1   Rarity Can Increase Aesthetic Value

Russow (1981) invites us to compare two individual whales: one belonging to an endangered species of blue whale (*Balaenoptera musculus*), the other a common species of right whale (*Eubalaena australis*). By hypothesis, let's assume that both organisms enjoy the same level of sentience, have the same capacity for flourishing, play the same functional roles in their ecosystems, and are members of the same biotic communities. In these morally relevant respects the two individuals are indistinguishable. Recall from Chapter 7 on methodology in philosophical inquiry that universalizability (judging similar cases similarly) is a logical requirement of ethical judgments. Hence, if the two whales are identical in their *morally relevant* properties, there is no ethical justification for treating them differently.

We can use a hypothetical case, as in Section 7.2 to test our reasoning about this situation. Suppose that we are confronted with a choice about which whale to save from a tragic situation. Both animals are locked in individual pockets of water which are surrounded by expanses of sea ice. The ice is rapidly closing in and will soon prevent access to the surface, at which point the animals will drown. Fortunately, we are able to break one whale free. Unfortunately, there is not enough time to save them both. Which animal should we rescue?

From a strictly ethical perspective there is no rational basis for choosing one whale over the other. This is a classical moral dilemma in which you are damned if you do and damned if you don't. However, in terms of their conservation value the animals are far from equal. Many environmentalists would be outraged if a member of an endangered species were to be sacrificed in favor of a member of a common one. But as we have seen, placing such value on rarity makes no sense from a strictly ethical perspective (see Section 9.2.5 for further discussion).

Russow and Sober point out, however, that rarity often enhances the value of artwork. To illustrate, they cite examples of renowned paintings whose value is enhanced when items from the same artist or period are scarce. Perhaps an even more illustrative example is the value of heritage-listed architecture. Buildings can have a high degree of aesthetic value, especially when they are good representatives of a particular historical period or school of architecture. For example, in many contemporary North American cities, good examples of Victorian architecture are often heritage protected. Little attention was paid to their destruction when this style of building was common. However, as buildings from the period became scarce, heritage societies started speaking out in favor of their protection. It is now seen as something of a tragedy when good examples from this period are lost. The point that Russow and Sober are making is that the value which environmentalists place on rarity aligns much better with our treatment of aesthetically valuable objects than it does with our treatment of ethically valuable organisms.

11.2.2 Aesthetic Value Is Sensitive to Authenticity of Origin

In our presentation of the environmentalist agenda (Chapter 1) we noted that domesticated species tend to be regarded as less valuable than their naturally occurring counterparts. Russow (1981) illustrates this attitude with the example of laboratory bred strains of mice. Strains from genetically distinct lineages are no less distinctive[1] than naturally occurring subspecies, like the Florida panther (see Section 9.3.2). Yet, engineered strains of mice are allowed to go extinct without any objection from environmentalists. Presumably, such

---

[1] Arguably, laboratory mice strains are genetically *more* distinctive than naturally occurring subspecies, due to the extreme genetic manipulation that is often done to create the strains. Targeted gene knockouts, crispr cas9 gene editing, and GFP reporter gene transformations are just a few examples of such manipulations. These techniques have resulted in some truly amazing genetic strains mice that are vastly different than wild populations and subspecies.

strains are considered less valuable because of the 'unnatural' influence on their evolution.

Environmentalists also have tended to prefer relatively unaltered or 'pristine' environments over ones that have been more heavily impacted by humans. This issue has emerged in debates over restoration ecology. In his influential article "Faking Nature" (1982), philosopher Robert Elliott argues that a restored landscape is inherently less valuable than the one it was constructed to resemble. He describes an actual case in which a mining company proposed to restore a landscape to its former state after stripping it of precious metals. The restoration was to be so meticulous that nature lovers would discern no impact once the project was complete. However, members of the Environmental Commission responsible for evaluating this proposal argued that perfect restoration is impossible, even in principle:

> even if, contrary to the overwhelming weight of evidence before the Commission, successful rehabilitation of the flora after mining is found to be ecologically possible on all mined sites on the Island . . . the overall impression of a wild, uncultivated island refuge will be destroyed forever by mining.
>
> (quoted in Elliott, 1982, p 82)

Their point was that *the very knowledge* that the site had been reconstructed by human hands would rob it of value. Elliot argues that this sentiment reveals that, as in the case of artwork, the value of a natural landscape depends on the process by which it originated. Natural landscapes, he claims, are authentic only if they were created by ecological, evolutionary, and geological processes that unfold over extended periods without intervention by humans.

It is difficult to justify this sentiment in terms of the values that were explored in *any* of the previous chapters of this book. By hypothesis, the two ecosystems are no different in their ability to provide ecosystem services, in their provision of medicines or food, in the recreational opportunities that they afford, etc. So there is no instrumental reason to prefer the original habitat over the restored one. Nor is this judgment justified in terms of the intrinsic values that are often associated with ecological wholes. In Chapter 9, we noted that the very distinction between natural and unnatural is hopelessly confused. On the one hand, humans are sometimes regarded by environmentalists as a part of nature. This sentiment is expressed, for example, in the frequent call from environmentalists for people to 'get back to nature.' On the other hand, they are seen as somehow separate from nature. But even if this issue could be sorted out, the inference from natural origin to enhanced value is fallacious for a further reason: it is guilty of the naturalistic fallacy that was outlined in Section 9.2.1, and/or the origin fallacy outlined in Section 9.2.3.

Once again, this component of the environmentalist agenda looks to be grounded in an aesthetic, not an ethical judgment. Russow and Sober note that authenticity of origin is a familiar component of aesthetic value. To illustrate, consider the role that discoveries of forgery have on the value of artwork. When it comes to aesthetically valuable items, the quality of our experience requires that we are encountering the authentic object that was produced by the accredited artist. For instance, suppose that the artwork that you admired during your visit to the Louvre, and always assumed to have been painted by da Vinci, turned out to be a very good replica of the original painting which, it turns out, was locked in a basement vault. It doesn't matter how convincing the replica might be. Most people would feel that the quality of their aesthetic experience is undermined unless they are viewing the actual Mona Lisa. It therefore appears that aesthetic judgment is sensitive to authenticity of origin in a way that mirrors environmentalist intuitions about the value of 'natural' species and ecosystems.

II.2.3 *The Importance of Context to Aesthetic Value*

In our summary of the objectives that define the environmentalist agenda (Chapter 1), it was noted that in situ conservation is generally preferable to ex situ conservation. This issue arose again in Chapter 4 of this book, when it was noted that various germ plasms are already being maintained under climate-controlled conditions in secure facilities. We suspect that this is not what most environmentalists have in mind when calling for biodiversity conservation. But this raises the question of whether environmentalists are really prioritizing the conservation of these species for human use. If so, then there should be no objection to the highly clinical, but effective means by which this goal is currently being achieved.

Similar issues arise in cases where endangered animals are placed in zoological parks to ensure their protection and facilitate breeding. In some cases, this is the most effective conservation strategy at anyone's disposal. Yet, environmentalists typically do not condone these sorts of intervention, except perhaps occasionally, or on a temporary basis. Again, this attitude is difficult to justify on strictly ethical grounds. Consider an individual who needs to be moved to a hospital in order to receive life-saving treatment. We wouldn't hesitate to move them. By the same token, if the reason for valuing species is because of their intrinsic moral worth, environmentalists shouldn't balk when they are preserved in seed banks or zoos.

However, as before, the importance of context makes sense if the reason for valuing these endangered species is because of their aesthetic, rather than their moral value. As Sober (1986) points out, many great works of art depreciate in aesthetic value when they become decontextualized. His examples include frescos and architectural monuments whose significance is attached to a particular place. For instance, imagine if Michelangelo's masterpiece were somehow removed from the Sistine Chapel. Some forms of graffiti art also degrade in aesthetic value when they are taken out of context.[2] This has recently become a topic of discussion with the removal of street artist Banksy's work by cutting away entire sections of building so that they can be transported to the auction house. Interestingly, removing Banksy's paintings from their original context increased

---

[2] See e.g. http://bit.ly/2dt0vky.

their monetary value while simultaneously decreasing their aesthetic value.

11.2.4 Shared Intuitions about the Duty to Conserve Artwork

Up to this point, we have considered three respects in which the value that environmentalists place on species and ecosystems looks more like aesthetic valuation than ethical valuation. Of course, there are a number of objections that might be raised against this analogy. Philosophers working in the field of environmental aesthetics point out that natural entities lack an author who intentionally created them. It is also unclear whether there are culturally supplied standards for assessing the value of a species or ecosystem, as there are for particular genres of artwork. These differences suggest, to some, that the aesthetic value found in nature is different in kind from the value recognized in artwork. This topic will be explored in more detail in Section 11.5, where we discuss some developments in the field of environmental aesthetics. For the time being, let us accept (if only provisionally) that the value of certain species and ecosystems is entirely aesthetic, not grounded in some additional property that might be of instrumental benefit or intrinsic moral value (e.g. sentience). What does this imply about our duty to conserve such items?

Russow and Sober take it for granted that artistic masterpieces and culturally significant artworks ought to be conserved. Interestingly, neither philosopher offers an argument to support this claim. Instead, they rely on a common-sense moral intuition which (they assume) will be shared by the majority of their readers. Russow puts the point as follows:

> Most of us believe that the world would be a poorer place for the loss of bald eagles in the same way that it would be poorer for the loss of the Grand Canyon or a great work of art. In all cases, the experience of seeing these things is an inherently worthwhile experience.
>
> (1981, p. 142)

Russow goes on to add an important qualification to this sentiment:

> We believe that diminishing the aesthetic value of a thing for mere
> economic benefit is immoral, but that aesthetic value is not
> absolute – that the fact that something has aesthetic value may be
> overridden by the fact that harming that thing, or destroying it, may
> result in some greater good. That is, someone who agrees to destroy
> a piece of Greek statuary for personal gain would be condemned as
> having done something immoral, but someone who is faced with a
> choice between saving his children and saving a "priceless"
> painting would be said to have skewed values if he chose to save the
> painting.
>
> *(1981, p. 142)*

Put simply, the claim is that aesthetically valuable objects command
an intermediate degree of moral significance: they cannot be harmed
in the name of mere economic benefit, but they are morally subordinate to basic human needs. Sober concurs that a society must reach a
certain level of material comfort before the duty to conserve artwork
starts to apply. For example, imagine a society that spends a considerable amount of money conserving precious examples of rare architecture while it does nothing to address a significant homelessness
problem. Sober would argue that the conservation of beauty is unwar-
ranted in such cases. However, he agrees with Russow that once a
certain degree of affluence is attained, the duty to conserve artwork
and cultural items kicks in.

Putting these ideas together, we can reconstruct the following
argument for the conservation of biodiversity on aesthetic grounds:

Premise 1:   Certain species and ecosystems have the same type
and degree of aesthetic value as great works of art.

Premise 2:   Most people intuitively recognize that great works of
art deserve an intermediate degree of moral signifi-
cance. Specifically, it is generally considered wrong
to destroy or decrease the aesthetic value of a great

	artwork merely for economic gain, provided that a certain level of affluence is attained.
Conclusion:	It should, therefore, generally be considered wrong for members of sufficiently affluent societies to destroy or decrease the aesthetic value of certain species or ecosystems merely for economic gain.

There are a few important things to note about this argument.

First, as mentioned earlier, Premise 1 is based on an analogy between the beauty that exists in artwork and that which is found in nature. If one accepts that great artworks ought to be protected in order to preserve their aesthetic value then, as a matter of logical consistency, one ought to extend the same consideration to certain natural objects. The strength of Premise 1, therefore, depends on how closely analogous these two modes of valuation turn out to be. This issue will be addressed in Section 11.5, where we discuss one of the most prominent theories of natural beauty to have been developed within the field of environmental aesthetics.

A second thing to note is that our conservation duties are limited to 'great' or culturally important works of art. It would be absurd to demand that every artwork demands equal protection. Presumably, the same point holds for species. As Russow admits, there are some species which are by no means aesthetically significant. She singles out the hapless snail darter (*Percina tanasi*) as a case in point. This implication alone might be unpalatable to some environmentalists. In particular, there is the problem of whether to conserve 'unscenic' examples of nature, as philosopher Uriko Saito (1998) describes them. This issue will be explored in more detail in Section 11.4.

Third, it is important to keep in mind that, as it has been presented so far, premise 2 rests entirely on a shared moral intuition: that great works of art possess an intermediate degree of moral significance – above economic gain, but below basic human needs. One sort of worry is that this intuition might be highly culturally specific. It is conceivable that some affluent cultures might, despite having met the necessary material requirements, nonetheless continue to prioritize economic gain over aesthetic value. Alternately, we can imagine that in some cultures the value of certain culturally important artworks might trump human life. This is just to say that this argument is only compelling to the extent that this normative intuition is widely shared.

A related worry is that, even in our own (Western) culture, this normative intuition might not withstand careful scrutiny. Recall from our earlier methodological chapter (Chapter 7) that, according to the method of reflective equilibrium, such intuitions must be balanced against general moral principles. Achieving consistency can require the revision of certain intuitions, even when they are strongly held. This raises the question of whether the intuition to which Russow and Sober appeal, regarding the duty to conserve aesthetically valuable objects even in the face of economic loss, survives scrutiny. We now consider this question in more detail.

11.3   THE SUPERFICIALITY OBJECTION

Another potential reason why aesthetic value is an unpopular reason for conserving biodiversity is because aesthetic values are often seen as superficial or frivolous. This is most apparent in cases where they come into conflict with more 'serious' economic concerns. For example, philosopher Robert Loftis (2003) notes that protection of the Arctic National Wildlife Refuge represented a loss of over $800 million to the State of Alaska. According to Loftis, there would be no way to justify such a large economic sacrifice if this region offered only aesthetic benefits. On his view, aesthetic value is simply too frivolous to legitimately influence important policy decisions. Loftis offers the following analogy:

> If a doctor had to choose between giving one of two patients a heart, she could not justify her decision by saying that one of the patients was more beautiful than the other (or more sublime, or more in possession of any other positive aesthetic characteristic.) A doctor

certainly couldn't let aesthetic characteristics outweigh non-aesthetic characteristics, like the likelihood of survival past five years. But if a doctor cannot make a decision regarding who gets a heart based on aesthetics, how can environmentalists ask thousands of loggers to give up their jobs and way of life on the basis of aesthetics?

(2003, p.43)

We hope that the reader shares this intuition with us: Obviously, it would be immoral to base decisions about human life on judgments about beauty. Lofits maintains that conservation decisions often negatively impact human welfare, for example, in the form of lost economic opportunities. Therefore, he concludes that it would be morally impermissible to base conservation decisions on judgments about beauty.

In a second thought experiment, Loftis invites us to consider whether it would be morally acceptable to donate large sums of money to a particular person simply because she is beautiful. As a matter of fact, he notes, many of us already do this. We happily pay for the privilege of looking at movie stars and supermodels, making them exceptionally wealthy in the process. Loftis notes that although this practice is familiar, it is far from morally laudable. Indeed, many of us feel slightly ashamed about the disproportionate amount of money and attention that gets showered upon beautiful people. But what, then, is the pertinent difference between this practice and a conservation program that spends large sums on the conservation of pandas or polar bears, just on account of their beauty?

This objection can be understood as a direct challenge to the second premise of the argument that was outlined earlier. Recall that, according to this premise, objects of considerable aesthetic value are more morally significant than the economic benefits that might be gained from their destruction. To support this claim, Russow and Sober presented us with examples in which a great artwork is sacrificed in the name of personal benefit. Loftis' examples seem to tug our intuitions in an opposing direction. That is, we intuitively recognize that the superficial doctor is morally objectionable. Likewise, the salaries of supermodels and movie stars strike us as egregious. It would therefore appear that our intuitions are in conflict about the ethical standing of beauty. If so, then according to the method of reflective equilibrium (discussed in Section 7.1.4), we are left with two options. In order to achieve consistency in our convictions, either we must reject the claim that beautiful objects ought to take priority over personal profits, or, apparently, we must start advocating for the special treatment of beautiful people.

Thankfully, this moral dilemma can be avoided. There are several reasons why human beauty does not provide an adequate test case for thinking about our duties to conserve art or nature. Consider, first, the example of the superficial doctor. As Loftis describes the case, the doctor ignores considerations about which patient is more likely to survive a heart transplant. In other words, the doctor is prioritizing aesthetic value above human health and welfare. Recall that, according to the argument that was attributed earlier to Russow and Sober, aesthetic value should not be assigned this level of moral significance. It was argued, rather, that aesthetic value commands an *intermediate* level of moral significance – below basic human needs, but above economic benefits. This explains why the decision of the superficial doctor strikes us as morally objectionable: because he fails to assign the appropriate level of significance to human life. In fact, we would be just as quick to condemn the doctor if a life-saving treatment was allocated on the basis of social status, wealth, or almost any other factor. Hence, it does not follow from our views about this case that aesthetic value is a uniquely superficial type of consideration when human life is *not* at stake.

Turning to Loftis' second example, there are many reasons why people might feel uncomfortable about the inflated salaries of movie stars and supermodels. Most of us operate with an intuitive sense of justice which reacts negatively to gross inequities in the distribution of wealth, especially when they are not based on merit. The allocation of resources to beautiful people triggers this sentiment. On this view, we do not necessarily reject the expenditure of funds on beautiful objects. For instance, many of us are comfortable with the payment of large sums to conserve exceptional artwork. Rather, it is the fact that certain *people* receive such *disproportionately* large sums that triggers a sense of outrage. Again, there is nothing special about the fact that these decisions are being based on beauty. Many people are similarly outraged by the salaries paid to professional athletes or to corporate CEOs.

Another important thing to note about Loftis' thought experiment is that beautiful people will not cease to exist if we suddenly refuse to lavish them with such exaggerated rewards. This is an important disanalogy with artwork and species. In those cases, failing to invest in conservation means that the items are lost forever.

Finally, one might argue that the analogy between beautiful people and beautiful species breaks down for a very different reason. Recall that Russow and Sober identified authenticity and rarity as important contributors to aesthetic value. It seems entirely plausible that even popular movie stars and supermodels lack these properties. Most of us are aware that actors and models undergo all sorts of 'beauty enhancements' (makeup, digital touch-ups, surgery, etc.) to maintain their appearance. Indeed, the prototypical Hollywood star is the living embodiment of *in*authentic beauty. At the same time, there appears to be no shortage of beautiful people for Hollywood producers to choose from. As handsome as Tom Cruise might be, he is much more replaceable (and therefore less unique as an *aesthetic* object) than the northern white rhino (*Ceratotherium simum cottoni*) or the hairy-nosed wombat (*Lasiorhinus krefftii*). On this view, the reason that many of us are outraged by the salaries of movie stars and models is not because we deny the importance of conserving aesthetic value, but rather because the beauty of these individuals is often inauthentic and, on the whole, somewhat common.

11.4   THE PROBLEM OF UNAPPEALING SPECIES AND ECOSYSTEMS

There is yet another reason why aesthetic values tend not to enter explicitly into debates about conservation. As noted earlier, aesthetic values might provide only limited support for the conservation of biodiversity. After all, we feel obligated to conserve only a select few pieces of artwork because, frankly, most examples are of mediocre quality. What does this imply about the conservation of biodiversity? How many species or ecosystems are sufficiently beautiful to demand conservation?

A popular complaint from environmentalists is that so-called 'charismatic megafauna' already receive an inordinate amount of attention. This derogatory label refers to the very limited range of species that most people care about (pandas, bald eagles, marmots, and the like). The vast majority of animals, plants, and fungi fail to conform with popular notions of beauty. This is to say nothing of what E.O. Wilson (1987) called "little things that run the world," which most people never even see. If conservation priorities were relegated to our shared aesthetic values, the thinking goes, then the majority of species on earth would be neglected.

To compound this worry, a number of psychological studies reveal that even minor physical differences among species can have large impacts on our aesthetic judgments. For example, David Stokes (2007) compared people's responses to similar-looking species of penguin and found that a small patch of warm coloration confers a major advantage. Body size (Knegtering et al., 2011) and neotenous characteristics (Gould, 1980, Lawrence, 1986) exert a similarly positive influence on aesthetic judgments about animals. When it comes to forest ecosystems, people prefer less 'cluttered' environments to those containing decaying logs and other important habitats (Brown and Daniel, 1986, Ribe, 1989). The worry, in all of these cases, is that aesthetic values tend not to align with ecologically significant features.

In response to these concerns, it is important to keep in mind that aesthetic value is not being proposed as a replacement for all other kinds of value. For example, if the extinction of a species were to impact human health, then its aesthetic appeal should not even come into consideration. Many of the objections against the prioritization of charismatic megafauna involve just this sort of trade-off: some more ecologically significant species is neglected in favor of one that is cuter, more majestic, or whatever. Insofar as 'ecological significance' is understood in terms of human health and welfare, then even a proponent of aesthetically informed conservation would not condone the protection of a charismatic species over a more important one.

But where does this leave us when it comes to species or ecosystems that make no contribution to the human health and welfare? In the first part of this book, it was argued that many species in existence might fall into this category. Let us suppose that only a small handful of these 'non-essential' species are regarded as aesthetically valuable according to our shared aesthetic standards. Let us also allow that most of these species are non-sentient, and therefore do not obviously fall under the umbrella of intrinsic moral value. Does this mean that we are left without any reason whatsoever to conserve them?

One way to deal with these objections is to simply 'bite the bullet' and acknowledge that aesthetic value provides only limited support for conservation. In this respect, aesthetic value is perhaps similar to every other kind of value that has been explored in previous chapters of this book. It was found that each of those values (ecosystem services, medicinal benefits, intrinsic moral value, etc.) applies to some entities and not others. No single factor, up to this point, has provided blanket support for the environmentalist agenda.

However, most proponents of aesthetic value offer a very different response to this challenge, arguing that our more common aesthetic judgments have the capacity for expansion. Aldo Leopold puts the point as eloquently as anyone:

Our ability to perceive quality in nature begins, as in art, with the pretty. It expands through successive stages of the beautiful to values as yet uncaptured by language.

(1949, p. 96).

Callicott develops the parallel to art appreciation, noting that people's aesthetic judgments often undergo a process of maturation:

Among gallery-goers there are also those whose taste is limited to the pretty – to naïve, realistic still life or portrait painting, for example. Then there are those capable of appreciating successive stages of the beautiful present in 'fine art,' whether pretty or not. And finally there are serious and studied aesthetes who are alert to values beyond the beautiful: such subtler aesthetic qualities in painting are composition, colour combination, technique, expression, humor, historical allusion, and so forth.

(1989, p. 240)

The idea is that, just as with the appreciation of artwork, people's appreciation of nature is enhanced with the appropriate knowledge or education. When this happens, a broader range of species are recognized as aesthetically valuable. It follows that our shared aesthetic responses are not necessarily so shallow, since most people have the capacity to appreciate a much broader range of species and ecosystems than they currently do. The fact that 'charismatic' organisms are so popular reflects, on this view, a general lack of edification rather than a paucity of aesthetic value in nature.

This response brings us to the point where most philosophers working in the field of environmental aesthetics enter the debate. As mentioned, the central preoccupation of this field has been to provide an account of what makes natural objects beautiful. We can now appreciate the significance of this question. It has just been proposed that the acquisition of certain knowledge can enable a person to *recognize* a broader range of aesthetically valuable objects in nature. This claim presupposes that there is some fact of the matter about which species ought to be recognized as beautiful. In other words, it assumes that there is some standard of correctness for evaluating the accuracy of aesthetic judgments about nature, just as there are for evaluating Felicity's judgment of Gaugin. Whether similar aesthetic standards can be found in the case of species and ecosystems is a question to which we now turn.

11.5 ENVIRONMENTAL AESTHETICS AND THE NATURAL ENVIRONMENTAL MODEL

The discipline of environmental aesthetics is a relative newcomer within the field of aesthetics. Nonetheless, there has emerged a diversity of theories attempting to explain why certain natural objects are aesthetically valuable. We do not have the space for even a cursory review of this discipline.[3] Instead, we shall focus on one of the most influential and well developed examples: Allen Carlson's Natural Environmental Model, which locates the standards for natural beauty in criteria that are supplied by scientific ecology and evolutionary theory. As he explains,

> What I am suggesting is that the question of what to aesthetically appreciate in the natural environment is to be answered in a way analogous to the similar question about art. The difference is that in the case of the natural environment the relevant knowledge is the commonsense/scientific knowledge that we have discovered about the environment in question.
>
> *(1979, p. 269)*

To understand how Carlson arrives at this position, it is helpful to revisit an example that was presented earlier in this chapter. Recall the disagreement between Felicity and Sean about the aesthetic merit

---

[3] A number of recent anthologies provide an overview of the main positions in environmental aesthetics. In particular, see Allen Carlson and Arnold Berleant (eds.), *The Aesthetics of Natural Environments* (Broadview Press, 2004); Allen Carslon and Sheila Lintott (eds.), *Nature, Aesthetics, and Environmentalism: From Beauty to Duty* (Columbia University Press, 2008). See also Glen Parsons, *Aesthetics and Nature* (Continuum Press, 2008) for an introduction to this discipline.

of Gaugin's artwork. Felicity thought that the work was entirely overrated. Sean, in his attempt to challenge Felicity's judgment, invoked the standards of post-impressionist painting, explaining how Gaugin's work exemplifies them particularly well. Gaugin's work has aesthetic merit, he might note, regardless of whether Felicity has a personal preference for artifacts from this period. Hence, there is room to argue that her aesthetic judgment is mistaken.

Let us now consider an analogous case, where the focal object is a rare species of insect.

> **Biodiversity judgment**: Tony and Cass are watching a nature documentary about a species of critically endangered bumble bee (Suckley's cuckoo bumble bee, *Bombus suckleyi*). This bee exhibits an unusual behavior that is of considerable interest to naturalists – they kill the queen of another bee species, and then raise their young in the hive that is still tended by the other species' worker bees. Suppose that Tony and Cass are informed that this bee offers no instrumental benefit to humans. After seeing examples of its nest parasitism behavior and learning about their significance to naturalists, Tony turns to Cass and says, "I see no justification for protecting this species. Its value is totally overrated."

Here, Tony is expressing the same sort of judgment toward a natural entity that Felicity expressed toward the work of Gaugin. The question is whether there are similar grounds for Cass to challenge Tony's judgment.

Carlson, like many philosophers working in environmental aesthetics, would point to a disanalogy between the two cases. Unlike works of art, entities found in nature are not created with any sort of intention. This is important for Carlson because he takes artistic intentions to define the boundaries of an artwork. For example, Gaugin did not intend for us to consider the color of frames in which his canvases were mounted or the shade of wallpaper surrounding his paintings in evaluating his work. These elements should therefore not be included in our aesthetic assessment of Gaugin's work. However, objects found in nature possess no corresponding intention to specify their boundaries. For Carlson, this creates a problem when it comes to the resolution of aesthetic disagreement. In order for Cass and Tony to engage in meaningful dialogue, there needs to be some non-arbitrary way of identifying the object of their aesthetic judgments. Are they to consider a single species of bee in isolation? Should they be taking into account the species on which it parasitizes, or, perhaps certain components of a larger ecosystem? Carlson calls this the "what" of an aesthetic judgment. Since there is no artistic intention to specify the *what* of natural objects, he notes, we require some other way to individuate them for the purposes of evaluating aesthetic judgments.

Gaugin's work also belongs to a particular cultural period that is associated with distinct standards of beauty. It would be inappropriate to judge his work according to the standards of hyper-realism or abstract expressionism, because Gaugin did not operate in either of these traditions. Carlson calls this the "how" of aesthetic judgment: the set of standards or criteria that legitimately apply to an object and determine its relative aesthetic merit. Since Gaugin painted before the move to pure abstraction, if we evaluate his work as failed abstract expression we get something wrong. Once again, natural objects pose a challenge in this regard. They are not created in a particular cultural period, so it is difficult to identify any specific aesthetic tradition to which they belong. So, in the context of our running example, to which set of standards might Cass appeal to in her defense of the aesthetic value of Suckley's cuckoo bumble bee? The answer is far from obvious.

This brings us to the role of the biological sciences (evolution, ecology, and natural history) as a basis for judgments about natural beauty. According to Carlson, these disciplines supply objective criteria for establishing the *what* and the *how* of aesthetic appreciation: "Such knowledge," he claims, "yields appropriate boundaries of appreciation, particular foci of aesthetic significance, and relevant acts of aspection" (2008, 127). Let us first consider an example of how biological science is supposed to provide the *what* of aesthetic judgment. Historically, sea anemones were classified as a type of plant. Visitors to the seashore thus admired their shape and color by classifying them together with flowers. Carlson would point out that these aesthetic judgments were mistaken because, as we now know, sea anemones are in fact animals. When viewed in this light, their beauty arguably takes on a different significance. There is a sense in which it is more striking to see an *animal* that resembles a plant, at least in terms of its gross morphology and color, than it is to see yet another species of flower.

Carlson further argues that the biological sciences provide legitimate standards for evaluating the *how* of natural beauty: "Just as the knowledge provided by art critics and art historians enables us to aesthetically appreciate art, that provided by naturalists, ecologists, geologists, and natural historians equip us to aesthetically appreciate nature" (2008, 127). Again, Carlson offers little in the way of a demonstration of this idea. However, the philosopher Ned Hettinger (2005) offers an example that Carlson would surely endorse.

Hettinger describes an actual legal case in which scientific experts invoked aesthetic considerations to justify conservation of the Delhi Sands Flower-loving Fly (*Rhaphiomidas terminates*). This was a controversial decision, in part, because this endangered species of insect stood in the way of a large development project – the construction of a hospital that would have destroyed its only known habitat. Advocates for development attempted to discount the value of the fly by portraying it in disparaging terms: "a creature that spends most of its life underground, living as a fat, clumsy, enigmatic maggot" (quoted in Hettinger, 2005, p. 75). However, scientists familiar with the fly's natural history offered a more informed account of its aesthetic value. As Hettinger explains,

> They portrayed the inch-long fly as able to hover like a hummingbird above flowers and to use its straw-like mouth to extract nectar. Females of the species were described as telescoping their bodies three inches into the sand to deposit a clutch of eggs.

Said one defender, "It's a fly you can love. It's beautiful. Nothing is too wonderful to be true in the world of insects."

(2005, p. 75)

There are several things to note about this positive account of the Delhi fly. First, its admirers are drawing a behavioral comparison to other species (hummingbirds) which are more commonly regarded as beautiful. This highlights one potential way in which biological information can inform aesthetic judgments: by identifying similarities between lesser-understood organisms and the ones that most people already consider beautiful. A second role for biological information is hinted at by the phrase, "nothing is too wonderful to be true in the world of insects." This claim presupposes a comparative background of insect phenotypes, where the Delhi fly is thought to occupy a unique place in the catalogue of evolutionary possibilities. For it to go extinct, in other words, would be to lose an important representative in the panoply of insect diversity. It is in light of these scientifically informed comparisons that, according to the Natural Environmental Model, the portrayal of the Delhi fly as an 'enigmatic maggot' was a mistaken judgment – on par with Felicity's judgment about Gaugin.

11.5.1 Some Challenges Specific to the Natural Environmental Model

A wide range of objections have been raised in opposition to the Natural Environmental Model, and we only have space to consider a few of the more pressing ones here. One objection claims that, contra Carlson, the biological sciences do not provide objective criteria for identifying the *what* of aesthetic judgments – especially in the case of holistic entities such as subspecies and ecosystems. As we argued in Section 9.3.2, the boundaries that scientists draw around these objects are often arbitrarily defined by pragmatic concerns facing a particular investigator. The Natural Environmental Model naïvely assumes that since these disciplines are 'scientific,' they must be in the business of carving nature at its joints. Most philosophers of biology and working biologists would deny that this is true for many of the entities that ecologists study.

Another objection to the Natural Environmental Model is that it fails to comprehensively describe the *how* of aesthetic judgments about nature. Opponents point to all sorts of examples where the appreciation of natural beauty is independent of scientific information. One can enjoy the vibrant color of a sea anemone, for example, without an accurate understanding of its taxonomic classification. Hence, Carlson's model offers, at most, only a partial account of the criteria that inform our judgments about natural beauty.

Perhaps a more serious objection concerns the scope of Carlson's theory. Earlier, we were wrestling with the question of whether broadly unappealing species and ecosystems possess sufficient aesthetic value to occasionally demand conservation. This concern motivated the search for a philosophical theory of aesthetic value – a theory that could identify certain entities as aesthetically valuable given the right body of information, regardless of whether most people currently recognize them as beautiful. The Natural Environmental Model fulfills this role *too well*. The sciences of evolution, ecology, and natural history have a unique story to tell about each and every species. If these stories are the basis for the *what* and the *how* of aesthetic value, then it would seem to follow that *every* species is equally aesthetically valuable – at least, as far as the Natural Environmental Model is concerned. To his credit perhaps, Carlson embraces this implication of his theory (assigning it the title *"positive aesthetics"*). However, as environmentalists, we should be deeply concerned. What we require is some theory that provides rationally compelling reasons why certain species should be protected on aesthetic grounds. It does no good to be told, simply, that all species should be conserved because all are beautiful in their own way. The very credibility of aesthetic value as a basis for conservation requires that some species can be identified as lacking this property. Otherwise, aesthetic value cannot serve as a basis for making decisions about how to allocate limited resources. It remains to be seen whether some modification to the Natural Environmental Model can accommodate this important constraint.

11.6 OUTSTANDING CHALLENGES FOR AN AESTHETIC DEFENSE OF CONSERVATION

In this chapter we have wrestled with an issue that often lies below the surface of conservation debates. Although environmentalists do not hesitate to present species and ecosystems in an aesthetically appealing light, they often stop short of arguing that aesthetic value provides a sufficient reason to conserve them.

We have considered several explanations for this discrepancy between our 'hearts' and our 'minds,' as it were. One possibility is that aesthetic value is widely conflated with personal preference. In reply to this worry, we pointed out that standards of correctness for aesthetic judgments already inform debates over the value of artwork. Some of those standards emanate from culturally shared values, while others have a possible basis in human biology. Regardless of their origin, it is mistaken to simply assume that aesthetic values are necessarily idiosyncratic to the individual.

Note that it is a further question whether an aesthetically valuable object ought to be conserved simply on account of its beauty. In this chapter, we have appealed to a widely held moral conviction: that it would be wrong to allow a great artwork, like the Mona Lisa, to be destroyed simply because one is reluctant to pay for its conservation. This sentiment applies on the proviso that people's basic human needs are already satisfied, and that the expenditure of conservation funds would not generate undue suffering. However, if someone agrees with this sentiment, and also admits that the aesthetic value of certain natural objects are on a par with is the great artworks occasionally produced by humans, then they ought also to agree that it would be wrong to allow a great 'work of nature' – be it a species or an ecosystem – to be destroyed simply because they are reluctant to pay for its conservation. This is just to say that the normative 'oomph' of the argument from beauty to duty, as it has been considered so far, rests on an intuition about the moral significance of great artwork.

We can now start to see where the challenges emerge for this line of argument. One set of challenges surrounds the identification of genuinely beautiful objects in nature. What we seem to require is an account of natural beauty that has the capacity to sway people into recognizing that certain items are not just beautiful, but *exceptionally* so. A second set of challenges surrounds the normative issue as to why there is a moral duty to conserve items that fall into this category. With these considerations in mind, there appear to be two very general ways to rationally defend the conservation of natural beauty.

The first option involves an appeal to aesthetic values that most people recognize regardless of their education or background. This would include an appreciation for charismatic megafauna, a few exceptional plants, a handful of other species, and possibly not much else. One benefit of this approach is that it points to a fairly obvious moral principle (utility maximization) as the basis for conservation. Up to this point, we have been relying on the shared moral intuition that exceptional natural beauty is just as morally significant as great artwork. Following philosophers like Loftis, we might inquire whether this intuition is grounded in some general moral principle, and if so, what is it? The principle that an action is right only if it maximizes net utility is standardly recognized in most policy settings. This principle could therefore supply the normative premise in an argument from natural beauty to conservation duty. The only catch, it would seem, is that this argument is restricted to just those species that are sufficiently appealing to the majority of people. Beyond those species to which we have a moral duty to protect (e.g. sentient animals) and those which provide essential ecosystem services, this argument provides only limited additional support for the environmentalist agenda.

A very different line of argument is favored by most practitioners of environmental aesthetics. The primary objective of this field, as noted, is to develop a philosophical theory of aesthetic value. Ideally, such a theory would supply intersubjective standards for judging species and ecosystems. An advantage of such a theory is that it would potentially extend to items in nature that are commonly neglected.

As we have seen, one of the more popular attempts to develop such a theory focuses on certain *dis*similarities between artwork and nature. The Natural Environmental Model appeals to the biological sciences to both identify the aesthetic objects and to supply standards for their assessment. An issue for this particular model is that the biological sciences might not supply objective criteria for the individuation of many of the items (e.g. subspecies and ecosystems) that most people aesthetically admire. However, an even bigger problem is that a biological story can be provided for every organism. Rather than providing criteria for resolving aesthetic disputes, the appeal to science pushes the problem back a step. Instead of asking which items in nature are the most beautiful, we are left wondering which *scientifically portrayed* items are the really beautiful ones?

Suppose, however, that some future theory is able to overcome these problems. That is, suppose we were in possession of an account of the *how* and the *what* of aesthetic value in nature. The question remains as to why it ought to be protected. If the theory in question reveals that natural beauty is essentially different from artistic beauty, then presumably it would not be an option to rely on our shared intuitions about the moral significance of artwork. Likewise, an appeal to utility maximization does not obviously justify the protection of entities whose aesthetic value is not apparent to the majority of people. Perhaps a solution to the problem of why it is important to conserve 'unscenic' natural beauty can be found in discussions about the importance of funding the so-called fine arts – artistic pursuits that are appreciated by a relatively small sector of society (see Carroll, 1987, Feinberg, 1994, Manning, 1994, Brooks, 2000). However, this issue remains an open field for future investigation, and, for that reason, we think environmentalists ought to develop this line of argument before relying too heavily on it for support.

11.7 FURTHER READING

Carlson, A. (2008). *Nature and Landscape: An Introduction to Environmental Aesthetics*, New York: Columbia University Press.

Carroll, N. (1993). "On Being Moved By Nature: Between Religion and Natural History," in *Landscape, Natural Beauty and the Arts*, S. Kemal and I. Gaskell (ed.), Cambridge: Cambridge University Press.

Hargrove, E.C. (1989). *Foundations of Environmental Ethics*. Englewood Cliffs: Prentice Hall.

Paden, R. Harmon, L.K. and Milling, C.R. (2013). "Philosophical histories of the aesthetics of nature." *Environmental Ethics* 35: 57–77.

Thompson, J. (1995). "Aesthetics and the value of nature." *Environmental Ethics*, 17: 291–305.

12 How Far Do Intrinsic Value Defenses Get Environmentalists?

12.1 INTRODUCTION

In Part I of this book we explored the instrumental value defenses that we environmentalists sometimes use as a defense of biodiversity conservation. As summarized in Chapter 6, such defenses get us some of what we are after in the environmentalist agenda, but not everything. We also saw that such defenses might cause problems for some parts of the environmentalist agenda. As a result of these shortcomings, or possibly all along, many environmentalists turn to defenses based on claims about the intrinsic value of biodiversity. Part II of the book has focused on these claims. What do they mean? How are they justified? Do they do a better job of defending the environmentalist agenda? And so on. In this chapter we take stock of where we have gotten to. Table 12.1 summarizes what the major ethical positions appear to mean for the individual parts of the Environmentalist Agenda.

12.2 ANTHROPOCENTRISM

Although we described the first part of the book as 'instrumental value defenses,' another way to view the same material is that it was a defense based on the anthropocentrist position about what has intrinsic value. Everybody agrees that thriving human lives are intrinsically valuable, and that in various ways conserving biodiversity helps humans to thrive. So anthropocentric reasons for conserving biodiversity will be uncontroversial as far as they go. In Chapter 6 we reviewed how far arguments for conserving biodiversity based on such an anthropocentric view about intrinsic value are able to support the environmentalist agenda. As we saw there, adopting an anthropocentrist position on intrinsic value gets environmentalists some of what

Table 12.1 *Summary comparison of the intrinsic value defenses presented in Part II in comparison to the goals of the environmentalist agenda as laid out in Chapter 1.*

	Anthropocentrism	Sentientism	Ecoholism	Aesthetic Value
	(Only humans count morally)	(Only sentient animals count morally)	(Ecological wholes like species and ecosystems count morally)	(Particularly beautiful species or ecosystems have an equivalent moral significance to cherished artworks)
Philosophical Merit	That humans count morally is not a controversial position. Things that help humans meet their needs and satisfy their preferences have some moral justification. How this gets operationalized depends on the merits of sentientism and ecoholism.	By various extensionist arguments, there are strong reasons for adopting this position. Doing so places moral constraints on how humans ought to meet their needs and satisfy their preferences.	This position is contentious, both in terms of its philosophical underpinning and in terms of how it can be operationalized to make actual decisions.	Less controversial among philosophers than it perhaps is among the members of the broader population who often think of aesthetic value as merely a matter of idiosyncratic taste.

Element of the Environmentalist Agenda

Element of the Environmentalist Agenda	Anthropocentrism	Sentientism	Ecoholism	Aesthetic value
Section 1.4.1 Preference for Preventing Extinction	Anthropocentrism *might support* this preference if humans actually hold it, but conservation goals may be outweighed by other competing human interests.	Sentientism *probably doesn't support* this preference. Non-sentient species are only of indirect concern, insofar as they affect sentient animals.	Ecoholism *probably supports* this preference, because ecological wholes like species are morally considerable.	Aesthetic value *probably supports* this preference, but it is constrained to only species or ecosystems of exceptional beauty.
Section 1.4.2 Preference for 'Natural' Over Modified Habitats	Anthropocentrism *might support* this preference if humans actually hold it, but conservation goals may be outweighed by other competing human interests.	Sentientism *does not seem to speak to* this preference directly. Habitat modification is only morally relevant if it affects sentient animals, and this might be positively or negatively depending on the modification.	Ecoholism *probably supports* this preference because such modification is often viewed as a moral harm to ecosystems, which are seen as being morally significant in their own right.	Aesthetic value *supports* this preference, since it recognizes authenticity of origin as a contributing factor.

Table 12.1 (*cont.*)

	Anthropocentrism	Sentientism	Ecoholism	Aesthetic Value
Section 1.4.3 A Preference for Preservation Over Conservation	Anthropocentrism *might support* this preference if humans actually hold it, but conservation goals may be outweighed by other competing human interests.	Sentientism *does not seem to speak to* this preference directly. This is an issue only to the extent that either preservation or conservation affect sentient animals.	Ecoholism *probably supports* this preference because ecosystems are directly morally considerable and modifying ecosystems is often defined as harm to them.	Aesthetic value *supports* this preference because it recognizes context as a contributing factor.
Section 1.4.4 Preference for Wild Over Domesticated Populations	Anthropocentrism *might support* this preference if humans actually hold it, but conservation goals may be outweighed by other competing human interests.	Sentientism *does not obviously support* this preference. The degree of sentience is what is important, not the degree of domestication.	Ecoholism *probably supports* this preference because species are directly morally considerable and domesticating species would probably be defined as harm to them.	Aesthetic value *might support* this preference, in cases where wild species are more rare or beautiful than domesticated.

	Anthropocentrism	Sentientism	Ecoholism	Aesthetic value
Section 1.4.5 Preference for Native Over Introduced	Anthropocentrism *might support* this preference if humans actually hold it, but conservation goals may be outweighed by other competing human interests.	Sentientism *does not obviously support* this preference. The degree of sentience is what is important, not whether they are native or introduced.	Ecoholism *probably supports* this preference. Ecosystem health is often defined in reference to a pristine condition that is reduced if species are introduced.	Aesthetic value *supports* this preference, since it recognizes authenticity of origin as a contributing factor.
Section 1.4.6 Preference for Historical vs. Changed Communities and Ecosystems	Anthropocentrism *might support* this preference if humans actually hold it, but conservation goals may be outweighed by other competing human interests.	Sentientism *does not seem to speak to* this preference. Change is only morally relevant if it affects sentient animals, and this might be positively or negatively depending on the change.	Ecoholism *probably supports* this preference. Ecosystem health is often defined in reference to a pristine condition that is reduced if these conditions are changed.	Aesthetic value *supports* this preference, since it recognizes authenticity of origin as a contributing factor.
Section 1.4.7 Preference for Ecological Wholes Over Individual Sentient Animals	Anthropocentrism *might support* this preference if humans actually hold it, but conservation goals may be outweighed by other competing human interests.	Sentientism *probably does not support* this preference.	Ecoholism *probably supports* this preference. Ecological wholes matter morally, individual sentient animals might matter as well, but less so.	Aesthetic value *probably supports* this preference given that it is the species or ecosystem and not necessarily a token organism per se that people admire aesthetically.

Table 12.1 (cont.)

	Anthropocentrism	Sentientism	Ecoholism	Aesthetic Value
Section 1.4.8 Preference for In Situ vs. Ex Situ Conservation	Anthropocentrism *might support* this preference if humans actually hold it, but conservation goals may be outweighed by other competing human interests.	Sentientism *might support* this preference to the extent that sentient animals flourish better in the wild than in captivity. Sentientism *doesn't seem to speak to* this preference with regard to non-sentient organisms.	Ecoholism *probably supports* this preference. Ex situ conservation might be acceptable as a transient tool, but in situ conservation seems to clearly be the goal of ecoholism.	Aesthetic value *supports* this preference, since it recognizes authenticity of origin as a contributing factor.

we want, but certainly not everything on the environmentalist agenda. As long as we environmentalists remain cognizant of the limitations and implications of the anthropocentrist position, it is a strong and easily defended position.

12.3 SENTIENTISM

Starting from the traditional ethical position of anthropocentrism, philosophers have used an extensionist argument to say that if what makes humans morally considerable is that they have the capacity to experience pain and pleasure, and to make plans for the future, then at least some animals are also morally considerable because they have the same mental capacities. Judging from the proliferation of laws and the rise of popular movements aimed at the ethical treatment of animals, this extensionist approach seems to be a successful philosophical project. Its success greatly enlarged the scope of moral considerability and encompasses large parts of the natural world. Although sentient organisms comprise a relatively small part of the world's biodiversity, the sentientist position greatly expands the non-sentient parts of the world that matter *instrumentally*. That is, some species or ecosystem might be of little use or interest to us humans, but it might still be indirectly important because of our moral duties to other sentient organisms. The sentientist position gets us environmentalists some of the environmentalist agenda, almost certainly more than the anthropocentric view, but, just like anthropocentrism, it doesn't get us everything.

It's important to note that, if we are correct in judging that the sentientist philosophical project is a success, that means that anthropocentrism is, in some sense, a failure. That is, if sentientism is right, then acting either *solely* in the interests of humans, or uncritically placing humans' interests above the interests of other sentient animals, is morally wrong. In other words, if the sentientist position is correct – and, as we said, we think it probably is – it means that we environmentalists can't just pretend that it doesn't exist. It means we can't just conserve biodiversity for our own human interests, as discussed in Part I of this book. Doing so would be morally wrong. At a minimum, we'd have to carefully consider the similar interests, or even moral rights, of all sentient animals in our conservation decisions.

Note as well that the sentientist position also raises significant challenges for some parts of the environmentalist agenda. For example, it is much more difficult to see how controlling or culling sentient animals to protect non-sentient organisms is a morally acceptable conservation tool. It's also difficult to see how to justify differential treatment between two equally sentient species just because one is, say, rare, or non-native. There are active philosophical projects aimed at addressing such thorny issues. For example, co-author of this book Gary Varner (2011) has been attempting to justify so-called 'therapeutic hunting' from a sentientist position. But until or unless such projects succeed, the sentientist position necessarily limits parts of the environmentalist agenda, and may require environmentalists to take dramatically different stances on other parts of the environmentalist agenda.

12.4 ECOHOLISM AND BIOCENTRIC INDIVIDUALISM

As we discussed in Chapters 9 and 10, attempts to justify ecoholism have taken two distinctly different approaches. In one, the extensionist approach, philosophers and scientists try to make ecological wholes seem like individuals, in the sense of being the sorts of things that had independent, morally relevant interests. This extensionist approach seems to have failed as a philosophical project, and it seems unlikely to us that the approach will ever yield the kind of conclusions that environmentalists would like it to.

In the second approach, philosophers have given up on the extensionist approach and tried to justify the position that ecological wholes matter morally by appealing to a very different sort of ethical theory (e.g. communitarian ethics). In Chapter 10 we gave reasons to think that such an approach suffers from a variety of practical and theoretical problems. There are active philosophical projects aimed at overcoming these objections, but so far none seem to us to be successful. It is not necessary for the reader to take our word for this conclusion. What is essential is that if environmentalists want to employ an ecoholism defense, they need to at least be cognizant of the fact that such approaches are controversial and are likely to face the kinds of objections that we raised in Chapters 9 and 10. Environmentalists do themselves no favors by naïvely appealing to such defenses.

We haven't said a lot about biocentric individualism throughout the book. This is because it is a position held by very few environmental philosophers, and it suffers from substantially the same criticisms as ecoholism.

12.5 AESTHETIC INTRINSIC VALUE

In Chapter 5 we discussed ways to defend the conservation of biodiversity based on our enjoyment of biodiversity, or on biodiversity's power to transform our enjoyment value. Those defenses were properly placed in Part I of the book because they consider 'beauty' as a form of instrumental value. In Chapter 11, we considered whether it could be argued that aesthetic value is really a form of intrinsic value. It was argued that this idea conflicts with the popular conception of beauty being solely in the eye of the beholder. On the contrary, there are culturally and perhaps biologically shared criteria for appreciating beautiful artifacts, and it is plausible that similar criteria inform our appreciation of certain species and ecosystems. Since many people recognize a duty to protect aesthetically valuable artifacts, at least on the part of members of affluent societies, so too should beautiful entities in nature be conserved.

An important challenge confronting this approach involves identifying exactly which species or ecosystems are of the greatest aesthetic value, and therefore most deserving of protection. In some cases, this judgment might appeal to culturally specific values. In other cases, it might depend on values that are shared more broadly among cultures. The extent to which scientific information should inform judgments about aesthetic value remains an important topic for debate. Nevertheless, as seen in Table 12.1, an aesthetic defense might actually support a good deal of the environmentalist agenda. However, as we pointed out in Chapter 11, aesthetic intrinsic value is not the same as moral intrinsic value, and so might carry different, perhaps weaker, duties toward the preservation, or conservation, of biodiversity.

12.6 CONCLUSIONS

At a bare minimum, the all-inclusive claim that "biodiversity has intrinsic value" seems unlikely to be supportable. On the other hand, it is equally unlikely to be the case that all and only human interests matter, morally speaking. What started out as a claim meant to move away from such an anthropocentric position, and toward a moral status for biodiversity, seems to have landed somewhere in between. Biodiversity per se doesn't possess intrinsic value, but some other animals do. This enlargement of the circle of moral considerability gives environmentalists some powerful arguments for supporting certain kinds of conservation activity, such as direct conservation of sentient species, but it causes some difficulties for other parts of the environmentalist agenda (see Table 12.1).

13 Conclusions and Personal Reflections

It was with some trepidation that we took on the cause of writing this book. We are all conscious of the very real likelihood that readers will take great exception to what we have said here. The book is likely to make many readers uncomfortable because we challenged some cherished positions on the conservation of biodiversity. And if that is true, we suppose, there is a real likelihood that you have stopped reading before you got to this chapter. On the off chance that this is not the case, we thought readers might find it helpful to know that these are difficult arguments, about which even the authors of this book don't always agree. So we thought that we would end the book with some of our individual reflections on our own positions and how we came to these, followed by some of our collective views and a very brief synopsis.

13.1 JONATHAN NEWMAN

I am an academic ecologist who studies plant–insect and plant–fungal interactions in temperate grasslands, with a focus on invasive species and climate change impacts. In my 25+ years of postdoctoral experience, I have co-authored one previous book, *Climate Change Biology* (Newman et al., 2011) and about 125 other scientific publications, only one of which involved philosophy or environmental ethics.[1] I have been a journal editor for *Journal of Ecology* and *Journal of Animal Ecology*, and I have been on the editorial boards of the journals *Behavioral Ecology* and *Global Change Biology*. I am a philanthropic donor to Greenpeace[2] Canada; and I consider myself to be an environmentalist.

---

[1] Garcia and Newman (2016).

[2] I certainly don't agree with all of Greenpeace's environmental positions (e.g. I am not anti-GMOs), but I think it's a good thing that someone is out there, agitating on behalf of the environment.

I was trained as an ecologist, at a time[3] when ecology and conservation biology were more distinct disciplines than is my impression of them today. Nevertheless, moving into my first faculty position in the mid-1990s, I was assigned to teach conservation, and did so regularly until the mid-2000s when I started teaching a broader course on environmental science.

Conservation biology then, and now, described itself as a 'value-laden discipline.' There was, and is, clearly, an 'ethical component' to the motivation of conservation biologists. Conservation textbooks contained chapters on the justification for taking conservation action. And I took all of this on intellectually, in a distinctly non-critical and non-reflective way. And I taught it to my students.

In 2002, I was fortunate to take part in the FLAD–NSF International Bioethics Institute in Lisbon, Portugal.[4] The Institute was jointly funded by the US National Science Foundation and by a private Portuguese foundation.[5] Led by philosopher Gary Comstock,[6] the institute was restricted to faculty members in the life sciences from the US and Europe. The goals of the institute were:

1) To assist life science faculty members in integrating discussions of ethics into existing science courses.
2) To acquaint faculty in the life sciences with ethical theory.
3) To assist faculty in constructing pedagogical materials, such as case studies and classroom exercises.

The idea was that if biology students only learned about ethics in philosophy classes, they would not think of ethics as a necessary and integral part of their chosen discipline. They would view it as 'something apart from biology.' The institute was intellectually intense. We lived together, dined together, and discussed the intellectually challenging area of moral philosophy from early morning until bedtime every day. And we were taught by some well-known philosophers. Gary

---

[3] BA 1985, PhD 1990.   [4] Because the internet never forgets: http://bit.ly/2bJZrFc
[5] FLAD is the Fundação Luso-Americana (the Luso-American Foundation).
[6] Gary Comstock is currently professor of philosophy at North Carolina State University: http://faculty.chass.ncsu.edu/comstock/

Comstock himself has written extensively on, for example, the morality of GMOs.[7] Other notable instructors included Peter Sandøe,[8] Tom Regan,[9] and Gary Varner.[10]

Like many of the other students taking part in the Institute, I was stimulated but still rather confused. This was all new to me, and pretty difficult stuff. I left Lisbon and returned to my position as University Lecturer in Ecology at Oxford University, and Cephalosporin Fellow in Biology at St. Peter's College. I more or less immediately got together with my friend and colleague, the tutor for philosophy at St. Peter's, Tim Mawson,[11] and we formed a reading group. I got four biology undergraduates and Tim got four philosophy undergraduates, and we read a number of books and key papers together over the course of the next couple of years. All were on animal and/or environmental ethics.

In my attempts, feeble though they were at the time, to put into practice what I had learned in Lisbon, and what I was continuing to learn through my reading group, I began incorporating environmental ethics into my conservation course at Oxford. As I continued to read widely on the topic, I regularly bothered Gary Varner via email for help, reading suggestions, and discussion. In 2004, my wife, animal welfare researcher Georgia Mason, and I moved to the University of Guelph, in Ontario, Canada. In 2006, Georgia ran a symposium on the subject of whether fish feel pain or not. Gary had written some things on this subject and was invited as a speaker to the symposium. While

---

[7] A not so easy to find, but very interesting synthesis of that work can be found in: Comstock, G. 2000. *Vexing Nature? On the Ethical Case against Agricultural Biotechnology*. Kluwer Academic Publishers.

[8] Peter Sandøe is the director of the Danish Centre for Bioethics and Risk Assessment, and Professor of animal ethics at the University of Copenhagen: http://bit.ly/2bRrK7O

[9] Hopefully the reader will recognize Tom Regan's name from Chapter 8 of this book. Tom Regan, was professor emeritus at North Carolina State University and author of the seminal book *The Case for Animal Rights* (1983), among many others: http://tomregan.info

[10] Hopefully the reader will recognize Gary Varner's name as a co-author of this book! At the time, Gary's thinking was synthesized in *In Nature's Interests? Interests, Animal Rights and Environmental Ethics* (1998), which I read enthusiastically and I questioned Gary quite closely about his arguments.

[11] Tim Mawson is a moral philosopher and member of the faculty of philosophy at Oxford University: http://bit.ly/2rEEg2t

Gary was visiting, I pitched him the idea of writing a book on environmental ethics for environmentalists. Why?

Reflecting on the Institute in Lisbon, now a decade and a half later, I distinctly remember being asked by a classmate if I thought that culling animals like deer to save endangered plants was ethically permissible. I answered, without much critical reflection, "of course it is." Now I am not so sure. Through the years, as I thought more deeply about the topic, I slowly began to question my initial positions – positions I had adopted through teaching conservation biology over the previous 10 years. This is, after all, the function of ethics. Ethics is the analysis of arguments leading to decisions about what is right and wrong. Its function is to cause us to question our status quo moral positions. I found myself deeply influenced by the sentientist positions we discussed in Chapter 8. I began to see it as an ethical problem to sacrifice sentient animals to conserve non-sentient plants. This position put me at immediate odds with most – perhaps all – of my conservation biology colleagues.

I find the sentientist arguments rational, coherent, and consistent. I applied a sort of modified method of reflective equilibrium (see Chapter 7) to my own moral views. I thought to myself, what sort of ethical commitments follow from these sentientist ethical theories? And it certainly seemed to me that some of the implications were that it wasn't necessarily obvious that culling sentient animals to protect non-sentient plants was morally permissible. However, this caused me some disequilibrium in that my rock bottom moral intuition told me (and sometimes still does) that protecting rare species of plants was a moral obligation that we humans share. Continuing with the method of reflective equilibrium, I now needed to go back and show where I was wrong about sentientism being the right way to think about morality, or that sentientism didn't contain the moral commitments that I thought it did, so that I could preserve my rock bottom moral intuition about conserving rare plants. Or, if I was unable to do either of these, I had to admit that perhaps my moral intuition about plants was wrong. The problem was, I couldn't find a rational, coherent, or consistent explanation of why the sentientist position was wrong. I struggled with this disequilibrium for a number of years, and I'm still not terribly thrilled with where I have landed. But I think I have landed at a place where I have to give up on my moral intuition and accept that plants and other non-sentient, even non-living components of the world are not directly morally considerable. They matter only in so much as they affect the lives of sentient animals, to whom I believe we do have ethical duties. Another moral commitment that I think follows from this position is that most meat eating is probably morally wrong. I say this as a person who loves eating meat and who hasn't completely abandoned eating it!

As I said, I still find this position somewhat unsettling. It is difficult to give up on one's moral intuition. This is where I am right now. And I am hoping that smart environmental philosophers are able to show that we can get all or most of the environmentalist agenda by reasoning as strict sentientists. People like Gary Varner have active research projects aimed at doing just that. They haven't yet found the argument that I personally find convincing, but the projects are intellectually stimulating and perhaps they will find that argument.

So, why write this book, and why did Gary and Stefan agree to join me in this project? While I was coming to terms with the implications of my ethical reasoning, I engaged repeatedly in discussions with my academic colleagues in conservation biology. There I found the same few entrenched arguments repeated time and again, and I found myself making the same set of counterarguments time and again. It seemed to me that conservation biologists were only dimly aware that environmental ethics existed as a field of study, and were pretty unaware of any of the arguments going on in that discipline. I was frustrated with the general level of, and quality of, discussion and saw a need to familiarize my colleagues with these standard arguments and counterarguments so that we could raise the level of discourse. As for why Gary and Stefan agreed to join me in this project, I am not sure, and they probably regretted that decision at some point during the writing process!

13.1.1   Where Am I Now in My Thinking?

I think that objective intrinsic value exists in the world, and that it is limited to sentient animals. I believe that we first and foremost have a moral duty to respect those individuals and to consider their interests in our decision making. All the rest of nature has instrumental value and/or aesthetic value. In accepting this position, I have had to accept some unpalatable intellectual commitments that accompany the position. For example, I have had to accept that there will be times where the value of developing nature for human needs and wants outweighs the instrumental value we may achieve by leaving nature undeveloped. I have had to accept the logic of species introductions and removals, if such management approaches are likely to improve the instrumental value of nature. And I have had to accept the fact that sometimes wholesale ecosystem reconfiguration or replacement will be more valuable to us, and other sentient creatures, than leaving that system untouched. These conclusions do not mesh well with my sympathy for much of the environmentalist agenda that we laid out in Chapter 1. My sympathy remains, but I have come to view a number of these goals as *strongly held preferences* rather than any sort of moral responsibility.

13.1.2   Additional Reading

Below are readings that I have found valuable for one reason or another. Some I found persuasive, some I found challenged my worldview at the time, some just made me think a bit differently about the difficult issues we addressed in this book.

Regan, T. (ed.). 1984. *Earthbound: Introductory Essays in Environmental Ethics*. Prospect Heights, IL, Waveland Press.

Kirkman, R. 2002. *Skeptical Environmentalism: The Limits of Philosophy and Science*. Bloomington, IN, Indiana University Press.

Maier, D.S. 2012. *What's So Good about Biodiversity? A Call for Better Reasoning about Nature's Value*. New York, Springer.

Morris, J. (ed.) 2000. *Rethinking Risk and the Precautionary Principle*. Oxford. Butterworth-Heinemann.

13.2   GARY VARNER

I have been a professor of philosophy at Texas A&M University since 1990, but I have been thinking about environmental ethics ever since I was a child. Of course, I didn't start out with all the specialized vocabulary that is now de rigueur: 'anthropocentrism,' 'sentience,' 'ecoholism,' and so on; but I remember thinking from a very young age that there was something unethical about how human beings have been commandeering the Earth at the expense of other life forms. When my family moved from our ancestral home in central Ohio to the Mojave Desert in northern Los Angeles County, I was enthralled by the forests of Joshua trees around my home in the Antelope Valley and by the looming San Gabriel Mountains. I learned to love camping there, and to this day my default summer vacation venues are the arid landscapes of the southwestern United States.

I read Aldo Leopold during high school in California, and in college I majored in philosophy, because I wanted to sort out my beliefs about how humans should live on Earth, and I wanted to rationally defend my intuitive belief that humans shouldn't be commandeering the Earth to the extent that we are. The field of environmental ethics was brand new then (I started my master's program in 1980, the year after the journal *Environmental Ethics* was founded), and at the time I leaned toward ecoholism. For my doctoral dissertation at the University of Wisconsin, I worked on the concept of interests, because it seemed to me that the starting point of ethical thinking was concerning oneself about the strivings and experiences of other sentient individuals. As I looked for convincing, rational arguments for extending intrinsic value to species and ecosystems, however, I found the arguments wanting, for some of the reasons articulated (albeit more clearly with my coauthors than I ever did on my own) in Chapter 9 of this book. So, over the years I have moved back toward a more traditional moral theory.

In my first book, *In Nature's Interests? Interests, Animal Rights, and Environmental Ethics* (1998), I defended as best I could a version of biocentric individualism, based on an extensionist strategy. In Chapter 3 of that book I argued that the best way to account for some of our intuitions about the well-being of humans and other sentient animals would involve invoking the kind of 'biological' interests discussed in Section 9.3 of this book. I argued that if that was so with regard to sentient animals, then those 'biological interests' of non-conscious organisms should count for something too. I also defended a hierarchy of interests, however, one that places the lives of sentient organisms above those of the non-sentient, and the satisfactions of especially complex and long-term interests (which I then called *"ground projects"*) above more simple and short-term, but still conscious, preference interests. (My argument for that hierarchy was based on what I thought to be a hierarchical relationship among the three categories of interests.) And I included a chapter responding to what I characterized as the "dogma" that animal rights and animal welfare views are incompatible with the environmentalist agenda. Some of my arguments there are reflected in Chapter 8 of this book.

As reviews of *In Nature's Interests?* came out, a troubling pattern emerged. Almost every review by a philosopher faulted my key argument in defense of extending the concept of morally significant interests to non-conscious organisms, and they all faulted it in the same way. So, in a review of Nicholas Agar's book *Life's Intrinsic Value* (Agar, 2001), I publicly recanted that argument (Varner, 2003). Specifically, I admitted that the intuitions about sentient animals' and humans' interests that I had argued required invoking the moral significance of non-conscious, biological interests, could just as well be accommodated by what is called an *externalist account* of well-being. The idea is that in making a judgment about, say, a sentient, non-human animal, you imagine yourself having to choose among possible lives for that animal, based on what you know now about how the animal's life will go under various scenarios, and you ask yourself which life you would choose to subsequently experience yourself. This is an 'externalist' account because it doesn't involve literally taking the animal's point of view (the animal is incapable of taking into account all of the considerations that you are capable of considering), and that's why, I had argued, we need to invoke the moral significance of biological interests.

The next step in my changes in moral thinking began when, in 2001, I taught a graduate seminar on "The Work of Peter Singer." The seminar started with R.M. Hare's (1981) *Moral Thinking: Its Levels, Method, and Point*, because Hare had been Singer's dissertation advisor at Oxford. With that seminar, I started a project critically appraising how far Hare's two-level utilitarianism supports Singer's abolitionist conclusions in animal ethics. That project produced my 2012 book, *Personhood, Ethics, and Animal Cognition: Situating Animals in Hare's Two-Level Utilitarianism* (Varner, 2012).

I was sympathetic to Hare's criticisms of the method of reflective equilibrium, which we discussed in Section 7.1.4. As we noted in Section 7.1.3, Hare argued that the logic of moral discourse implies utilitarianism. But Hare thought that, for various reasons, real-world utilitarians need an "intuitive level system" of rules (what I call ILS rules). Hare reserved the label "critical level thinking" for explicitly utilitarian thinking that is equivalent to what is commonly called act utilitarianism. On Hare's theory, we should rely on ILS rules under normal circumstances, but we have to do our best at explicitly utilitarian thinking when we consider modifications to those ILS rules, when our ILS rules conflict or offer no guidance, and in certain extraordinary circumstances.

In *Personhood, Ethics, and Animal Cognition* I defended, on utilitarian grounds, a revised version of the hierarchy of interests that I had defended in *In Nature's Interests?* Although Hare himself avoided using the concept of 'personhood,' I argued that a utilitarian has good reasons for thinking that the life of an individual with "a biographical sense of self" is more (as I put it) "*morally charged,*" meaning that this cognitive capacity makes its life able to go well (and also to go badly) in significant ways that it can't for an individual that lacks this cognitive capacity. Thus, 'personhood' replaced 'ground projects' in my earlier hierarchy of moral value.

13.2.1   Where Am I Now in My Thinking?

Working within Hare's conceptual framework for a decade convinced me that I had already been thinking like a utilitarian – albeit a Harean, two-level utilitarian – for some time, if not all of my life. So, I am now working on a sequel to my 2012 book that will apply that ethical framework to a range of ethical issues regarding our treatment of animals, including the keeping of companion and working animals, animal agriculture, and research using animal models, but also how well the environmentalist agenda, as set out in Chapter 1 of this book, can be embraced from a sentientist perspective.[12]

I don't expect the embrace to be perfect. For instance, like Jonathan Newman, I don't think that the preservation of *every* endangered species can be justified from a sentientist perspective. I think that there will be times where developing wildlands for various purposes is justified, that sometimes introducing exotic species and removing indigenous ones will be justified, etc., in terms of the instrumental value of such policies to humans and other sentient animals.

Hare's particular version of utilitarianism also has an implication that runs contrary to an important, base-line moral intuition that I held for most of my life: the intuition that moral value is what we described in Section 1.6.1 of this book as "objective intrinsic value." That is, for most of my life I thought that the moral value of nature that I lamented humans' destroying "exists in nature independently of human valuers." Under the influence of Hare's theory, however, I now believe that morality is a construct of the logical requirements that our language places on moral judgments. So I now believe that

---

[12] The new book is under contract with Oxford University Press with the working title *Sustaining Animals: Envisioning Humane, Sustainable Communities.*

intrinsic value is what we described in Section 1.6.1 as 'non-objective' and 'relational.'

That needn't worry me, though, if – as I *hope* – the logical requirements on moral judgments as described by Hare are universal in human languages. For that would ensure that, in our terminology from Section 1.6.1, those logical requirements are 'hard-wired' into our judgments about intrinsic value, i.e. that intrinsic value is of type 2.B.i in our taxonomy in Section 1.6.1 ("'hard-wired' into our judgments about intrinsic value"), rather than of type 2.B.iii ("idiosyncratic"), or even type 2.B.ii ("influenced by culturally shared norms"). If that's so, then everybody's moral judgments will converge if they are thinking logically and attending to the same facts. If there is a Chomsky-style 'universal grammar' that has (my term) 'a moral module' that embodies the logical requirements on moral judgments as articulated by Hare, then that will certainly be so.

I'm well aware, however, that "*hoping* that something is true" doesn't make it a bit more likely!

13.2.2 Additional Reading

Below are two books that were pivotal in my own development as an ethicist, and the two books that I have published prior to this one.

I read Bryan Norton's 1988 book while on a camping trip during my time as a visiting assistant professor at Washington University in St. Louis the year after I finished my PhD. That book inspired me to think, for the first time, that an *anthropocentric* stance could pretty fully embrace the environmentalist agenda.

That same year, I first read Hare's *Moral Thinking* (1982) as part of a directed readings course with a graduate student there. I had read some of Hare's other works while a master's student at Georgia, and my undergraduate advisor at Arizona State (Ted Humphrey) had made Hare recommended reading, so I ended up re-reading *Moral Thinking* several times. In my 2012 book, I think that I extended his theory in some useful ways, especially his treatment of those 'intuitive level rules.'

Hare, R.M. 1982. *Moral Thinking: Its Levels, Method and Point.* New York: Oxford University Press.

Norton, Bryan. 1988. *Why Preserve Natural Variety?* Princeton, NJ: Princeton University Press.

Varner, Gary. 1998. *In Nature's Interests: Interests, Animal Rights, and Environmental Ethics.* New York: Oxford University Press.

Varner, Gary. 2012. *Personhood, Ethics and Animal Cognition: Situating Animals in Hare's Two-Level Utilitarianism.* New York: Oxford University Press.

13.3   STEFAN LINQUIST

13.3.1   In What Sense Am I an Environmentalist?

An ongoing concern for us, as authors, has been that our critique of the justification for the environmentalist agenda might lead some readers to scrutinize our individual commitments to environmentalism. I would like to think that readers of this book are immune to the ad hominem fallacy of evaluating the person rather than their argument. However, in reality, I recognize that debates over environmentalism are fraught with distrust. In the current political climate, to even question the foundations of environmentalism can invite speculation about one's ambitions or ideological motives.

My academic training is in theoretical biology and the philosophy of biology. Some of my research interests – for example, on the existence of resilient generalizations in ecology – bear upon environmental issues. I also teach undergraduate courses in environmental philosophy. However, my understanding of environmentalism has mostly been shaped by experiences outside the university.

From 2005–2015, I was involved in the creation of a public education facility (the Ucluelet Aquarium) on the west coast of Vancouver Island (Linquist, 2018). This remote corner of British Columbia has been a hotbed for environmental controversy since 1993, when area residents staged an organized protest against logging in Clayoquot Sound (Magnusson and Shaw, 2002). That event established a tradition of environmental activism in the region which has coexisted with various industries (mostly aquaculture, logging, and tourism), as well as the five local Nuu-Chah-Nulth First Nations. The result is a microcosm for many of the environmental challenges facing society on a larger scale. In my role as 'aquarium philosopher' I have discussed matters of science and ethics with members of several (often opposing) stakeholder groups. The result has been a series of ongoing conversations that inform my understanding of the environmentalist agenda and the challenges facing it.

While working on this book, three particular stakeholder groups often came to mind. The first group includes environmental activists and certain eNGOS who campaign publically on behalf of the environmentalist agenda. In my experience, these organizations appeal to both instrumental and intrinsic values to defend biodiversity conservation. My sense is that these environmentalists will find our critique of ecoholism particularly challenging. The idea that 'pristine' ecosystems have some kind of intrinsic value is the unquestioned starting point for much of their reasoning.

This axiom is also a source of friction with the second stakeholder group who came to mind: the many 'green' industry representatives who advocate for sustainable growth. It might come as a surprise to some readers that representatives from the aquaculture and logging industries also view themselves as environmentalists, in a sense. They tend to cite instrumental rather than intrinsic values as reasons for conserving biodiversity, with cost–benefit analysis as their preferred mode of decision making. My sense is that this audience will welcome our discussion of the precautionary principle, given the popular misconception that it provides a decisive objection to most industrial practices. However, I suspect that our discussion of intrinsic value will receive a mixed reception. On the one hand, it might be regarded as a sign of right-minded thinking that, according to our analysis, species, ecosystems, and many organisms do not obviously possess intrinsic moral value. On the other hand, our analysis locates sentient organisms squarely within the realm of ethical concern. This conclusion is bound to have implications for the practice of aquaculture, assuming that fish are indeed sentient (Braithwaite, 2010). So, one potential upshot of our discussion in this book is a critique of 'sustainable' industries, such as aquaculture, that appeals exclusively to anthropocentric values.

This point perhaps deserves emphasis, because the public debate surrounding aquaculture in British Columbia (a case with which I am somewhat familiar) reflects a broader range of environmental conflicts found elsewhere throughout the world. Currently, the aquaculture industry is criticized for a variety of ethical and instrumental reasons. When presented to the public, these objections tend to shade into one another as if to form a single wall of criticism. Advocates for aquaculture respond, naturally, by singling out the most obviously flawed objections to their industry. After all, when trying to push through a wall it makes sense to start with the weakest bricks. If our analysis in this book is sound, then we would expect aquaculture defenders to attack the ecoholist idea that pristine ecosystems are intrinsically valuable. A second, slightly less obvious weakness is a reliance on the precautionary principle. The worry, however, is that the dismissal of these weaker arguments will be perceived, perhaps mistakenly, as a vindication of aquaculture or other such industries. Effectively, the removal of those weaker bricks might be seen as having caused the entire wall to crumble. That would be a bad thing if, for example, these industries violate animal welfare concerns or if their practices are on balance detrimental to human societies. The point is that environmental opposition to industry is potentially weakened when good arguments are presented alongside the bad.

The third stakeholder group that has come to mind while writing this book are the five First Nations who've inhabited Clayoquot Sound for millennia. I do not pretend to understand how these stakeholders might react to the arguments explored in this book. Indeed, it is unlikely that there is such a thing as 'the' Nuu-Chah-Nulth perspective. Undoubtedly, it is an oversimplification to generalize about even members of these First Nations – let alone indigenous communities as a whole.

One possibility is that some First Nations readers might balk at our critique of ecoholism and the precautionary principle, as I expect of environmental activists. This expectation is based on the idea that these two groups sometimes share similar values. Occasionally, a comparison is drawn between the ecoholist idea of a biotic community and the popular indigenous view of interconnection among all living things. However, on closer consideration, I doubt that these two value systems can be so easily superimposed. For one thing, the ecoholist tradition involves, by its own admission, a break from anthropocentric moral frameworks. As we argued in Chapter 10, this leaves open the question of how to reconcile conflicts of interest, for example, when an increase in human flourishing imposes a cost on other species. A value system that recognizes intrinsic value in ecological wholes seems poorly equipped to adjudicate such trade-offs (Justus et al., 2009). By contrast, indigenous value systems could not have survived for millennia without useful action-guiding principles for resolving or avoiding these tensions.

My limited understanding of indigenous value systems leads me to believe that they are, above all, deeply connected to the specific locations in which they evolved. As a member of the Ahousaht Nation once explained to me, "Even if they were to remove every tree from this hillside, and destroy every salmon in our rivers, our people will still be here, because this place is who we are." I am not sure that the arguments that we have considered in defense of the environmentalist agenda share much in common with such an acutely place-based value system.

Returning to the question at hand, I see myself as an environmentalist in the sense that I consider it a worthwhile objective to find common ground among these three stakeholder groups, broadly construed. This requires an honest attempt to articulate and critique the arguments used by each group to justify their preferred actions and policies. My hope is that, in this book, we have made at least a small degree of progress on this front. I suppose that there is one important respect in which our efforts could be seen as biased, since we have focused our critique on just the environmentalist agenda, while paying less critical attention to the two alternative viewpoints of 'sustainable' development or indigenous philosophy. It might therefore appear to some readers that these alternatives are getting off easy. But in our defense, much of the work in environmental philosophy (not to mention a sizable body of work in ecology and economics) is directed in opposition to sustainable development. And for reasons that I have touched upon, we are hardly in a position to articulate and critique the principles of indigenous philosophy. Instead, we have chosen to focus on the environmentalist agenda partly because it seems deserving of closer examination, and partly because our educational backgrounds place us in a good position to do so.

13.3.2   *What Did I Learn from Working on This Book?*

When I accepted Jonathan Newman's invitation to participate in this project, I had very little sympathy with intrinsic value arguments for biodiversity conservation. Too often, environmentalists appeal to the work of philosophers who, it is often claimed, have established that ecosystems or species possess some special property that bestows moral significance. As we discuss in Part II of this book, Western ethical frameworks evolved to recognize persons, not nature, as morally significant. This obstacle has motivated two procrustean strategies that seem intent on extending that framework indefinitely outward. One strategy involves the personification of ecological wholes, portraying species or ecosystems in an organismic guise to make it seem, if you squint hard enough, as if they possess something like an interest (e.g. Vucetich et al., 2015). The inconvenient truth is that the sciences of ecology and evolution simply do not bear out such efforts, as we have discussed in Chapters 9 and 10. The alternative approach has been to 'de-personify' our ethical framework, which means the abandonment of human-centered values. One problem with this approach is that it leaves us ethically rudderless, since the continuation of one form of life often requires the destruction of another (Grey, 1993). Others point out that non-anthropocentric value systems provide no basis for adjudicating conflicts of duty and are therefore highly impractical (Justus et al., 2009). More generally, the problem with the depersonification of value is that it is difficult to avoid begging the question about which kinds of entity are morally significant. The entire approach of attempting to locate intrinsic value in ecological wholes has therefore always struck me as a non-starter.

However, my interactions with Gary Varner have resulted in a more nuanced understanding of intrinsic value. The idea that *sentient* organisms possess objective intrinsic value (independent of any valuer) now looks to be a strong and defensible position. A potential avenue for future research is to work out the implications of this idea for environmental ethics, as Gary has done in some of his writings. Even more liberating is the recognition that intrinsic value can also be generated by social and cultural practices – what we have called relational intrinsic value – as in the case of aesthetically valuable artifacts. This is not the same kind of intrinsic value that tends to get invoked in the context of extensionist arguments. In those cases, the possession of some morally significant property (e.g. sentience) automatically confers moral significance on the entity in question. By contrast, in the case of socially generated values, the moral duty to preserve an item depends on your relation to the culture in question. For members of a culture who value cedar trees as sacred objects, for instance, the duty to preserve them is internal to their value system and perhaps in no need of justification. To a cultural outsider, however, the same duty might rest on a very different set of principles. For example, we might see the preservation of another culture's sacred objects as a requirement of the Kantian idea of autonomy or, more generally, as a requirement of respect and tolerance for cultural diversity. I do not take this to be a developed philosophical position. However, my aim has been to gesture toward an avenue of investigation that looks promising. The connection between aesthetic and environmental value strikes me as a fruitful area for building bridges across conflicting value systems.

More surprising, to me, has been the discovery that the case for biodiversity's instrumental value is less compelling than I might have imagined before embarking on this project. I used to see medicinal and agricultural benefits as a compelling reason to conserve all manner of biodiversity. However, arguments reviewed in Chapter 4 force me to reconsider this position. Likewise, I used to see the precautionary principle as, at the very least, a useful heuristic for environmental decision making. Now, in light of Chapter 3, I see it as more of a vague and misleading slogan. My faith in the idea that biodiversity should be conserved because of its role in providing ecosystem services was already shaken by the work of Mark Sagoff (1998, 2008). Now, given the many methodological challenges that were discussed in Chapter 2, I no longer see this as a blanket defense for conserving biodiversity. I have to confess that these conclusions do not sit well with me, yet I see no obvious way to reject them.

13.3.3   Additional Reading

In our wildest moments of ambition, we sometimes imagine that this book will help to advance the public debate over important environmental issues. It has never been our aim to provide anything resembling a final answer to the questions raised in each of our chapters. With this in mind, it is perhaps helpful to recommend a few of the many excellent works that readers might find enlightening to pursue. Perhaps my favorite book on the concept of biodiversity and its cultural and epistemic development is David Takacs' *The Idea of Biodiversity* (1996). A colleague from the Geography department lent me a heavily marked and worn-out photocopy of this book when I started working at Guelph. Even more amazingly, she insisted that I return her shabby copy after only a few weeks. In my view, this work is justly deserving of such high regard. Another book which I consider essential for anyone interested in the history of environmentalism is Donald Worster's *Nature's Economy* (1977). It provides an engaging history of the ecosystem concept as well as a sober discussion of Aldo Leopold's influence on environmental thought. While on the topic of excellent historical scholarship that I wish I'd read sooner in my life, William Cronon's *Changes in the Land* (1983), along with his article on wilderness, are a must-read for anyone interested in popular conceptions of pristine nature.

The field of environmental aesthetics contains many fruitful avenues for exploration. One important question concerns whether some aesthetic values might be common among human societies. I consider Stephen Davies' *The Artful Species* (2012) to be the best thing going on this topic. It would be encouraging to see collaboration with anthropologists who could help to develop and test his suggestions. Another under-explored connection surrounds the reasons why it is important to provide public funding for the arts. As we discussed briefly in Chapter 11, the aesthetic defense of conservation usually begins with our broadly shared intuition that it is important to preserve so-called great artworks. The extension to biodiversity then hinges on whether certain species or ecosystems are comparable to these exceptional artifacts. However, an alternative approach would be to explore reasons for allocating public funds to the fine arts, even those which might turn out to be something less than great. This might provide a sound basis for conserving a broader range of entities in nature on account of their *potential* aesthetic value. This line of argument, if successful, might also relieve environmentalists of having to provide a fully developed theory of intrinsic aesthetic value – something that proves to be no easy task. Although I have not pursued these ideas in any depth, the seminal articles by Joel Feinberg and Richard Manning provide an extremely helpful starting point. Jerrold Levinson's volume, *Aesthetics and Ethics: Essays at the Intersection* (1998) also contains a few insightful gems.

Cronon, W. 1983/2003. *Changes in the Land: Indians, Colonists, and the Ecology of New England*. New York: Hill and Wang.
Cronon, W. 1998. The trouble with wilderness, or getting back to the wrong nature. In J.B. Callicott and M.P. Nelson (eds.) *The Great*

New Wilderness Debate, Athens, GA: University of Georgia Press, pp. 414–442.

Davies, S. 2012. *The Artful Species*. Oxford: Oxford University Press.

Feinberg, J. 1994. Not with my tax money: The problem of justifying government subsidies for the arts. *Public Affairs Quarterly* 8:101–123.

Levinson, J. 1998. *Aesthetics and Ethics: Essays at the Intersection*. Cambridge, UK: Cambridge University Press.

Manning, R.N. 1994. Intrinsic value and overcoming Feinberg's Benefit Principle. *Public Affairs Quarterly* 8:125–140.

Takacs, D. 1996. *The Idea of Biodiversity: Philosophies of Paradise*. Baltimore: Johns Hopkins Press.

Worster, D., 1977/1994. *Nature's economy: A history of ecological ideas*. Cambridge: Cambridge University Press.

13.4 DON'T AGREE TO DISAGREE

As is hopefully obvious from reading this chapter, our individual ideas about why we should conserve biodiversity have changed over the years, and quite dramatically so. As we have engaged with the ideas and evidence – individually, with each other, and with our students and colleagues – we have each changed our views. These changes have taken many years and have, at times, meant that our intellectual positions were at odds with our sympathies, passions, and intuitions. These periods of dissonance have been difficult, but necessary for the evolution of our thinking. We don't expect you to immediately (or even eventually) agree with either our personal views (Sections 13.1 to 13.3) or with the views of others that we presented throughout this book. Indeed, we would be disappointed if you did so. What we hope is that you don't simply adopt an 'agree to disagree' type reaction. That would be intellectually lazy. What we hope is that we have caused you to think, and to continue to engage carefully and critically with these ideas, and others, and that you will construct and reconstruct your own understanding of these issues. It is important to sort out not only *what* you think about conserving biodiversity, but also *why* you think that way, and whether you *ought* to think that way. Doing so can be difficult, and takes considerable time, but that is how we will advance the level and quality of discussion.

13.5 WHY OUGHT WE CONSERVE BIODIVERSITY?

It should now be apparent that there is no simple answer to this question; indeed, simple answers are almost certainly wrong at some level of analysis. Still, we authors remain committed to the idea that we ought to conserve biodiversity. It may well be that there are examples of biodiversity that lack instrumental value, as well as intrinsic value. And in these cases, we may have to admit that, perhaps, our desire to conserve it is no more than a personal preference on our parts. And even when biodiversity has instrumental value, that value might be less than the alternatives.

We hope that by carefully presenting the arguments, and the standard objections, we have helped the reader to more effectively engage in arguments about how we should live in relationship to the land.

References

Abby, E. (1968). *Desert Solitaire, a Season in the Wilderness*. New York, NY: Ballantine.

Agapow, P.-M., Bininda-Emonds, O.R.P., Crandall, K.A., et al. (2004). The impact of species concept on biodiversity studies. *The Quarterly Review of Biology, 79,* 161–179.

Agar, N. (2001). *Life's Intrinsic Value: Science, Ethics, and Nature.* New York, NY: Columbia University Press.

Aiken, W. (1984). Ethical issues in agriculture. In: Regan, T. (ed.) *Earthbound: New Introductory Essays in Environmental Ethics.* 1st edn. New York, NY: Random House.

Allen, R. (1980). *World Conservation Strategy. Living Resource Conservation for Sustainable Development.* Gland, Switzerland: International Union for Conservation of Nature and Natural Resources.

Andreoni, J. (1989). Giving with impure altruism: applications to charity and Ricardian equivalence. *The Journal of Political Economy, 97,* 1447–1458.

Appleton, J. (1988). Prospects and refuges revisited. *Landscape Journal, 3,* 91–103.

Appleton, J. (1996). *The Experience of Landscape.* Chichester, UK: Wiley.

Aristotle (1941 [4th century BCE]). *Politics,* translated by Benjamin Jowett. *The Basic Works of Aristotle.* R. McKeon. New York: Random House, 1113–1316.

Ayres, R.U. (1998). The price-value paradox. *Ecological Economics, 25,* 17–19.

Barnosky, A.D., Matzke, N., Tomiya, S., et al. (2011). Has the Earth's sixth mass extinction already arrived? *Nature, 471,* 51–57.

Belaoussoff, S. and Kevan, P.G. (2003). Are there ecological foundations for ecosystem health? *The Environmentalist, 23,* 255–263.

Bell, G. (2001). Neutral macroecology. *Science, 293,* 2413–2418.

Bell, T., Newman, J.A., Silverman, B.W., Turner, S.L., and Lilley, A.K. (2005). The contribution of species richness and composition to bacterial services. *Nature, 436,* 1157–1160.

Biddinger, G.R., Calow, P., Delorme, P., et al. (2008). Managing risks to ecological populations. In: Barnthouse, L.W., Munns, W.R. and Sorensen, M.T. (eds.) *Population-Level Ecological Risk Assessment.* 1st edn. Boca Raton, FL: Taylor & Francis.

Black, H.C., Nolan, J.R., and Nolan-Haley, J.M. (1990). *Black's Law Dictionary*. 6th edn. St. Paul, MN: West Publishing Co.

Borris, R.P. (2017) Bioprospecting: an industrial perspective. In: Paterson, R. and Lima, N. (eds.) *Bioprospecting: Success, Potential and Constraints*. Cham, Switzerland: Springer International Publishing.

Botkin, D.B. (1990). *Discordant Harmonies: A New Ecology for the Twenty-First Century*. New York, NY: Oxford University Press.

Bracken, M.E.S., Friberg, S.E., Gonzalez-Dorantes, C.A., and Williams, S.L. (2008). Functional consequences of realistic biodiversity changes in a marine ecosystem. *Proceedings of the National Academy of Sciences of the United States of America*, 105, 924–928.

Braithwaite, V. (2010). *Do Fish Feel Pain?* Oxford, UK: Oxford University Press.

Brooks, A.C. (2000). Public subsidies and charitable giving: crowding out, crowding in, or both? *Journal of Policy Analysis and Management*, 19, 451–464.

Brown, T.C. and Daniel, T.C. (1986). Predicting scenic beauty of timber stands. *Forest Science*, 32, 471–487.

Caldeira, M.C., Hector, A., Loreau, M., and Pereira, J.S. (2005). Species richness, temporal variability and resistance of biomass production in a Mediterranean grassland. *Oikos*, 110, 115–123.

Callicott, J.B. (1980). Animal liberation: a triangular affair. *Environmental Ethics*, 2, 311–338.

Callicott, J.B. (1982). Hume's is/ought dichtomy and the relation of ecology to Leopold's land ethic. *Environmental Ethics*, 4, 163–174.

Callicott, J.B. (1987). Conceptual foundations of the land ethic. In: Callicott, J.B. (ed.) *A Companion to a Sand County Almanac: Interpretive and Critical Essays*. 1st edn. Madison, WI: University of Wisconsin Press.

Callicott, J.B. (1988). Animal liberation and environmental ethics: back together again. *Between the Species*, 4, 163–169.

Callicott, J.B. (1989). *In Defense of the Land Ethic: Essays in Environmental Philosophy*. Albany, NY: State University of New York Press.

Callicott, J.B. (1994). Moral monism in environmental ethics defended. *Journal of Philosophical Research*, 19, 51–60.

Callicott, J.B. (1995). Animal liberation: a triangular affair. In: Elliot, R. (ed.) *Environmental Ethics*. 1st edn. Oxford: Oxford University Press.

Callicott, J.B. (1999). Holistic environmental ethics and the problem of ecofascism. In: Callicott, J.B. (ed.) *Beyond the Land Ethic: More Essays in Environmental Philosophy*. 1st edn. Albany, NY: SUNY Press.

Callicott, J.B. (2008). Leopold's land aesthetic. In: Carlson, A. and Lintott, S. (eds.) *Nature, Aesthetics, and Environmentalism: From Beauty to Duty*. 1st edn. New York, NY: Columbia University Press.

Canter, P.H., Thomas, H., and Ernst, E. (2005). Bringing medicinal plants into cultivation: opportunities and challenges for biotechnology. *Trends in Biotechnology*, 23, 180–185.

Cardinale, B.J., Duffy, E., Srivastava, D., et al. (2009). Towards a food-web perspective on biodiversity and ecosystem functioning. In: Naeem, S., Bunker, D.E., Loreau, M., Hector, A. and Perring, C. (eds.) *Biodiversity, Ecosystem Functioning, and Human Well-being: An Ecological and Economic Perspective*. 1st edn. Oxford: Oxford University Press.

Cardinale, B.J., Duffy, J.E., Gonzalez, A., et al. (2012). Biodiversity loss and its impact on humanity. *Nature*, 486, 59–67.

Cardinale, B.J., Gross, K., Fritschie, K., et al. (2013). Biodiversity simultaneously enhances the production and stability of community biomass, but the effects are independent. *Ecology*, 94, 1697–1707.

Cardinale, B.J., Matulich, K.L., Hooper, D.U., et al. (2011). The functional role of producer diversity in ecosystems. *American Journal of Botany*, 98, 572–592.

Carlson, A. (1979). Appreciation and the natural environment. *The Journal of Aesthetics and Art Criticism*, 37, 267–275.

Carlson, A. and Lintott, S. (2008). *Nature, Aesthetics, and Environmentalism: From Beauty to Duty*. New York, NY: Columbia University Press.

Carroll, N. (1987). Can government funding of the arts be justified theoretically? *Journal of Aesthetic Education*, 21, 21–35.

Carter, A. (2000). Humean nature. *Environmental Values*, 9, 3–37.

Ceballos, G., Ehrlich, P.R., Barnosky, A.D., et al. (2015). Accelerated modern human–induced species losses: entering the sixth mass extinction. *Science Advances*, 1, e1400253.

Cerda, C., Barkmann, J., and Marggraf, R. (2013). Application of choice experiments to quantify the existence value of an endemic moss: a case study in Chile. *Environment and Development Economics*, 18, 207–224.

Chase, J.M. and Myers, J.A. (2011). Disentangling the importance of ecological niches from stochastic processes across scales. *Philosophical Transactions of the Royal Society of London B: Biological Sciences*, 366, 2351–2363.

Chomitz, K.M., Alger, K., Thomas, T.S., Orlando, H., and Nova, P.V. (2005). Opportunity costs of conservation in a biodiversity hotspot: the case of southern Bahia. *Environment and Development Economics*, 10, 293–312.

Costanza, R., dArge, R., deGroot, R., et al. (1997). The value of the world's ecosystem services and natural capital. *Nature*, 387, 253–260.

Costanza, R., Norton, B., and Haskell, B. (eds.) (1992). *Ecosystem Health: New Goals for Environmental Management*. Washington, DC: Island Press.

Costello, C. and Ward, M. (2006). Search, bioprospecting and biodiversity conservation. *Journal of Environmental Economics and Management*, 52, 615–626.

Costello, M.J., May, R.M., and Stork, N.E. (2013). Can we name Earth's species before they go extinct? *Science*, 339, 413–416.

Craig, W.J. (2009). Health effects of vegan diets. *The American Journal of Clinical Nutrition*, 89, 1627S–1633S.

Culver, M., Johnson, W.E., Pecon-Slattery, J., and O'Brien, S.J. (2000). Genomic ancestry of the American puma (*Puma concolor*). *Journal of Heredity*, 91, 186–197.

Daily, G.C. (1997). *Nature's Services: Societal Dependence on Natural Ecosystems*. Washington, DC: Island Press.

Daniels, N. (2013). *Reflective equilibrium* [Online]. Available: http://stanford.io /2e1aeMe.

Darwin, C. (1904 [1871]). *The Descent of Man, and Selection in Relation to Sex*. New York, NY: J.A. Hill and Company.

Darwin, C. (2003 [1859]). *On the Origin of Species by Means of Natural Selection*. Toronto, ON: Broadview.

Davies, S. (2012). *The Artful Species: Aesthetics, Art, and Evolution*. Oxford, UK: Oxford University Press.

Deacon, T.W. (1998). *The Symbolic Species: The Co-Evolution of Language and the Brain*. New York, NY: W.W. Norton.

deLaplante, K. and Picasso, V. (2011). The biodiversity-ecosystem function debate in ecology. In: Delaplante, K., Brown, B. and Peacock, K.A. (eds.) *Handbook of the Philosophy of Science. Volume 11: Philosophy of Ecology*. 1st edn. Oxford, UK: Elsevier.

Di Minin, E., Fraser, I., Slotow, R., and MacMillan, D.C. (2013). Understanding heterogeneous preference of tourists for big game species: implications for conservation and management. *Animal Conservation*, 16, 249–258.

Dias, D.A., Urban, S., and Roessner, U. (2012). A historical overview of natural products in drug discovery. *Metabolites*, 2, 303–336.

Diffey, T.J. (2000). Arguing about the environment. *British Journal of Aesthetics*, 40, 133–148.

Diggle, S.P., Griffin, A.S., Campbell, G.S., and West, S.A. (2007). Cooperation and conflict in quorum-sensing bacterial populations. *Nature*, 450, 411–414.

Druce, H.C., Mackey, R.L., and Slotow, R. (2011). How immunocontraception can contribute to elephant management in small, enclosed reserves: munyawana population as a case study. *PLoS One*, 6, e27952.

Duffy, J.E., Srivastava, D.S., McLaren, J., et al. (2009). Forecasting decline in ecosystem services under realistic scenarios of extinction. In: Naeem, S., Bunker, D.E., Hector, A., Loreau, M., and Perring, C. (eds.) *Biodiversity, Ecosystem Functioning, & Human Wellbeing: An Ecological and Economic Perspective*. Oxford, UK: Oxford University Press.

Dutton, D. (2009). *The Art Instinct: Beauty, Pleasure, and Human Evolution*. New York, NY: Oxford University Press.

Ehrenfeld, D.W. (1972). *Conserving Life on Earth*. New York, NY: Oxford University Press.

Ehrenfeld, David. (1978). *The Arrogance of Humanism*. New York: Oxford University Press.

Ehrlich, P.R. and Ehrlich, A.H. (1992). The value of biodiversity. *Ambio*, 21, 219–226.

Eijgelaar, E., Thaper, C., and Peeters, P. (2010). Antarctic cruise tourism: the paradoxes of ambassadorship,"last chance tourism" and greenhouse gas emissions. *Journal of Sustainable Tourism*, 18, 337–354.

Elliott, R. (1982). Faking Nature. *Inquiry*, 25, 81–93.

Farnsworth, N.R., Akerele, O., Bingel, A.S., Soejarto, D.D., and Guo, Z. (1985). Medicinal plants in therapy. *Bulletin of the World Health Organization*, 63, 965.

Feinberg, J. (1994). Not with my tax money the problem of justifying government subsidies for the arts. *Public Affairs Quarterly*, 8, 101–123.

Fennell, D.A. (2015). *Ecotourism*. 5th edn. Abingdon, UK: Routledge.

Ferré, F. (1996). Persons in nature: toward an applicable and unified environmental ethics. *Ethics and the Environment*, 1, 15–25.

Firn, R.D. (2003). Bioprospecting – why is it so unrewarding? *Biodiversity & Conservation*, 12, 207–216.

Flader, S.L. (1974). *Thinking Like a Mountain: Aldo Leopold and the Evolution of an Ecological Attitude toward Deer, Wolves, and Forests*. Columbia, MO: University of Missouri Press.

Food and Agriculture Organization of the United Nations (2013). *FAO Statistical Yearbook 2013: World Food and Agriculture*. Rome: FAO.

Frankham, R., Ballou, J.D., Dudash, M.R., et al. (2012). Implications of different species concepts for conserving biodiversity. *Biological Conservation*, 153, 25–31.

Garcia, R.K. and Newman, J.A. (2016). Is it possible to care for ecosystems? Policy paralysis and ecosystem management. *Ethics, Policy & Environment*, 19, 170–182.

Gardner, A. (2015a). The genetical theory of multilevel selection. *Journal of Evolutionary Biology*, 28, 305–319.

Gardner, A. (2015b). More on the genetical theory of multilevel selection. *Journal of Evolutionary Biology*, 28, 1747–1751.

Gaston, K.J. (2008). Bliodiversity and extinction: the importance of being common. *Progress in Physical Geography*, 32, 73–79.

Gertler, B. (2015). "Self-Knowledge." Stanford Encyclopedia of Philosophy, Edward N. Zalta ed. [Online]. Available: http://stanford.io/2eHShDV.

Ginsburg, J. (2001). US Wild Horses: To Many Survivors on Too Little Land? *National Geographic News* [Online]. Available: http://bit.ly/2dzqvfs.

Gleason, H.A. (1926). The individualistic concept of the plant association. *Bulletin of the Torrey Botanical Club*, 53, 7–26.

Goodnight, C. (2015). Multilevel selection theory and evidence: a critique of Gardner, 2015. *Journal of Evolutionary Biology*, 28, 1734–1746.

Goodpaster, K.E. (1978). On being morally considerable. *The Journal of Philosophy*, 75, 308–325.

Goodpaster, K.E. (1979). From egoism to environmentalism. In: Goodpaster, K.E. and Sayre, K.M. (eds.) *Ethics and Problems of the 21st Century*. 1st edn. Notre Dame, IN: University of Notre Dame Press.

Gould, S.J. (1980). *The Panda's Thumb: More Reflections in Natural History*. New York, NY: WW Norton & Company.

Grantham, T.A. (1995). Hierarchical approaches to macroevolution: recent work on species and selection and the "effect hypothesis." *Annual Review of Ecology and Systematics*, 26, 301–321.

Green, J.L., Harte, J., and Ostling, A. (2003). Species richness, endemism, and abundance patterns: tests of two fractal models in a serpentine grassland. *Ecology Letters*, 6, 919–928.

Grey, W. (1993). Anthropocentrism and deep ecology. *Australasian Journal of Philosophy*, 71, 463–475.

Griffin, J.N., O'Gorman, E.J., Emmerson, M., et al. (2009). Biodiversity and the stability of ecosystem functioning. In: Naeem, S., Bunker, D.E., Hector, A., Loreau, M., and Perring, C. (eds.) *Biodiversity, Ecosystem Functioning, & Human Wellbeing: An Ecological and Economic Perspective*. Oxford: Oxford University Press.

Griffith, G.W. (2012). Do we need a global strategy for microbial conservation? *Nature*, 469, 275.

Grifo, F., Newman, D., Fairfield, A., Bhattacharya, B., and Grupenhoff, J. (1997). The origins of prescription drugs. In: Grifo, F. and Rosenthal, J. (eds.) *Biodiversity and Human Health*. Washington, DC: Island Press.

Groom, M.J., Meffe, G.K. and Carroll, C.R. (2006). *Principles of Conservation Biology*. 3rd edn. Sunderland, MA: Sinauer Associates.

Gunn, A.S. (1980). Why should we care about rare species? *Environmental Ethics*, 2, 17–37.

Gunn, A.S. (1984). Preserving rare species. In: Regan, T. (ed.) *Earthbound: Introductory Essays in Environmental Ethics*. 1st edn. Prospect Heights, IL: Waveland Press, Inc.

Hardin, G. (1969). The economics of wilderness. *Natural History*, 78, 20–27.

Hare, R. (1981). *Moral Thinking: Its Levels, Method, and Point*. New York, NY: Oxford University Press.

Hare, R.M. (1973a). Review: Rawls' Theory of Justice – I. *The Philosophical Quarterly*, 23, 144–155.

Hare, R.M. (1973b). Review: Rawls' Theory of Justice – II. *The Philosophical Quarterly*, 23, 241–252.

Hargrove, E.C. (1992). *Foundations of Environmental Ethics*. Upper Saddle River, NJ: Prentice-Hall.

Harvey, A.L. (2008). Natural products in drug discovery. *Drug Discovery Today*, 13, 894–901.

Hector, A., Bell, T., Connolly, J., Finn, J., Fox, J., Kirwan, L., Loreau, M., McLaren, J., Schmid, B., and Weigelt, A. (2009). The analysis of biodiversity experiments: from pattern toward mechanism. In: S. Naeem, D.E. Bunker, A. Hector, M. Loreau, and C. Perrings (eds.), *Biodiversity, Ecosystem Functioning, and Human Wellbeing: An Ecological and Economic Perspective*. New York: Oxford University Press, pp. 94–104.

Hendriks, I.E. and Duarte, C.M. (2008). Allocation of effort and imbalances in biodiversity research. *Journal of Experimental Marine Biology and Ecology*, 360, 15–20.

Hepburn, R.W. (1966). Contemporary aesthetics and the neglect of natural beauty. In: Williams, B. and Montefiore, A. (eds.) *British Analytical Philosophy*. London: Routeledge and Keegan Paul.

Hettinger, N. (2005). Allen Carlson's environmental aesthetics and the protection of the environment. *Environmental Ethics*, 27, 57–76.

Hillebrand, H., Bennett, D.M., and Cadotte, M.W. (2008). Consequences of dominance: a review of evenness effects on local and regional ecosystem processes. *Ecology*, 89, 1510–1520.

Hooper, D.U., Adair, E.C., Cardinale, B.J., et al. (2012). A global synthesis reveals biodiversity loss as a major driver of ecosystem change. *Nature*, 486, 105–108.

Hooper, D.U., Chapin, F.S., Ewel, J.J., et al. (2005). Effects of biodiversity on ecosystem functioning: A consensus of current knowledge. *Ecological Monographs*, 75, 3–35.

Hooper, D.U. and Vitousek, P.M. (1998). Effects of plant composition and diversity on nutrient cycling. *Ecological Monographs*, 68, 121–149.

Howard-Snyder, F. (2011). "Doing vs. Allowing Harm." In: Edward N. Zalta (ed.) *Stanford Encyclopedia of Philosophy* [Online]. Available: http://stanford.io /2eWW5Vj.

Hubbell, S.P. (2001). *The Unified Neutral Theory of Biodiversity and Biogeography.* Princeton, NJ: Princeton University Press.

Hume, D. (1978 [1739–40]). *A Treatise of Human Nature.* Oxford, UK: Oxford University Press.

Hume, D. and Beauchamp, T.L. (1957 [1751]). *An Inquiry Concerning the Principles of Morals.* Indianapolis, IN: Bobbs-Merrill.

Hursthouse, R. (2011). Virtue ethics and the treatment of animals. In: Beauchamp, T.L. and Frey, R.G. (eds.) *The Oxford Handbook of Animal Ethics.* 1st edn. Oxford, UK: Oxford University Press.

Huth, H. (1948). Yosemite: the story of an idea. *Sierra Club Bulletin,* 33, 47–78.

Isbell, F.I., Losure, D.A., Yurkonis, K.A., and Wilsey, B.J. (2008). Diversity-productivity relationships in two ecologically realistic rarity-extinction scenarios. *Oikos,* 117, 996–1005.

Jamieson, D. (1999). *Singer and His Critics.* Malden, MA: Blackwell Publishing.

Jamieson, D. (2007). The transformative power of biodiversity. *Bioscience,* 57, 709–710.

Jamieson, D. (ed.) (2008). *A Companion to Environmental Philosophy.* Oxford, UK, Blackwell.

Jax, K. (2006). Ecological units: definitions and application. *The Quarterly Review of Biology,* 81, 237–258.

Jax, K. (2007). Can we define ecosystems? On the confusion between definition and description of ecological concepts. *Acta Biotheoretica,* 55, 341–355.

Johnson, E. (1981). Animal liberation versus the land ethic. *Environmental Ethics,* 3, 265–273.

Johnson, W.E., Onorato, D.P., Roelke, M.E., et al. (2010). Genetic restoration of the Florida panther. *Science,* 329, 1641–1645.

Jonsson, M., Dangles, O., Malmqvist, B., and Gueérold, F. (2002). Simulating species loss following perturbation: assessing the effects on process rates. *Proceedings of the Royal Society of London. Series B: Biological Sciences,* 269, 1047–1052.

Justus, J., Colyvan, M., Regan, H., and Maguire, L. (2009). Buying into conservation: intrinsic versus instrumental value. *Trends in Ecology & Evolution,* 24, 187–191.

Kant, I. (1948 [1785]). *The Moral Law: Kant's Groundwork of the Metaphysics of Morals. Translated with commentary by H.J. Paton.* New York, NY: Hutchinson's University Library (Reissued by Harper Torchbooks, 1964).

Kareiva, P. and Levin, S.A. (eds.) (2003). *The Importance of Species: Perspectives on Expendability and Triage*. Princeton, NJ: Princeton University Press.

Katz, E. (1991). Defending the use of animals by business: animal liberation and environmental ethics. In: Hoffman, M., Frederick, R., and Petry Jr, E.S. (eds.) *Business, Ethics, and the Environment: The Public Policy Debate*. 1st edn. New York, NY: Quorum Books.

Kearns, C. (2010). Conservation of biodiversity. *Nature Education Knowledge*, 3, 7.

Kheel, M. (1985). The liberation of nature: a circular affair. *Environmental Ethics*, 7, 135–149.

Kirkby, C.A., Giudice-Granados, R., Day, B., et al. (2010). The market triumph of ecotourism: an economic investigation of the private and social benefits of competing land uses in the Peruvian Amazon. *PLoS One*, 5, e13015.

Kiss, A. (2004). Is community-based ecotourism a good use of biodiversity conservation funds? *Trends in Ecology & Evolution*, 19, 232–237.

Knegtering, E., van der Windt, H.J., and Uiterkamp, A.J.S. (2011). Public decisions on animal species: does body size matter? *Environmental Conservation*, 38, 28–36.

Kneitel, J.M. and Chase, J.M. (2004). Trade-offs in community ecology: linking spatial scales and species coexistence. *Ecology Letters*, 7, 69–80.

Kricher, J. (1998). Nothing endures but change: ecology's newly emerging paradigm. *Northeastern Naturalist*, 5, 165–174.

Krüger, O. (2005). The role of ecotourism in conservation: panacea or Pandora's box? *Biodiversity & Conservation*, 14, 579–600.

Larson B. (2011). *Metaphors for Environmental Sustainability: Redefining our Relationship with Nature*. New Haven, CT: Yale University Press.

Lawler, S.P., Armesto, J.J., and Kareiva, P. (2002). *How relevant to conservation are studies linking biodiversity and ecosystem functioning?* In: Kinzig, A.P., Pacala, S.W., and Tillman, D. (eds.) *The Functional Consequences of Biodiversity: Empirical Progress and Theoretical Extensions*. 1st edn. Princeton, NJ: Princeton University Press.

Lawrence, E.A. (1986). Neoteny in American perceptions of animals. In: Hoetage, R. J. (ed.) *Perceptions of Animals in American Culture*. 1st edn. Washington, DC: Smithsonian Institution.

Lazari-Radek, K.d. and Singer, P. (2014). *The Point of View of the Universe*. Oxford, UK: Oxford University Press.

Lehman, H. (2000). Ecosystem health as a moral requirement. *Journal of Agricultural and Environmental Ethics*, 12, 305–317.

Leopold, A. (1949). *A Sand County Almanac, and Sketches Here and There*. New York, NY: Oxford University Press.

Leopold, A. (1966). The round river. In: Leopold, A. (ed.) *A Sand County Almanac with Essays on Conservation from Round River*. New York, NY: Oxford University Press.

Leopold, A. (1979). Some fundamentals of conservation in the Southwest. *Environmental Ethics*, 1, 131–141.

Leopold, A.S., Cain, S.A., Cottam, C.M., Gabrielson, I.N., and Kimball, T.L. (1963). *Wildlife Management in the National Parks and Monuments of Arizona*. Washington, DC: US Department of the Interior, National Park Service.

Leopold, L. (1987). Foreword. In: McCabe, R.A. (ed.) *Aldo Leopold: The Professor*. Madison, WI: University of Wisconsin Press.

Lewontin, R.C. (1970). The units of selection. *Annual Review of Ecology and Systematics*, 1, 1–18.

Li, J.W.-H. and Vederas, J.C. (2009). Drug discovery and natural products: end of an era or an endless frontier? *Science*, 325, 161–165.

Linquist, S. (2018). Today's awe-inspiring design, tomorrow's plexiglas dinosaur: how public aquariums contradict their conservation mandate in pursuit of immersive underwater displays. In: Minteer, B.A., Collins, J.P., and Maienschein, J. (eds.) *The Ark and Beyond: The Evolution of Zoo and Aquarium Conservation*. 1st edn. Chicago, IL: University of Chicago Press.

Linquist, S., Gregory, T.R., Elliott, T.A., et al. (2016). Yes! There are resilient generalizations (or "laws") in ecology. *The Quarterly Review of Biology*, 91, 119–131.

Linzey, A. (1998). Sentientism. In: Bekoff, M. (ed.) *Encyclopedia of Animal Rights and Animal Welfare*. 1st edn. Westport, CT: Greenwood Press.

Lo, Y.S. (2001a). The land ethic and Callicott's ethical system (1980–2001): An overview and critique. *Inquiry*, 44, 331–358.

Lo, Y.S. (2001b). Non-Humean holism, un-Humean holism. *Environmental Values*, 10, 113–123.

Lo, Y.S. (2006). Making and finding values in nature: from a Humean point of view 1. *Inquiry*, 49, 123–147.

Loftis, J.R. (2003). Three problems for the aesthetic foundations of environmental ethics. *Philosophy in the Contemporary World*, 10, 41–50.

Maclaurin, J. and Sterelny, K. (2008). *What Is Biodiversity?* Chicago, IL: University of Chicago Press.

Magnusson, W. and Shaw, K. (2002). *A Political Space: Reading the Global through Clayoquot Sound*. Kingston, ON: McGill-Queen's University Press.

Maguire, L.A. and Justus, J. (2008). Why intrinsic value is a poor basis for conservation decisions. *Bioscience*, 58, 910–911.

Maier, D.S. (2012). *What's So Good about Biodiversity?: A Call for Better Reasoning about Nature's Value*. London, UK: Springer Science & Business Media.

Manning, R.N. (1994). Intrinsic value and overcoming Feinberg's benefit principle. *Public Affairs Quarterly*, 8, 125–140.

Manson, N. (2002). Formulating the precautionary principle. *Environmental Ethics*, 4, 263–274.

Marino, L., Lilienfeld, S.O., Malamud, R., Nobis, N., and Broglio, R. (2010). Do zoos and aquariums promote attitude change in visitors? A critical evaluation of the American zoo and aquarium study. *Society & Animals*, 18, 126–138.

Maslin, M. (2004). *Global Warming: A Very Short Introduction*. Oxford: Oxford University Press.

May, R.M. (1973). Time-delay versus stability in population models with two and three trophic levels. *Ecology*, 54, 315–325.

May, R.M., Lawton, J.H., and Stork, N.E. (1995). Assessing extinction rates. In: May, R.M. and Lawton, J.H. (eds.) *Extinction Rates*. 1st edn. Oxford, UK: Oxford University Press.

McCann, K.S. (2000) The diversity–stability debate. *Nature* 405: 228–233.

McCabe, R.A. (1987). *Aldo Leopold, the Professor*. Madison, WI: Rusty Rock Press.

McCarthy, E.M. (2006). *Handbook of Avian Hybrids of the World*. Oxford, UK: Oxford University Press.

McCauley, D.J. (2006). Selling out on nature. *Nature*, 443, 27–28.

McChesney, J.D., Venkataraman, S.K., and Henri, J.T. (2007). Plant natural products: back to the future or into extinction? *Phytochemistry*, 68, 2015–2022.

McGill, B.J., Dornelas, M., Gotelli, N.J., and Magurran, A.E. (2015). Fifteen forms of biodiversity trend in the Anthropocene. *Trends in Ecology & Evolution*, 30, 104–113.

Meine, C. (1988). *Aldo Leopold: His Life and Work*. Madison, WI: University of Wisconsin Press.

Midgley, M. (1983). *Animals and Why They Matter*. Athens, GA: University of Georgia press.

Moss, A., Jensen, E., and Gusset, M. (2015). Evaluating the contribution of zoos and aquariums to Aichi Biodiversity Target 1. *Conservation Biology*, 29, 537–544.

Moyel, B. (2005). Making the precautionary principle work for biodiversity: avoiding perverse outcomes in decision-making under uncertainty. In: Cooney, R. and Dickson, B. (eds.) *Biodiversity and the Precautionary Principle: Risk and Uncertainty in Conservation and Sustainable Use*. 1st edn. London, UK: Earthscan.

Myers, N. (1993). Biodiversity and the Precautionary Principle. *Ambio*, 22, 74–79.

Myers, N. (1996). Environmental services of biodiversity. *Proceedings of the National Academy of Sciences*, 93, 2764–2769.

Naeem, S., Chapin III, F., Costanza, R., et al. (1999). Biodiversity and ecosystem functioning: maintaining natural life support processes. *Issues in Ecology*, 4, 1–11.

Naeem, S., Loreau, M., and Inchausti, P. (2002). Biodiversity and ecosystem functioning: the emergence of a synthetic ecological framework. In: Loreau, M., Naeem, S., and Inchausti, P. (eds.) *Biodiversity and Ecosystem Functioning: Synthesis and Perspectives*. 1st edn. Oxford, UK: Oxford University Press.

Naess, A. (1973). The shallow and the deep, long-range ecology movement. A summary. *Inquiry*, 16(1–4), 95–100.

Naidoo, R. and Adamowicz, W.L. (2005). Biodiversity and nature-based tourism at forest reserves in Uganda. *Environment and Development Economics*, 10, 159–178.

Newman, D.J. and Cragg, G.M. (2012). Natural products as sources of new drugs over the 30 years from 1981 to 2010. *Journal of Natural Products*, 75, 311–335.

Newman, D.J., Kilama, J., Bernstein, A., and Chivian, E. (2008). Medicines from nature. In: Chivian, E. and Bernstein, A. (eds.) *Sustaining Life: How Human Health Depends on Biodiversity*, 1st edn. Oxford, UK: Oxford University Press.

Newman, J.A., Anand, M., Henry, H.A.L., Hunt, S., and Gedalof, Z. (2011). *Climate Change Biology*. Wallingford, UK: CABI.

Norton, B.G. (1986). Conservation and preservation. *Environmental Ethics*, 8, 195–220.

Norton, B.G. (1987). *Why Preserve Natural Variety?* Princeton, NJ: Princeton University Press.

Norton, B.G. (1994). *Toward Unity among Environmentalists*. Oxford, UK: Oxford University Press.

Nussbaum, M.C. (2004). Beyond 'compassion and humanity': justice for nonhuman animals. In: Sunstein, C.R. and Nussbaum, M.C. (eds.) *Animal Rights: Current Debates and New Directions*. Oxford, UK: Oxford University Press.

Odenbaugh, J. (2015). Nothing in ethics makes sense except in the light of evolution? Natural goodness, normativity, and naturalism. *Synthese*, doi: 10.1007/s11229-015-0675-7.

Passmore, J. (1974). *Man's Responsibility for Nature*. New York, NY: Charles Scribner's Sons.

Pearce, D. (1998). Valuing the environment. In: Pearce, D. (ed.) *Economics and Environment: Essays on Ecological Economics and Sustainable Development*. 1st edn. Cheltenham, UK: Edward Elgar.

Pearce, D. (2005). Paradoxes in biodiversity conservation. *World Economics*, 6, 57–69.

Pearce, D. and Puroshothaman, S. (1995). The economic value of plant-based pharmaceuticals. In: Swanson, T.M. (ed.) *Intellectual Property Rights and Biodiversity Conservation: An Interdisciplinary Analysis of the Values of Medicinal Plants*. 1st edn. Cambridge, UK: Cambridge University Press.

Pereira Di Salvo, C.J. and Raymond, L. (2010). Defining the precautionary principle: an empirical analysist of elite discourse. *Environmental Politics*, 19, 86–106.

Petchey, O. L., A. Hector and K. J. Gaston (2004). How do different measures of functional diversity perform? *Ecology* 85(3): 847–857.

Pollan, M. (2001). The Year in Ideas: A to Z; Precautionary Principle. *New York Times*, p. 92. http://nyti.ms/2eHtYV6.

Ponte, L. (1976). *The Cooling: Has the Next Ice Age Already Begun? Can We Survive It?* New York, NY: Prentice-Hall.

Primack, R.B. (2002). *Essentials of Conservation Biology*, 3rd edn. Sunderland, MA: Sinauer Associates.

Principe, P.P. (1996). Monetizing the pharmacological benefits of plants. In: Balick, M.J., Elisabetsky, E., and Laird, S.A. (eds.) *Medicinal Resources of the Tropical Forest: Biodiversity and Its Importance to Human Health*. 1st edn. New York, NY: Columbia University Press.

Raiffa, Howard (1968). *Decision Analysis: Introductory Lectures on Choices under Uncertainty*. New York: Random House.

Raup, D.M. (1991). A kill curve for Phanerozoic marine species. *Paleobiology*, 37–48.

Rausser, G.C. and Small, A.A. (2000). Valuing research leads: bioprospecting and the conservation of genetic resources. *Journal of Political Economy*, 108, 173–206.

Rawls, J. (1971). *A Theory of Justice*. Cambridge, MA: Harvard University Press.

Regan, T. (1976). Feinberg on what sorts of beings can have rights. *The Southern Journal of Philosophy*, 14, 485–498.

Regan, T. (1981). The nature and possibility of an environmental ethic. *Environmental Ethics*, 3, 19–34.

Regan, T. (1983). *The Case for Animal Rights*. Berkeley: University of California Press.

Regan, T. (2004). How to justify violence. In: Best, S. and Nocella Ii, A. (eds.) *Terrorists or Freedom Fighters?: Reflections on the Liberation of Animals*. 1st edn. New York, NY: Lantern Books.

Ribe, R.G. (1989). The aesthetics of forestry: what has empirical preference research taught us? *Environmental Management*, 13, 55–74.

Ricklefs, R.E. (2008). Disintegration of the ecological community. *The American Naturalist*, 172, 741–750.

Ripple, W.J. and Beschta, R.L. (2012). Trophic cascades in Yellowstone: The first 15 years after wolf reintroduction. *Biological Conservation*, 145, 205–213.

Ritter, L., Totman, C., Krishnan, K., et al. (2007). Deriving uncertainty factors for threshold chemical contaminants in drinking water. *Journal of Toxicology and Environmental Health, Part B*, 10, 527–557.

Rodman, J. (1977). I. The liberation of nature? *Inquiry*, 20, 83–131.

Rollin, B.E. (1981). *Animal Rights and Human Morality*. Buffalo, NY: Prometheus Books.

Rollin, B.E. (1995). The new social ethic for animals. In: Rollin, B.E. (ed.) *Farm Animal Welfare: Social, Bioethical, and Research Issues*. 1st edn. Ames, IA: Iowa State University Press.

Rollin, B.E. (1999). *An Introduction to Veterinary Medical Ethics: Theory and Cases*. Ames, IA: Iowa State University Press.

Rolston III, H. (1975). Is there an ecological ethic? *Ethics*, 85(2), 93–109.

Rolston III, H. (1979). Can and ought we to follow nature. *Environmental Ethics*, 1, 7–30.

Root, R.B. (2003). The expendability of species: a test case based on the caterpillars on goldenrods. In: Kareiva, P. and Levin, S.A. (eds.) *The Importance of Species: Perspectives on Expendability and Triage*. 1st edn. Princeton, NJ: Princeton University Press.

Rosindell, J., Hubbell, S.P. and Etienne, R.S. (2011). The unified neutral theory of biodiversity and biogeography at age ten. *Trends in Ecology & Evolution*, 26, 340–348.

Ross, W.D. (1930). *The Right and the Good*. Oxford, UK: Oxford University Press.

Rosser, A.M., Tareen, N., and Leader-Williams, N. (2005). The precautionary principle, uncertainty and trophy-hunting: a review of the Torghar population of Central Asian Markhor *Capra falconeri*. In: Cooney, R. and Dickson, B. (eds.) *Biodiversity and the Preuationary Principle: Risk and Uncertainty in Conservation and Sustainable Use*. London: Earthscan.

Routley, R. (1973). Is there a need for a new, an environmental, ethic. Proceedings of the XVth World Congress of Philosophy, 1973, 205–210.

Russow, L.-M. (1981). Why do species matter? *Environmental Ethics*, 3, 101–112.

Rutberg, A.T. (2013). Managing wildlife with contraception: why is it taking so long? *Journal of Zoo and Wildlife Medicine*, 44, S38–S46.

Sagoff, M. (1984). Animal liberation and environmental ethics: bad marriage, quick divorce. *Osgoode Hall Law Journal*, 22, 297.

Sagoff, M. (1998). *The Economy of the Earth: Philosophy, Law, and the Environment*. Cambridge, UK: Cambridge University Press.

Sagoff, M. (2008). On the economic value of ecosystem services. *Environmental Values*, 17, 239–257.

Saito, Y. (1998). The aesthetics of unscenic nature. *The Journal of Aesthetics and Art Criticism*, 56, 101–111.

Sandin, P. (1999). Dimensions of the Precautionary Principle. *Human and Ecological Risk Assessment: An International Journal*, 5, 889–907.

Sapontzis, S. (1987). *Morals, Reason, and Animals*. Philadelphia, PA: Temple University Press.

Sarkar, S. and Margules, C. (2002). Operationalizing biodiversity for conservation planning. *Journal of Biosciences*, 27, 299–308.

Sax, D.F. and Gaines, S.D. (2003). Species diversity: from global decreases to local increases. *Trends in Ecology & Evolution*, 18, 561–566.

Sax, D.F., Gaines, S.D., and Brown, J.H. (2002). Species invasions exceed extinctions on islands worldwide: a comparative study of plants and birds. *American Naturalist*, 160, 766–783.

Schaler, J.A. (2009). *Peter Singer under Fire: The Moral Iconoclast Faces His Critics*. New York, NY: Open Court Publishing.

Schläpfer, F., Pfisterer, A.B., and Schmid, B. (2005). Non-random species extinction and plant production: implications for ecosystem functioning. *Journal of Applied Ecology*, 42, 13–24.

Schläpfer, F. and Schmid, B. (1999). Ecosystem effects of biodiversity: a classification of hypotheses and exploration of empirical results. *Ecological Applications*, 9, 893–912.

Schläpfer, F., Schmid, B., and Seidl, L. (1999). Expert estimates about effects of biodiversity on ecosystem processes and services. *Oikos*, 84, 346–352.

Schmidtz, D. and Willott, E. (2002). *Environmental Ethics: What Really Matters, What Really Works*. 2nd edn. Oxford, UK: Oxford University Press.

Schoener, T.W. (1983). Simple models of optimal feeding-territory size: a reconciliation. *American Naturalist*, 121, 608–629.

Schwartz, M.W., Brigham, C.A., Hoeksema, J.D., et al. (2000). Linking biodiversity to ecosystem function: implications for conservation ecology. *Oecologia*, 122, 297–305.

Schweitzer, A. (1955). *The Philosophy of Civilization*. New York, NY: Macmillan.

Schwitzgebel, E. and Cushman, F. (2012). Expertise in moral reasoning? Order effects on moral judgment in professional philosophers and non-philosophers. *Mind & Language*, 27, 135–153.

Shrader-Frechette, K. (1996). Individualism, holism, and environmental ethics. *Ethics and the Environment*, 1, 55–69.

Simpson, R.D., Sedjo, R.A., and Reid, J.W. (1996). Valuing biodiversity for use in pharmaceutical research. *Journal of Political Economy*, 163–185.

Singer, M.G. (1961). *Generalization in Ethics: An Essay an the Logic of Ethics, with the Rudiments of a System of Moral Philosophy*. New York, NY: Knopf.

Singer, P. (1975). *Animal Liberation: A New Ethics for Our Treatment of Animals*. New York, NY: Random House.

Singer, P. (1990). *Animal Liberation: A New Ethics for Our Treatment of Animals. New* revised *edition*. New York, NY: Avon Books.

Singer, P. (2004). Humans are sentient too. *The Guardian*, 30 July. www.theguardian.com/education/2004/jul/30/research.highereducation.

Singer, P. (2009). Reply to David Schmidtz. In: Schaler, J.A. (ed.) *Singer under Fire: The Moral Iconoclast Faces His Critics*. 1st edn. Chicago, IL: Open Court.

Singer, P. (2011). *Practical ethics*. Cambridge, MA: Cambridge University Press.

Sinnott-Armstrong, W. (2008). Framing moral intuitions. In: Sinnott-Armstrong, W. (ed.) *Moral Psychology, Vol 2: The Cognitive Science of Morality: Intuition and Diversity*. Cambridge, MA: MIT Press.

Slovic, P. (2000). *The Perception of Risk*. London: Earth Scan Publications Ltd.

Smith, K.K. (2000). Mere taste: democracy and the politics of beauty. *Wisconsin Environmental Law Journal*, 7, 151.

Sober, E. (1986). Philosophical problems for environmentlism. In: Norton, B. (ed.) *The Preservation of Species*. 1st edn. Princeton, NJ: Princeton University Press.

Sober, E. and Wilson, D.S. (1998). *Unto Others: The Evolution and Psychology of Unselfish Behavior*. Cambridge, MA: Harvard University Press.

Soulé, M.E. (1985). What is conservation biology? *Bioscience*, 35, 727–734.

Soulé, M.E. (1996). Are ecosystem processes enough? *Wild Earth*, 6, 59–60.

Srivastava, D.S. and Vellend, M. (2005). Biodiversity-ecosystem function research: is it relevant to conservation? *Annual Review of Ecology Evolution and Systematics*, 36, 267–294.

Stokes, D.L. (2007). Things we like: human preferences among similar organisms and implications for conservation. *Human Ecology*, 35, 361–369.

Stone, C.D. (1972). Should trees have standing – toward legal rights for natural objects. *Southern California Law Review*, 45, 450–501.

Swanson, T. (1998). *Intellectual Property Rights and Biodiversity Conservation: An Interdisciplinary Analysis of the Values of Medicinal Plants*. Cambridge, UK: Cambridge University Press.

Taylor, P.W. (1986). *Respect for Nature: A Theory of Environmental Ethics*. Princeton, NJ: Princeton University Press.

Thomson, J.J. (1976). A defense of abortion. In: Humber, J.M. and Almeder, R.F. (eds.) *Biomedical Ethics and the Law*. New York, NY: Plenum Press.

Turner, D. and Hartzell, L. (2004). The lack of clarity in the precautionary principle. *Environmental Values*, 13, 449–460.

Turner, R.K., Pearce, D. and Bateman, I. (1993). *Environmental Economics: An Elementary Introduction*. Baltimore, MD: The Johns Hopkins University Press.

van Wyk, B.-E. and Wink, M. (2004). *Medicinal Plants of the World: An Illustrated Guide to Important Medicinal Plants and Their Uses*. Portland, OR: Timber Press.

Varner, G.E. (1991). No holism without pluralism. *Environmental Ethics*, 13, 175–179.

Varner, G.E. (1998). *In Nature's Interests?: Interests, Animal Rights, and Environmental Ethics*. Oxford, UK: Oxford University Press.

Varner, G. (2003). Book review: Life's Intrinsic Value. *Environmental Ethics*, 25, 413–416.

Varner, G. (2011). Environmental ethics, hunting, and the place of animals. In: Beauchamp, T.L. and Frey, R.G. (eds.) *The Oxford Handbook of Animal Ethics*. 1st edn. Oxford, UK: Oxford University Press.

Varner, G.E. (2012). *Personhood, Ethics, and Animal Cognition: Situating Animals in Hare's Two Level Utilitarianism*. Oxford, UK: Oxford University Press.

Vellend, M., Baeten, L., Myers-Smith, I.H., et al. (2013). Global meta-analysis reveals no net change in local-scale plant biodiversity over time. *Proceedings of the National Academy of Sciences*, 110, 19456–19459.

Vellend, M. et al. (2011). Measuring phylogenetic biodiversity. In: Anne E. Magurran and Brian J. McGill (eds.), *Biological Diversity: Frontiers in Measurement and Assessment*. Oxford, UK: Oxford University Press, 194–207.

Vucetich, J.A., Bruskotter, J.T., and Nelson, M.P. (2015). Evaluating whether nature's intrinsic value is an axiom of or anathema to conservation. *Conservation Biology*, 29, 321–332.

Wardle, D.A., Zackrisson, O., Hornberg, G., and Gallet, C. (1997). The influence of island area on ecosystem properties. *Science*, 277, 1296–1299.

Welchman, J. (2009). Hume, Callicott, and the land ethic: prospects and problems. *The Journal of Value Inquiry*, 43, 201–220.

Wentsel, R., Beyer, N., Forbes, V., Maund, S., and Pastorok, R. (2008). A framework for population-level ecological risk assessment. In: Barnthouse, L.W., Munns, W.R., and Sorensen, M.T. (eds.) *Population-Level Ecological Risk Assessment*. 1st edn. Boca Raton, FL: Taylor & Francis.

White, Jnr., Lynn. (1967). The historical roots of our ecologic crisis. *Science*, 155 (3767), 1203–1207.

Whyte, I.J. (2002). The elephant management dilemma. In: Schmidtz, D. and Willott, E. (eds.) *Environmental Ethics: What Really Matters, What Really Works.* 2nd edn. Oxford: Oxford University Press.

Whyte, J. (2007). Only a Reckless Mind Could Believe in Safety First. *The Times.* http://bit.ly/2eyqxlY.

Wilkins, J.S. (2009). *Species: A History of the Idea.* Berkeley: University of California Press.

Williams, G.C. (1966). *Adaptation and Natural Selection: A Critique of Some Current Evolutionary Thought.* Princeton, NJ: Princeton University Press.

Wilson, E.O. (1984). *Biophilia.* Cambridge, MA: Harvard University Press.

Wilson, E.O. (1987). The little things that run the world (the importance and conservation of invertebrates). *Conservation Biology,* 1, 344–346.

Wilson, E.O. (ed.) (1988). *Biodiversity.* Washington, DC: National Academy Press.

Wilson, E.O. (1999). *The Diversity of Life.* Cambridge, MA: Harvard University Press.

Wilson, E.O. (2006). *The Creation: An Appeal to Save Life on Earth.* New York, NY: Norton.

World Tourism Organization (2002). *Tourism Market Trends: World Overview & Tourism Topics 2002 Edition.* Madrid, Spain: UNWTO.

World Tourism Organization (2010). *Tourism and Biodiversity – Achieving Common Goals towards Sustainability.* Madrid, Spain: UNWTO.

Zavaleta, E.S. and Hulvey, K.B. (2004). Realistic species losses disproportionately reduce grassland resistance to biological invaders. *Science,* 306, 1175–1177.

Zhu, F., Qin, C., Tao, L., et al. (2011). Clustered patterns of species origins of nature-derived drugs and clues for future bioprospecting. *Proceedings of the National Academy of Sciences,* 108, 12943–12948.

Zotchev, S.B., Sekurova, O.N., and Katz, L. (2012). Genome-based bioprospecting of microbes for new therapeutics. *Current Opinion in Biotechnology,* 23, 941–947.

Index